A History of Modern Britain
1815 to 1970

by the same author

A History of Modern Europe
Modern European History 1789–1973
British History 1714 to the Present Day
Europe and Beyond 1870–1973

A History of Modern Britain

1815 to 1970

SECOND EDITION

Herbert L. Peacock, M.A.

HEINEMANN EDUCATIONAL BOOKS
LONDON

Heinemann Educational Books Ltd
London Edinburgh Melbourne Auckland
Singapore Hong Kong Kuala Lumpur
Nairobi Ibadan Johannesburg
Lusaka New Delhi

ISBN 0 435 31710 5

Published by Heinemann Educational Books Ltd
48 Charles Street, London WIX 8AH
Printed Offset Litho in Great Britain by Cox & Wyman Ltd
London, Fakenham and Reading

Contents

PART TWO – SPECIAL STUDIES

Preface

THE aim of this history is to give a comprehensive account of British social and political developments since 1815. The first part comprises a history of the whole period, while in the special studies in the second part I have dealt with particularly important social, political and economic developments in a more detailed way. There is also a chapter on the outstanding scientific and technological advances during the period. I hope that the general scope and approach will make it useful, in different ways, both for 'O' and 'A' level work and as a book for general reference.

I am greatly indebted in the preparation of the manuscript to the following: Professor O. R. Macgregor, of Bedford College, London, for his advice on the early nineteenth century; Mr L. W. White, formerly Headmaster of Beckenham Grammar School, for his invaluable help at all stages and in particular for his contribution to the sections on the Empire and Commonwealth; Mrs Diana St John, lecturer in history at Hammersmith College of Further Education, for her extensive reading of the whole manuscript; Mr Frank Greenaway of the Science Museum, South Kensington, for his contribution to the chapter on the history of science and technology.

I must also acknowledge help and advice from Mr John Roberts, Headmaster of Newcastle under Lyme High School, Mr Paul Richardson, formerly history master at Manchester Grammar School and now of my publishers; Mrs Susan Stewart; and Mr Alan Hill, chairman of Heinemann Educational Books.

H. L. Peacock.

Preface to the Second Edition

In this second edition a number of small revisions have been made and fuller treatment has been given to the period of the Labour Government administration 1964–70. Some treatment has also been given to major events post-1970, but these matters are, in general, still too close to us for a complete and balanced account to be given in a book of this kind.

December 1973   H.L.P.

List of Maps and Diagrams

Illustrations

Acknowledgements

THE following have given permission for the reproduction of the photographs appearing on the pages listed below:

Architects' Journal, 366
Associated Press, 225, 345
The British Council, 101
British Petroleum, 327
General Post Office, 392
International Wool Secretariat, 307
Keystone Press Agency, 190, 271, 277, 345, 385
London Electrotype Agency, 90
Mansell Collection, 39
Radio Times Hulton Picture Library, 3, 6, 20, 22, 25, 27, 48, 50, 62, 65, 66, 73, 82, 91, 99, 106, 110, 126, 132, 135, 140, 142, 155, 165, 169, 179, 181, 193, 197, 214, 219, 222, 227, 231, 232, 246, 251, 257, 258, 263, 292, 296, 315, 333, 334, 339, 353, 359, 360, 363, 371, 379
The Ronan Picture Library, 375
The Science Museum, 9, 12, 184, 313, 370, 373, 374, 377, 382, 384, 388, 390, 395
University Library Cambridge, 109
The Weaver Smith Organization, 393

PART ONE

The History

1. Britain in 1815

FOR BRITAIN the Battle of Waterloo was the triumphant conclusion of a struggle which had lasted for almost 150 years. Since the reign of Louis XIV Britain and France had been engaged in a series of wars in four continents and since 1793 the fighting had been almost continuous. During this last stage it had taken on a new bitterness, for the French Revolutionaries and later Napoleon had not only challenged British international influence and economic prosperity, but had threatened her whole political and social structure. In 1815 this threat had been removed; the upstart emperor had been banished to St Helena and the old ruling families of Europe had returned to the lands and thrones from which he had ejected them. Britain was confirmed in her possession of the valuable colonies she had captured during the war and her navy dominated the world's trading routes. Almost alone in Europe the country had escaped the turmoils of revolution and the ravages of invasion; in commerce and industry she had no rivals.

But this economic predominance was a sign that Britain was passing through a revolution of her own. It was certainly less rapid but in many

The end of the French Wars; Wellington and Blucher meet on the battlefield of Waterloo.

ways more profound than anything that had happened in Europe since 1789. In 1801 the population of the British Isles was 16,000,000; by 1851 it had increased to 27,000,000 and the improvement in the standard of living had more than kept pace with this growth. Such a growth was only possible because of fundamental economic changes which in their turn brought about reforms in the social and political structure of the country. Britain, defender of the *status quo* in Europe against the French Revolutionaries, was in fact the most rapidly changing country in Europe in 1815 and for several decades to come.

The land

In 1815 most people in Britain still lived and worked in the countryside. Even those who lived in the towns were closely bound up with country life. Most large scale industries – brewing, distilling, leatherwork, shipbuilding and the manufacture of woollen textiles – depended upon the produce of the land. In 1801 there were only fifteen towns with a population of more than 20,000 people and of these only London could be called a city in the modern sense. The balance between country and town was to change very rapidly in terms of population in the next generation; nevertheless in 1815 and for many years to come the country interest was still dominant in Britain. All political power and all social status depended upon the possession of land. The landowning classes ran local government as Lords Lieutenant and Justices of the Peace; they dominated the higher ranks of the established church and they officered the army and navy. Above all they controlled Parliament. Their monopoly of political power lasted not only until the Reform Bill of 1832 but for many years afterwards. For well over half the century landowners dominated both Houses of Parliament, and throughout the century they provided most of the leaders in both the great political parties.

Changes in the countryside

The landowning interests were determined to preserve this social and political structure, but unlike the aristocracy in Europe they were not blindly reactionary. They did not feel it was beneath their dignity to take an active interest in the commercial exploitation of their estates. During the eighteenth century the landowners led the way in introducing new farming methods, experimenting with new crops and using new machinery and stockbreeding methods. Lord 'Turnip' Townshend won his nickname because of his interest in new crops and the famous East Anglian landowner Coke of Holkham was said to have increased the value of his rentals from £2,000 to £20,000 by putting into practice the latest farming methods.

In order to apply these agricultural reforms the landowners had also given fresh impetus to the enclosure movement. Throughout central and southern England in the early eighteenth century the arable land was still generally divided into a series of great unfenced fields which were in turn split into strips. Any one farmer might own a scattered collection of these strips. Such a system made it very uneconomical to introduce new machinery and impossible to use new crops. At the same time the practice of grazing all animals on the unfenced common land prevented the selective breeding of pedigree herds. The enclosure movement consolidated the strips into self-contained farms and fenced the common land, a change which was essential for the introduction of new methods which would increase yields and so increase the rents the landowners could levy.

Enclosures could only be carried out by act of Parliament but the land-owners were able to use their influence there and in local government to push the bills through and silence any opposition. Hundreds of acts were passed in the late eighteenth century so that by 1815 most of the old open fields had been broken up and the enclosure of the common grazing grounds was completed during the next two decades. Many of the small yeomen farmers could not afford the cost of hedging and ditching or the loss of grazing rights which the enclosure movement involved. They were forced to sell out, and their holdings were taken over by the bigger landowners who turned the land into large farms which they leased to wealthy tenant farmers. During the French wars the high price of grain had helped the less efficient yeomen farmers to survive, but after 1815 the collapse of corn prices ruined them in thousands and they were faced with the choice of becoming landless labourers or moving into the towns.

In his *Rural Rides*, William Cobbett (see Chapter 2) lamented the dis-appearance of the yeoman farmer who had always been regarded as the backbone of English society. He also regretted the way in which the profits of commercial farming and the social status which landowning conveyed had attracted men with little understanding of the duties and responsibilities of their privileged position. 'The war and the paper system,' he wrote, 'has brought in nabobs, Negro-drivers, admirals, governors, commissioners, loan jobbers, lottery dealers, bankers, generals, stockjobbers. . . . You can see but few good houses not in the possession of one or other of these.' Cobbett was exaggerating, but the point he was making was substantially true. The disappearance of the yeoman farmer, and the new commercial attitude towards the land, had created a growing gulf in the English country-side: between the landowners and wealthy farmers on one side and the impoverished labourers on the other. It led to sporadic outbursts of violence and disorder amongst the workers, which were ruthlessly suppressed by the magistrates.

The landowners were also able to use their position as magistrates to enforce oppressive game laws which became even harsher after 1815. Landlords were allowed to set lethal mantraps and spring guns, and poachers could be sentenced to transportation for life. Penalties for all sorts of crime, and especially for crime against property, were disproportion-ately ferocious; in 1815 over 200 crimes were still punishable by death.

A parish poorhouse in 1810.

However, this extreme harshness gradually fell into disrepute, and juries were increasingly unwilling to find men guilty of minor offences which carried the death penalty.

Distress in the countryside

The demand for home-grown grain during the war brought a rapid increase in corn prices and handsome profits for the farmers. But the farm workers did not share this prosperity. Their wages rose, but always more slowly than the price of food, so that although the demand for labour actually increased with the enclosures, even those in regular employment could not exist without some form of poor relief.

The landlords were well aware that it was not in their own interests to drive the mass of people in the countryside below subsistence level. Even in the 1790s there were signs that rural poverty would lead to widespread unrest. They therefore used their control of local government to forestall violence by alleviating poverty, but without having to bear the full costs themselves. In 1795 the magistrates of Speenhamland in Berkshire agreed upon a new system of poor relief. They proposed to supplement the labourers' wages by grants of food and money according to the size of their families and the current price of bread. The cost of this relief was to be born by the parish rates. This system of warding off widespread starvation and the danger of revolt was soon adopted throughout Southern England. (In the North this 'outdoor relief', as opposed to the 'indoor relief' given to the residents of the parish poor house, was only used to help those who were temporarily out of work, and not to supplement wages.)

The Speenhamland system had many evil effects. The farmers knew that wages would be subsidized from the rates and refused to pay their workers properly. On the other hand many ratepayers who were not employers found the burden of the rates enormously increased, especially in bad years. Worst of all the worker knew that however hard he strove he could never earn a living wage. In Cobbett's words: 'A labouring man in England, with a wife and only three children, though he never loses a day's work, though he and his family be economical, frugal, and industrious in the most extensive sense of these words, is not now able to procure for himself by his labour a single meal of meat from one end of the year to the other. Is this a state in which the labouring man ought to be?'

Transport and travel

The miserable conditions of village life led the more adventurous individuals to seek their fortunes in the towns but most villagers would never travel beyond the local market in their whole life. Journeys in the early nineteenth century were slow, uncomfortable and even dangerous at the best of times and in winter it was impossible to reach many areas by wheeled transport. Yet by 1815 the situation was certainly a great deal better than it had been a generation earlier. At least some of the credit for this must go to the turnpike trusts of which there were some 3,000 controlling 20,000 miles of road. In return for the right to levy tolls these trusts were supposed to maintain and improve stretches of the most important routes. Yet, although some of them did excellent work, many more were either unprofitable or negligent and the profusion of different authorities led to appalling inefficiency and made travel expensive. There were, for instance, twenty-three trusts on the main London to Holyhead road each charging separate tolls.

The most effective trusts were those which employed proper road engineers of whom the three outstanding individuals were James Metcalfe, Thomas Telford and John Macadam. In the late eighteenth and early nineteenth centuries these men laid roads which were properly surfaced and drained and Macadam gave his name to the cheap and effective method of road making he devised. Thanks to the work of these men and to the local committees which drained and paved the main streets in the towns, the first thirty years of the nineteenth century were the golden age of the horse-drawn coach. Along the main routes there were strings of inns and staging posts between which regular coach services could average 10 m.p.h. In 1817, for instance, it was possible to take a scheduled journey from London to Liverpool in 32 hours and passengers were requested by the owners not to tip the driver if it took longer.

But these improvements in road transport could only affect the lives of a few people. A journey from London to York cost about 90s. for a good seat which was as much as many ordinary workers earned in several months. Certainly the coaches were quite unsuitable for the transport of heavy goods over long distances and in remoter areas a good deal of trade was still carried on with pack animals. The great significance of the railways after 1830 was that they provided cheap fast transport for both passengers and goods in a way that was impossible on the roads until the invention of the internal combustion engine.

Water transport

Since transport overland posed such difficulties goods were carried wherever possible by water. In the eighteenth and early nineteenth centuries there was a flourishing coastal trade especially in bulky goods such as grain, timber, iron and coal. Barges and smaller boats pushed far up the estuaries which were improved by dredging and there were several thousand miles of navigable river. But obviously neither the coastal trade nor the river boats could satisfy the demands of commerce in a period of rapid industrial expansion, and during the second half of the eighteenth century the main industrial and commercial centres were linked by a system of canals. One of the earliest, the Bridgewater Canal, had halved the price of coal in Manchester, and the great inland waterways in the North and the Midlands built by Brindley, Rennie and Telford played a major part in the development of British industry. Some of them were outstanding works of engineering – such as the Leeds–Liverpool Canal which climbed 500 ft over the Pennines and the Huddersfield Canal which passed through 5,000 yards of tunnels. Yet the canals had many drawbacks. Once again there was a multiplicity of authorities and frequently barges could not pass from one canal to another. There could be no scheduled deliveries and goods could seldom travel at more than three miles an hour. The canals certainly fulfilled a useful purpose in Lancashire, Cheshire, Yorkshire and the Midlands, but the canals in the rural south were never profitable and by the early nineteenth century many canal companies were exploiting their monopoly by charging high prices for their services. Within a dozen years of the Battle of Waterloo dissatisfaction with the inadequacies of the canal companies led merchants in Manchester and Liverpool to launch their famous railway company.

The towns and industry

During the eighteenth century the towns were commercial rather than industrial centres. Of course there was a good deal of manufacturing done in them, but whether they were market centres or great ports such as London, Bristol and Liverpool, their real wealth came from trade. Industry in fact was very often found *outside* the towns. In Yorkshire the handloom weavers combined their craft with farming, and throughout the villages and hamlets of England womenfolk supplemented their incomes by carding and spinning wool. Frequently villages were centres for a particular industry. There were coalmining villages clustered around the pitheads, and iron-smelting villages. In the late eighteenth century there were cotton-

Eighteenth Century Industry: the Darby iron works in Coalbrookdale.

manufacturing villages high up in the Lancashire valleys, where the streams flowed swiftly enough to provide power to drive the new machinery. (Arkwright had first used water power to drive a textile factory at Cromford in 1771. After that the use of water-powered machinery spread rapidly, especially in the cotton industry.)

A dominant feature of the nineteenth century was the urbanization of industry. The industrial villages grew into towns, and the old towns themselves became centres of manufacture as well as commerce. The use of the new steam power meant that the factories could now be set up in the main centres of population. Later the development of the railways was to encourage a further concentration of industry at the railheads; but in 1815 the double process by which manufacturing was drawn into factories and factories themselves were concentrated in industrial towns had only just begun. Metalwork and leatherwork, carpentry and the weaving of woollens were still mainly domestic crafts and resisted factory organization for many years.

The factory system

Large scale factory production was first applied in the brewing industry, and by 1815 had spread to flour-milling and sugar-refining. There were also large units in iron-smelting and refining. However, the most important development of factory methods at this time was in the production of cotton textiles. The application of steam power to the machinery of Arkwright, Crompton and Cartwright transformed the cotton industry within a generation. Watt patented his rotary steam engine in 1783, and four years later the first steam engine was used to drive a cotton mill. By 1800 the Boulton and Watt works in Birmingham had turned out 500 engines, which were at work all over the country (see p. 361). In 1805 a handloom cotton weaver might have earned 23s. a week; in 1818 his wages had fallen to 8s. The new machinery had ousted the old domestic craftsman.

Even for those who found work in the factories there were problems. Working conditions had been harsh under the old domestic system. The craftsman had had to labour long hours to get a living wage and children had been grossly overworked throughout the eighteenth century. Yet there had been some individual freedom. In the factories the workers found themselves regimented and disciplined and their labour was more intense, more monotonous and more concentrated. At the same time the drawing together of dissatisfied wage earners into factories and urban slums increased the possibility of social unrest. In the years immediately after 1815 this was particularly true. Over 200,000 soldiers and sailors were suddenly demobilized and thrown on to the labour market. The Government terminated its contracts for the manufacture of uniforms and arms and there was widespread unemployment. The sufferings of the people were intensified by the bitter winter of 1816. There was distress in both the towns and the countryside, but it was the industrial workers who were better placed to act together against the authorities, and it was from them that the most violent outbursts came in the post-war years (see Chapter 2).

The armed forces

Britain's success in the French wars was closely related to her industrial and commercial strength. The English forces had been supplied with their cannon and men-of-war, their bayonets and their boots, by the most advanced industrial state in Europe. Even more important, the country's long established position as a naval and trading power had preserved her from invasion and had earned her the money to subsidize allies in Europe.

Of the two services, the navy was by far the more highly regarded. Yet British warships could only be manned through the efforts of the press gangs, which combed the streets of the seaports and even the inland towns for able-bodied men. Naval discipline was still savage despite the reforms of Nelson and other humane commanders, and pay and living conditions were generally worse than in the merchant service. However, the quality of the officers had improved since the seventeenth century when courtiers and royal favourites were granted high commands without any training. By 1815 the officers were mostly the sons of gentlemen of modest means, or of merchants and professional men, and they regarded their service as a full-time career. This element of professionalism, which was lacking in the army, kept the navy at a high pitch of efficiency throughout the nineteenth century. It was the effectiveness of the navy which allowed British statesmen from Canning to Palmerston and Disraeli to carry out their high-handed and aggressive foreign policies with such confidence.

The state of the army was very different. Traditionally a standing army was regarded as a dangerous force which might fall into the hands of an arbitrary monarch. Eighteenth century governments begrudged the cost of maintaining troops, and Britain fought no prolonged campaigns in Europe after the great victories of Marlborough. It was not until the Pensinsular War, 1808–14, that Britain once more mobilized large armed forces. The officers were the sons of the aristocracy and of the wealthier merchants who could afford to buy commissions. Under Wellington's stern discipline they became reasonably efficient, but they remained amateurs who regarded the business of fighting as an interlude in their social lives. Their disregard for professional methods would certainly have been unthinkable in Napoleon's armies. Even Wellington was astounded to see officers carrying umbrellas into battle as a protection against the rain, and Picton, one of the heroes of Waterloo, wore a top hat in place of his military shako which gave him a headache.

The rank and file of the army were regarded as the very lowest strata of society. To Wellington they were 'the scum of the earth' who joined the army to escape destitution or the gallows. On seeing a draft of men sent out to him in the Peninsula he commented: 'I don't know what effect these men will have on the enemy, but, by God, they terrify me.' Wellington did do something to improve their conditions. Discipline remained severe but was not quite so pointlessly savage. Soldiers were housed in properly built barracks instead of being billeted amongst the civilian population, and this certainly reduced the unpopularity of the army. But once victory was assured in 1815 the old mistrust revived. Once again it became a disgrace for an honest working man to enlist as a soldier. The armed forces were cut back to a small force for home and colonial garrison duties. It was not until after the disastrously mismanaged Crimean campaigns, and the disturbing successes of the Prussian army later in the nineteenth century, that British governments came to grips with the problem of army reform.

The monarchy

The common soldier occupied the lowest order in society; at its head was the king. But in 1815 the monarch was neither a glorious nor a popular figure. The reign of George III had begun at the climax of British success in the Seven Years War, but it had been marred by the loss of the American colonies. The King's reputation had been damaged early in the reign by his association with unpopular courtiers and advisers, and by the high-handed actions of his ministers in the struggle with John Wilkes, the hero of the London mob. The political influence of the Crown declined and after 1811 the King was incapable of even his ceremonial duties. He suffered from bouts of apparent insanity and his authority was formally delegated to his eldest son George, the Prince Regent and the future King George IV.

High life and low life in Regency London:
(above) *dancing at Vauxhall Gardens,*
(below) *a dog fight at the Westminster Pit.*

Whatever his failings, George III had at least maintained something of the dignity and moral reputation of the throne. These were soon destroyed by his profligate son. The Regent was the leader of the fashionable world of London, Bath and Brighton. He and his friends, such as the famous fop Beau Brummel, lived in a world of unbridled extravagance and luxury which made them utterly remote from the condition of the ordinary people. The only point of contact between the debauched Prince and the mass of his subjects was a common interest in horse racing and prizefighting. When the impoverished blanketeers (see p. 19) of Lancashire tried to carry a petition to London to seek the Regent's help, they were showing a pitifully misplaced faith in their monarch. The political caricaturists and radical agitators, who knew more of him, found in his way of life and that of his imitators an endless supply of material for their revolutionary pamphlets and cartoons. Even amongst the ruling classes the Regent was regarded as a thoroughly disreputable character. Wellington, whose language was not particularly refined, said of him, 'He speaks so like old Falstaff, that, damn me, if I was not ashamed to walk into a room with him.' On the floor of the House of Commons Henry Brougham, the radical politician, denounced his 'utter disregard of an insulted and oppressed nation' and the way in which he and his circle 'proceeded from one wasteful expenditure to another, decorated their houses with the splendid results of their extravagance and associated with the most profligate of human beings'.

The Regency age had some attractive features. It was an age of elegance in both painting and architecture. The Nash Terraces around Regent's Park in London, the Crescent in Bath and the many small but beautifully proportioned town houses in Brighton and the other south coast resorts bear witness to this. Certainly it would be unfair to suggest that the wealthy classes as a whole modelled their lives on the Prince Regent. Yet it was a period in which social divisions seemed to be getting greater rather than less. The ruling classes exploited their control of Parliament to pass legislation such as the Corn laws (p. 15) to their advantage and against that of the mass of the people. As magistrates they executed the law in terms of narrow class interest, and as leaders of the Church they failed to take the message of Christianity into the new industrial towns. Thirty years after the fall of the Bastille there were few signs of Equality or Fraternity in British society, while Liberty existed only in a very attenuated form.

Freedom of the Press

Yet there was quite remarkable liberty in some fields. The invention of the steam-driven printing press in 1814 brought about a great growth in the circulation of newspapers. By 1816 there were 252 papers in Britain, and although most of these were concerned with local affairs, the London papers and those of the northern industrial towns carried a good deal of political news and comment. The laws of libel and the sense of public propriety were much less strict in those days. *The Times* made the most outspoken comments on the death of George IV in 1830, and no twentieth century newspaper proprietor would dare to publish the scathing caricatures by James Gillray and George Cruikshank which were so popular then. The Government did make some attempts to control the Press. During the years of acute unrest between 1815 and 1821 there were 121 prosecutions for seditious and blasphemous libel, and a heavy stamp duty was imposed to limit the circulation of the radical news-sheets. But the opposition Press could not be suppressed and the Government found it increasingly difficult to get convictions in the courts.

This freedom of the Press was the envy of European liberals who enjoyed no such liberty under the reactionary restored monarchies in their own countries. It did mean that many people, beyond the tiny minority that had the right to vote, could be informed of and involved in political affairs.

The British people in 1815
In retrospect, the early Industrial Revolution appears to be a time of squalor and suffering, of poverty and disease, of appalling living conditions and inadequate food. On the other hand there were a number of improvements in everyday things which made life more comfortable and more healthy. Brick, stone and tiles replaced wood, plaster and thatch as building materials; pottery and china crockery replaced wooden bowls and pewter mugs. Cheap cotton clothes made laundry easier and changes of clothing more frequent. Food was probably of a better quality and more plentiful. Certainly many contemporaries thought that life was getting better and that it was definitely superior to that led elsewhere in Europe. One foreign visitor, L. Simond, wrote at this time: 'If I were asked . . . for a summary of what I have seen in England, I might probably say that its institutions present a detail of corrupt practices. . . . On the other hand, I should admit very readily that I have found the great mass of the people richer, happier, and more respectable that any other with which I am acquainted'.

There is still a good deal of controversy as to whether the workers were 'worse-off' or 'better-off' in the early nineteenth century than they had been a generation or so before. In fact there is probably no simple answer in these terms. There were some sections of society, such as the handloom weavers, whose standard of living was steadily deteriorating; others, such as those forced from domestic industry into the factories, were no worse off materially but found their new way of life psychologically less acceptable. Finally there were those whose lives were improving but not fast enough to keep pace with their new aspirations. It was this group, the intelligent artisans, rather than the depressed rural labourers and the declining domestic craftsmen, that probably posed the most formidable challenge to established society in the first half of the century.

2. Crisis and Repression, 1815–21

THE THREE leading politicians in the years immediately following 1815 were Lord Liverpool, Prime Minister from 1812 to 1827, Lord Sidmouth, the Home Secretary, and Lord Castlereagh, the Foreign Secretary. They were rigid conservatives who saw the threat of revolution in any form of popular discontent. They had already been alarmed by the activities of the secret Luddite movement in Nottinghamshire in 1811. The aim of the Luddites (named after the mysterious Ned Ludd) was to smash the new machines which were replacing the skilled workers in the Nottingham hosiery industry. Their successful activities were imitated by bands of handloom weavers in Lancashire and Cheshire, where the new power-looms were attacked and destroyed. After the war there were outbreaks of machine-smashing in the countryside as well, notably at Littleport in the Isle of Ely. Lord Liverpool's reaction was to make machine-breaking a capital offence.

The Government and the economic crisis of 1816
The causes of distress have already been explained. Liverpool, following the prevailing economic ideas of *laissez faire*, had no constructive policy to offer. No aid was to be expected for industry and none for the poor beyond the Speenhamland system. The Prime Minister publicly declared that 'the evils inseparable from the state of things should not be charged on any Government; and, on inquiry, it would be found that by far the greater part of the miseries of which human nature complained were at all times and in all countries beyond the control of human legislation.' Nothing could be done! Lord Sidmouth agreed with these views. In 1812 he had stated: 'Man cannot create abundance where Providence has inflicted scarcity.' And in 1817, a year of great post-war distress, he declared that 'the alleviation of the difficulties is not to be looked for from the intervention of Government and Parliament.'

The Corn Laws
The Government's policy of non-intervention applied especially to industry. Their attitude towards agriculture was quite different. The landed interest still dominated Parliament and it was from this group that the leading politicians were drawn. With the end of the war and the resumption of imports of grain, the price of wheat had fallen from 126s. 6d. a quarter

in 1812 to 65s. 7d. in 1815. From 1813 to 1815 hundreds of farmers who had borrowed money to expand the area of land under cultivation on the security of high prices were unable to repay, and found themselves in debtors' gaols. This led to a severe loss of rent by the landlords who raised a cry of protest in Parliament. Lord Liverpool came to their aid with the Corn Law of 1815.

The aim of the law was to keep up wheat prices by forbidding the import of foreign grain until the home price rose above 80s. a quarter. For the next two years wheat prices rose, reaching 96s. 11d. in 1817, a year of poor harvest, dear bread and unemployment. But in the long run even this legislation failed, and prices fell to 44s. 7d. between 1821 and 1825. There was some improvement thereafter but prices did not rise above 73s. As a result the wheaten loaf was too dear for the poorly paid agricultural labourers and the unemployed workers in the towns, but it was still too cheap to prevent numerous bankruptcies amongst farmers.

Financial policy of Liverpool

The Government's financial policy also aroused resentment from the more articulate sections of the working class under the influence of Radicals like William Cobbett. This was especially the case over income tax. It had been introduced in 1797 to meet the heavy costs of the French war. In 1815 the tax was bringing in about £15 million, one quarter of the total Government revenue. Yet Liverpool, influenced by *laissez faire* doctrines, and under pressure from the wealthier classes, both landed and commercial, removed income tax altogether and increased duties on articles of ordinary consumption to make up the loss in revenue. This substitution of indirect for direct taxation placed an extra burden on the working classes and was vigorously attacked by Cobbett and his followers.

Cobbett also denounced the return to the Gold Standard by an act of 1819. The Government took this step to check the inflation produced by the banks issuing bank notes without having reserves that would enable them to convert the paper into gold on demand. The rise in prices was to some extent checked by the Act, and the economy stabilized. Cobbett's criticism was that with a fall of prices, the *actual* burden of the National Debt was increased. However, the Tory Governments did succeed in reducing the total of the National Debt by more than £60 million by the year 1830.

The Radicals

The difficulties of the working class were given publicity by a number of would-be reformers of the social and political system. These were generally known as 'Radicals' although they were not an organized party and did not even agree amongst themselves. Nevertheless, they had a common hatred of the evils which the war and the Industrial Revolution had produced. Above all, they loathed the Government of Lord Liverpool and demanded the extension of the right to vote to many more people.

There were already a few Radicals in Parliament. Such members as Joseph Hume and Sir Francis Burdett constituted a radical wing of the Whig party, while 'Orator' Henry Hunt, Francis Place, William Cobbett, Major John Cartwright and others were intensely active outside Parliament in these years. Robert Owen, factory owner, philanthropist and early socialist was also concerned with these same problems of social and political justice. Owen stood apart from most other radicals in the immediate post-war years, though he was to gain an increasing influence with the working class from about 1820 onwards.

William Cobbett (1763–1835)
Of all these radicals William Cobbett not only had the most astonishing and colourful career, but probably exercised the most stirring influence over the labouring population in town and country. He was the first great modern agitator to give the working class or the 'masses', a sense of their political and social rights both as individuals and as a class.

He ran away from his life as a ploughboy, and became first a soldier, and then a teacher of English and pamphleteer in America. At that time he was an outright Tory in all his sympathies and was an outspoken opponent of the rebellious American colonists. Later he also opposed the French Revolution and crossed swords with its greatest English supporter, Thomas Paine. In all this there was no sign of his later radicalism. His journal, the *Political Register*, was established to fight democratic ideas and Jacobinism. Gradually, however, his views changed. He became increasingly aware of the injustice of the English social system. The *Political Register* began to change its tone as Cobbett realized that his Tory friends would not remedy the evils he observed. He soon became a serious nuisance to his former allies especially when, during the Napoleonic Wars, he denounced the Duke of York for selling commissions in the army to royal favourites, and bitterly attacked the army authorities for allowing German mercenaries to flog British soldiers who were demanding arrears of pay. The Government ordered his prosecution. He was fined £1,000 (a huge sum in those days) and sent to Newgate prison for two years.

These experiences made Cobbett more active than ever. In 1816 he founded a twopenny version of his *Political Register*, cheap enough to be bought by the workers. In one year it reached a circulation of about 60,000 and was read aloud by the literate to the illiterate in working men's clubs and political organizations. In this 'twopenny trash' as his opponents called it, Cobbett took up the cause of parliamentary reform, denounced the Poor Law, the factory system and all its consequences, condemned the Corn Laws and Lord Liverpool's cabinet and quarrelled with a number of his fellow Radicals. In 1816 he went to America again for a few years in order to escape arrest, but his *Political Register* continued to be published by his supporters in Britain. When he returned to England, he began to write his *Rural Rides* – an account of his journeys through England in which he observed the good and bad in English agriculture and exposed the sufferings of the labouring population. *Rural Rides* appeared in the Register from 1821, and was published in book form in 1830. Besides his intense political activity in the years 1815–30, he wrote half a dozen other books of considerable merit and importance.

The Spa Fields riots

The years 1816–21 were marked by mass meetings and marches, a new and alarming phenomenon to contemporary British political leaders. The first demonstration occurred in London at Spa Fields in 1816, a year of great distress and unemployment. The demonstration was organized by a group influenced by Thomas Spence (1750–1814) who had advocated the nationalization of all land and the imposition of a single tax to replace all other forms of taxation. Amongst the leaders of this Spa Fields demonstration was Arthur Thistlewood, an avowed republican.

The first meeting took place peacefully, and was followed on the same day by another addressed by 'Orator' Hunt, who had no sympathy with Spence's ideas and spoke for the Radical programme of parliamentary reform instead. These protest meetings stirred up popular feeling to fever pitch, and a large mob began to parade through the London streets, some seizing guns from a gunsmith's shop and preparing to march on the Tower of London. Some wore French revolutionary 'caps of liberty' and carried pikes in the Jacobin manner. Lord Sidmouth and his colleagues, who had spies planted in the organization, declared that a general rising was threatened. The Houses of Parliament appointed 'Committees of Secrecy' to investigate the disturbances.

Suspension of Habeas Corpus and the spy system

The reports of the 'Committees of Secrecy' led to the suspension of the Habeas Corpus Act, which guaranteed the subject against imprisonment without trial. The suspension was for one year, but was renewed for another year in 1818. This was a serious limitation on individual freedom and had last been used by the Government during the war years from 1794 to 1801. A number of radical journalists and agitators were imprisoned during 1817–18. All public meetings had to be authorized by the magistrates; licences were necessary for reading-rooms, public houses and coffee houses which could be closed by order if it were suspected that Radical meetings had taken place on the premises. Sidmouth sent out more Government agents, headed by the infamous Oliver, to infiltrate Radical organizations, pretending to be sympathizers. In addition magistrates in the industrial areas were advised to use agents of their own. These measures of the Home Office were not as effective as had been hoped. London juries particularly tended to show leniency in cases of high treason. For instance, the Spenceans who had organized the Spa Fields demonstration were acquitted on this charge. But as nothing was done to deal with the basic causes of discontent, the extremists became even more desperate. In 1818 Thistlewood was sentenced to a year's imprisonment in Horsham gaol for challenging Lord Sidmouth to a duel.

The Blanketeers, 1817

The discontented workers in the Midlands and the North had seen all the efforts of the Londoners fail. The Radicals were divided and alarmed. Cobbett had fled to America, others were in prison or in hiding. The northern weavers decided to act on their own, and organize a march from Manchester to London early in 1817. The weavers were to march in groups of ten, each man with a blanket on his back and a petition to the Prince Regent fixed to his arm. They were to request the Prince Regent to do something to remedy the ills of the cotton industry. The march was preceded by an open-air meeting in St Peter's Fields, Manchester, and about six hundred men set out. Many were arrested by the militia before they reached Stockport; about four hundred reached Macclesfield, but only one man got to London – and he duly presented his petition. There was a sequel typical of the times. Some blanketeers were imprisoned in Manchester, and four of their sympathizers were arrested for plotting to set fire to the city to avenge them. They had been deliberately led on to this plot by a local spy and informer.

Activities of Oliver the spy

The chief Government spy, Oliver, was active in the north throughout 1817. He and other agents reported that the masses were about to rebel. These reports fell on willing ears – the Duke of Northumberland had compared the march of the blanketeers to the march of the Marseillais to Paris during the French Revolution. The Government arrested still more Radical leaders.

Oliver's method in the North was to pretend that he was a delegate from the London 'physical force' group of the Radicals. He was most successful in Derbyshire, where the condition of the unemployed frame-knitters was appalling. Under the leadership of Jeremiah Brandreth, a small band of men, seizing what arms they could find, set out to march on Nottingham hoping for wide support there. Near Nottingham the insurrectionists were met by a band of soldiers and captured. Thirty-five of them were tried at Derby for high treason. Brandreth and two others were hanged.

There is no proof that Oliver had deliberately stirred up Brandreth's futile insurrection, but certainly his general activities had contributed to the state of unrest which led to it. There is also no proof that Lord Sidmouth deliberately planned such provocation through Oliver. In fact Oliver was used without much care. The local magistrates were not told that he was in their midst, and frequently local informers were spying on the Government spy.

In 1818 trade improved, unemployment fell and with it popular unrest.

The suspension of Habeas Corpus was not renewed. But in 1819 another industrial depression set in and things were as bad as ever.

The Peterloo Massacre, 1819

The depression of 1819 produced another outburst of Radical agitation led by men like 'Orator' Hunt and Major John Cartwright who demanded manhood suffrage and the repeal of the Corn Laws. In August 1819, the Manchester radicals decided to hold a mass meeting in St Peter's Fields. The principal speaker was to be Hunt. The organizers had taken every precaution to make it non-violent, yet the local magistrates were worried by rumours of revolt and held the Yeomanry in readiness. Thousands of men, women and children converged on the meeting-place peacefully, though with banners flying. Only the aged and infirm carried sticks. Altogether it was an orderly and respectable gathering. Orator Hunt, who knew that the magistrates intended to arrest him, offered to give himself up before the meeting began, but this was refused and the meeting took its course. Half-way through, the magistrates decided it was illegal and sent in the Yeomanry to arrest Hunt, who allowed himself to be taken without resistance. However, the Yeomanry had had some difficulty in reaching the platform, and were surrounded by angry protesters. They drew their sabres and at the same time a troop of Hussars was sent to their assistance. The soldiers no longer used the flats of their sabres, but began to strike out in all directions. The crowd attempted to escape, and there was a general panic. In ten

A political cartoonist's version of the Massacre of Peterloo.

minutes the field was cleared, but 400 people, including 113 women, were wounded, and 11 killed.

This 'massacre of Peterloo', as it was bitterly called, was denounced from many different quarters. Even the moderate Whigs joined with the Radicals in protest. The Tory Lord Mayor of London and the Common Council addressed a letter of protest to the Prince Regent; Manchester itself was seething with anger; Cobbett returned from America and Henry Hunt, released on bail, was greeted by a crowd of 25,000 in London. The Government, however, were quite unabashed – the Prince Regent congratulated the magistrates on their action, and the lord-lieutenant of Yorkshire was dismissed for having organized a protest. Oliver the spy was judiciously appointed by the Government as Inspector of Buildings in South Africa. Meanwhile, when discontent turned to violence in the industrial areas of Scotland in April 1820, the Government used force again. The Tenth Hussars were used to disperse a crowd of Glasgow workers marching on the Carron iron works at Falkirk. It was the aftermath of Peterloo that Cobbett had in mind when he described the state of England: 'Gaols ten times as big as formerly; houses of correction; treadmills; the hulks; and the country filled with spies of one sort and another.'

The tragedy of Peterloo might well have provoked more violent demonstrations, but the northern industrial workers who were most outraged by it were still only a minority of the population. As it was, Liverpool was able to impose still more restrictions on political liberty.

The Six Acts
These restrictions were embodied in the Six Acts, devised by Sidmouth and introduced into the Commons in 1819 by Lord Castlereagh. The Acts imposed even more stringent regulations than those of 1817 (see p. 18). Meetings for the purpose of presenting petitions were restricted to the residents of the parish in which the meeting was to be held. Magistrates were given power to convict offenders at once instead of committing them to the Assizes. They could search private houses if they considered it necessary, suppress all armed drilling and ban any meeting of which they disapproved. Another regulation was aimed especially at Radical publications such as Cobbett's *Register*, Richard Carlile's *Republican*, and the cheap reprints of Thomas Paine's *Rights of Man* and *The Age of Reason*. The heavy tax on newspapers was now extended to periodical publications of all kinds. However, this last regulation was not very successful; Cobbett continued to publish his *Register* without the official stamp, and other papers appeared in a similar way. Their editors were repeatedly fined and sent to prison, but the 'unstamped press' still flourished.

The Cato Street Conspiracy, 1820
In 1820 Arthur Thistlewood and some sympathizers among the Spencean Philanthropists produced a desperate plan to murder the whole Cabinet

The arrest of the Cato Street Conspirators.

and seize control of London. Edwards, a Government spy, helped them to prepare the scheme. It was probably this agent who arranged for a false newspaper advertisement of a Grand Cabinet Dinner. This advertisement stirred the conspirators to action, but they were raided by police as they were making their final preparations in a barn off the Edgware Road. Thistlewood, who killed one of the men sent to arrest him, was executed together with the other leaders. The whole affair was used by the Government to justify the Six Acts. And indeed the conspiracy did frighten many of the middle class so much that they once more gave the Government their support.

The Queen's affair

The Liverpool administration regained some popularity over the Cato Street conspiracy, only to lose it again through the curious affair of Queen Caroline. The Prince Regent had secretly married Mrs Fitzherbert in 1785. Some years later he committed bigamy by marrying Princess Caroline of Brunswick. After a little while they separated and the Prince Regent tried to divorce Caroline by charging her with loose conduct while on her travels in Italy. For the Prince Regent to make such a charge was an unmatchable piece of hypocrisy, and in fact a parliamentary inquiry into her conduct proved nothing. When the Regent became King in 1820 he determined to prevent Caroline becoming Queen, and sought the dissolution of his marriage by Act of Parliament. This, however, led to a full inquiry into the conduct of both the Prince Regent and his wife – an unsavoury business which further damaged his reputation. Caroline returned to England and was given a rousingly sympathetic reception by the people of London. The House of Lords meanwhile passed the Bill of Pains and Penalties which would have led to a dissolution of her marriage, but the majority was so slight that Lord Liverpool would not introduce it into the Commons. The coronation took place. Caroline tried to force her way into Westminster Abbey, urged on by a sympathetic mob. She gave up the attempt and – conveniently for the new King – died a month later.

The 'Queen's Affair' did great harm to the monarchy; the Radicals took up the Queen's cause against George IV; William Cobbett acted as one of her close advisers and carried on constant propaganda on her behalf.

Some comments on the Liverpool administration in the years 1815–21

The immediate post-war years were a time of poverty, tragedy and suffering for the working class and of increasing privilege and prosperity for the upper classes. The Government's policies made no concessions to mass pressure, but relied on repressive measures such as the Six Acts. The prevailing ideas of *laissez faire* prevented any sort of constructive policy being formed to ease the post-war difficulties.

The House of Commons could give no leadership. Attendance was poor, even on important occasions, and the standard of debating low. The smug representatives of the landed interests could only summon 163 members out of a total of more than 600 to vote on the debates over Government spies in industrial areas. Other matters, such as the Corn Laws and foreign affairs, always interested Liverpool himself much more than these serious matters of personal liberty. Apart from a handful of Radicals, the opposition was also quite ineffectual in these years. Parliament and Government still represented the 'old order'; as yet they had not come to grips with the new problems presented by Britain's emerging industrial society.

3. The Enlightened Tories

BETWEEN 1820 and 1824 British exports increased by about 40 per cent. The new prosperity this brought helped to damp down the Radical agitation. At the same time Liverpool, under pressure from a powerful minority of his younger colleagues, made a number of new Cabinet appointments. Sir Robert Peel replaced Sidmouth at the Home Office in 1822, George Canning became Foreign Secretary on the suicide of Castlereagh and William Huskisson became President of the Board of Trade.

Liverpool and the old Tories had strong reasons for making these changes. They hoped that the policies of the new men would so please the industrial middle class that they would continue to accept the old parliamentary system, with its narrow electorate based on the landed interest.

Characteristics of the Enlightened Tories
The new men had one thing in common – they all understood the importance of industry and overseas trade. Canning (see Chapter 5) did much to establish British trade with the South American republics when they broke away from Spain and Portugal. Huskisson and the new Chancellor of the Exchequer (Robinson) swept away outdated restrictions, monopolies and taxation. Sir Robert Peel was a most effective reformer of the law and later of the system of finance and taxation.

These new men differed in another important way from their aristocratic colleagues. Both in background and interests they were nearer to the middle class and were prepared to appeal for their support. George Canning, for instance, shocked Wellington and his friends by addressing large public meetings and explaining his policy to them.

William Huskisson
Among the most progressive of the new men was William Huskisson. He became President of the Board of Trade in 1823 and succeeded Canning as M.P. for Liverpool. Huskisson really began the policy of free trade which became the basis of the British economy in the nineteenth century. During the Napoleonic Wars the movement towards free trade, which had started as early as 1784 under the Younger Pitt, was not only halted, but reversed. To raise money for the war the Government had imposed heavy duties on imported raw materials, and taxed a wide range of commodities in common use, such as glass, metal goods, books, paper, silk, woollen and cotton

Parkside Station on the Liverpool–Manchester Railway where Huskisson was killed by the Rocket steam locomotive in 1830.

goods, and even candles and domestic servants. When income tax was abolished in 1816, these taxes were increased in order to make up for the loss of revenue (see p. 16).

Huskisson saw that this policy damaged trade and hindered prosperity and so he attacked the system of indirect taxes and duties. Firstly, many commodities which had been refused entry to Britain altogether were now allowed in at moderate duties. Secondly, he reduced the excise duties on everyday manufactures by 30 per cent. Thirdly, he cut the very high customs duties on many luxury goods. This not only encouraged trade but also made smuggling unprofitable and allowed the Government to reduce expenditure on the vast army of customs officers who patrolled the coasts. Fourthly, he reduced the duties on a number of basic imports, such as cotton, a matter of great importance to his trading and manufacturing constituents in the north. Huskisson also negotiated reciprocal treaties with the United States and other Powers by which Britain agreed to reduce tariffs on their goods if they did the same for British exports.

Huskisson also tackled the old Navigation Acts. These Acts, passed in the seventeenth century against the Dutch, were supposed to prevent British cargoes being carried in any but British ships. By the 1820's they were completely out of date and merely provoked retaliation from other countries. Huskisson's Reciprocity Act of 1823 led a number of countries to agree with Britain on equal facilities in their trading relationships.

Huskisson foresaw a great future for the British Empire as a trading community, and he did much to aid the development of the colonies. For instance, he maintained a high protective duty on timber imports from other countries in order to safeguard the Canadian products. He also introduced preferential duties which aided exports from the colonies to the home country. He promoted emigration to Canada, New Zealand and Australia. He also delivered a final blow at the old Mercantile System, which had lost Britain the American colonies, by allowing British colonies to trade directly with European countries. These changes reflected Huskisson's well-founded confidence that Britain had the industrial power to compete freely with other countries to her own advantage.

Huskisson's battle with the old restrictive policies was of the greatest importance for the development of Britain in the nineteenth century. He was killed when he stepped in the path of a locomotive at the opening of the Manchester and Liverpool Railway in 1830, a tragically ironic end to the man whose policies in helping trade and industry expand had made the railways so essential to Britain.

Sir Robert Peel

Sir Robert Peel was the son of a wealthy Lancashire cotton manufacturer who had himself shown interest in factory reform and secured the passing of the first (but ineffective) Factory Act in 1819. The younger Peel, after a brilliant academic career at Harrow and Oxford, entered Parliament in 1809. He represented an Irish borough bought for him by his father, who hoped to see his son become Prime Minister. In 1812, again thanks to his father's influence, he was appointed Chief Secretary for Ireland. Liverpool promoted him to this post not only for his marked abilities as an administrator, but also because at that time he strongly opposed any change in the laws relating to Roman Catholics, a question which was already a violent issue in Ireland. The old Tories regarded Peel as the safest of the younger men and one who would continue to bolster up the domination of Ireland by the Protestant landlords.

In 1822 Peel became Home Secretary. During the next eight years he carried out highly important reforms. For many years past Radicals inside and outside Parliament had been demanding reform of the barbarous criminal laws. Some improvement in prison conditions had been achieved by the reformer John Howard (1726–90), but during the wars conditions in the prisons had deteriorated and individuals from all parties pressed for reform. Under the influence of Jeremy Bentham, Sir Samuel Romilly (1756–1818) led these demands. As Solicitor General in the Government of 1806, he fought to reduce the number of capital offences, but his only success was the abolition of the death sentence for pickpockets in 1808. Romilly committed suicide in 1818 and his work in Parliament was carried on by Sir James Mackintosh. But he too met with solid opposition from the old Tories. He managed to outlaw man-traps and spring-guns on landlords' estates, but apart from that could do little more than keep the question of penal reform before Parliament.

Sir Robert Peel was open to reasoned persuasion on penal reform. He consulted both the great Radical philosopher, Jeremy Bentham (see Chapter 6), and another strong advocate of criminal law reform, Henry Brougham. Over two hundred offences carried the death penalty in 1820 and in 1813 there had been a gruesome mockery of justice when a boy of 13 was hanged for stealing a sheep. Over four hundred offences (including the formation of a trade union) could be punished by transportation to the convict settlements of Australia. This barbarous severity defeated its own ends, for if a man intended to commit a crime he might as well risk hanging for a big crime as a small one. On many occasions humane juries refused to convict a proved offender rather than see a man publicly hanged for a petty crime. Impressed by such arguments Peel came to the conclusion that reform was necessary on the grounds of both humanity and efficiency. In 1823 he introduced four Bills which, by concentrating on the more flagrant abuses, secured the assent of Parliament. About 180 crimes were removed from the capital list. The death penalty was abolished for such offences as cutting the banks of rivers or the hop-binds in the hop fields, or impersonating a Greenwich pensioner. One of these Acts of Parliament put an end to the ghastly custom of burying suicides near the highways with a stake driven through their bodies. Such were the practices against which Romilly, Mackintosh, Brougham and Bentham had agitated for so long. At that time Peel's action was regarded as distinctly courageous, and even he was not able to sweep all the barbarities away. Public hanging, for example, continued for another thirty years.

Peel also initiated a number of reforms in the administration of prisons and the classification and separation of prisoners. No longer were debtors

The unreformed prisons: prisoners at Brixton gaol on the treadmill.

and petty offenders herded together in the same room as violent criminals in the bad old prisons like Newgate and Clerkenwell. Peel also put an end to the employment of paid Government spies and *agents provocateurs*, a decisive break with the policies of 1815–21.

The term 'bobby' is a reminder that it was Peel who pioneered the present police system of Britain. In forming the Metropolitan Police Force in 1829 he was following his reforms of the penal law by the next logical step, namely, the creation of an efficient police system not only to catch the criminal but to deter him. Until that time the only detectives were the Bow Street Runners, organized by a private business. The 'runners' were frequently in league with criminals, and they wore a red uniform which could be seen at a considerable distance. The only preventive force were the parish night-watchmen who were often old and decrepit and, particularly in London, almost useless for controlling crime. Peel had already set up an organized police force in Ireland and he used this experience when he set up the system in London. Peel also established the principle that the police should carry no firearms. Gradually other local authorities copied the Metropolitan force as the criminals were driven out of London into the provinces.

Repeal of the Combination Laws, 1824
Two major reforms of the 1820's were achieved in spite of, rather than with the aid of, the Liberal Tories. The first of these, the repeal of Pitt's laws of 1799 and 1800 against the trade unions, was passed by Parliament in 1824. This was the work of the Radical tailor of Charing Cross, Francis Place, and his friends in the House of Commons, Joseph Hume and Sir Francis Burdett. In 1824 Hume, following Place's suggestion, secured the appointment of a parliamentary committee to inquire into the trade union question. This committee was skilfully packed with Hume's supporters. Place himself selected the skilled artisans who were to appear before the committee to give evidence. He rehearsed them in the library of his workshop in Charing Cross, so that they were ready for the committee's questions. These men, drawn from London and large industrial towns, made a great impression on the committee by their education, speech and general moderation. Place had chosen them for this very reason, and the aggressive, militant agitators were kept well away from the committee's proceedings. Place felt convinced that once the trade unions were allowed normal existence they would shun violence and the workers would set about helping the employers to increase production and consequently their own prosperity. This line of argument appealed to the wavering Whigs and Tories and, in the more relaxed conditions of 1824, with trade expanding and unemployment at a low level, Parliament passed an act giving remarkable freedom to form unions.

The results of this Act were the opposite of what Place had expected. Trade unions which had been forced to disguise themselves as friendly societies for sickness and unemployment benefits now came out into the open in their hundreds. The speculative boom in industry in 1824 meant greatly increased profits for the employers, and the trade unions demanded increased wages and threatened to strike. The cost of living had risen fast in this period. The standard loaf which cost about 8d. in 1822 rose to 11d. in 1824, and this added force to the trade union demands. Many wage increases were made in 1824, but in the following year the boom collapsed and there was once again bankruptcy and unemployment.

The supporters of Liverpool's Government demanded the outlawing of the trade unions once again, but Place, Hume, Burdett and their supporters waged a vigorous and effective campaign to prevent this. Nevertheless, although the trade unions remained legal, a number of serious obstacles were put in their way by the amending Act of 1825. Trade unions were not allowed to 'molest' or 'obstruct' employers or other workers. This, of course, made strikes extremely difficult to carry out, for the courts, controlled by judges and magistrates who were incliend to regard all trade unionists as conspirators, were likely to interpret these legal terms widely. However, despite these difficulties, the years after 1825 witnessed a rapid growth in the trade union movement.

Catholic emancipation

When the struggle between the Stuarts and their Protestant opponents had ended in the flight of James II and the accession of William III in 1688, the Roman Catholics lost a number of political rights. Although some of these rights had been restored, many were still withheld. The religious problem these laws produced was particularly acute in Ireland and had grown worse with the 1800 Act of Union between England and Ireland. Here the problem was economic as well as religious. The country was four-fifths Catholic but most of the landlords and all the Government office holders were Protestant. No Catholic could be elected to Parliament. This meant that the Catholics of Ireland, whether peasant or merchant, had no legal means of voicing their grievances except when they could win the support of the Radicals in Britain. Although they were aware of the economic abuses of the Protestant landowners, Peel and most of his colleagues were bitterly opposed to releasing Catholics from the restrictive laws. They feared (correctly, as events proved) that Catholic emancipation would be the beginning of a process which would lead to the complete independence of Ireland from the British Crown.

The protest against these disabilities was led by one of the most effective Irish agitators of the nineteenth century, a lawyer called Daniel O'Connell. His aim was to secure the repeal of the Act of Union and to re-establish an independent Irish Parliament dominated by the Catholic majority. He did not want a complete break from England in such matters as foreign policy, but demanded an Irish parliament to conduct the internal affairs of the country. Catholic emancipation was an essential step towards this goal.

In 1823 O'Connell formed the Catholic Association. This organization soon became remarkably powerful. Even poorer Catholics gave a penny a month to the funds, a contribution known as the 'Catholic rent'. The Catholic priesthood strongly supported O'Connell's movement. Soon Catholic emancipation had become a nation-wide demand in Ireland, impossible for the English Parliament to ignore.

The County Clare election

Although Catholics could not be elected as M.P.s, O'Connell put himself forward as a candidate in an election in County Clare in 1828 against Vesey Fitzgerald, an Irish Protestant landlord who was in fact quite popular. Such was O'Connell's influence with the forty-shilling freehold voters that they marched to the poll with the priests at their head, and O'Connell was triumphantly elected.

In 1827 Lord Liverpool resigned and there followed a number of short-lived ministries. Canning, his immediate successor, died in 1828 and was followed by Goderich (formerly F. J. Robinson, the Chancellor of the Exchequer) who was unable to hold the Government together for more than a few weeks. Finally Wellington agreed reluctantly to form a Government. Huskisson and his Liberal Tory supporters were thrown out of the Government but Peel, who had refused to serve under Canning, now came back in. Peel and Wellington were both opposed to Catholic emancipation so that the County Clare election was fought just at a time when O'Connell had lost his few supporters in the English Government.

Repeal of the Test and Corporation Acts; the Catholic Emancipation Act

Just before the County Clare election Lord John Russell, leader of the younger Whigs, had secured the abolition of the Test and Corporation Acts. These had been passed in the reign of Charles II to prevent anyone who was not a communicant member of the Church of England from holding the most important offices in the state or being members of the local corporations. For years they had not affected Protestant Dissenters who were freed from penalties for holding such offices by an Annual Act of Indemnity. The repeal of these Acts focused further attention on the position of Catholics.

With the election of O'Connell for County Clare, Wellington faced the possibility of civil war in Ireland, unless concessions were made. Although O'Connell personally was opposed to violence, he might well be unable to control his more extreme followers. Wellington was not prepared to risk this and had to reverse his position. He had forced his own brother the Marquess Wellesley to resign from the Lord Lieutenancy of Ireland because of his support for Catholic emancipation, but now Wellington and Peel had to persuade the Tory Party and Parliament to accept the measure demanded by O'Connell. Peel persuaded the King, George IV, while Wellington himself browbeat the House of Lords into acceptance by threats of civil war and turmoil. Peel had to rely on the support of the Whigs to secure the passing of the Catholic Emancipation Act by the House of Commons.

However, Wellington and his friends were not entirely finished with the matter. Peel, as Home Secretary, deliberately passed O'Connell over when the first Catholic barristers were appointed in Ireland. Wellington also, on a technical argument, forced O'Connell to fight the County Clare election all over again before he could take his seat in the House of Commons. Wellington also disenfranchised the forty-shilling freehold voters in Ireland and raised the qualification for the franchise to £10.

Position of the Tory Party in 1830

By 1830 the position of the Tory party, which had governed Britain for nearly fifty years, was critical. The old Tories, especially the Irish landlords, were embittered by Wellington's change of face over Catholic emancipation. The Liberal Tories, like Huskisson, refused to work with him and were drawn towards the Whigs. Wellington's opponents in his party were only waiting for an opportunity to make him pay for what they regarded as his political treachery. Their opportunity came with the revival of the parliamentary reform movement in England.

The impetus for this revival came from the 1830 July Revolution which overthrew Charles X of France and the successful revolt of the Belgians against the Dutch king. Wellington had no sympathy with the Belgian or French revolutionary movements, and in this respect the more progressive Tories and Whigs were against him. The year 1830 was one of widespread hardship and unemployment recalling the worst days of the period immediately after 1815. There were outbreaks of rick-burning in the southern countryside, while in the north working men openly prepared for revolution. In these circumstances the Whigs took up more strongly the demand for parliamentary reform in the hope of staving off serious social disturbance. On the death of George IV and the accession of William IV in 1830 a general election took place and the Whigs increased their representation. Lord Grey then raised the question of parliamentary reform, but Wellington replied that 'the system of representation possessed the full and entire confidence of the country'. In reply a combination of the progressive Tories, the Whigs and the old Tories, who thirsted for political revenge against Wellington and Peel, defeated the Government in the Commons and forced Wellington to resign. The King asked Lord Grey to form a Government and after fifty years of unsuccessful opposition, the Whigs were once more in office. This dramatic change at Westminster was soon to have far-reaching effects for the rest of the country.

4. The Foreign Policy of Castlereagh and Canning

The Congress of Vienna, 1814–15

During 1814 and 1815, with some interruption when Napoleon escaped from Elba, the representatives of the Great Powers met at Vienna to re-settle Europe after the turmoil of the Revolution and the Napoleonic Wars.

The leading personalities attending the Congress were the Czar Alexander I of Russia, Prince Metternich for Austria, King Frederick William III of Prussia, Talleyrand for France and Lord Castlereagh for Britain. The main problems facing the Congress were how to guard against further French aggression, how to meet the territorial demands of the victorious Powers and how to maintain an effective alliance among themselves to preserve the settlement.

The first problem was met by strengthening the small states on France's eastern frontiers. The Austrian Netherlands (Belgium) were united with Holland as a barrier on the north-east, the direction taken by the French Revolutionary Armies of 1792. In Northern Italy the King of Sardinia was restored to power and given control of the formerly free republic of Genoa. Prussia was granted large areas along the Rhine.

The second question led to some conflict amongst the allies. There was a serious dispute over the fate of Poland and Saxony, both former allies of Napoleon. The Czar Alexander demanded the whole of the Grand Duchy of Warsaw and the Prussians agreed to this provided they obtained the whole of the Kingdom of Saxony. Castlereagh allied with Metternich and Talleyrand against Alexander and forced him to be content with less than his first demands, while Prussian demands were also reduced to Danzig and Posen, Western Pomerania and about two-fifths of the Saxon kingdom. Austria obtained Venetia and Lombardy in northern Italy and part of the Adriatic coast. Sweden gained Norway from Denmark as compensation for her loss of Finland to Russia and as a punishment to Denmark for her alliance with Napoleon. In Germany Napoleon had drastically reduced the number of small independent States. The Congress recognized that this could not be reversed and set up a new German Confederation of thirty-nine states. Britain made important additions to her empire, gaining Cape Colony, Ceylon, Mauritius, Trinidad, Tobago and St Lucia, Heligoland, Malta, and a protectorate over the Ionian Islands.

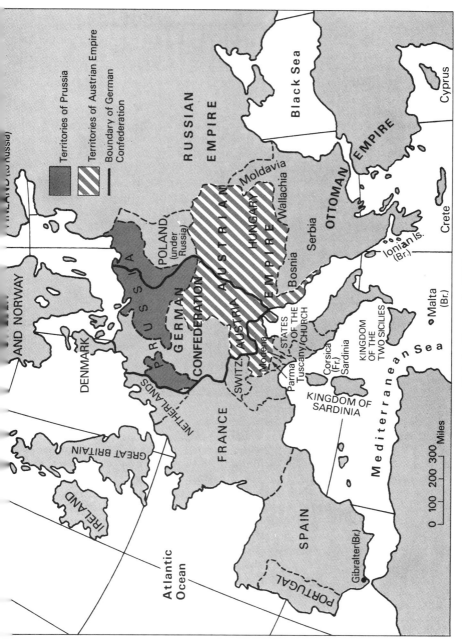

FIG. 1. Europe in 1815

Lord Castlereagh

The British Foreign Secretary had played a large part in creating the alliance which had defeated Napoleon and he was equally important in drawing up the settlement at Vienna. Castlereagh did a good deal to reduce the demands of the other powers. In Britain, however, he was regarded by many as a reactionary whose main aim was to restore pre-revolutionary Europe under despotic kings and their henchmen.

This criticism did not do justice to him. In the face of Prussian opposition, he urged strongly that France should not be forced back to the frontiers of 1789, but that the frontiers won by the revolutionary armies of 1792 should be accepted by the Congress. He had no love for revolutions and their conquests, but he saw the need to bring France gradually into the European political system which he was attempting to create. He believed that a policy of revenge would make France more likely to try to overthrow the settlement and in any case he saw in a revived France a vital counterbalance to the power of the eastern European despots.

Castlereagh and the Holy Alliance

In 1815 the Czar Alexander put forward a plan for what he called the Holy Alliance. It was, however, more in the nature of an agreement than an alliance, for it did not bind the signatories to any specific obligations. The sovereigns of Europe were to promise to keep their countries in constant accord and to rule their peoples on the basis of the principles of Christian brotherhood. This declaration was signed by all the powers of Europe except Great Britain and the Pope. Castlereagh adopted a hardheaded, realistic attitude to what he called the 'sublime mysticism and nonsense' of the Czar's proposal.

Yet Castlereagh himself was anxious to find a way to maintain the peaceful co-operation of the victorious Powers after the Congress. He was largely responsible for the creation of the Quadruple Alliance of 1815 between Great Britain, Austria, Russia and Prussia. At first France was not admitted to the alliance, for the allies were not prepared to recognize France as an equal. The alliance guaranteed the arrangements already made at Vienna and its members also agreed 'to renew their meetings at fixed periods for the purpose of consulting upon their common interests'. Their declared purpose was to maintain the 'repose and prosperity of nations and . . . the peace of Europe'.

Although the system of periodic meetings did in time break down, the peace of Europe was maintained for a long period – in fact, no major war occurred until the outbreak of the Crimean War in 1854. Castlereagh's idea of the periodic meetings of the Great Powers was something new in the affairs of Europe, and Castlereagh looked forward to the time when all disputes could be settled by such peaceful means.

Castlereagh and the Congresses

Castlereagh envisaged a conciliatory role in international affairs for Great Britain. This was demonstrated at the first congress, that of Aix-la-Chapelle in 1818. The Congress decided upon the withdrawal of the army of occupation from France and her admission to the Quadruple Alliance, which thus became the Quintuple Alliance. There were already revolutionary stirrings in a number of European states, especially in Spain, where a liberal revolution broke out in 1818. Castlereagh, while detesting what he called 'the revolutionary pest', was anxious to prevent the intervention of the members of the Quintuple Alliance in the affairs of Spain. In particular he suspected the motives of the Czar Alexander who wished to send an army through Western Europe to suppress the Spanish revolt. Over this Castlereagh and Metternich agreed, for the Austrians greatly feared the extension of Russian influence further into Europe. Eventually Castlereagh persuaded the other four Powers to sign a declaration of non-intervention in the internal affairs of other nations. This special declaration affirmed their 'invariable resolution never to depart, either among themselves or in their relations with other States, from the strictest observation of the principles of the rights of nations'. This declaration remained the keynote of British policy, but it meant little to the other powers, as events at later congresses were to show.

In 1820 and 1821 revolts broke out in Naples, Portugal and Spain. The revolutionaries hoped to force the despotic rulers restored by the Congress of Vienna to introduce constitutional government. At the same time in South America the old colonies of Spain and Portugal broke away and established national Governments of their own. These revolts produced a very complicated situation in Europe. The Austrians had a special treaty with the King of Naples by which Austria would help him to suppress any revolutionary movement. This treaty was part of Metternich's design to prevent the spread of revolution in states close to Austrian territory. The British Foreign Secretary recognized Austrian rights under the treaty, but he, like Metternich, wanted to prevent either Russia or France intervening in Spain. In this he was following the traditional policy of safeguarding Britain's interests in Gibraltar and the Western Mediterranean. He was also determined to keep both Spain and the former Spanish colonies as markets for British trade. In fact by using the support of Prussia and Austria he managed to prevent Russia and France taking any action either in Spain itself or in South America.

All these problems had arisen at the Congress of Troppau in October 1820, to which Castlereagh sent an observer, not a plenipotentiary. While Castlereagh got his way over Spain and her former colonies, he could not prevent Austria, Prussia and Russia from issuing the Troppau Protocol. In this the Powers declared that states which had undergone a revolution which threatened other states were no longer members of the European system. They went further and declared their right to intervene by peaceful means 'or if need be by arms to bring back the guilty State' into the European alliance.

Castlereagh condemned the Troppau Protocol because it would lead to 'extensive interference in the internal transactions of other States' and his resistance prevented further attempts to bring back the former colonies of Spain and Portugal to the control of the mother countries. The Congress of Laibach, January 1821, was really a continuation of the Congress of Troppau. As a result of the Congress Metternich dispatched an Austrian army to Naples to restore King Ferdinand and crush the revolutionaries. The restoration of such an outrageously bad ruler by force of arms provoked a good deal of Radical protest in Britain and Castlereagh was held to be partly responsible for the whole affair.

The foreign policy of George Canning

Before the meeting of the next congress, that of Verona in October 1822, Castlereagh committed suicide and was succeeded as Foreign Secretary by George Canning. The Duke of Wellington was sent to Verona to represent Great Britain and, in general, continued Castlereagh's policy. Canning's first great problem arose from the political situation in Spain, where the Liberal revolution had imposed more effective parliamentary control over the despotic Ferdinand VII. The Czar Alexander I still wished to send troops into Spain to suppress the Liberal movement, but neither Canning, Metternich, nor the French were prepared to let the Russians into Western Europe. However, having resisted Russian intervention in Spain, Canning was faced with an ultra-royalist Government in France which proposed to send a French army to carry out anti-Liberal policies there. The Great Powers, except for Britain, withdrew their ambassadors from Spain, and the French army prepared to march over the Pyrenees. Canning instructed Wellington to withdraw from the Congress of Verona. He feared that if despotic governments were restored in Spain and Portugal they would try to recapture their colonies where Britain was already building a most profitable trade. His resistance was reinforced by President Monroe's famous Doctrine of 1823 which made it plain that the United States would oppose any interference by European Powers in the American Continent. Thus between them Canning and Monroe assured the survival of the new states of Latin America. Canning made it clear that Great Britain would resist attempts to reconquer them, and the power of the British navy in the Atlantic made his protests effective. However, he was unable to prevent the French restoring the absolute monarchy in Spain itself.

Canning and the Greek War of Independence

In 1821 the Greeks revolted against their Turkish masters and once again Canning had to face the problems of big Power rivalries, and in particular Alexander's expansionist ambitions. Britain saw the Russian attempts to replace the Turks in the Balkans and to seize Constantinople as a threat to

their own interests in the Middle East. Alexander was eager to give direct
Russian assistance to the Greeks, but both Canning and Metternich
indicated their disapproval. This checked Alexander but, when he died in
1825 and was succeeded by Nicholas I, the problem arose in a more acute
form. Nicholas was even more determined to take part in the Greek
struggle. Canning's position at home was complicated, for there was
strong support for the Greek cause, and Canning himself had considerable
personal sympathy for the Greeks. He therefore adopted a more positive
policy, giving help to the Greeks and preventing unilateral intervention by
Nicholas. In 1827 he negotiated the Treaty of London with Russia and
France; by this the Powers made joint representation to Turkey that
Greece, while remaining in the Turkish Empire, should be granted self-
government. This solution pleased neither the Greeks nor the Turks and,
when the latter refused to negotiate, tension mounted between them and
the London Treaty Powers. In 1827 the Turkish Fleet was destroyed by a
joint British, Russian and French naval force at the Battle of Navarino,
which appears to have begun when the Turks fired a few shots across the
bows of the allied force. Naturally, it greatly assisted the Greek cause.

Canning died before the battle of Navarino was fought, and was
succeeded by Wellington who approved neither the London Treaty nor the
battle. He reversed Canning's policy, and Britain withdrew from the
alliance. The outcome was that Russia declared war on Turkey in 1828
and forced the Turks to sign the Treaty of Adrianople (1829). In 1832
Greece became an independent Kingdom with Otto of Bavaria as King. Its
independence was recognized by all the Great Powers. The situation which
Canning had feared had now come about; although Russia had made no
territorial acquisitions, her influence in the Balkans had increased immensely and her threat to the Turkish Empire was greater than ever. This
was a problem left for Palmerston, Disraeli and all British Foreign
Ministers down to 1914.

5. The First Reform Bill, 1832

Introduction

The system of parliamentary representation was based on the privileges of the landowners. In the eighteenth century they had been able to control Parliament and not unnaturally they controlled it in their own interest especially in such matters as taxation. But by 1832 the old parliamentary system was no longer adequate, either in the system of election or the composition of the House of Commons. The growth of industry and commerce had produced a class of newly rich who had little connection with the land. They were regarded by the old landlord class with contempt as the uncultured, self-made upstarts of the new industrial society. The landed interests were, however, gradually forced to accept a number of middle-class members into the House of Commons.

The electoral system before 1832

The existing electoral system had evolved in the sixteenth and seventeenth centuries and was totally unsuitable in the nineteenth. The rapid growth and widespread redistribution of population in the eighteenth century had resulted in a gross inequality in parliamentary representation. Towns whose population had expanded enormously during the century were still regarded for parliamentary purposes as small and insignificant boroughs; while great cities like Leeds, Manchester and Birmingham had no representation at all in 1831. Conversely, there were the 'rotten' boroughs which were now almost deserted but had full representation in Parliament. For instance, Gatton in Surrey had only six houses and one elector, while Old Sarum, near Salisbury, was nothing but a mound of earth represented by two members. Most of Dunwich had, through coast erosion, fallen into the sea, but it too still returned its two members to Parliament.

As well as the 'rotten' boroughs, there were the 'pocket' boroughs, so called because some wealthy patron had the power to nominate his own candidates as borough representatives. Sometimes these boroughs had been specially created by the Crown, as in Cornwall, in the hope that they would return 'King's men' to the House of Commons. Their patrons often regarded these 'pocket' boroughs as financial investments, for nominations were readily bought and sold in an age when membership of the House of Commons opened the way to appointment to valuable sinecures.

Even in boroughs with a reasonable number of voters there was corruption, for the right to vote was a valuable possession. Money and gifts openly changed hands in elections, so those with the vote did everything possible to prevent any additions to the franchise so that the financial value of their votes could be maintained. As the poll in a general election took fifteen days, there was ample opportunity for bribery on a grand scale. (The most expensive election ever fought was that for the County of York in 1811, when £200,000 was spent.) This state of affairs tended to keep the number of voters in the boroughs very small, and sometimes the corporations alone had the right to vote. In 1820 the borough of Totnes in Devon had only seventy-eight voters, Rye in Sussex had fourteen and its neighbour Winchelsea had seven. Altogether fifty-six towns had less than forty voters each, and about 160 landlords were able to nominate 300 M.P.s to the House of Commons – nearly half the membership.

The Middlesex Election: a cartoon from 1806. Middlesex was one of the few seats with an electorate running into thousands before 1832.

In the counties the position was rather better. The franchise was wider, for the forty-shilling freeholder possessed the vote. In general, the less corrupt members of the House of Commons were drawn from the counties and the county members were more inclined to combat acts of injustice or tyranny by King or Government. This was not true in all counties, for in Scotland the county constituencies were as restricted and as open to bribery and corruption as the English boroughs. Here again the number of voters was very small – thirty-two, for instance, in Invernesshire. Altogether there were forty-five M.P.s representing Scottish counties and boroughs, many of whom had purchased their seats.

The distribution of seats was very uneven. From Cornwall, which was very thinly populated, forty-two members were returned; Dorset had eighteen and Somerset sixteen borough members, whereas in other counties, such as Cambridgeshire, Cheshire or Durham there were two county and two borough members. The result was that a very unrepresentative group of voters controlled the composition of the House of Commons.

This was the state of affairs in 1832. But it would be wrong to assume that a corrupt system inevitably produced corrupt Members of Parliament. Methods which from a twentieth-century point of view are corrupt were widely accepted as a normal means of entering Parliament. The system produced some of the most brilliant and upright statesmen in British history. The Pitts, Sir Robert Peel and Lord Palmerston were first elected by 'pocket' boroughs, but their personal standards were high. The boroughs they first represented were the means by which they gained entry to Parliament and thereby important political experience.

The movement for parliamentary reform after 1815
In the years 1815–21 the merchants and factory owners were as alarmed as the landlord interests by the waves of popular discontent. This alarm kept the two classes united for some years against the Radical leaders. But with industrial expansion after 1821 the new middle class began to protest at the weight of national taxation that they had to bear, in contrast to the landed interest which had been singled out for special protection by the Corn Laws. Taxation of raw materials for industry was especially irksome to the factory owner. Besides, the Corn Laws of 1815, while favouring the landlords by keeping up rents and the value of land, raised the cost of living for the factory workers and spread discontent in the industrial areas. These were all obstacles to the smooth running of industry on which the profits of the middle class depended. In the 1820's, therefore, some sections of the middle class allied themselves with the Radical Members of Parliament. These M.P.s were demanding a reform of Parliament which would certainly give the middle classes a much greater share in politics. Only by breaking into the old landlord preserve of Parliament itself could industry protect and promote its interests.

The 'enlightened Tories' of the late 1820's, such as Peel and Huskisson, tried to appease the middle class by economic and social reforms, while Canning pursued a foreign policy in the interests of British trade. However, far from heading off the demand for parliamentary reform these concessions made the middle classes even more anxious for political rights.

Divisions in the Whig and Tory Parties

The increasing divisions of opinion on the reform question in the Whig and Tory Parties also aided the reformers. Some Whigs allied themselves with the old Tories on many issues, and this left the Whig leader Lord Grey and the younger Whigs such as Lord John Russell with no alternative but to support the progressive reforms of Peel and Huskisson. In the 1820's Lord Grey was not in favour of wholesale parliamentary reform, but was hoping to replace the Tory landed gentry in Parliament by Whig aristocrats in alliance with the richer merchants and factory owners. At the time this was as far as he was prepared to go. But there were far more radical men in the Whig party who disagreed with Grey's moderation. The leaders of this faction were Henry Brougham and Lord Durham, the latter popularly known as 'Radical Jack'. Both Brougham and Durham were prepared to make a clean sweep of the whole 'rotten' and 'pocket' borough system, and bring the middle class right into the parliamentary system.

The 'Philosophic Radicals'

Even more adventurous than Brougham and Durham were the 'Philosophic Radicals', or followers of the doctrines of Jeremy Bentham (see p. 46). They had strong support outside Parliament among the professional and manufacturing classes, and their spokesman in the House of Commons was Joseph Hume. Bentham had actually proposed to extend the vote to all men over 21, but even his followers regarded this as too radical to be practical. However, working-class leaders such as William Cobbett, Henry Hunt and Sir Francis Burdett were quite prepared to demand manhood suffrage, and founded the National Political Union to this end. Finally quite outside Parliament and beyond both Cobbett and Hunt was the revolutionary society, the National Union of the Working Class, which was founded in 1830 and had considerable support in the northern industrial towns.

Political developments which helped the cause of Reform

The success of Daniel O'Connell's campaign for Catholic emancipation in 1829 (see pp. 29–31) aided the cause of parliamentary reform both directly and indirectly. It showed that strongly entrenched interests could be defeated even with a Tory Government in power. It also led to the break-up of the old Tory party and the defeat of Wellington. The result was the formation of an all-Whig Government for the first time in many years.

Events abroad in 1830 also helped the movement for parliamentary reform. The overthrow of Charles X in France and the revolts in Belgium,

Poland and Italy heartened the reformers and frightened many of their opponents into a readiness to make concessions.

The Birmingham Political Union
In 1830 a Birmingham banker and currency reformer, Thomas Attwood, established the Birmingham Political Union to agitate for reform. His example was followed by sympathizers in other large industrial towns and Francis Place and Sir Francis Burdett organized the local societies into one movement known as the National Political Union. They proposed a union of the working and middle classes in the cause of reform, and began to put forward candidates for Parliament. Their hopes were encouraged by the election of 'Orator' Henry Hunt as M.P. for Preston in 1829. Both Place and Attwood urged the middle class to refuse all tax payments until Parliament accepted the demands of the reformers. This really alarmed the Whig Government, and compelled Grey to move forward from his half-hearted approach to the question of the rotten and pocket boroughs.

The Labourers' Riots, 1830
In 1830 there were widespread riots in the south of England. They were provoked by unemployment and near starvation which recalled the worst days after Waterloo. The rebellious labourers were treated as harshly by the new Whig Home Secretary, Lord Melbourne, as they had been by Sidmouth in 1815–21. Although the rioters killed not a single person, nine were hanged and 450 men and boys were transported. There was, however, one important result. The Whigs had seen the spectre of revolution very close at hand, and many came to regard parliamentary reform as the only political safeguard against it.

Introduction and passage of the Reform Bill, 1832
Henry Brougham, Lord John Russell and Lord Durham led the campaign for parliamentary reform in Lord Grey's Government. The inclusion of these men in the Cabinet showed that Grey had changed his own views. Grey then appointed Lord Durham, the most Radical of all, as chairman of the special committee of four to draw up the scheme for electoral reform. Durham in turn selected Lord John Russell to introduce the Bill into the House of Commons in March 1831. Having much of the inspiration of Durham behind it, the Bill went further than many Radicals outside Parliament had dared to hope. It proposed nothing less than the complete abolition of the rotten boroughs.

The Second Reading of the Bill opened the debate. There was fierce opposition from the Tories, and the reading was carried by a majority of only one vote. However, during the committee stage of the bill in which every clause was discussed, Grey was twice defeated. He resigned, demanding a general election, and the new King, William IV, agreed to this. The Whigs were returned stronger than before with a majority of 136. The Bill, slightly altered, was then passed by the House of Commons, but rejected by the House of Lords in October 1831.

There was an immediate outburst of popular fury at the action of the Lords. A number of peers who had voted against the bill were set upon by mobs and their houses were damaged. At Bristol the crowds looted the Mansion House and burned down the Bishop's Palace. In the northern counties there was much drilling and arming, and in the southern counties another outburst of rick-burning and general disorder. Although the Whigs were alarmed by these signs of potential revolution, they now used this fear to play upon the minds of the Tory opposition. Increasing numbers of employers believed that only the passage of the Bill could forestall popular revolution.

A third Bill, slightly amended, was introduced in December 1831. This passed all stages in the House of Commons and two readings in the House of Lords. But in the Committee stage Tory opposition again developed over certain details. Grey then asked William IV to create fifty new Whig peers to give a clear Whig majority in the House of Lords and he resigned when the King refused to agree to more than twenty.

The King then asked Wellington to form a Government. The Duke had been an outright opponent of the Bill but in the hope of meeting the situation by partial concessions to the reformers, he was prepared to accept a Reform Bill in a very reduced form and to attempt to push it through the House of Lords. This was too much for the Tories who already regarded him as a traitor over Catholic emancipation, and he was unable to form a Government. Grey therefore returned to office. Wellington and many Tories stayed away from the debates in the Lords, so that Grey would not need his fifty new peerages, and as a consequence the Reform Bill was passed June 1832. Wellington had managed to save the Tory House of Lords from the Whigs, but he had been defeated by the reformers both inside and outside Parliament. Upon the resignation of Grey, Attwood, Place, Hunt, Cobbett and many others had whipped up an immense popular campaign in the country which had been decisive. Particularly effective was Attwood's campaign to secure the non-payment of taxes and Place's appeal to bank depositors to withdraw their money. Wellington had been defeated once more by a combination of Radicals, Whigs and his opponents in the Tory Party itself.

Changes made by the Reform Bill

By the Reform Act of 1832 the borough franchise was given to all those who possessed or occupied a house of £10 annual value. This was essentially a middle-class and not a working-class enfranchisement. In the countryside the vote was retained by those holding freehold land of 40s. annual value, and given to copyholders of land of £10 annual value, and to tenants-at-will of land valued at £50 annually. Boroughs with a population of less than 2,000 lost both M.P.s, and those of between 2,000 and 4,000 lost one

M.P. This released 143 seats in the House of Commons for redistribution to the counties and large towns, some of which (for example, Manchester and Sheffield) could elect members of their own for the first time. Similar changes were made for Scotland and Ireland.

Immediate results of the Reform Bill

In several respects the Reform Bill was less far-reaching than all the agitation suggested. Only one-sixth of the adult male population of Britain now had the vote, the number of electors rising from about 435,000 to 652,000 in England and Wales. In the countryside the landlord class was still in a very strong position, for as voting remained open a landlord could tell how his tenants voted. Over the next thirty years bribery, intimidation and corruption continued in general elections, chiefly because of the absence of a secret ballot. The Reform Bill made the parish overseers responsible for compiling the lists of those entitled to vote in elections and these lists were to be publicly displayed. But the overseers were frequently illiterate and often inefficient. Names were frequently included incorrectly in the lists or others which should have been included were omitted, and anyone objecting to overseer's lists could run himself into considerable legal costs.

In general, the class composition of the House of Commons remained much the same after 1832 as it had been before. The industrial interests of the big towns were better represented but the landed interests were still dominant. In the Parliament of 1841–46 over 70 per cent of the members were drawn from the landed class.

The Reform Bill and the English party system

The use of the terms 'Whig' and 'Tory' for the party groupings before 1832 can give a false impression of party unity which did not then exist. There were constant shifts and changes of personal political loyalties. Before 1832 the terms 'Whig' and 'Tory' were applied to broad tendencies of opinion rather than to close party ties in the present-day sense. For example, after the election of 1830 when Grey became Prime Minister, nobody seemed quite clear at first about the real result of the election. The Treasury officials who recorded it listed the new Members of Parliament under at least eight headings, such as Friends (of Wellington), Foes, Moderate Ultras, Doubtful Favourables, Doubtful Unfavourables, the Huskisson Party, etc. Nowhere do the terms 'Whig' or 'Tory' appear. The party whips had the task of holding the loyalty of enough M.P.s to the Government to enable it to continue in office. In their attempts to obtain or retain the support of members, who were virtually independent of party control, they had to use persuasion, bribery or intrigue.

The Reform Bill of 1832 marked the end of this old loose form of party organization and the beginning of the modern political party. Before 1831 the meeting-places for the leading Tories and sympathizers had been a number of London clubs, such as White's in St. James But after its foundation in 1831, the Carlton Club became the first party headquarters of the Tories. A number of party officials (at first unpaid) worked at the Club. They had to co-ordinate the work of the party in Parliament and to attempt to hold it together on the most important matters of policy. During and before elections it was their task to see that their party supporters were on the local electoral lists, and to check the electoral qualifications of any potential opponents. The officials at the centre increasingly relied upon and supervised the activities of party agents in the localities. The amount of local party propaganda greatly increased as time went on, for there were now more voters to be won over. In fact, after 1832, the two main parties had to recognize the existence of a wider 'public opinion'. In the Tory Party, these developments owed a great deal to the work and influence of Sir Robert Peel, who was anxious to produce a far more coherent and disciplined party than had existed before. His methods and ideas were a distinct break from those of Wellington and the eighteenth-century politicians.

The Whigs also took party organization more seriously after the Reform Act. In general, the employment of local agents and central officials, and the regular meetings of the party leaders to work out policy and tactics in Parliament, followed almost the same lines as the Tories. Their political centre in London was the Reform Club, established in 1836.

Summary

While the Reform Bill did not bring about the sweeping changes in voting power demanded by many of the Philosophic Radicals and the organized sections of the working class, it was important as a break with the strict eighteenth-century view of politics. In the House of Commons there was undoubtedly an increase in the proportion of men gaining their livelihood from business, but they were still a small minority compared with those connected with the land. The £10 household franchise was not given in the counties at all, which meant the exclusion of a considerable section of the middle class itself. Indeed, by increasing the county representation in Parliament, the power of the landlords was actually increased. The working class, who had done so much to frighten both Whigs and Tories into accepting the reformers' demands, were excluded altogether from the franchise. Finally the old system of open voting, with all its possibilities of unfair practices, remained. A motion during the reform debates for the secret ballot received only one vote in the House of Commons! All these shortcomings of the first Reform Bill were to produce further demands from the working class and many of the middle class for more far-reaching parliamentary reform. But the changes did make Parliament much more open to pressures from outside, and the Reform Act was followed by a spate of social reform such as the country had never seen before.

6. The Whigs and Social Reform, 1832-41

Introduction

The Whigs were returned to power with a clear cut majority in the Parliament of 1833. On viewing the new House of Commons, Wellington gloomily remarked that 'he had never seen so many bad hats in his life'. However, the new Parliament showed more signs of life and earnestness than a good many of its predecessors. Between 1833 and 1841 the old ideas about the role of government changed and parliamentary intervention in the economic and social affairs of the country increased. The Government was forced to respond to the pressure of its Radical and middle-class supporters and adopt some of the ideas of the great social reformers of the age.

Jeremy Bentham (1748–1832)

Among the theorists of this period Bentham was pre-eminent. Although not a public orator or agitator himself, many reforms in this period were influenced by his ideas. He was the brilliant son of a successful lawyer; he was educated at Westminster School and at the age of thirteen went up to Oxford. His first important work was published in 1776, entitled *A Fragment on Government*. In this he criticized the widely accepted idea that English law and government could not be improved upon. Bentham's greatest and most widely read work, *Introduction to the Principles of Morals and Legislation*, which followed in 1789, expounded the basic theories of what became known as Utilitarianism. According to Bentham, human action is governed by the 'pain and pleasure' principle. Happiness consists in the avoidance of pain and the achievement of pleasure, and all laws should be directed towards the attainment of these simple aims. They should have as their object only that which achieves 'the greatest good of the greatest number'. All laws and institutions should be tested by one basic question: What is their utility or usefulness? If they cannot be justified on these grounds, then they must be swept aside, irrespective of their origin. Thus Bentham challenged tradition, class privilege and vested interests of all kinds.

In another of his critical works, *The Rationale of Punishments and Rewards*, Bentham attacked the barbarous and inefficient English penal system. He also made a close study of the English Poor Law, found it most unsatisfactory, and made criticisms of it which were later accepted by a Whig

Government. His fame as a great thinker spread to many countries. He was made a French citizen by the revolutionary Government in 1792, and corresponded with leading statesmen all over the world. In 1817 he published his *Catechism of Parliamentary Reform* which analysed the serious shortcomings of the British electoral system. He demanded annual general elections, the vote for all men over twenty-one, the secret ballot and equal electoral districts. His theories were taken up by the Philosophic Radicals, especially after 1815. His influence was seen most clearly in the social reforms of Peel in the 1820's, in the Reform Bill of 1832 and in the Whig reforms of 1833–41. He died in June 1832, on the day before the Reform Bill was passed by Parliament.

Robert Owen (1771–1858)

Robert Owen was an outstanding reformer and thinker of another kind. A mixture of self-made business man, idealist and agitator, he was laughed at by his opponents as a crank. Born at Newtown, Montgomeryshire, he worked for a time as a draper's assistant, and from this humble beginning he became, in 1800, the owner of a large cotton mill on the Clyde at New Lanark. There he put his ideas on factory and social organization into practice. He reduced the hours of work; employed no children under ten years of age at a time when it was common for children to work in factories and workshops from the age of five; set up a school for his employees' children; and built excellent houses. By these changes he produced willing workers and a happy factory settlement – something that astonished the hundreds of distinguished visitors (including the Czar of Russia), who came to inspect such an amazing phenomenon. At the same time Owen was able to show an increase in production from the factory and very good profits. Owen was attempting to prove to other factory owners that they only had to follow his example in order to produce a happy and well-organized industrial state. He was seeking to show that the worst evils of the Industrial Revolution need never have occurred, and that it was not too late to make amends. Owen toured the country tirelessly, addressing meetings in which he described his experiments and ideas.

In 1813 Owen published *A New View of Society* in which he argued that men's characters were made for them by education and environment and that by the application of his ideas, mankind's problems would be solved. Owen failed to persuade other factory owners to follow his methods but he did for a time enlist the sympathy of a number of prominent people, including the Duke of Kent (the father of the future Queen Victoria) who was a member of a committee formed by Owen for the improvement of factory conditions. Owen's influence was behind the 1819 Factory Act introduced by Sir Robert Peel the elder.

By 1820 Owen was advocating the establishment throughout Britain of 'Villages of Co-operation' where the workers would produce goods for their own local needs and exchange surplus products for those of other

Robert Owen's school for the children of his workers at New Lanark.

parishes in a nation-wide federation. This type of production would replace capitalist competition by co-operative and profit-sharing work in which all wealth would be shared by the community. He was not interested in parliamentary reform, and soon became disillusioned with his prospects in Britain. He emigrated to the United States and in Indiana established New Harmony, a community where co-operation, profit-sharing and human brotherhood were to replace the old motives of profit and self-advancement. However, this attempt at a new type of society was a failure. Various disputes arose within it and the material temptations of the rapidly expanding society in the United States proved too strong for its members.

During the years 1820–30, Owen's influence in Britain was seen most clearly in the establishment by working people of co-operative societies. By 1830 there were more than 300, though not all co-operators were enthusiastic for the type of society Owen envisaged. The modern co-operative retail movement really has its origin in the town of Rochdale where in 1844 a small group of weavers established a co-operative shop in Toad Lane. Their scheme was to buy goods directly from the wholesalers and re-sell without profit. The later development of the movement, which rapidly spread to many towns in Britain, took the form of the 'dividend' paid to the customer out of the retail profits, in proportion to the amount of his purchases during the year. By the middle of the century the Co-operative Wholesale Society had been established, and the movement set up its own factories and productive units.

Owen had turned from the capitalist to the wage-earner, and became convinced that only through the trade unions could he achieve his new co-operative commonwealth. A number of the early trade unions which flourished after 1825 gave him their support and it was Owen who made the first great attempt to unite them into one nation-wide movement.

The Abolition of Slavery, 1833

Through the untiring work of William Wilberforce, Granville Sharp and other members of the Evangelical Group in the Church of England, the Government had abolished the slave trade in 1807. But the reformers regarded this as only the first step towards ending slavery itself in the British West Indies and South Africa.

Powerful interests opposed this reform, in particular the sugar planters of the West Indies. A healthy slave was worth about £50 to his owner. The planters feared that abolition would give a great advantage to their rivals the slave-owners of the southern United States. There was also genuine fear of social unrest, for the slaves were accustomed to the organized life of the plantations and were quite unused to working as independent families. Wilberforce and his great supporter in Parliament, Thomas Fowell Buxton, founded the Anti-slavery Society in 1823 and from that time onwards the question was constantly raised in Parliament. George Canning had secured the passing of a resolution that the home Government should recommend improvements in the treatment of slaves to the colonial authorities, but despite pressure from London nothing was done. Another advance in 1828 gave coloured people who were not slaves legal equality with white settlers in the British colonies. The humanitarians pointed out that conditions among West Indian slaves had become worse since Britain's abolition of the slave trade in 1807. As the supply of slaves had decreased, those already there were severely overworked and between 1807 and 1830 their numbers declined by more than 100,000.

On 7 August 1833, the Emancipation Act was passed. £20 million was given to the slave owners in compensation, and the transition of the slaves to the status of free wage-labourers was spread over seven years. They were to work part of the day for their masters and the remainder was to be their own time. This scheme worked badly and in fact all slaves had become free labourers by 1838. The owners claimed that the compensation was insufficient, covering only half the market value of their slaves. Many West Indian planters were ruined, and in South Africa the Dutch Boers undertook their Great Trek away from Cape Colony and British control (1836).

The Factory Act, 1833

Working conditions in the early factories were appalling. The factories were mostly old buildings with insufficient space for the machinery and no protection for the workers. Ventilation and hygiene were neglected. There were exceptions, such as the factories of enlightened employers like Owen and John Fielden, but these were rare cases. Whole families, including children barely five years old, were employed in the workshops, and parents were often made responsible for the work of their children. Both adults and children had sometimes to work eighteen hours a day. In the factory towns hundreds of workers were housed in back-to-back houses without sanitation and light, often without proper foundations and constructed with walls of single brick, the work of speculative builders and the property of extortionate landlords.

These conditions were regularly denounced by such critics as Cobbett, Owen and Lord Ashley (later Earl of Shaftesbury). Ashley and Owen both investigated them at first hand, and Ashley brought young and crippled children to his London home to give evidence to the Commission of Inquiry set up by Grey's Government in 1833. Owen also gave evidence before this Commission, claiming that he had found children as young as four years old in the factories. At the same time there was violent agitation in the northern towns for an improvement of working conditions. At last a Factory Bill was introduced into the Commons by another leading reformer of this period, Lord Althorp. This was passed by the House of Commons and was known as the 'Children's Charter' because it affected mainly the work of children and young persons in factories.

Children spinning yarn in about 1820.

The main provisions of the Factory Act of 1833, which applied to *all* textile factories except silk, were as follows:

(1) Children under 9 years were not to be employed in textile factories. (2) Children between 9 and 13 years old were not to work more than twelve hours a day, with a total of forty-eight a week. (3) Young people of 13 to 18 were not to work more than twelve hours a day or sixty-nine a week. (4) Night-work between 8.30 p.m. and 5.30 a.m. was prohibited for all workers under 18. (5) Four Government inspectors were appointed to see that the law was carried out.

Importance and effectiveness of the Factory Act

The Factory Act of 1833 was not the first – there had been others in 1802, 1819, 1826, and 1830. These, however, had only applied to the cotton industry, and lacked adequate means for their enforcement. The great difference in 1833 was the appointment of inspectors who had the right to enter any factory and report to the magistrates any infringement of the Act. Four inspectors were scarcely enough for the whole country, but at least the principle of inspection had been accepted – another drastic break from the ideas of *laissez faire*. Employers frequently evaded the Act, especially as it was difficult to prove a child's true age until the compulsory registration of births and deaths introduced in 1836. However, the regular reports that the inspectors had to make to Parliament proved conclusively that conditions were often appallingly bad, and in need of further reform.

The first Government grant to education, 1833

Elementary education for the children of the working class was very haphazard. The Dame Schools, run by elderly ladies who made a small charge for instruction in reading, writing, arithmetic and the Bible, gave some education to a few children. Elsewhere there might be charity schools, established by the efforts of private subscribers. In many industrial areas there were no schools for the poor at all.

However, some individual reformers had already attempted to improve the education of the poorer classes well before 1815. Andrew Bell and Joseph Lancaster had both introduced the monitorial system by which a master taught monitors, they in their turn teaching the younger children. In 1808, a number of Non-Conformists formed the British and Foreign Schools Society to promote Lancaster's ideas. In 1811 the Church of England entered the field in support of Andrew Bell with the formation of the National Society. These two bodies became bitter rivals for the control of elementary education during the nineteenth century. Bentham foreseeing this danger had proposed a separate State system of elementary schools entirely free of denominational teaching, but his influence here did not prevail. Through the influence of both Nonconformity and the Church of England in the Whig and Tory parties, the Government decided instead to help the existing societies. In 1833 £20,000 was granted to this work. In 1839 the Government increased this to £30,000, but on condition that a committee of the Privy Council was set up to supervise its expenditure. The first school inspectors were appointed soon afterwards.

The Poor Law Amendment Act, 1834

Under the terms of Gilbert's Act, 1782, an unemployed man who applied for poor relief from the parish had to be found work near his home. But the coming of the Industrial Revolution was accompanied by unemployment on such a scale that often no work could be found. When war broke out with France in 1793 prices rose and the value of wages declined, so that even those in work could scarcely support themselves. To meet this situation the Speenhamland system (see p. 6) soon spread all over the country, though in the north such relief was only given to the unemployed and not as a supplement to bad wages. The Speenhamland system was first introduced from a genuine desire to help the poor; but the system encouraged employers to pay the lowest possible wages in the knowledge that their labourers would have them increased by the poor law authorities. The better workers resented it bitterly; the weaker ones came to depend upon it. Naturally, it led to a great increase in the local rates from which the Speenhamland payments were made. The national total of poor rates in 1795 was about £2 million, and had risen to just under £8 million by 1830.

In 1832 Grey's Government appointed a Royal Commission to report on the state of the Poor Law. The Commission, which contained a number of Benthamites or Utilitarians, made drastic proposals for reform. It recommended the abolition of all outdoor relief (i.e. outside the workhouse) for able-bodied persons. Such relief was to be confined to the sick, aged and infirm to assist with maintenance and doctor's fees. For the able-bodied labourer seeking assistance the workhouse test was to be strictly applied. This meant that no labourer could gain assistance unless he was willing to enter a workhouse. In the workhouse conditions were to be sufficiently harsh and unattractive to discourage applications and to encourage every possible effort by the labourers to find work. Husbands and wives were to be separated to prevent the further begetting of children while they were chargeable to the rates, and even the children were to be separated from their parents. These proposals were accepted by Grey's Government and embodied in the Poor Law Amendment Act of 1834.

For the purposes of poor relief and the building of workhouses, parishes were grouped into 'Unions'. In this way the rates could be spread over a wider area and could be more fairly imposed on both the poorer and richer parishes. Boards of Guardians, elected by those paying the poor rate, were to supervise the whole administration within the union. A number of full-time Poor Law officials, such as the workhouse masters, were appointed, and they were answerable in the first place to the Board of Guardians. At the centre supervising and enforcing the new law throughout the country were three Commissioners and their secretary, the fanatical Benthamite, Edwin Chadwick.

Some comments on the new Poor Law

Within two years of the passing of the Act the national total of poor rates had been halved. This was highly satisfactory to the middle class and the aristocracy. But no administrators have been more violently hated by the people than Chadwick and the 'three Pashas of Somerset House'. The sharp change from the old outdoor system of relief to the stringent work-house test was too much for those who suffered it. The new workhouses soon became known as the 'Bastilles' and some of them were attacked and burnt down in the 1830's. Few writers of this period had anything good to say of them, and the criticisms of novelists like Dickens did much to force a more humane administration of the law as the century progressed. Chadwick and the Commissioners genuinely believed that the old system had corrupted the labourers and that nothing but moral good would come from the change. One of Chadwick's colleagues, J. Kay-Shuttleworth, wrote about the new Poor Law: 'The effect of the law is almost magical and I may confess to you privately that I have lived a life of high moral and intellectual enjoyment in effecting and witnessing this mighty change.'

However, even Chadwick and the Commissioners were unable to have everything their own way. By 1836 they had achieved the introduction of the new system in the southern counties, and they turned their attention to the north. Here poor relief had been mainly used to assist workers during unemployment and not to add to wages. This unemployment relief was now to disappear entirely and the temporarily unemployed were to be forced into the workhouses. The working people reacted violently against the new law, helped by a number of sympathetic employers among whom factory owners John Fielden and Richard Oastler were most prominent. Another leader of the anti-Poor Law agitation was a Methodist minister, J. R. Stephens, whose powerful and violent oratory led to the destruction of some of the northern workhouses. The local Boards of Guardians were terrified by this agitation, and a number were sympathetic towards it. Chadwick and the Commissioners found it impossible to make progress and for several years to come poor relief in the north continued to be paid as a form of unemployment benefit to those out of work. All the Commissioners could do was to take advantage of any periods of full employment to get workhouses built.

The Municipal Corporations Act, 1835

In 1833 Grey had appointed a Commission to examine English local government. Its report disclosed a state of inefficiency, corruption and chaos.

The Commissioners reported that 246 towns in England and Wales were chartered towns with a mayor and corporation. They varied in size from places which were little more than hamlets to very large towns. Some large towns, such as Manchester and Birmingham, which had developed from very small beginnings during the Industrial Revolution, had no corporation at all and were still under the control of a lord of the manor. In the majority of towns there was no elective system whatsoever. Seats on the corporation were often handed down from father to son in certain families, other members being co-opted by the existing corporation. Funds entrusted to the corporations for the furtherance of education and town improvements were frequently misused. The money found its way into the pockets of the members of the corporation, or was spent on lavish annual dinners and other social events.

Many corporations had no responsibility for the health of their towns. Such things as sewage disposal, refuse collection, paving, lighting were managed by separate committees appointed by Acts of Parliament. The areas which these committees were supposed to supervise did not always coincide with the boundaries of the corporate towns, so that there were hundreds of overlapping administrative boundaries and much conflict between different authorities.

By the Municipal Corporations Act of 1835 the borough councils were to be elected. All male ratepayers voted for councillors elected for a three-year period. This was more democratic than the national franchise and the Scottish local franchise, for it went beyond the £10 householder. The councils elected the mayor and the aldermen, the latter forming one quarter of the council and sitting for six years. The council's accounts were to be properly audited and to be published annually. The councils could also take over the duties of the various local committees already mentioned, but only if these committees dissolved themselves voluntarily. The Municipal Corporations Act of 1835 was the beginning of modern local government. The Act of 1835 established the principle that the councils were directly responsible to the ratepayers.

The Whigs and the Trade Unions

Many working-class leaders and Radical propagandists denounced the Reform Bill as a fraud perpetrated upon the mass of the people who had worked so hard to secure it. The years of Whig rule were a time of recurrent economic crisis and unemployment, the worst period for the agricultural and industrial workers being the years 1836–37. These conditions, combined with low wages and the new Poor Law, led to widespread working-class agitation and attempts to develop various strong and independent labour movements. By 1832 there were a number of very large trade unions notably the Cotton Spinners' Union and the Operative Builders' Union. The latter had a membership of 60,000 in 1832.

In the early 1830's Robert Owen became the main inspiration of trade union activity. He had given up hope of converting his fellow employers to his views and had turned his attention to direct working-class action. In

October 1833, he launched the Grand National Consolidated Trades Union which aimed at uniting the workers of every trade into one gigantic trade union. It is estimated that during the following year it achieved the enormous membership of half a million. Not only did Owen mean to improve the immediate bargaining power of the workers, but he saw this gigantic organization as a basis for his co-operative commonwealth in which the workers themselves would take over and run all important industries. Numerous trade unions became affiliated to the Grand National, which had branches throughout Britain, in the countryside as well as in the towns.

The Whigs were alarmed. One popular newspaper had declared that the trade unions had dispensed with their (the politicians') services, implying that the trade unions intended to take over the conduct of the country's affairs and ignore Parliament. Some Government supporters demanded a return to the past and the complete banning of the trade unions, but the Government decided to make a harsh example of some trade unionists in order to browbeat the remainder into abandoning the G.N.C.T.U. In the village of Tolpuddle in Dorsetshire six farm labourers were arrested in 1834 for secretly enrolling members into a lodge or union branch with the purpose of joining Owen's organization. They were convicted on the purely technical grounds of having sworn an illegal oath of loyalty and secrecy. They were sentenced to seven years' transportation. Owen aroused a furious national campaign of protest against the sentences passed on the 'Tolpuddle Martyrs', with no immediate results. But in 1836 the six labourers were pardoned, and after some delay brought home from Australia to England.

In other parts of the country members of the G.N.C.T.U. were arrested on the grounds of 'molestation' of other workers and employers, or of 'illegal conspiracy'. A number of ancient statutes were invoked to justify the actions taken by the magistrates. At the same time Owen began to have differences with his supporters (his attitude was somewhat dictatorial) and the Union's finances were on the point of collapse. A nation-wide strike was called in 1834, and for some time this brought large sections of industry to a standstill. But the weight of authority on the side of the Government, the victimization of numerous local leaders, the financial and organizational difficulties in a period of slow communications, the application of the new workhouse test for relief, the impossible task of maintaining the strikers from Friendly Society or trade union funds for a long time – all these factors helped the Whig Government's outright opposition to Owen's activities. As a drift back to work began the employers presented to the workers the 'Document'. This was a signed pledge to be given by the worker that he would in no way support the Union or its members. As this was made the condition of regaining employment, the Grand National Consolidated Trades Union collapsed by the end of 1834.

The Whig Government and its first Home Secretary, Lord Melbourne, earned the hatred of large sections of the working population. The case of the 'Tolpuddle Martyrs' seemed to show that, in their attitude to the working class the Whigs were no better than the Tories of the pre-1832 Governments.

Other Whig reforms
The pace of reform slackened during the premiership of Lord Melbourne, who was not at heart a reformer but a moderate old fashioned aristocrat. In 1837 William IV died and was succeeded by his niece Victoria, a girl of 18, who reigned for the remainder of the century. Melbourne regarded it as his principal duty to instruct the young Queen in the affairs of state and the responsibilities of the Crown. She came to rely upon her 'dear Lord Melbourne' as a kind of political father, and when, in 1839, Lord Melbourne resigned through lack of adequate support in the House of Commons, she hated the task of requesting Peel to form a Government. In the so-called 'Bedchamber Question' which followed she showed that obstinacy and self-will which were to create considerable difficulties for her ministers throughout the century. Peel requested that the ladies-in-waiting who had been appointed by Melbourne, not only for their personal qualities but because they were Whigs, should be changed. This was reasonable, for Peel feared that these ladies would influence the Queen against him, but she refused to make the change, and Peel resigned. Lord Melbourne rather unwillingly returned to office and remained there till 1841 when he again resigned and was succeeded by Peel. Meanwhile in 1840 Victoria had married her cousin, Prince Albert of Saxe-Coburg, whose guidance later enabled her to meet the needs of English political life more adequately. While he was unpopular with the rather insular English politicians and social figures of the early Victorian years, he gave considerable services to the nation, notably in the encouragement of science and industry.

/ The Whig reforms of the period 1836–41, though less striking than those of 1832–5, were of considerable importance. The compulsory registration of births, marriages and deaths in 1836 made it easier to enforce the Factory Acts relating to young workers. It also enabled a more accurate estimate of the size and distribution of the population to be made, and provided essential statistics for future social legislation. In the same year the Government passed an act allowing limited liability companies to be formed – that is, companies in which the shareholders were no longer liable to repay the entire losses of the company in case of failure. This Act encouraged enterprise and investment though also a certain amount of risky speculation. An example of this was the first 'railway mania' of 1837, when no less than forty-two railway companies were formed by act of Parliament. Some of these failed, but nevertheless the Whig Government continued to give its blessing to railway development, and considerable progress was made. In 1837 the farthest distance a Londoner could travel by train was to Tring in Hertfordshire, but in 1838 he could travel to Birmingham./

In 1840 the penny post was introduced. This reform was mainly due to the work of Rowland Hill, one of the most remarkable men of the nineteenth century. His first interest was in educational reform, and Dr Arnold of Rugby was directly influenced by his ideas. He later invented the first successful rotary printing press, and then became an ardent promoter of emigration to the colonies and worked with Edward Gibbon Wakefield (see p. 337). Finally he made a detailed study of the English postal system and proved conclusively that the old system of payment according to the distance a letter or parcel was sent was, in fact, losing revenue to the Post Office. In his work *Post Office Reform: Its Importance and Practice*, he advocated the use of an adhesive stamp and a standard charge according to weight. Eventually the Government accepted the idea, and in 1840 the penny stamp for a weight of half an ounce came into operation. Hill was given a post in the Treasury in order to supervise the change-over to the new system. Its results were remarkable. The business of the Post Office increased tenfold by 1860, and the benefits to trade, industry and social life were enormous. The Post Office really supplemented the tremendous advantages for travel and business which the railways were bringing about. It is not surprising that on his death in 1879 Rowland Hill was buried in Westminster Abbey.

In 1836 the Marriage Act allowed persons who objected to the publication of banns to be married in church or chapel or before a registrar. In the same year the Government introduced the Tithe Commutation Bill by which the old tithe to be paid to the Established Church by farmers was replaced by a rent charge based on the average price of corn for the previous seven years. This proved to be a considerable relief to many farmers. Also in 1836 the Stamp Duty on newspapers was reduced from fourpence to one penny per issue. This duty, associated with the repressive period immediately after 1815, had been most unpopular and had hindered wider circulation. Moreover, with the rapid growth of industry and commerce and the development of more organized advertising, the old duty was unpopular among business men.

Summary

The Whigs had aroused great opposition amongst the working class. They ran into difficulties over the new Poor Law, over finance and over Ireland (see p. 63). After 1835 they were handicapped by a small majority in the House of Commons which would have restricted their actions even if Melbourne had wanted further social reform. They showed neither sympathy with, nor real understanding of, the Chartist Movement (see pp. 69-75). Their attitude to the trade unions, typified by the affair of the 'Tolpuddle Martyrs', consolidated working-class opinion against them. On the other hand, with Palmerston at the Foreign Office, they had conducted a successful international policy, they had stimulated trade, and above all they had been responsible for a number of vital social and administrative reforms.

7. Robert Peel and the Repeal of the Corn Laws

Introduction

Peel's work as Home Secretary in the years 1822–30 had met with strong resistance from the old Tories. His change of policy over Catholic emancipation in conjunction with Wellington was the product of political necessity rather than deeply-felt principle. His attitude to the Reform Bill was quite clear, for he had opposed it to the last. However, after the defeat of his party in 1830 he was prepared to help to weld it into a coherent organization and, after 1832, as leader of the party he was the main inspiration of its new organization based on the Carlton Club.

He was Prime Minister for the first time for a brief period in 1834–5. Divisions in the Whig Party over the Irish question had led Melbourne to resign though the Tories were still in a minority. During Peel's first administration the most important development was his statement of the new Tory programme in the Tamworth Manifesto. This was his election address to his constituents at Tamworth in the Midlands in 1834, in which he accepted the changes made by the Reform Bill of 1832 as a 'final and irrevocable settlement'. He declared that if the Reform Bill meant 'a careful review of institutions, civil and ecclesiastical . . . the firm maintenance of established rights, the correction of proved abuses and the redress of real grievances', then he and his followers would act in this spirit. The Tamworth Manifesto thus established the 'Conservative' programme, to use the new party label. Because the Manifesto clearly recognized the need for reform of proved social abuses, it was a further break from the old unchangeable Toryism which Peel himself had challenged as Home Secretary in the 1820's.

In 1839 he again made a brief attempt to form a Government, but the Bedchamber Question (see p. 55) put an end to this. However, in 1841 Peel had a decisive majority in the House of Commons.

The state of Britain in 1841

When Peel became Prime Minister in 1841 the country was in a serious social and economic position. Trade had slumped and working conditions were deteriorating. A series of bad harvests since 1837 had caused suffering to both farmers and labourers. The workhouses, now operating under the new Poor Law of 1834 (see p. 51), were crammed with paupers in the rural districts. The situation in the towns was scarcely better, and conditions in 1841–2 were some of the worst on record. In the country agricultural wages were about 10s. a week, whilst in the towns the highest wage for a skilled worker was 18s. These compared unfavourably even with the difficult period immediately after Waterloo. About one Englishman in every eleven was a pauper, and in Birmingham about one-fifth of the population was on poor relief. In Manchester 116 mills were closed down and 50,000 people were receiving poor relief. It is therefore not surprising that the Chartist Movement (see pp. 69–75) reached its peak in these years and that the Government had to hurry troops into the northern towns to suppress disturbances caused by unemployment and near starvation.

Despite the earlier work of Huskisson, the Whigs had not developed a full free trade policy. Manufacturers were still handicapped by heavy import duties on many raw materials, and duties on such common needs as corn, sugar, tea and butter added considerably to the cost of living. The consequent hardships are vividly described by great contemporary writers such as Dickens, Kingsley and Charlotte Brontë. The young Disraeli, the future leader of the Conservatives, was at this time writing *Sybil or the Two Nations*, in which he described the conditions of the poor and criticized the failure of the upper classes to do anything about them. From a different approach, Frederick Engels, the pioneer with Karl Marx of modern Communism, was studying them for his revealing work, *The Condition of the Working Classes in 1844*.

Peel was fully aware of the situation and was determined to change it.

Free trade

Peel's aim, as he himself expressed it, was to 'make this country a cheap country for living'. He saw the need to liberate British trade from the stranglehold of more than 1,000 import duties. These duties were not originally 'protective' duties to safeguard British manufacturers and producers from competition, but were imposed to raise revenue for the Government. The Whig Governments, with their unbalanced budgets, had not dared to remove them for fear of making things worse. There were also many export duties on manufactured goods, imposed for the same revenue-raising purpose. The Budget of 1842 was introduced into the Commons by Peel himself. Peel reduced the duties on 750 imported articles, and abolished a great number of export duties. Peel claimed that these changes would reduce the cost of living and at the same time increase both overseas trade and the home production of manufactured goods. This was a statement of the general aims of the British free trade policy which was to continue up to the Great War of 1914–18.

Income tax

Peel's first instalment of free trade (or 'freer trade' to be more accurate) meant a loss of income to the Exchequer of nearly £2½ million. To make up for this Peel – even against the opposition of a section of his own party – re-introduced income tax, which had been abolished in 1815 on the insistent demands of the wealthier classes. This bold measure imposed a tax of 7d. in the £ on incomes over £150 per annum. This tax fell almost entirely on the middle and upper classes. It represented a completely new financial development in time of peace, and meant that the *direct* taxpayer had to contribute a substantial part of the Government's revenue. The change was a financial success, for in 1844 the Government's income exceeded expenditure by £2 million – a great contrast to the bankrupt finances of the Whigs – and in the long run the move towards free trade encouraged industrial expansion and fuller employment.

This success enabled Peel to meet the arguments of his opponents and to go further. The Budget of 1844 removed more duties to the value of £400,000, and in those of 1845 and 1846 a further 450 duties were lifted; sugar duties were reduced and all remaining export duties abolished. By 1846 more than three-quarters of the duties existing in 1841 had been abolished, yet the Government's income had actually risen well above that of 1841. This had been achieved by the steady expansion of trade encouraged by these measures, and by the operation of the income tax.

The Bank Charter Act, 1844

With the development of the railways and the rapid expansion of trade, the decade 1840–50 was a time of heavy speculation and risky business ventures. Numerous unsound railway companies and dubious insurance concerns were floated and the banks were far too inclined to lend money for speculation. One of the worst episodes was the 'railway mania' of the years 1845–6, in which hundreds of new railway companies were formed, many under the inspiration of the 'Railway King', George Hudson. Many unwise investors were ruined when these collapsed. This led to a lack of confidence in English money and credit, which did much harm abroad. Peel, in the Commons debate on this problem, declared that he saw in the House one business man whose liabilities were £50,000 but whose actual assets were no more than £3,000. Peel aimed to restrain such speculation in order, as he put it, to 'inspire confidence in the medium of exchange'. The situation was complicated by the fact that the Bank of England had no monopoly of note issue, and the so-called 'country banks' could issue their own notes and give unlimited credit.

Sir Robert Peel had had considerable financial experience; he had been a member of the Bullion Committee which had met in 1819 and had advised the return to a gold standard (see p. 16). He now put his experience to good use in devising the Bank Charter Act of 1844. By this statute the Bank of England could only issue £14 million of bank notes without the equivalent gold or bullion security. Above that figure all notes had to have their counterpart in gold (75 per cent) and silver (25 per cent). This was designed to check the Bank's lending powers and prevent it from extending too much credit to the country banks. Secondly, all other banks were limited in their total issue of notes to £8½ million. The Act achieved most of its objects, and such was the stability of English money, that by the middle of the century the City of London had become the monetary centre of the world.

It was difficult for Peel to secure the passing of the Bank Charter Act. He had to educate his own party to accept this amount of control and to gain the support of the House of Commons by reasoned argument against speculative interests. In this case, the one-sided composition of the House actually helped him in his reforms. The landed interests which still dominated the House (see p. 43) supported him against the middle-class business interests who were opposed to the Act.

Social reform during Peel's second ministry

Since the passage of the 1833 Factory Act, Lord Shaftesbury and his supporters had campaigned for further legislation to improve the conditions of factory workers. Something had been achieved to protect the interests of young workers in 1833, but Shaftesbury, backed by Fielden and Oastler, demanded further factory regulations for adult workers. These men mounted a campaign to secure a ten-hour working day for women and children. In this way they hoped to make a ten-hour day effective for men, whose work in the factories could scarcely be carried on without the accompanying work of women and children. A special committee, known as the Ten Hours' Committee, was set up to organize the agitation. In 1840 Shaftesbury secured the appointment of a committee of the House of Commons to inquire into the working of the 1833 Factory Act, and another to consider the conditions of children in the mines and other industries which were outside the scope of the 1833 Act. Shaftesbury expected very little support from Sir Robert Peel, who appeared to him cold, reserved and lacking in the moral fervour and enthusiasm necessary for carrying through such reforms. Nevertheless, official committees were set up by Peel, in which Edwin Chadwick, the fervent Benthamite and poor law reformer (see chapter 6), took a leading part.

The Mines Act, 1842

The Report of the Commission on the Employment of Women and Children in Mines, 1842, was a devastating document. It brought to light the most appalling conditions. Children as young as five years old were being employed in the mines as trappers – that is, opening and shutting the ventilating doors in the mine galleries. They worked in these unhealthy and lonely conditions for as long as twelve hours at a stretch. Young people, both boys and girls, had to fill the coal trucks, and haul or push them to the bottom of the shaft. In the very low galleries (the Commissioners found some no more than thirty inches high) they had to crawl on hands and knees chained to the trucks. In addition the Davy safety lamp was not yet

LETTING CHILDREN
DOWN A COAL MINE
From a Plate in the *Westminster
Review*

Female and child labour in the mines.

compulsory in mines, and explosions and other disasters were common.

This report faced the public and Parliament with the existence of conditions hitherto unknown to the vast majority of the privileged classes. Even the coal-owners themselves could not stand out against the cry of horror which arose from the ranks of the religious philanthropists. Lord Shaftesbury was able to secure the passing of the 1842 Mines Act, which forbade the employment of women and girls and of boys under 10 years old in underground workings. Inspectors were allowed, but with very limited powers; and the coal-owning interests in Parliament had gained enough support to reduce the age limit from the thirteen years originally proposed by Shaftesbury.

Factory reform

In 1844 Peel's Home Secretary, Sir James Graham, introduced a Bill to limit to twelve the hours worked by women in factories. He also proposed that children should be allowed in the factories at the age of eight instead of nine, but that their hours were to be reduced from nine to six-and-a-half daily. This, however, did not satisfy the Ten Hours' Committee. It appeared to them a retrograde step. Shaftesbury and his supporters were demanding that the working hours for women and young persons, aged 13 to 18, should be reduced to ten. Sir Robert Peel himself opposed this, arguing that it would reduce England's competitive power in Europe. Graham's proposals therefore became law by the Factory Act of 1844. In 1847, after Peel's fall from power, Fielden's Factory Act achieved the ten hour maximum. In 1850 Shaftesbury secured an amendment to the 1847 Act by which the normal working day was to be 10½ hours, but with a Saturday half holiday for women and young persons.

General comment on factory reform
Factory reform in these years was never a simple, clear-cut party question. Many factory owners, both Whig and Tory, opposed factory legislation on the grounds that it would lead to a loss of profits and give advantages to foreign manufacturers when British production costs rose. They resented increasing Government interference in private industry and there was also a widely held theory, propounded by the economist Nassau Senior, that all profits were made in the last hour of work and that to reduce hours would inevitably lead to the total loss of profits. Nassau Senior, who was an opponent of the trade unions and a fanatical supporter of the new Poor Law, found ready support from factory owners. But three things defeated him – the sheer force of the humanitarian movement led by men such as Shaftesbury, the actual expansion of industry after the Factory Act of 1833, and the willingness of the landed interests in the House of Lords and Commons to vote for restriction on their political rivals among the manufacturing classes.

In 1842 Chadwick made his report on the 'Sanitary Condition of the Labouring Population', and in 1844 that on 'The Health of the Towns'. While nothing important was done in Peel's administration, these reports did lead to the first Public Health Act in 1848 which permitted local boards of health to be set up to improve sanitation, water supply and drainage.

Peel and Ireland
After Catholic emancipation in 1829 O'Connell supported the Whigs in Parliament on most questions, and he had supported the passage of the Reform Bill of 1832. He hoped in return to gain Whig support for further reforms in Ireland. But the Whigs themselves were divided on Irish affairs, while the House of Lords, still Tory-dominated, opposed any further concessions. O'Connell now turned to a vigorous campaign against the payment of tithes by the peasantry to the Anglican Church in Ireland. There was also a widespread campaign against the payment of rents to extortionate landlords. By the mid-thirties arson and murder were common

occurrences in Ireland. Lord Grey retired from the Whig leadership when he disagreed with his colleagues over the use of force to quell these outrages. Lord Melbourne, who became Prime Minister in 1835 (see p. 55), had to rely on O'Connell's support in the House of Commons, and a number of concessions were granted which made Ireland rather more peaceful in the years 1835–41. In 1836 the Whigs' Tithe Commutation Act substituted a fixed money rent for the old tithe payments to the Anglican Church, and this change reduced the burden on the peasants. The police force in Ireland was also reformed and Irishmen were admitted to it. Catholics were appointed to an increasing number of posts and O'Connell himself was chosen Lord Mayor of Dublin.

This mild policy helped to reduce the violent agitation, but when Peel came to office in 1841 O'Connell at once demanded the repeal of the Union between England and Ireland and the establishment of a separate Irish Parliament. O'Connell was trying to repeat the tactics which had, through threats of violence and revolution, forced Wellington and Peel to agree to Catholic emancipation in 1829. But history did not repeat itself and O'Connell himself was not prepared to incite the Irish to open violence, although a series of vast and threatening meetings were held in Ireland during the years 1841–3.

Peel won in this trial of nerves. He banned a mass meeting which O'Connell had called at Clontarf at the very climax of his campaign for the repeal of the Union. O'Connell, faced with the possibility of bloodshed, abandoned the meeting and ordered his followers to accept the Government's decree. Although his supporters accepted his advice, there is no doubt that the Clontarf fiasco lost O'Connell much of the prestige he had so far enjoyed among the Irish. O'Connell was arrested, tried on a charge of sedition, and sentenced to a fine of £2,000 and a year's imprisonment. However, the House of Lords, to whom he had appealed, reversed the sentence and O'Connell was freed. He died in 1847, by which time his programme had already been superseded by that of the revolutionary Young Ireland Movement.

The Anti-Corn Law League

In 1839 one of the most powerful and successful movements of the nineteenth century was launched. This was the Anti-Corn Law League, led by Richard Cobden and John Bright. Richard Cobden was a calico manufacturer in Manchester, a fervent believer in Free Trade and a master of argument on economic matters. John Bright, a manufacturer in Rochdale and a member of the Quaker Society, was a brilliant orator who combined logical argument with rousing emotional appeal. Manchester was the centre of the agitation for Corn Law Repeal, and the 'Manchester School' was the name given to the ardent free-traders of the nineteenth century. Both Cobden and Bright convinced their listeners that their motives were not selfish and that both the middle and working class would benefit by the abolition of the Corn Laws. Bright effectively denounced those members of the Establishment who advised the poorer classes from a position of privilege: 'A fat and sleek dean, a dignitary of the Church and a great philosopher, recommends for the consumption of the people swedes, turnips and mangelwurzel; and the hereditary Earl Marshal of England recommends hot water and a pinch of curry powder.' Bright saw the struggle essentially in class terms – an alliance of the working and middle classes in conflict against a landed aristocracy. In the conditions of the 'hungry forties' his approach proved very effective.

An Anti-Corn Law League Bazaar in the Theatre Royal, Covent Garden, May 1845.

The Anti-Corn Law League had the strong support of British manufacturers, for it seemed to them that the Corn Laws kept bread prices high and caused both labour discontent and demands for higher wages. Once these laws were removed, they held that the price of bread would fall, the real value of wages would increase and labour relations would improve. The supporters of repeal also thought that the abolition of the Corn Laws would help towards general free trade, and thus assist the expansion of Britain's trade with the world.

Starving Irish peasants at the gates of a workhouse in 1846.

Methods and organization of the Anti-Corn Law League

The organization and propaganda of the League was highly effective. This was largely because it dealt with a question which, at least on the surface, united both capitalists and their employees. Strong financial support enabled it to publish two newspapers. In 1843 over 9,000,000 pamphlets were distributed by a staff of 800. The political meetings organized by the League were the largest known in Britain up to that time. So effective were these meetings that the opponents of the League, especially the landlords, denounced the movement as unconstitutional and attempted to have it declared illegal. *The Times*, representing Government and landlord interests, was its persistent opponent. The landlords argued that, if the protective duties of 1815 were removed altogether, Britain would be flooded with cheap foreign corn and prices would fall to such an extent that farmers would be ruined.

Sir Robert Peel and the Corn Laws

Sir Robert Peel had taken office in 1841 pledged to maintain the Corn Laws, but every one of his free trade measures made it more and more difficult to defend them. The arguments of Cobden and Bright became unanswerable, and by 1845 Peel had come to realize that the Corn Laws must go. He hoped, however, to be able to wait till the next general election and to make the repeal of the Corn Laws the main issue. This would have happened in 1848, or whenever he decided before that date to go to the country. But the tragic events of 1845 and 1846 forced his hand. In the first place the summer of 1845 was very wet and the greater part of the English wheat crop was ruined. This was followed by disaster in Ireland, where potato rot turned the crop into black slime almost overnight. It was impossible to supply the starving Irish with English grain, and soon the Irish workhouses were full and the people dying in thousands.

The only way to relieve the frightful distress in Ireland was to allow the free import of corn into the British Isles. But even when Peel himself urged this course upon his Cabinet he met with strong opposition and decided to hand in his resignation. Lord John Russell then tried to form a Whig Government, but failed, and Peel came back with the intention of forming a ministry which would unanimously support repeal. However, his position in the House of Commons in 1846 was extremely difficult. His opponents in his own party outnumbered his supporters, and he was therefore dependent on the support of the Free Trade Whigs under Lord John Russell. Peel did have the support of the Duke of Wellington who, although not entirely convinced of the necessity of repeal, decided to put loyalty to Sir Robert above his own feelings and those of the Protectionist Tories. This ensured the passage of the Repeal Act through the House of Lords in June 1846, after the Commons had supported Peel at the conclusion of several months of heated debate. The Repeal reduced the duties on wheat, oats and barley immediately and led to their complete abolition after a few years. Peel had triumphed, but faced the wrath of his enemies in the Tory Party. What had happened to the Duke of Wellington after Catholic emancipation in 1829 now happened to Peel. The Corn Laws were repealed on 25 June 1846, and Peel resigned four days later after defeat on a Coercion Bill for Ireland. His defeat was largely brought about by a rising young politician, Benjamin Disraeli. Peel died in 1850.

Benjamin Disraeli (1804–81)

The case for the landlords had found a brilliant exponent in Benjamin Disraeli, son of a Christian Jew, Isaac d'Israeli, who had himself been a literary figure of some distinction. Benjamin Disraeli had entered Parliament in 1837 as member for Maidstone, and the garrulous mixture of colourful sense and nonsense which marked his maiden speech had caused him to be howled down by a derisive House of Commons. Moreover, he struck an alien note in the still predominantly aristocratic House, with his rings worn over white kid gloves, his yellow waistcoat and red and gold trousers. As this flashiness brought him no benefit he toned down his dress and became a somewhat more sober supporter of Peel, in the hope of being promoted to office.

However, even at this time his own ideas were quite different from those of his leader. In his novel *Sybil, or the Two Nations* he described the Britain of the Chartists and Radicals, with whom he avowed considerable sympathy, and he even supported a number of Chartist demands in the House of Commons. *Sybil* also expressed his attitude towards the aristocracy. He admired the aristocracy for its dignity, its standards of education and culture, and its devotion to the public good, but he demanded that it should take up popular causes and attempt to understand and lead the masses. He despised the new commercial class quite as much as Radicals like Cobbett had done. Disraeli therefore cut a curious figure as a Tory who wished to reconcile Toryism and the working class without actually giving the latter any political power.

Disraeli had hoped to be included in Peel's Government of 1841, but he was passed over, and from that moment carried on a campaign against Peel as a traitor to Tory principles. In particular he attacked Peel's free trade policies and at the time of the Repeal of the Corn Laws the Protectionists were only too delighted to have in Disraeli a spokesman whose wit and sarcasm gave Peel some very uncomfortable moments in the House of Commons. Another leading opponent of repeal was Lord George Bentinck, a Tory M.P. who gave up horse racing at the time of the Corn Law debates in order to devote his attention to the campaign against Sir Robert Peel. Through the efforts of Disraeli and Bentinck repeal was delayed six months from January to June 1846.

Almost immediately after the repeal the Whigs, Radicals and Protectionists combined to defeat Peel on the Coercion Bill. Peel remained in the House of Commons, but the Tory Party split in two. The former Peelite Tories such as Gladstone and Sir James Graham joined the Whigs after Peel's death and this regrouping of political forces was the origin of the Liberal Party with its Free Trade programme. On the other hand, Disraeli had achieved a good deal for himself, for he was now second in command to Stanley (later the Earl of Derby) in the Tory Party, and in 1852 served as Chancellor of the Exchequer for a brief period.

Effects of the Corn Law repeal

The Protectionist fear that the repeal of the Corn Laws would ruin agriculture proved unfounded. For the next thirty years the English farmer got a good price for his corn, and it was not till the new wheat-growing areas of Canada and the United States were developed that competition from foreign producers hit British agriculture. In fact, after 1846 both landlords and farmers improved the productivity of their land. Better wages on the land and in industry and a rapidly increasing population produced a high demand for English agricultural products. On the other hand, the fall in prices which Cobden and Bright had anticipated did, not take place. Wheat prices remained high for many years, though never as high as before the repeal. The repeal helped the Irish to some extent, but not before irreparable damage had been done. Starvation and emigration reduced the population of Ireland from 8,000,000 in 1815 to 4,000,000 by 1850. Finally, the free exchange of corn now encouraged other countries to lift some of their duties on English industrial products, and so contributed to the rapid expansion of English trade and industry in the mid-century.

8. The Chartist Movement

Introduction
The Chartist Movement was the first organized effort to form a political force which would challenge outright the two established political parties. Its origins were working class, its challenge strong and at times violent. While its ultimate fate was apparently dismal, it had a number of lasting effects on English political and social life.

Causes of the rise of Chartism
There were two main grievances behind the Chartist agitation. First there was the workers' disappointment with the 1832 Reform Bill, and second there was the hardship to the working class which resulted from the Poor Law Amendment Act. These two were closely related; for when the Poor Law began to operate in the north in the bad years of the later 30's the workers found just how little political power they had to improve their conditions. On both these issues the workers had middle-class allies, for the leading opponents of the Poor Law were men like Fielden, Oastler and Stephens (see p. 52) and many Radicals had attacked the limited nature of the Great Reform Bill. Thus the earlier Radical agitations merged into the Chartist Movement.

London Working Men's Association
In June 1836, a number of skilled craftsmen met in London and established the London Working Men's Association. Among these men was a future leader of Chartism, William Lovett. The organization listed its political demands under six main headings: universal male suffrage, equal electoral districts, annual parliaments, payment of M.P.s, the secret ballot in elections, and no property qualification for candidates. Soon the Association had more than a hundred societies affiliated to it throughout the country, for naturally these demands were popular with the working class. In 1838 William Lovett called the six points the 'People's Charter', and at a vast meeting in Birmingham in 1838 the Chartist Movement was established.

Composition of the Chartist Movement
Beneath the apparent unity of the Chartist Movement there were, from the very first, considerable differences of opinion, especially about the means by which the Charter was to be achieved. William Lovett represented the

skilled London craftsmen whose education and intelligence led them to advocate persuasion rather than force. Lovett believed, among other things, that a system of popular education run by the State would solve most social and political problems. Another moderate leader was Thomas Attwood, a banker and leader of the Birmingham Political Union.

In contrast to these moderate Chartists were the more extreme groups, mainly in the smaller northern industrial towns which had suffered from miserable conditions since the end of the Napoleonic Wars. Feargus O'Connor, editor of the *Northern Star*, the influential Chartist newspaper published in Leeds, used physical force as a threat though he never seemed ready to use it in fact. On the other hand there was no doubt about the revolutionary aims of another of the leading Chartists, the young George Julian Harney. Believing in the need for a revolution on the continental pattern, Harney had much support among the Chartists of the northern towns, especially in Newcastle, where he remained throughout this period a popular figure among the working class. The Chartist Movement also contained many Socialist followers of Owen, who wanted to use the Chartist Movement to establish their co-operative commonwealth (see p. 48). Another leader, Bronterre O'Brien, a Radical newspaper editor, agitated for a form of Socialism based on the nationalization of industry and was also a supporter of physical force. He only supported petitions to Parliament, he declared, in the manner of a character in Le Sage's story of Gil Blas, 'who presented a petition to his victim with one hand, while pressing a blunderbuss to his head with the other'.

Possibly even more divisive than the disagreement on the use of force were the differences in the leadership and its aims in different localities. For example, after the failure of the first petition of 1839, purely local forms of Chartism developed in such towns as Manchester and Leeds, and from 1842 onwards the Leeds Chartists abandoned the agitation for the People's Charter and concentrated on gaining seats on the local council. In these efforts they had considerable success and brought about many local improvements. However, such regional differences weakened Chartism from the first.

The First Chartist petition, 1839
One thing which united them all at first was the Charter, with its six demands. In 1839 a Chartist Convention of fifty-three delegates met in London. Such was the optimism and enthusiasm generated by the support they were receiving in the North that some of the delegates wished the convention to proclaim a new government for Britain. A huge petition was drawn up and signed by supporters throughout the country. The Convention moved to Birmingham, where it was considered easier to organize a strike or an insurrection if Parliament rejected the petition. During the organization of the petition, O'Connor's influence had greatly increased, and in 1839 his *Northern Star* had a circulation of over 30,000 copies weekly.

In Birmingham itself the Chartist leaders, including Lovett, O'Brien and Harney, all spoke at mass rallies in the Bull Ring, despite the fact that the local magistrates had forbidden the use of this popular meeting-place. Police were called in from London, there were severe clashes with the demonstrators, and eventually soldiers were used to disperse them.

In July 1839, the first Chartist Petition was presented to Parliament. It contained about 1,280,000 signatures. In Parliament, Thomas Attwood was the principal speaker for the six points of the Charter, but it was overwhelmingly rejected by both Whigs and Tories.

Attempted insurrection

The rejection of the petition faced the Chartists with the first really big clash between the moderates and those prepared to use physical force. The Chartist Convention disbanded in August 1839, after long and fruitless debate. In the meantime two of the leaders, Lovett and J. R. Stephens, were sentenced to imprisonment on charges of disorder and sedition. The physical force advocates were now prepared to act on their own, and a special committee of five made plans for a general rising of the working classes.

The Newport rising

The first outbreak came in the town of Newport in Monmouthshire, where the local leader was a well-known Radical named John Frost. O'Connor opposed this plan and warned the leaders of police spies in the movement. However, Frost and his supporters persisted, and staged an armed attack on the town on 3 November 1839, in order to release an imprisoned Chartist leader from the local gaol. With 4,000 men, rather unruly and totally untrained, Frost moved on the town, and was met by about thirty soldiers and a number of special constables, who barricaded themselves in the local hotel. The Chartist force attempted to break into the hotel but were beaten back by volleys from the soldiers and police, leaving twenty-four dead behind them. Thus the general insurrection had failed in its first move, and Frost's supporters in other parts of the country abandoned their revolutionary projects. Frost and two others were captured and sentenced to death, but the penalty was commuted to transportation for life. In 1840, O'Connor, Bronterre O'Brien, Lovett and Harney were all in prison, and the movement seemed to have failed in the face of the Whig Government's show of force. At the same time the economic revival sapped a good deal of the popular support.

Second Chartist Petition, 1842

The Chartists, however, were by no means defeated, and after his release from prison O'Connor became even more firmly established as a popular leader. A new petition, six miles long, was drawn up and signed, it was claimed, by about 3,000,000 persons. When this petition was unfolded on the floor of the House of Commons it looked 'as though it had been snowing paper'. The second petition, demanding once again the six points, was rejected by the House of Commons on a vote of 287 to 49.

This rejection led to the adoption of new methods. A general strike began at Ashton-under-Lyne and spread rapidly to the other northern industrial towns. Workers supporting the strike went round the industrial towns knocking out the boiler-plugs in the factories to prevent non-strikers from working. The violent disturbances that followed were known as the 'Plug Riots'. However, when some of the extremists demanded that the strike should become a general rising of the people O'Connor lost his nerve and denounced the strike in the *Northern Star*. O'Connor's change of heart assured the failure of the strike. Over 1,500 Chartists were arrested and 79 transported to the penal settlements in Australia.

Chartism and the Anti-Corn Law League
The Chartist movement was also weakened by its attitude to the Anti-Corn Law League. The Chartist leaders denounced the League as an organization of the employing classes whose only interest was to lower the price of corn in order to reduce the workers' wages. This policy divided the Chartists from a powerful and successful organization whose avowed aims were in the interests of both the manufacturing and working classes.

An attempt was made in 1843 by a Birmingham Chartist and merchant, Joseph Sturge, to bridge the division between the Chartist working class and the middle-class supporters of the League. He proposed the formation of a new organization to combine opposition to the Corn Laws with agitation of a lawful kind for an extension of the franchise. At first William Lovett and some other Chartist leaders supported this idea, but their demand that all six points of the Charter should be adopted was rejected by Sturge's middle-class supporters, and these efforts to broaden the class basis of the movement failed.

The years 1842–5
During this period there was some economic recovery and less unemployment. This improvement, though by no means startling, tended to reduce support for the Chartists. The circulation of the *Northern Star* fell from 13,000 in 1841 to only 9,000 in 1843. Other organizations gained ground at the expense of the Chartists, especially the new Owenite Co-operative Movement, the Anti-Corn Law League, the Ten Hours' Committee (see p. 61) and the trade unions. The Chartists themselves were sidetracked into an attempt to meet the economic rather than the political demands of their supporters. A Chartist Convention of 1845 set up a Chartist Land Co-operative Society which in 1847 became the National Land Company. The sum of £80,000 was raised and an estate was purchased in Hertfordshire and named O'Connorsville. The idea behind this scheme was to settle tenants on the land and, from the rentals obtained, to purchase more and

more land so that eventually a large number of small thriving farms could be set up throughout the country. But the scheme was a failure and Chartist agitation declined during the economic revival of 1846.

Revival of Chartism, 1848

The last Chartist revival was mainly due to another economic depression in 1847, and was assisted by the election of O'Connor as M.P. for Nottingham. The 1848 risings in France, Italy, Germany and the Austrian Empire created a sense of revolutionary optimism which encouraged the Chartists, some of whom had direct connection with the European insurgents. At home, a new Chartist petition (the third) was organized, a National Assembly was called, and O'Connor worked out a constitution for a British republic with himself as president. Finally, a great mass meeting was arranged for 10 April on Kennington Common, to be followed by the presentation of the third petition to the Houses of Parliament.

The Government and its middle-class and aristocratic supporters were alarmed at these developments. The young Queen herself dubbed all Chartists as 'red republicans' and certainly encouraged her Government to take strong repressive measures. O'Connor's tide of oratorical violence had never been stronger than at this time and he claimed that the number of signatures on the third petition was between four and six million. The Duke of Wellington was given the task of guarding the capital against revolution. He brought a mass of troops into London and enrolled a number of special constables including Louis Napoleon the future ruler of France.

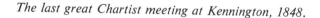

The last great Chartist meeting at Kennington, 1848.

The meeting on Kennington Common was forbidden by the Government, but it took place nevertheless. It was undoubtedly a very large gathering, though estimates vary between 25,000 and 125,000. O'Connor was due to speak, and on his arrival the police interviewed him and persuaded him to abandon the march on Westminster. After the meeting had been addressed in very bad weather by O'Connor and other leaders, the third petition was taken to the House of Commons in a cab. The number of signatures was found to be less than 2 million, and included many forgeries. It was rejected by Parliament like the first two charters.

Last insurrectionary plans

There followed the last efforts of the revolutionary elements in the movement to bring about a rising of the working classes. A small group of fanatics, greatly over-estimating their own influence and chances, planned to lead an insurrection in London on 18 August 1848. But, owing to the presence of a Government spy named Powell, the whole conspiracy was disclosed to the authorities, and the leaders were arrested at their headquarters. Five of them were sentenced to transportation for life. Neither Lovett, O'Connor nor even Harney had supported this insurrectionary group. The old leaders attempted to keep Chartism alive after 1848, but with little success. O'Connor's Land Company failed; some leaders such as Harney took up the theories of class war propounded in the Communist Manifesto by Marx and Engels; others joined middle-class movements for the gradual extension of the vote to working people – a movement which helped to achieve the Second Reform Bill of 1867 (see p. 96). In 1852 O'Connor was committed to an asylum and he died in 1855. About 50,000 of his old supporters followed the funeral procession. It was the last flicker of the Chartist movement.

Some causes of Chartist failure

The Chartist failure was hardly surprising. It is inconceivable that Parliament, dominated by the aristocracy and wealthy middle classes, could have accepted the six points, for there is little doubt that, had a full working-class vote been allowed in the elections of, say, 1841, the whole composition of Parliament would have been changed. Why, then, were three petitions presented to Parliament which had no real hope of success? One motive was, of course, to rouse 'public opinion' outside Parliament and, perhaps, to demonstrate to the working class what a useless instrument Parliament was for the furtherance of their aims. The natural result was violence and the threat of revolution, but the army and the police were securely under the control of the wealthier classes represented in Parliament. The few Chartist attempts at revolution were defeated with great ease, and the Chartists themselves never reached any general agreement on the need for violence.

Some Chartist leaders were avowed Socialists and attacked the whole social and economic structure. The Parliament of 1842, dominated by the Tory Party, was firmly convinced that the Chartists meant to put an end to private property rights. The speeches of Bronterre O'Brien, James R. Stephens, O'Connor and Harney were frequently outright attacks on the wealthier classes and all that they stood for. This lost them the support of those who sympathized with their strictly political aims.

The repeal of the Corn Laws and the other reforms introduced by Peel led to an improvement in living standards and this sapped the support for the Chartist agitation. The growing trade union and co-operative movements in the years 1844–50 also drew many workers away from Chartism. These movements, with their schemes for sickness insurance, unemployment benefits and non-profit trading in clothes and foodstuffs, offered something much more definite than the apparently unattainable ideals of Chartism.

Conclusion

Were the Chartists a complete failure? Certainly none of their demands were met before or immediately after 1848. On the other hand, all the points of the Charter except that of annual elections were achieved in the following century. Indeed, many former Chartists who had turned from the Charter to more limited reform movements lived to see the general principle of a vote for the working man accepted in 1867.

Their agitation had drawn attention to the hardships of the poor, had awoken sympathy in many surprising places and had frightened the upper classes into reconsidering their attitude to social reform. In some ways the movement seems strangely modern, demanding political changes which were only fully achieved in the twentieth century. On the other hand many of the supporters of the movement were drawn from the small industrial cities and decaying outwork industries and in their economic thinking they were looking back to the 'good old days' before the factories and the new Poor Law. But whichever interpretation one applies to the Chartist Movement, there is no doubt that it was the most important example of working-class activity in politics before the emergence of the Labour Party.

9. Lord Palmerston

PALMERSTON'S impact on nineteenth-century Britain was probably greater than that of any other single statesman. His energy was proverbial. He rarely slept more than four hours a night, he wrote all his foreign dispatches by hand, and was in the habit of jumping over the railings of his London house for exercise even when he had reached the age of eighty. In manner he was buoyant, friendly and rather aggressively outspoken. He was no respecter of persons and was often on very bad terms with his sovereign – although it must be admitted that Palmerston was not the only minister with whom Queen Victoria was on bad terms. He gloried in the power of Britain and did much to promote it. His ideas on social and economic affairs were reactionary and after the Reform Bill of 1832 he was a principal obstacle to any further parliamentary reform. His most popular idea on home affairs was that beer-shops should be set up for the sale of beer at twopence a pint.

In foreign policy, which he guided for thirty years, he generally supported the struggles of liberal rebels against tyranny, but it was no coincidence that this policy almost invariably strengthened the trade, power and influence of Britain. 'It may be true,' he declared, 'that trade ought not to be enforced by cannon balls, but on the other hand trade cannot flourish without security.' He created a popular interest in foreign policy and, on one occasion engaged in public debate with a leading Chartist. However, Palmerston did not always support liberty, nationalism and democracy abroad. His actions were often contradictory and sometimes unjust, though never without colour or interest.

Early career
He was born in 1784, the son of the second Viscount Palmerston. After a public school and university education he succeeded to his father's Irish peerage in 1802. As an Irish peer, he was not excluded from the House of Commons, and in 1806 he was elected as a Tory for the pocket borough of Newtown, Isle of Wight. In 1809 he was offered the post of Chancellor of the Exchequer, but preferred the less ambitious office of Secretary at War, in which he was responsible for all the financial business of the army. In this post he remained till 1828, being generally regarded as a safe Tory and an able administrator without much political ambition. At this time Palmerston was a supporter of the 'enlightened Tory' group led by

Huskisson. When Wellington dismissed Huskisson in 1828 (see p. 30) Palmerston resigned. In the meantime he had come round to support for the limited franchise changes which resulted in the Reform Bill of 1832, and in 1830 joined Grey's Whig ministry as Foreign Secretary. It is from this point that his impact upon the political life of Britain and Europe was really felt.

The Belgian question, 1830–9

Palmerston had been dissatisfied with Britain's undistinguished part in international affairs during Wellington's premiership. Now he was faced with a major problem fraught with both opportunity and danger. In 1815 the Vienna settlement had united Belgium and Holland into the Kingdom of the United Netherlands. This arrangement had not proved satisfactory. The Belgians suffered from the favouritism shown by King William I to his fellow Dutch nationals in military and political affairs. Religious, political and economic discontent led to a rising in Brussels in 1830 and the Dutch troops were expelled from the city. The Great Powers were immediately concerned as this was a breach of the Vienna treaties which they had guaranteed. The French especially were involved, for the revolution of 1830 in France which had replaced Charles X by the more liberal Louis Philippe, had been the signal for the Belgian revolt.

Palmerston had been pleased to see a parliamentary government of a sort set up in France in 1830, and he hoped to work with the Government of Louis Philippe to counterbalance the power of the despotic eastern states, Prussia, Russia and Austria. On the other hand, the Belgians expected help from Louis Philippe, and Palmerston suspected that France might attempt to annex the country.

There was obvious danger of a general European war over the Belgian question. Prussia and Austria were almost certain to support the Dutch, for both states were alarmed lest the revolutionary example set by Belgium should spread to their own domains. Talleyrand and Palmerston met in London and persuaded the Dutch and Belgians to accept an armistice. At this point the Belgians chose Louis Philippe's second son, the Duc de Nemours, as their King. This was quite unacceptable to Palmerston, and by a combination of threats and intrigue he persuaded Louis Philippe to disown the arrangement. The Belgians then elected someone more acceptable to Palmerston – Leopold of Saxe-Coburg, the uncle of the future Queen Victoria – but the Dutch objected to the arrangement and sent large forces into Belgium. In reply the French invaded the country, with Palmerston's agreement, but once the ·Dutch forces had been ejected, it took the combined pressure of Palmerston and the governments of Austria and Prussia to secure the withdrawal of the French forces. Louis Philippe once more gave in to pressure, as the safety of his throne depended upon good relations with Great Britain. A combined British and French force then drove out the remnants of the Dutch forces holding out in Antwerp.

It was not till 1839, however, that the Dutch finally recognized Belgian independence, which was guaranteed at the same time by all the Great Powers.

Portugal and Spain

At the same time as the Belgian crisis, revolutions occurred in Spain and Portugal. Britain had always been closely concerned in the affairs of the Iberian Peninsula, for the British position at Gibraltar and British naval and commercial interests in the Mediterranean could be influenced for good or bad by the political situation in these countries. In 1833, both in Spain and Portugal, there was a political struggle between the constitutional queens (Maria in Portugal and Isabella in Spain) and their uncles Miguel and Carlos, who both favoured absolute rule. Palmerston obtained the support of Louis Philippe for British policy, and in 1833 a Portuguese fleet under the command of a British officer defeated the forces of Miguel. In 1834 Palmerston engineered a treaty of alliance between Portugal, Spain, Great Britain and France by which the four countries agreed on joint action against Miguel and Carlos. This led to the flight of the despotic uncles from Portugal and Spain, though Carlos was to return and provoke the 'Carlist' Civil Wars later in the century.

Mehemet Ali

The problem of Mehemet Ali and the Turkish Empire arose directly from the Greek War of Independence which ended in 1832 in the Sultan's unconditional recognition of Greek independence. The Pasha of Egypt, Mehemet Ali, nominally a subject of the Sultan, had given assistance against the Greeks on condition that the Morea and Crete should both be conceded to him by the Sultan. Having lost the Morea, Mehemet Ali demanded control of the greater part of Syria. When the Sultan refused, Mehemet Ali's son, Ibrahim Pasha, invaded Syria and took it by conquest. The Turks sent an army against him, but were heavily defeated at the battle of Konieh. The Sultan appealed for help to the Czar of Russia, Nicholas I, who sent Russian troops into European Turkey to protect Constantinople against a possible attack by Mehemet Ali's forces.

Palmerston decided that he could not allow Russia the dangerous privilege of 'protecting' the Turkish Empire, and he persuaded Louis Philippe to join with Britain in sending a naval force to the Aegean in 1833. The Sultan was persuaded, or intimidated, to make peace with Mehemet Ali and to grant him control of Syria and Palestine. By this settlement Palmerston made the presence of Russian troops in Constantinople unnecessary, and had apparently once more brought the Sultan under Western control.

But Russia did not go away empty-handed. By the Treaty of Unkiar-Skelessi in July 1833, Russia and Turkey signed a defensive alliance in which the Sultan agreed to close the Straits to the warships of all nations, on the demand of Russia. Although this part of the treaty was secret, Palmerston got to know of it, and determined to break it as soon as possible.

The crisis of 1839-41

By 1839 the Turkish armies had been considerably strengthened and the Sultan decided to wrest control of Syria from Mehemet Ali. He launched an attack on Syria, but the armies of Mehemet Ali proved more formidable than expected. They had been reorganized by French officers, on the initiative of Thiers who was at this time head of the French Government. Thiers hoped to extend French influence in the Middle East and even to gain a part of Syria for France in return for supporting Mehemet Ali.

Two problems now faced Palmerston after the crushing defeat of the Turks: how to prevent Russia from intervening alone on the side of the Turks and how to prevent the French from achieving their aims in the Eastern Mediterranean. First he convened a conference of the Great Powers in London, deliberately omitting France. By the Convention of London, signed by Russia, Austria, Prussia and Britain, Mehemet Ali was offered the southern half of Syria, was recognized as the hereditary ruler of Egypt, and was ordered to make peace with the Sultan within ten days. When he refused these terms, an allied fleet captured Crete, a British squadron bombarded Alexandria, and British troops captured Acre on the coast of Syria. Russian troops also began to move south against Mehemet Ali. This use of force thwarted Mehemet Ali, frightened Louis Philippe who now dismissed Thiers, and brought about the second Convention of London. This time the Convention was signed by the French, whom Palmerston had invited to the Conference. Mehemet Ali lost both Syria and Crete to the Sultan, but his position as hereditary ruler of Egypt was confirmed. Thus Palmerston had controlled Russia, had strengthened the position of Turkey, and had crushed France's old imperial aims in the Middle East.

The Straits Convention, 1841

Palmerston was now in a great position to put an end to the Treaty of Unkiar-Skelessi, for the Sultan was under a great obligation to Britain who had taken the initiative in defeating Mehemet Ali. By the Straits Convention of July 1841, the Sultan agreed to close the entrance to the Black Sea to the warships of all nations while Turkey was at peace, and thus the exclusive agreement with Russia no longer held good. By 1841 Palmerston had achieved a remarkable series of successes in the Middle East.

Palmerston and the Far East

Palmerston's attitude towards weaker nations is one of the least admirable aspects of his work. For him British self-interest and the British sense of self-importance counted far more than considerations of political morality. Nowhere was this made more obvious than in the Opium Wars with China.

The East India Company and other British merchants had interests in the export of opium from Bengal to China. These interests were directly threatened when, in 1839, the Chinese Government seized British cargoes of opium at Canton and put an embargo on trade with Britain. Palmerston at once demanded compensation for losses to British traders and bombarded Canton when this was refused. After Peel's election victory in 1841, Palmerston was out of office for a time, but by the Treaty of Nanking 1842, the results Palmerston sought were achieved by his successor. Hong Kong was leased to Great Britain and five 'treaty ports' including Canton and Shanghai were opened to British traders, who were also exempted from the provisions of Chinese law and accorded about £6 million compensation for the Chinese confiscations.

During Palmerston's first period as Prime Minister, 1855–8, there were further complications with China. In 1856, the Chinese seized a trading vessel, the *Arrow*, which had an English registration but a Chinese owner living in Hong Kong and a Chinese crew. This vessel was engaged in opium-running and piracy. A joint British and French naval force bombarded and seized Canton in 1857, and bombarded Tientsin in the following year. The Chinese submitted, and by the Treaty of Tientsin in 1858 the opium trade was legalized. Several more ports were opened to British and French traders and Russia took the opportunity to seize all Chinese territory north of the Amur River.

Palmerston was violently attacked for these high-handed policies by his opponents in the House of Commons. In the general election, however, it was Palmerston who triumphed, while his critics, Cobden and Bright, lost their seats. 'Many objectionable members of the last House of Commons,' wrote Palmerston with his usual self-assurance, 'have been thrown out. On whatever grounds Palmerston's policies could be criticized (and they were obviously many), they were extremely popular with the middle-class voters enfranchised by the Reform Bill of 1832.

The Spanish marriages, 1846

The traditional British policy of preventing any union of the thrones of France and Spain was challenged towards the end of the reign of Louis Philippe. Louis Philippe wished to marry one of his sons to Queen Isabella of Spain, but Peel's Foreign Secretary protested against the proposed arrangement, and Palmerston, who was not a member of the Government fully supported his policy. Louis Philippe for his part refused to agree to a prince of the house of Saxe-Coburg as a husband for Isabella. Eventually it was settled that the Queen should marry a Spanish cousin and, after she had had children, Louis Philippe's son should marry her sister. In this way Peel's Government hoped to prevent the throne of Spain passing to the children of the French marriage.

After the fall of Peel in 1846 Palmerston again became Foreign Secretary Although he demanded that the marriages should take place as arranged

Queen Isabella in fact married an elderly cousin, Don Francis, who was unlikely to beget children, while her sister married Louis Philippe's son, at the very same time. Both Palmerston and Queen Victoria protested to Louis Philippe against what they regarded as a treacherous disavowal of an agreed policy. In England Palmerston aroused a public outcry against Louis Philippe which encouraged the King's opponents in France, and played an indirect part in his downfall in the revolution of 1848.

Palmerston and the revolutions of 1848

The year of revolutions, 1848, showed Palmerston at his best and his worst. All over Europe there were revolts – in Italy for unification and freedom from Austrian control; in France against the corrupt and in-effective Government of Louis Philippe; in Austria against the absolutism of Prince Metternich; and in Hungary, Bohemia and Croatia for national freedom for the subject peoples of the Austrian Empire.

In all these instances Palmerston was moved by the usual mixture of motives – the commercial interests of Britain and the maintenance of some sort of balance of power in Europe. Before the revolutions broke out, he continually emphasized the need to make some concessions to the liberal movements. Such concessions would, he contended, forestall outbreaks of violence. In particular he had urged the Austrian Emperor to make con-cessions to the Italians and Hungarians, and the King of Naples to do the same for his discontented subjects in Sicily. This intelligent advice was ignored.

When the revolutions broke out, British arms were allowed to reach the rebels in Sicily, and Palmerston expressed his approval of the new French Republic once he was sure that it had no hostile intentions towards Britain. To Hungary he gave no direct help, despite repeated appeals by the Hun-garians. English sympathizers had to witness the humiliating sight of the despotic Czar of Russia, Nicholas I, pouring troops into Hungary to aid his fellow sovereign in a ruthless suppression of the revolt. The un-conditional surrender of Hungarian forces led to hundreds of executions. Palmerston expressed his indignation, but was anxious to preserve the unity of the Austrian Empire as a counterweight to possible Russian ex-pansion in the Balkan Peninsula.

In 1850, General Haynau, who was mainly responsible for the brutal reprisals taken against the Hungarians, came to Britain on an official visit. As he was touring the brewery of Messrs Barclay and Perkins in South-wark, he was recognized by the workmen and chased by them for a considerable distance. Palmerston had already described the Austrians as 'the greatest brutes that ever called themselves by the undeserved name of civilized men'. On this occasion he showed his sympathy with the pursuers. 'General Haynau,' he said, 'was looked upon as a great moral criminal.' Queen Victoria, however, was indignant when Palmerston dispatched his comments to the Austrian Government without even allowing her to see them. This was only one of the numerous occasions on which Palmerston caused her annoyance, but his wide popularity in Britain protected him against royal displeasure.

The case of Don Pacifico, 1850

A new and weak nation, Greece, was brought under Palmerstonian pressure in the Don Pacifico affair of 1850. There had been disputes between Greece and Britain for some years, over the failure of the Greek Government to make justified payments to British traders. The Don Pacifico affair was really the culmination of a long series of such quarrels. Don Pacifico was a Portuguese Jew and merchant, born in Gibraltar, and therefore claiming British citizenship. His house in Athens had been attacked and

Lord Palmerston addressing the House of Commons, 1846.

destroyed by a mob, at the head of which were the sons of the Greek War Minister. Pacifico had claimed £20,000 compensation, but the Greek Government, rightly regarding the claim as excessive, refused to pay. The Greeks refused all Palmerston's demands for redress to Don Pacifico, and Palmerston finally sent a naval force to Athens and seized a number of Greek vessels as surety for compensation.

Palmerston's action led to international complications. As France and Russia were both guarantors, together with Britain, of Greek independence, they were furious that Palmerston had acted without consulting them, and the French Ambassador was recalled from London. There followed one of the most famous Commons debates of the nineteenth century. All Palmerston's old opponents, including Gladstone, spoke against him, but after a speech lasting five hours, in which Palmerston surveyed the whole of his foreign policy since 1830, the House defeated the motion of censure by fifty-six votes. It was in this speech that Palmerston made his famous comparison between the status of citizens under the ancient Roman Empire and that of the British citizen in the nineteenth century. 'As the Roman in days of old held himself free from indignity when he could say "Civis Romanus sum", so also a British subject, in whatever land he may be, shall feel confident that the watchful eye and strong arm of England will protect him against injustice and wrong.'

Recognition of Louis Bonaparte and the Crown

In 1848 Louis Napoleon had been elected President of the Second Republic and in 1851 he made himself absolute ruler of France by a successful *coup d'état*. A year later as a formality he changed his title from President to Emperor. Although many considered that the best British policy would have been one of neutrality, after the *coup d'état* Palmerston congratulated the French Ambassador in London on the course of events in France. As he had consulted neither the Government nor the Queen, the Prime Minister, Lord John Russell, dismissed him from office. Once more Palmerston had angered the Queen, as he had done during the Haynau and Don Pacifico incidents. Both she and Prince Albert believed that the monarch had the constitutional right to be consulted on foreign policy.

In 1852 Palmerston and his supporters revenged themselves on Lord John Russell, uniting against him to throw out the Militia Bill and force his resignation. In 1855 Palmerston regained office as Prime Minister with the specific purpose of pulling the country out of the ghastly impasse of the Crimean War – a task which he accomplished with considerable success (see Chapter 10).

Palmerston's policy towards Italy and Germany, 1859–65

Great events began to reshape the continent of Europe during Palmerston's second period as Prime Minister, 1859–65. Lord John Russell was Foreign Secretary, but it was Palmerston's ideas which guided foreign policy at this time.

In 1858, by the Treaty of Plombières between Napoleon III and Cavour, Prime Minister of the northern Italian Kingdom of Sardinia, the French Emperor secretly agreed to come to help Sardinia free northern Italy from Austrian domination. In 1859 war broke out between Sardinia and Austria, and French armies under Napoleon joined the Sardinians. The Austrians were defeated at the battles of Magenta and Solferino, but at this point, when Italian victory seemed certain, Napoleon suddenly made the armistice of Villafranca with Austria. Sardinia gained Lombardy, but not Venetia or the small states of Parma, Modena and Tuscany for which she had hoped. However, popular movements in the three duchies demanded union with Sardinia, and plebiscites held soon afterwards gave an overwhelming vote for union. At this point Palmerston made it quite clear that Britain would oppose any armed intervention in Italy designed to defeat the popular movement for union. This direct challenge to Austria was effective. In 1860 Modena, Parma and Tuscany became parts of the Kingdom of Sardinia, and Nice and Savoy were ceded to France.

Garibaldi and the Redshirts

In 1860 a popular revolt broke out in the island of Sicily against the rule of the despotic Bourbon Francis II of Naples. Conditions in the Kingdom of Naples had already been described by Gladstone after a visit there in 1851 as 'the negation of God erected into a form of government', and there was great sympathy in Britain for the Sicilians. At this point the great Italian, Giuseppe Garibaldi, organized an armed expedition by sea from the port of Genoa to give assistance to the Sicilian rebellion. His 'redshirts' consisted of volunteers from several nations. When the vessel carrying his volunteers arrived at Marsala on the western coast of Sicily he found a number of British warships anchored in the harbour and he sailed in under their protection. At this point the French Emperor Napoleon III, alarmed for the safety of the Pope in Rome, proposed to Russell that a joint British and French naval force should prevent Garibaldi from crossing the Straits of Messina to the mainland. Palmerston and Russell immediately opposed this suggestion, and Napoleon III gave way. Garibaldi successfully crossed to the mainland and entered Naples. Both Cavour and the King of Sardinia were now encouraged by Palmerston to go south and meet Garibaldi, and together they entered the city of Naples. Garibaldi, who had really hoped for an attack on Rome, accepted the proposed union of Naples with the Kingdom of Italy, leaving only Rome to the Pope.

In all these events Palmerston and Russell had played a conspicuous part. No one, including Napoleon III, dared to move against the British navy in the Mediterranean, and British official and popular sympathy encouraged the Italian nationalists. However, Palmerston was not motivated purely by a concern for Italian national liberty, for he was pleased to help in the creation of a Mediterranean state which would be friendly towards Britain and serve as a counter-weight to the power of Napoleon III.

Palmerston and the American Civil War, 1861–5

In 1861 the Civil War broke out between the Northern and Southern States of America. Palmerston maintained an official neutrality during the war, but two incidents involved a breach of this, first by America and then by Britain. In 1861, two Southern agents were travelling from Havana to Europe on a British ship, the *Trent*. Their purpose was to seek support in Europe for the Southern cause. However, the Northerners intercepted the

Trent and the two agents were removed. Palmerston protested strongly at this action against a vessel of a neutral state and, when the North refused to release the two agents, he sent troops to Canada in preparation for war against the North. At this point President Lincoln apologized and the two men were released.

The next incident involved a breach of neutrality by Britain herself. The Southern States had ordered the building at Birkenhead of a vessel, at first known as *No. 290* and later as the *Alabama*. This was apparently to be an unarmed merchant ship, but in fact was so constructed that it could be rapidly converted to a warship. Despite the protests of Lincoln's Government, the building continued, and Russell's grudging order to hold it up arrived after it had sailed for the South. Later, in 1872, Gladstone accepted the arbitration of an independent tribunal which met in Geneva and Britain paid compensation of £3,500,000 for the damage done to northern shipping by the *Alabama*.

Palmerston and Bismarck

In 1861 Bismarck became Chancellor of Prussia with the avowed aim of establishing Prussian control over north Germany. His first move was against the Duchies of Schleswig and Holstein. These territories had their own institutions although their dukes had for some time also been kings of Denmark. In 1863 there was a dispute over the succession to the duchies between Christian, the new King of Denmark, and a German claimant, the Duke of Augustenberg. Palmerston gave verbal assurances that Denmark would receive support if attacked, and this encouraged the Danes to resist the combined attack launched against them by Prussia and Austria, who at first backed Augustenberg. However, Bismarck effectively called Palmerston's bluff, for he guessed that Palmerston would not go to war over Denmark. Palmerston had spoken at an unfortunate moment for British diplomacy, for Bismarck had won the support of Russia, by helping to suppress the Polish revolt of 1863, Austria was Prussia's ally in the Schleswig-Holstein affair, and Napoleon III was heavily engaged in his attempt to establish a Latin Empire in Mexico. The balance of power, on which Palmerston's diplomacy depended, had already shifted decisively against him. His attitude to the Schleswig-Holstein question was, therefore, both ill-timed and ineffective.

Subsequently, in the Austro-Prussian War of 1866 Bismarck defeated his former ally and incorporated the whole of Schleswig-Holstein and much of north Germany into Prussia. Palmerston's defeat over Schleswig-Holstein marked the end of a long period in which Britain had played a dynamic and generally effective part in the affairs of Europe, and his prestige was already waning when he died at the age of eighty in 1865.

General comments on Palmerston's policy

Palmerston represented Britain when her international influence was at its greatest. He entered Parliament a year after the Battle of Trafalgar (1805) had ensured Britain's domination of the seas. He served in the Government of Lord Liverpool which saw the downfall of Napoleon at Waterloo and the rapid expansion of British trade and empire. He had witnessed the serious Radical discontents after 1815 and the very low ebb reached by the monarchy in the eyes of the people. Yet British parliamentary institutions had survived at a time when other monarchies were being challenged and, in some cases, overthrown. Palmerston was convinced that British parliamentary institutions were the best form of government, and he believed that other countries would do well to imitate them. This partly accounts for his approval of liberal revolutions on the Continent which seemed to be taking the countries concerned in the direction of a constitutional, limited monarchy.

His motives in foreign policy were, naturally enough, dominated by considerations of British self-interest. He successfully played off the other powers in both the Belgian and the Eastern Questions. In these disputes he was able to support diplomacy with force or the threat of force by the British navy, but in those circumstances where the balance of power had turned against Britain, and where land forces would have been needed to support his policy, as in the case of Schleswig-Holstein, he was reduced to ineffectual verbal protests. In the cases of Don Pacifico and of China, the navy was used ruthlessly against weaker states who had no support from other quarters. On the other hand Britain's naval domination in the Mediterranean enabled Palmerston and Russell to play a most important and effective part in the movement for Italian unification.

10. The Crimea, the Mutiny and the Second Reform Bill

THE outstanding political events of the mid-Victorian period were the Crimean War, the Indian Mutiny and the Second Reform Bill of 1867. Social reform also continued, but not at the pace of the years 1833–46. On the other hand, industry and trade made great progress and Britain became the financial and industrial centre of the world. In 1860 Britain's industrial production was four times that of the United States. It was also a period of great discoveries in technology and science, and of new and challenging ideas. These aspects are dealt with in Chapters 11, 29 and 33.

There were rapid political changes. In the space of twenty years there were nine Governments. The party system was changing as the result of the break-up of the old groups brought about by the repeal of the Corn Laws in 1846. The Conservatives split between the Disraeli Protectionists and the Peelite Free-Traders. The anti-Conservative forces were divided between the Whigs under Russell and the Radicals under Cobden and Bright. On two occasions Peelites and Whigs combined to form coalition Governments, and the clear-cut division between Liberals and Conservatives was not evident again until after 1868. The existence of a strong group of Irish M.P.s made the political situation even more unstable. The Irish Members in the Commons would support any party which would promise to further their aims.

The outstanding political figures of this period were Disraeli (leader of the Conservatives in the House of Commons), Lord Derby (Conservative leader in the Lords), Lord John Russell, Lord Palmerston (Whigs), Richard Cobden and John Bright (Radicals), and William Ewart Gladstone (at first a Conservative Free Trader, but later a leading Whig).

THE CRIMEAN WAR, 1854–6

Palmerston and his predecessors at the Foreign Office were all deeply concerned with the possible threat of Russia to the trading and imperial interests of Britain, and these interests were most vulnerable in India and the Eastern Mediterranean.

In 1852 a Whig-Peelite coalition under Lord Aberdeen came to power.

Lord Palmerston, who was out of favour with the Queen (see p. 83), was
Home Secretary and Lord John Russell Foreign Secretary. The Government was almost immediately confronted with a most serious crisis in
foreign affairs.

Causes of the Crimean War

The background of the Eastern Question has been dealt with in Chapter 9.
The Russians had extended their influence and power during and after the
Napoleonic Wars, and made every effort to increase it still further at the
time of the Greek War of Independence and the Treaty of Unkiar-Skelessi.
Russia was attempting to settle the problem of Turkey on her own terms,
and to gain access to the Mediterranean by agreements with Turkey which
gave Russia virtually free use of the Straits. There were difficulties too on
the Indian frontier, particularly in Afghanistan, where British interests were
constantly threatened by Russian intrigue. Fear and suspicion produced
violent anti-Russian feeling in all sections of British public opinion at this
time. Whigs, Radicals, new Conservatives and old Tories joined in the
general hatred of the Czar Nicholas I, who was seen as the embodiment of
tyrannical oppression. This feeling was especially strong in Britain after the
suppression of the Hungarian revolution of 1848 by Russian forces. Polish,
Hungarian and Russian refugees sought political asylum in London in these
years and strongly influenced British opinion.

Immediate causes of the Crimean War

Russian policy towards Turkey became increasingly aggressive in the
1840's. It was obvious that the Czar Nicholas was bent on the complete
destruction of the Turkish Empire in Europe. In 1844, on a visit to Britain,
Nicholas suggested that Britain and Russia should settle the fate of Turkey
between them. Britain was to take Egypt and Crete, and Russia to occupy
Constantinople. The independence of the provinces of Moldavia and
Wallachia, as well as Bulgaria and Serbia, was to be guaranteed by the
Great Powers and the immediate 'protector' of these territories would be
Russia. In 1853 Nicholas repeated rather similar proposals to the British
Ambassador in Moscow, Sir Hamilton Seymour.

  These suggestions looked attractive on the surface and might have
prevented war between Russia and the Western Powers, but Britain had a
number of reasons for opposing them. Russia would become the most influential power in the Balkans and the possession of Constantinople would
give her control of the entrance to the Black Sea and the Aegean. Russian
warships would also have free access to the Mediterranean.

  In 1853 the antagonism between France and Russia flared up over the
guardianship of the Holy Places in Palestine, sacred to all Christians.
During the French Revolution the French Roman Catholic monks, who
for many years had been allowed to care for the Holy Places, lost the
support of the revolutionary government which had turned against the

Catholic Church. The Greek Orthodox Church had then taken over the guardianship in place of the Catholic monks. In 1853, Napoleon III, anxious to gain the full support of the Catholic Church at home, persuaded the Sultan to recognize the ancient claims of the French monks. At once Nicholas I sent the aggressive and blustering Prince Menschikoff to Constantinople to put forward the counter-demand that the Greek monks should have their privileges maintained and that the rights of the Czar as the protector of all the Orthodox Christians in the Turkish Empire should be recognized. The second demand would have enabled Russia to intervene in the affairs of the Turkish Empire in the Balkans.

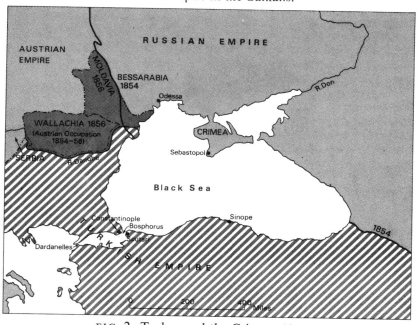

FIG. 2. Turkey and the Crimea, 1853–6.

The foremost opponent of Menschikoff in Constantinople was the British Ambassador, Lord Stratford de Redcliffe. At home the British Government, led by the mild and unaggressive Aberdeen and divided in its opinions, failed to give the Ambassador a clear lead. This suited Stratford de Redcliffe who was determined to frustrate Russian designs at all costs. He encouraged the Sultan to stand firm against Russian proposals on the understanding that Britain would support Turkey if war broke out. The result was that the British fleet moved to Besika Bay outside the Dardanelles in June 1853, and the Russians moved troops into the Turkish provinces of Moldavia and Wallachia in July 1853. The French agreed to support Britain with a squadron of their Mediterranean fleet.

At this point efforts were made by the Western Powers to prevent a general war breaking out. A conference of Austria, Prussia, France and Great Britain met in Vienna and drew up proposals (the Vienna Note) which were sent to the Czar and to the Sultan. A number of concessions were made to Russia, but the Turks, again encouraged by Stratford de Redcliffe, refused to accept them, and in October 1853, declared war on Russia. The Russian reply was to sink a Turkish fleet at Sinope in the Black Sea and to begin a general invasion of the Balkans. In March 1854, as allies of the Sultan, Britain and France declared war on Russia.

The Crimea

The threat which had provoked the British and French had been in the Balkans, but as soon as their troops began to disembark there the Russians withdrew without any major engagements. The allies therefore turned from defence to attack and at short notice sent the expedition on to the Crimean Peninsula which they believed would be hard for the Russians to defend and where their own superior sea-power would be of most use. However, from the moment the allied forces landed in September 1854 things went very badly. There were serious disagreements between the French and British commanders, and the supply system for the troops broke down. What has been described as 'the general insanity of the Crimea' was witnessed at its worst in the military hospital across the Black Sea at Scutari where, in the words of Lytton Strachey, 'Want, neglect, confusion, misery filled the endless corridors . . . There were no basins, no towels, no soap, no brooms, no mops, no trays, no plates.' However, when Palmerston became Prime Minister in 1855 he gave full support to the work of Florence Nightingale and her band of nurses in their efforts to break through the red tape and

The Crimean War: Florence Nightingale visiting the sick in the hospital at Scutari.

The Crimean War: Sir John Gilbert's romantic re-creation of the Charge of the Light Brigade.

obstruction of the allied commanders, and under her guidance the medical service was rapidly improved, reducing the death-rate in the hospital by forty per cent.

The war itself was slow, tedious and appallingly wasteful of life and effort. The allies' objective in the Crimea was the great Russian naval base of Sebastopol. But after winning the battle of the Alma River, a dispute broke out between the British and French commanders, and the opportunity to make an early attack on the fortress was lost. This enabled the Russian engineer Todleben to strengthen the defences of the naval base. This delay added many more months of hard fighting to the allies' campaign. In October and November that year the Russians launched a counter-offensive with the purpose of driving the allied troops back from the seige of Sebastopol. These sallies were defeated at the battles of Balaclava and Inkerman. Balaclava was the scene of the famous charge of the Light Brigade in which nearly six hundred men lost their lives through mis-understood orders and military bungling. By this time the British and French, inadequately supplied with clothing and tents, were suffering the rigours of a Russian winter. During the following summer they had to endure the equally unbearable heat of the Crimean summer.

The dispatches of *The Times* war correspondent, William Russell, brought home to the English people and Government the shocking state of things in the Crimea. As a result Aberdeen resigned and was replaced by the vigorous Palmerston, who reorganized the War Office and army supplies.

In September the allies captured the principal defence in front of Sebastopol, the Malakoff, and this compelled the Russians to evacuate the fortress. In March 1855 Nicholas I died and his successor Alexander II was faced with financial and administrative chaos and growing social unrest in Russia. He was anxious for a speedy peace so that he could devote himself to internal reforms, especially as the Austrians were threatening to join the war against him.

The Treaty of Paris, 1856

After preliminary negotiations at Vienna a final treaty was signed at Paris on 30 March 1856. The Conference was presided over by Napoleon III, who welcomed the chance to bring his capital and himself into the diplomatic limelight and raise the prestige of his régime.

By the Treaty of Paris the Straits Convention of 1841 was reaffirmed and the Dardanelles closed to warships of all foreign nations in times of peace; in addition the Russians were prohibited from building naval or military fortifications on the shores of the Black Sea. The Danube and the Black Sea were to be free to the merchant vessels of all nations. The provinces of Moldavia and Wallachia were to recognize the suzerainty of Turkey, but were to have their own internal self-government. Russia was to abandon her claim to be the protector of the Orthodox Christians in the Turkish Empire, but the Sultan was made to give assurances of better treatment for all his Christian subjects.

The allied aims had been achieved. Russian influence in the Balkans was reduced and her naval power was no longer a threat to the power of Britain and France in the Mediterranean. However, none of these undertakings lasted long. In 1858 Moldavia and Wallachia united under one ruler to form the state of Rumania, and in 1870, during the Franco-Prussian War, Russia declared that she was no longer bound by the terms of the Treaty of Paris which left her southern shores defenceless. The Sultan's guarantee of equal treatment for Moslems and Christians proved worthless. However, in 1856 the victory, though hard-won and costly, seemed very substantial to people in Britain and France. One direct result of the war was to focus attention in Britain on the out-of-date organization and methods of the British army, which had changed very little since the time of Waterloo.

THE INDIAN MUTINY, 1857

In May 1857 the Indian troops at Meerut mutinied and Delhi, the old capital of the Mogul Empire, fell to the rebellious soldiers. The sepoy regiments of the North-West Provinces followed suit and the English settlements at Cawnpore and Lucknow were soon isolated and under siege. At first only the Bengal army revolted but there was a serious danger that the mutiny would spread over the rest of India. The sudden outburst of revolt took the English in India completely by surprise, and it looked as though the Indian domains of Britain were about to fall away from her at one stroke. A major calamity had burst upon Britain with a ferocious suddenness, and shook Victorian complacency to the core.

India before the Mutiny

Important changes had been introduced into the administration of Britain's Indian interests by Pitt's India Act of 1784. The Governor-General, instead of being directly responsible to his Council in India, was now answerable for his actions to a Board of Control in Britain. This Board, of six members, was responsible for political decisions and changed when the Government changed. Trading policy was left in the hands of the East India Company. After this reform greater support in men and money was given to the Governors General and this enabled the British to expand their control much more rapidly. Successive Governors-General continued the work with great vigour. Lord Cornwallis (1786 – 1793) and the Marquess Wellesley (1798–1805) waged war on France's ally, Tippoo Sahib. Tippoo was finally crushed at the Battle of Seringapatam in 1799 largely because of the efforts of Wellesley's younger brother, the future Duke of Wellington. Wellesley also conquered the Carnatic and parts of Oudh while his successor Lord Hastings encroached on the frontiers of Nepal.

Under Lord William Bentinck (1828–35) there were important social reforms. He suppressed the practice of *suttee*, by which the widows of Hindus were burned on their husbands' funeral pyres, and wiped out the *thugs*, a sect of ritual murderers who were responsible for thousands of deaths a year. He also encouraged the use of English as the common language of the educational and administrative systems. Under Lord Auckland the British took up the offensive again. This time they attempted to set up their own nominee as Amir of Afghanistan to baulk the Russians. This policy ended in disaster when all but one member of the British expedition were wiped out in the Khyber Pass. However, the general advance continued and between 1843 and 1852 Sind, the Punjab and the whole of Burma were brought under British control.

The governor-generalship of Lord Dalhousie from 1848 to 1856 was of great importance. On the one hand he was responsible for many progressive reforms. He believed deeply that only Western technology could give hope to India in the future. He built railways, telegraph systems, roads, canals and schools. However, his fanatical Westernization inevitably aroused fears in traditional Indian society.

Even more sinister in Indian eyes, however, was his revival of the 'doctrine of lapse'. This was a custom practised under the Moguls, before the Europeans arrived in India, whereby states reverted to the Mogul if the the ruler died without heirs. Britain now claimed to have taken over the Mogul's rights and began to use the doctrine with such severity in states such as Jhansi (1854) and Nagpur (1853) that the Indian rulers believed there was a plan to oust them all in a short time. Such expansion, at times ruthless, produced serious discontent which developed to the point of open revolt. The peasantry benefited from British financial policy but, on the other hand, cheap factory-produced cotton goods from Britain were rapidly destroying the domestic spinning and weaving industries on which so many of them depended for part of their living. This meant that the peasantry became increasingly dependent on the produce of their land, and more and more indebted to the local moneylenders.

Many prominent Englishmen, among them General Sir James Outram who was given the task of annexing the kingdom of Oudh, doubted the wisdom of these annexations. The annexation of Oudh was an important grievance among the sepoys of the Bengal Army, many of whom came from Oudh. The sepoys had other more specific grievances as well. They were being prepared for service in Burma, against their contracted terms of service, and despite the fact that a Hindu would lose caste by crossing the 'Black Water' of the Bay of Bengal. Stories were spread by the Brahmins that the British were attempting to destroy the Hindu religion – and it was a fact that many British officers were attempting to convert their native troops to Christianity. Dalhousie's railway carriages were also an offensive innovation, for they led to the mixing of castes, which in the eyes of the Hindu was a religious crime. Then in 1856 the rumour was spread that the cartridges of the new Enfield rifle were greased with the fat of cows and pigs – the pig being unclean to the Moslem and the cow sacred to the Hindu. As the end of the cartridge had to be bitten off before loading, both Hindus and Moslems were incensed at this violation of their religious feeling.

Another complication was that the sepoys of the Indian Army had become increasingly privileged and increasingly undisciplined during the previous half-century. The proportion of British officers declined, especially when many British officers were withdrawn for campaigns in Burma, Persia, China and the Crimea. Indian regiments were often really controlled by religious committees drawn from all ranks and not by officers of the East India Company. Moreover, English defeats in Afghanistan and serious setbacks in the Crimea had destroyed the idea of British invincibility which had been built up since the days of Clive. This added force to the prophecy that the rule of the East India Company would end on 23 June, 1857 – exactly one hundred years after Clive's victory at Plassey.

The revolt by the sepoys at Meerut over the use of the greased cartridges suggested to the Victorian upholders of British rule that the revolt was the result of the blind religious prejudices of an ignorant sect refusing to accept enlightened Western standards. In fact the mutiny had wider significance. Both religious and economic factors played a very big part and modern Indian writers see the movement as a national revolt against British rule. This is, however, a matter of controversy. Of one thing there is little doubt: had the revolt spread as was intended, the position of the British in India would have been hopeless, for there were only 40,000 European troops in the whole continent. However, the Punjab supported Britain, as did the Nizam of Hyderabad and the rulers of Nepal and of Gwalior, while the sepoys of the Madras and Bombay commands were hardly affected.

Main events of the Mutiny

The main military problem in the first few months centred on Delhi, Cawnpore and Lucknow. At Delhi the small British force of 5,000 men held out just outside the city for two months against six times their number. A relieving force from the Punjab under John Nicholson finally reached the city and an attack was made on the walls. Nicholson himself was killed, but the city was recaptured after a further week of fighting. In reprisal for the wholesale murder of Europeans which the sepoys had committed the British troops acted with similar barbarity against the native population.

At Cawnpore the British force was compelled to surrender to Nana Sahib, the leader of another group of mutineers. He massacred first the men and then the two hundred women and children who were his prisoners. A relieving force under Sir Henry Havelock eventually recaptured the city. At Benares and Allahabad the British hanged thousands of their enemies on the trees surrounding the cities, while at Cawnpore every captured rebel was make to lick up two square inches of blood from the floor of the building in which the two hundred British women and children had been murdered. Then they were hanged. At Lucknow the besieged British force, outnumbered by thirty to one, held out till relieved by Havelock. In a courtyard of the city two thousand enemy sepoys resisted until they were exterminated by British fire.

The Indian Mutiny: rebel sepoys being blown to pieces at the mouth of British guns.

The atrocities and horrors on both sides in the Mutiny shocked enlightened opinion at home, but there were many who demanded still more
blood. This was resisted by Lord Canning, the Governor-General, known
afterwards as 'Clemency' Canning for his refusal to be swept into such a
policy. In this he had the direct support and encouragement of Queen
Victoria herself who deplored 'the un-Christian spirit shown . . . by the
public towards India.'

Results of the Mutiny
The British Government was compelled to accept the need for a thorough
change in the way India was governed. In the first place, by the Act of
1858 passed during Lord Derby's ministry, the East India Company was
abolished and all its powers, troops and territories were taken over by the
British Crown. A Secretary of State, with a Council of fifteen members
was made responsible to Parliament for Indian affairs, and the title of
Viceroy replaced that of Governor-General in order to stress the fact that
he was the direct representative of the Crown in India. The Queen also
issued a proclamation assuring her Indian subjects that it was her intention
to govern India for the benefit of all its people.

The atrocities committed during the Mutiny left a lasting mark on India
A great gulf was set between the British and the Indians – wider and more
formal than it had ever been in the time of the easy-going 'John Company'
While the British dropped the policy of annexing the Indian states by the
doctrine of lapse, they were determined to prevent Indians gaining re
sponsible positions. In the Indian Army, particularly, the proportion of
British officers and ranks to Indians was increased to one in three – and
the artillery was kept in British hands. Even in 1914 only about one
twentieth of the civil service posts of any importance were occupied by
Indians.

THE SECOND REFORM BILL, 1867

After 1832 only the Radicals had maintained a consistent demand for the
further extension of the franchise. The Chartists had made a powerful
effort to force the Governments of the day to accept the principle of man
hood suffrage, but their movement petered out in 1848. The middle-class
were content to share political power with the aristocracy after 1832 and
determined to resist any encroachment by the working class on their new
won political privileges. The Whig leader Lord John Russell typified this
attitude, and the Radicals appropriately named him 'Finality Jack' because
of his view that the 1832 Reform Bill was the final settlement of the franchise

Changes leading to further reform
However, certain important changes in the composition of the main
political parties in the mid-century helped to bring parliamentary reform

once more into the forefront of politics. The old Whig Party once dominated by the great landed aristocrats, gradually changed into the Liberal Party. Gladstone, the son of a Liverpool merchant and an ardent free-trader, who succeeded Russell as party leader, was nearer in sympathy to the merchants and industrialists, and had little respect for the aristocracy. Radicals such as John Bright and Richard Cobden were increasingly influential in the party. By 1865 Gladstone himself had come to the conclusion that further parliamentary reform was a necessity.

Since 1832 there had been a great increase in population and in the size of the new industrial centres. This alone would have made some redistribution of parliamentary seats necessary. In addition there had been a marked improvement in the standard of living and education of the skilled working men.

There was increasing pressure for parliamentary reform not only from radical and liberal politicians, but also from the independent organizations of the working class, especially trade unions. In 1866 the London Trades Council, representing all the main London Trades, began an organized campaign for manhood suffrage.

The political situation in 1866

Lord John Russell became Prime Minister in October 1865 on Palmerston's death and in the next year Gladstone, Chancellor of the Exchequer, introduced a Bill which would reduce the £10 borough qualification of 1832 to £7 and give the vote to the £14 tenant in the counties. This deeply disappointed the Radicals and the trade unions because it did not go far enough. On the other hand it went too far for the right wing of the Liberal Party, which opposed parliamentary reform under the leadership of Robert Lowe. His supporters were nicknamed the Adullamites by John Bright, after the Biblical story in which David escaped with his supporters to the cave Adullam. The 'Cave' as Lowe's supporters in the Commons were called, carried an amendment against the Government, which resigned and brought to an end the political career of Lord John Russell.

Lord Derby's Ministry and the passing of the 1867 Reform Bill

Lord Derby, leader of the Tory Party, now became Prime Minister, but the dominant figure in the new Cabinet was Disraeli. At once there were further popular demands for reform. A huge demonstration was planned to take place in Hyde Park in July 1866, and when the new Government had the gates of the park closed, the demonstrators broke down the railings and gained entry by force. Other meetings were held in Trafalgar Square, and John Bright conducted a nation-wide campaign for reform.

Disraeli's attitude to parliamentary reform differed considerably from that of the other leading members of his own party. He had for many years been a critic of the first Reform Bill, and had come to the conclusion that household suffrage was needed. On the other hand, he did not wish political power to fall into the hands of the working class, and when he brought forward his first proposals in March 1867, there were a number of 'fancy franchises' added to the principle of giving all rate-paying householders the vote in the boroughs. By these franchises, some people with certain financial qualifications or a certain standard of education were to receive an additional vote, thus preventing working-class domination. Although both Gladstone and Bright were also in favour of some of the 'fancy franchises', the debates on this question were exploited so successfully by the more progressive thinkers in both the main parties that the principle was finally dropped altogether. The vote was extended to all rate-paying householders and lodgers paying £10 rental in the boroughs, and in the counties went to the £12 leaseholders. Boroughs with less than 10,000 inhabitants lost one Member of Parliament, and the forty-five seats thus freed were redistributed to the larger towns and counties.

Effects of the Second Reform Bill
By the second Reform Bill 938,000 voters were added to the existing elec- torate of 1,057,000. The new voters were mainly the skilled workers in the towns. The wealthier farmers and landowners retained considerable political power in the counties. The fact that boroughs with only 10,000 inhabitants could still return their own Member of Parliament meant that these small constituencies still carried far too much weight in the parlia- mentary system. Nevertheless the Bill was a decisive move forward towards a truly democratic Parliament, and horrified the upholders of the old system, such as Robert Lowe. To him this was a fatal 'leap in the dark' which could only end in revolution and disorder.

Another important result of the second Reform Bill was to increase the importance of party organization. At general elections more public meetings were held to explain policies, and party discipline was improved in order to present a united front to the new electorate. In the election of 1868, the Liberal Party, led by Gladstone, carried out a political campaign through- out the country to win the new voters, while Disraeli who had taken Derby's place as Prime Minister in February 1868, was content with the old practice of writing an election address to his Buckinghamshire constituents. This partly explains why, although Disraeli introduced and passed the Reform Bill, it was Gladstone who won the election.

General comment on the mid-century
Britain's financial, industrial and commercial power expanded tre mendously in these years, and made her the richest nation in the world Nevertheless there were several disturbing developments. Army organiza tion was shown to be desperately out-of-date at the time of the Crimea The first great challenge to British imperialism, the Indian Mutiny, was a frightening blow to all those (and there were many) who regarded the growth of the British Empire as a God-ordained certainty. Finally, the

Lambeth in 1872. The Second Reform Bill extended the vote to at least some of the shopkeepers and working men of a town area like this.

second Reform Bill brought on to the political scene new popular forces whose impact was feared by all the upholders of the old order. It is not surprising that the thought and literature of the mid-Victorian age betrays a curious mixture of complacency and doubt.

11. The Victorian Outlook

In mid-nineteenth-century Britain rapid changes were taking place which affected every aspect of people's lives. Factory industry, the fast-growing new towns, the steamship, the telegraph, the vast railway expansion invading the most remote parts of the country – these and many other changes alarmed and horrified some people who saw the old rural England vanishing for good. Others, however, hailed these changes as splendid exciting evidence of a new age.

British achievements in manufacture and expanding trade produced a feeling of intense pride and self-confidence among many Victorians. As one writer put it 'What a satisfaction it is to every man going from the West to the East when he finds one of the ancient Druses clothed in garments with which our industrious countrymen provided him. What a delight it is in going to the Holy Land . . . to see four thousand individuals and scarcely be able to fix on one to whom your country has not presented some comfort or decoration!'

But mingled with this pride went doubts and uncertainties about the possible effects of these changes, for they brought new and alarming problems to be solved. We have seen in previous chapters what some of these problems were and how they were met. Not surprisingly writers and thoughtful men argued and put forward their views about how society should be properly organized. We have already met the Utilitarians, led by Jeremy Bentham, whose views had helped to shape the new Poor Law, and measures to improve public health. The strictly religious Evangelicals (Chapter 12) were another group that concerned themselves with social problems. While the Christian Socialists (Chapter 12) accepted the new industrial society and tried to achieve within it greater justice for working men. Amid all these changes, ideas and beliefs from the past were ruthlessly questioned and this included religious beliefs. 'O God,' prayed one eminent Victorian, 'if there is a God, save my soul, if I have a soul.'

One writer who well expressed the optimism and national pride of this period was the historian Thomas Babington Macaulay (1800–59). Macaulay had been a Member of Parliament and a minister. After losing his parliamentary seat in 1847 he gave his energies to writing. The first two volumes of his 'History of England' appeared in 1848 and sold 13,000 copies in four months. The later volumes completed in 1855 had even greater success. His work presented the Victorian middle class with a view of English

"THERE IS NO PLACE LIKE HOME."

Victorian self-satisfaction: A Punch cartoon drawn in 1849 shows a large and contented family at peace in England while the rest of Europe is torn by revolution and counter-revolution.

history that flattered them and made them feel important. 'In the course of seven centuries,' he wrote 'the wretched and degraded race have become the most highly civilized people that ever the world saw . . . have carried the science of healing, the means of locomotion and correspondence, every mechanical art, every manufacture, everything that promotes the con-venience of life to a perfection which our ancestors would have thought magical.' Macaulay in fact expressed everything which helped to make the Victorians feel proud, energetic and optimistic.

Very different from Macaulay was the Radical writer and thinker John Stuart Mill (1806–73). Mill was the son of a leading Utilitarian and grew up among a circle of hard-working reformers. As a youth he was a close friend of Francis Place. Mill believed strongly in individual liberty and parliamentary democracy, and had great faith in the power of human reason to secure the upward progress of mankind. In his great work *On Liberty* Mill argued for political democracy as opposed to tyranny of all kinds, including the tyranny of a wealthy and privileged upper class. He showed this belief in a practical way when he worked to secure competitive examinations for the civil service (see p. 129) in order to reduce the influence of patronage and privilege. He made a sympathetic study of Socialism and although he did not accept all its ideas, he was himself an outspoken critic of the power of property and wealth. On the other hand in the great debates of the time over the extension of the right to vote – particularly those leading up to the second Reform Bill of 1867 – he was cautious about the idea of a full working-class franchise. The working classes, he declared, were unfit 'for any order of things which would make any considerable demand on either their intellect or their virtue'. He feared too that unscrupulous politicians would be able to direct and manipulate working-class voters. In another way he was far ahead of the main political parties when he became the leading advocate of the equal status of women with men in society, including giving some women the right to vote.

Another writer with strong doubts and fears about the future of society was Thomas Carlyle (1795–1881). In many of his writings he tried to stir the Victorians out of complacency and into social action to improve the conditions of the mass of the people. He sympathized with the working men's discontents which gave rise to Chartism, though he disapproved of their aims. In his book *Chartism* he denounced Parliament and the richer classes for their failure to govern adequately – a failure which he regarded as the root cause of all social unrest. He had no faith in democracy and viewed with dismay the extension of the franchise to some working men in 1867. He felt that in doing this the middle and upper classes were abandoning their responsibilities. In place of popular democracy he wished to see the 'wise insight and ordering of a few'. Carlyle's desire that the leaders of the nation should undertake strong positive government led him to glorify the role of 'great men' in history, and among his writings are studies of both Frederick the Great and Oliver Cromwell. Many Victorians approved of these views, liking the idea that forceful and energetic actions could solve the problems that beset them. It is interesting to note that Carlyle's views led him to justify Governor Eyre's brutal suppression of the revolt in Jamaica in 1865, and that in this he was furiously opposed by John Stuart Mill, whose humanity and sense of justice were outraged by this event.

Another influential Victorian was Matthew Arnold (1822–88), the son of Dr Arnold, headmaster of Rugby. As an inspector of schools for thirty-five years he had great influence on the growth of British education. His wise and humane inspector's reports were highly critical of the shortcomings of both elementary and secondary education and suggested many remedies which were later applied. He went on official inquiries into the educational systems of France, Germany and other countries, trying by his reports to keep Britain abreast of her continental competitors. He was also a distinguished poet, searching as did his great contemporaries, Tennyson, Rossetti, Morris, Browning, Swinburne, for a new expression of beauty in a world which industry and commerce had disfigured in so many ways. In his work *Culture and Anarchy* Matthew Arnold attacked the self-satisfied middle-class materialists, intent on business and moneymaking. He used the term 'Philistine' to describe their outlook, which he held responsible for the decline of taste and the creation of so much pompous ugliness in furniture and architecture and so much sentimentality in art.

An even more severe critic, who was himself an artist and designer, was

William Morris (1834-96). He was an outstanding craftsman in many different fields of design, including furniture, interior decoration, typography and book production, and his influence on taste set in motion a sharp reaction against the elaborate and over-ornate mid-Victorian styles. But Morris was far more than a designer. He was a fierce opponent of the routine and degrading toil which the machine age was imposing on men. He envisaged a time when machinery would be controlled by man to produce more leisure time and this in its turn would lead to a revival of the non-machine-made arts and crafts. His concern with the evils of

A middle class Victorian interior showing the heavy and ornate decorations and furniture so popular at the time.

industrial society led him to Socialism, and he was an active member of the Socialist movement of the 1880's (Chapter 24), as speaker, writer, and organizer. In his book *News from Nowhere* he outlined the vision of the new Socialist commonwealth, in which co-operation between men and equality of rights and opportunities would replace the fierce and soul-destroying commercial competition and the tyranny of the rich over the poor.

Samuel Smiles (1812–1904): The gospel of work and self-help

The influence of the writings of Samuel Smiles on the Victorian period can hardly be exaggerated. His most important works were *Self-help* (1859), *Character* (1871), *Thrift* (1875), and *Duty* (1881). These very titles, whose dullness by no means reflects the real merits of the works themselves, express the cardinal Victorian virtues of will-power, determination and hard work. *Self-help* originated from some lectures given by Smiles to a group of young workers in Leeds who had established their own evening school for the purpose of 'self-improvement'. In its first five years *Self-help* sold 20,000 copies, and over 225,000 by the end of Smiles's life. None of the great novelists of the nineteenth century, including Dickens, achieved such a sale. *Self-help* went round the world, and was translated into numerous languages. The Arabic inscriptions on the walls of the Khedive's palace in Egypt were not passages from the *Koran* but from *Self-help*. The works of Smiles gratified those of all classes who were already successful and gave hope to those who were not. To be poor and satisfied in the Victorian period was considered almost as shameful as crime itself.

Smiles was not simply urging people to make money, although some supposed that this was his purpose. He emphasized that character formed by the knowledge of work well done was a great individual and national asset greater than 'worldly success'. In his early years Smiles himself was a Radical, and in the 1840's he supported the repeal of the Corn Laws and demanded a wider franchise and education for the working class. He came to the conclusion that until the working class was improved by the individual efforts of its members collective action was useless. 'No laws,' declared Smiles, 'however stringent, can make the idle industrious, the thriftless provident, or the drunken sober. Such reforms can only be effected by individual action.' His ideas on thrift were straightforward and simple – personal saving was not only good economics, but in itself led on to a virtuous life. 'A glass of beer a day is equal to forty-five shillings a year. This sum will insure a man's life for a hundred and thirty pounds, payable at death. Or placed in a savings bank, it would amount to a hundred pounds in twenty years.' This in itself would give a working man true independence of the Poor Law and other forms of charity.

However, he denounced the doctrines of *laissez-faire*. It was the duty of the State to provide the necessary minimum of protection to the people – especially in matters of public health. 'When typhus or cholera breaks out, they tell us that Nobody is to blame. That terrible Nobody! How much he has to answer for! More mischief is done by Nobody than all the world besides.'

Smiles never supported the ruthless commercialism of the nineteenth century by which the less successful were pushed to the wall. In his *Lives of the Engineers* he stresses the character and determination of the great English inventors rather than their money-making capacities. Even some trade unionists and Socialists had a good word for him when he declared that it was 'Far better and more respectable to be a good poor man than the bad rich one', and concurred when he wrote: 'The best culture is not obtained from teachers when at school or college so much as by our own diligent self-education when we have become men.'

From such views sprang the vast popularity in the Victorian period of the twopenny encyclopaedias, the weekly or monthly journals eagerly devoured by both the working and middle class, and the popular newspapers which rapidly developed in the second half of the nineteenth century.

The Monarchy and the family

The home and family were placed on a pinnacle of virtue by the Victorians. Only in the family could the best life be lived. 'Home,' said Samuel Smiles, 'is the first and most important school of character . . . From that source, be it pure or impure, issue the principles and maxims which govern society.'

Of course, this idealization of the home had more application to the middle class than to the poorer classes of the slums, but this high estimation of the family was encouraged by the fact that there was 'a family on the throne', and a very moral family. Queen Victoria and Prince Albert reflected every aspect of family propriety. Yet the facts of Victorian family life were not as simple and beautiful as the picture appears – children were under fierce and sometimes cruel subjection, often into adulthood. Queen Victoria ruled the life of her first child, the future Edward VII, and never allowed him any part in the government, even as a middle-aged man. Servants and wives were often under similar subjection. The difficulties in the way of divorce were supposed to have caused a considerable amount of undetected poisoning of husbands by wives in the Victorian period. Indeed, the appalling position of a woman married to a tyrannical and scheming husband was a frequent theme of Victorian literature. It was developed horrifically by Wilkie Collins in *The Woman in White*.

It is sometimes supposed that Queen Victoria's example had a beneficial effect on the whole moral life of the nation. On the other hand, in a work on the Victorian period, Sir Charles Petrie remarks: 'The Queen and Albert for twenty years gave an example of a dutiful, godly and serious life – but there is no reason to suppose that this affected the moral tone of the country. They set the tone of their immediate circle, but it is hard to believe that there was less betting at race meetings because the Queen never put a shilling on a horse.' Ultimately, the work of the Methodists and Evangelicals was much more important.

The Queen's attitude was often narrow and snobbish. At the Royal Levees, the aristocracy were readily accepted, but not the theatrical and the literary world, which were associated in the Queen's mind with immorality and 'free thought'. The wealthy merchant was also acceptable, but not the retail trader. These attitudes divided the Queen from a considerable and important part of her subjects.

Queen Victoria with a few members of her enormous family. The bearded figure is her grandson, the future George V and with him are his sons, the future Edward VIII and George VI.

The Prince Consort, whom she married in 1840, and who died through the blunderings of contemporary medicine in 1861, occupied a peculiar and difficult place in the Victorian scene. A man of energy, whose sound advice greatly improved the Queen's handling of State affairs, endowed with genuine understanding of science and commerce, he was nevertheless unpopular with both the aristocracy and the masses. His greatest fault in aristocratic eyes was his complete lack of any interest in sport. To a nation one of whose 'heroes' was the celebrated Squire Osbaldeston who killed one hundred pheasants in one hundred shots and rode two hundred miles in eight hours forty-two minutes at Newmarket in 1831, the Prince Consort was a German outsider with no appreciation of the true Britain. Such was the prejudice against him that during the Crimean War he was even suspected of being a traitor, and two London evening newspapers announced that he had been arrested for High Treason and was being sent to the Tower. However, his interest in science and commerce and his great work for the Exhibition of 1851 (see Chapter 29) made him popular with the commercial middle class. He did much to raise the prestige of the monarchy among that class on whose enterprise and ability the prosperity of Victorian Britain so much depended.

The Queen and the public

The position of the monarchy at the Queen's accession in 1837 was most insecure. It was widely believed that Victoria would be the last monarch to reign in Britain. She followed two sovereigns, George IV and William IV, who had gained no real respect. It had been possible for the literary critic and poet, Walter Savage Landor to write:

'When George IV from earth descended,
Thank God the line of Georges ended.'

Queen Victoria's dependence on Lord Melbourne and her obstinate use of the royal prerogative to defeat Peel over the Bedchamber Question (see Chapter 6), led to catcalls of 'Mrs Melbourne' from the London mob. She was also most unpopular with the Conservative aristocracy, and in 1839 she was hissed at Ascot races. Her marriage in 1840 freed her from too great dependence on her ministers, and at the same time the Prince Consort exerted a moderating influence on her outlook. This was especially apparent at the time of the Indian Mutiny, when the Queen's attitude of clemency reflected the Prince's views. But with his death in 1861, the Queen retired into a secluded and apparently permanent mourning.

After 1861 the Queen faced another period of dangerous unpopularity. A placard attached by some republican wag to Buckingham Palace announced 'This desirable residence to let – the owner having declined to do any business'. Republicanism was openly avowed by some prominent public figures including Sir Charles Dilke, John Morley and Joseph Chamberlain. The latter wrote to Dilke: 'The Republic must come and, at the rate we are going, it must come in our lifetime.' Between 1861 and 1864 the Queen made only one public appearance in London. In the year 1870 the only public ceremony she attended was the opening of London University – the very year of the fall of Napoleon III of France, of the appearance in a Trafalgar Square demonstration of the red Phrygian caps of the French Revolution of 1789 and the year of the establishment of a Republican Club by Charles Bradlaugh. Yet the Queen's retirement continued. Between 1861 and 1887 she very rarely stayed more than two nights at a time in London – a fact much resented by Londoners.

However, republicanism proved to be a passing phenomenon, and in 1897 it was Joseph Chamberlain himself who organized the Diamond Jubilee celebrations. The great change in public attitude arose from the rapid development of the British Empire, and Disraeli's work in building up the prestige of the Queen as its head. Disraeli drew the Queen more into public life and, by conferring on her the title of Empress of India, identified her with that vast extension of imperial power which pleased all classes. Imperialism was the salvation of the British monarchy. However, both Disraeli and Gladstone kept the Queen strictly to her constitutional rights and duties and allowed no extension of them.

12. The Welfare of the Body and Soul

PUBLIC HEALTH

In 1840 about one child in six died before the age of one and about a third of all children before the age of five. This appalling death-roll was due mainly to infectious diseases, the chief killers being typhoid fever, typhus, tuberculosis, scarlet fever, diphtheria and cholera (see below pp. 110–12). The death-rate for the whole country was about 23 per 1,000, whereas today it is less than half that figure. Although the figure of 23 per 1,000 seems appalling to us today, it caused no great alarm at the time – the death rate in London a century previously had been 80 per 1,000. However, in the slum areas of the industrial towns the death-rate could be as high as 39 per 1,000. The population of London rose from 865,000 in 1800 to 1,874,000 in 1841, and the housing conditions of the working class were as bad there as in other towns. Five out of every six workers had only one room for their families in filthy tenements. Water-closets were not used even by the middle class until 1840, and were unknown in the majority of workers' dwellings until much later in the century. Drinking water was supplied by private companies mostly using unfiltered Thames water. Up to the late sixties the London open drains ran into the river, and the increasing use of water-closets made the state of the river worse rather than better.

The development of sanitation was held back for many years by wrong ideas on the origins of infectious disease. What was known as the 'miasmatic' theory held the field for the first half of the nineteenth century. This theory held that marshy places and persons stricken with fever gave rise to a miasma which caused further disease. While this theory prompted demands for better sanitation, it failed entirely to consider, for instance, that bad water was the cause of cholera.

Edwin Chadwick secured the appointment of a special committee of three medical experts to investigate conditions of working-class life in a number of towns. His 'Report on the Sanitary Condition of the Labouring Population', published in 1842, contained the following description of housing and sanitary conditions among the working population of Leeds: 'With broken panes in every window-frame, and filth and vermin in every nook. With the walls unwhitewashed for years, black with the smoke of foul chimneys, without water, with corded bed-stocks for beds, and sacking for bed-clothes, with floors unwashed from year to year . . . while without, there are streets elevated to a foot, sometimes two, above the level of the causeway, by the accumulation of years, and stagnant puddles here and there with their foetid exhalations . . . undrained, unpaved, un-ventilated, uncared-for by any authority but the landlord, who weekly collects his miserable rents from his miserable tenants'. The first nationally organized inquiry into these matters came through the Poor Law Amend-ment Act of 1834. The Poor Law Commissioners set up a special commis-sion of inquiry which issued in 1844 the 'Report of the Commission for

A London street scene in the early nineteenth century: children play in a pile of refuse. A coffin is being carried into a house.

Inquiry into the State of Towns'. This disclosed on a national scale the tragic conditions in which the working classes lived and gave support to demands for reform. The cholera epidemics which occurred with disastrous regu-larity also frightened people into demanding better sanitation. Chadwick, again, was the inspiration behind this report.

Beginnings of reform

In 1847 the Metropolitan Commissioners of Sewers took over control of all sewage disposal from the numerous inefficient local bodies which had formerly had control in and around London.

In 1848, thanks to the work of Edwin Chadwick, the first Public Health Act was passed. This Act gave powers to local authorities to improve sanitation, but there was no compulsion. However, in 1866 the Sanitary Act *compelled* local authorities to take action to improve local health services. In 1858 a special Act of Parliament provided £3 million for the task of removing sewage from the Thames and having it pumped below London. The need for this work had been shown by the cholera epidemic of 1854 in London, which originated from polluted water drunk by people at the public pump in Broad Street. In 1866 towns such as Henley and Maidenhead, above London, were prohibited from discharging their sewage into the Thames. Another important step in providing a better water supply for London was taken by the Metropolitan Water Act of 1871, which provided that a water supply should be continuous. Previously the water companies had only provided water through the pumps at certain times of day. The quality of the water was greatly improved by adequate filtering. The supply of water to London remained in private hands until the Metropolitan Water Board was established in 1905. Some other large towns, however, established a public water supply by 1870.

With the complete coverage of all the London sewers by 1866 and the establishment of a better and continuous water supply, the London death-

Municipal improvement as a subject for the artist: George Scharf's painting of the laying of the water main in the Tottenham Court Road, London.

rate fell steeply. The various measures taken by Parliament in the years 1874–80 (Chapter 14), aided and encouraged these developments in all parts of the country. The death-rate dropped from 24 per 1,000 in 1870 to 19 per 1,000 in 1900.

Medicine

By the early nineteenth century there had been a number of important improvements in medical science such as the control of smallpox through vaccination pioneered by Edward Jenner. However, medical practice in general lagged far behind and the improvement in mortality rates was due more to better food and living conditions than the work of most doctors and hospitals.

Surgery was still very crude and the patient was conscious throughout the operation. At the beginning of the century Humphry Davy discovered the anaesthetic properties of nitrous oxide (laughing gas) but it was not until 1846 that the first operation using a general anaesthetic was performed in Britain. The next year Joseph Simpson introduced chloroform which was less disagreeable for the patient. From then onwards the surgeon could work slowly and with precision.

However, operations were still extremely dangerous because of the danger of infection. About 1865 Joseph Lister, a Glasgow surgeon (1827–1912) learned of the work of Louis Pasteur (1822–95) who had shown that fermentation was due to micro-organisms, that there were micro-organisms in the air that could produce putrefaction, and that some diseases were due to the multiplication of micro-organisms in the diseased animal. Lister realized that by killing the micro-organism in an operational wound infection might be prevented. His 'antiseptic' methods, using carbolic acid, were a great success and operational mortality gradually declined as their use spread. There was a still greater improvement when instruments and operating rooms were sterilized.

Anaesthetics and antiseptic methods improved the chances of mothers and infants surviving childbirth. After birth the child could also be protected not only by vaccination but by the introduction of other types of inoculation which have brought once widespread killer diseases such as diphtheria under control.

There were also important improvements in the standards of nursing. In 1833 the German Theodor Fleidner founded the order of Kaiserwerth Deaconesses in which educated young women devoted themselves to proper nursing. Their example was taken up in England by Elizabeth Fry who founded an Institute of Nursing Sisters and by several other groups of nurses in the best hospitals. The Kaiserwerth scheme was an inspiration to Florence Nightingale who made an enormous contribution to new standards both in the training and ward work of nurses.

Florence Nightingale's work in the Crimea (see Chapter 10) had an immediate effect in raising the status of nursing, and special subscriptions were raised in order to establish the Nightingale School of Nursing at St Thomas's Hospital. From this first professional training centre the nurses went out to other hospitals both in Britain and abroad. Florence Nightingale had an insight into the needs of the hospitals born of observation and experience. Long before the enunciation of the germ theory of disease by Pasteur and others, she fully grasped the importance of absolute cleanliness in everything to do with hospital treatment. It was necessary for her to declare what before her time had rarely been recognized – that dirt could give rise to illness. It was the determined application of 'fresh air, soap and water, and light' in the hospital at Scutari during the Crimean War that reduced the death-rate from 42 per cent to 24 per cent in a few months of 1855. Again, before scientific proof was given by Pasteur and Lister, she recognized that infection in hospitals could be carried from one patient to another by those attending them. She stressed the importance of providing the right conditions for the recovery of a patient and insisted that nursing should be more than mere giving of medicines. Her active work, her writings (which were numerous), her capacity to gain support and break through the hardest bigotry and opposition, resulted in the establishment of a recognized and efficient nursing service, adding immensely to the effectiveness of the great medical discoveries.

One area of medical treatment which has only improved very slowly has been the care of the mentally disturbed. In 1839 John Connolly made the first step forward by abolishing the use of chains and bars at his asylum at Hanwell and ceased to treat patients as if they were dangerous animals. Slowly some system of control was introduced into the admission and care of the mentally ill. Gradually doctors came to realize that many mental defects were forms of illness that could be cured and that even where there was no chance of a completely successful treatment the sufferers could still lead happy lives and did not have to be thrust out of sight and out of mind.

The development of National Insurance

Early forms of insurance were organized by working-class societies to provide sickness benefit for their members (see Chapters 2 and 28). During the Revolutionary and Napoleonic Wars and for many years afterwards these societies were often suspected of Radical aims, and were limited by legal restrictions. But towards the mid-nineteenth century these societies developed more rapidly in the industrial areas. The working class joined in great numbers and the membership, for example, of the Ancient Order of Foresters rose from 65,000 in 1845 to nearly 700,000 in 1886. Then the insurance companies took up the business of insuring the working-class family for small weekly premiums. By the early twentieth century, however, it became clear that such piecemeal social protection was inadequate and did not touch the poorest workers. There was a demand for a state system, especially after Bismarck introduced state schemes of insurance in Germany. In 1892 Joseph Chamberlain took a leading part in promoting such a scheme, but it was not until the Liberal administration of 1906–15 that the Government began to lay the foundations for a system of state welfare (see Chapter 17).

RELIGIOUS MOVEMENTS

Methodism

The Anglican Church in the eighteenth century was often guilty of smugness, inactivity and identification with a small ruling class. But there were always some of its members who tried to imbue it with a new life. John Wesley, above all, tried to take religion to those whom the Church had ignored, especially in the industrial towns and mining villages. Wesley's efforts to save the souls of the poorer classes by preaching honesty, purity and abstinence stemmed from the basic belief that God cared for all. Wesley began as a loyal member of the Church of England, but imbued a new dynamic spirit into religion. To the Wesleyan Methodists the Holy Spirit could directly and immediately affect the character of the individual when faith had entered the soul. The Church frowned on this view and disliked also the democratic implications of Wesleyanism. As the Methodist preachers were gradually excluded by the Church of England, they established their own chapels and also appointed laymen as preachers. Methodism made a direct appeal to the ordinary man which the Church did not. On the other hand, the political Radicals tended to distrust the Methodists because they thought they concentrated on personal conversion from sin to the exclusion of political action for the transformation of society. In this view they were mistaken for we now know that much trade union and political activity of the working class was derived from the Methodist communities in the industrial areas.

Methodism and literacy

The Wesleyans established their own Book Room in London from which the influence of their literature spread widely. They supported, together with other Nonconformists, the Religious Tract Society and the British and Foreign Bible Society. In 1815 the former had 124 local groups distributing religious literature and by 1854 the latter comprised 3,300 groups at home and abroad. The Methodist movement itself, besides supporting these societies, published a variety of magazines which not only propagated their own views of religion, but also included extracts from the great English novelists and poets. In this way, along with a considerable religious revival, they helped to encourage literacy among the people long before an adequate popular educational system existed. A section of Methodists, however, and other Nonconformists such as Unitarians and Strict and Particular Baptists continued to view the romantic novelists and poets as the brothers of Satan.

The Evangelical Movement

In the nineteenth century the spiritual enthusiasm of the Methodists produced a revival in the other Christian churches, in particular the Evangelical movement in the Church of England. This movement was represented and inspired by such men as William Wilberforce, the Earl of Shaftesbury and Bishop Ryle of Liverpool. They attempted to bring a loftier and less worldly tone to the Church and to bring about social improvements in the name of the Church and Christianity. William Wilberforce (1759–1833) (for his public career see p. 49) was associated with the evangelical 'Clapham Sect' – so named because they held their meetings in the Clapham district of London. Wilberforce planned and published, with the aid of the Clapham Sect, an important religious journal, the *Christian Observer*. This journal preached the strict observance of the Sabbath, conducted propaganda against wickedness in public life represented by such things as slavery, and brutal sports like cockfighting and duelling, and advocated improved education for the people, the reform of the prisons and better factory conditions. It represented the social conscience of the Evangelical movement in the Church of England.

The Earl of Shaftesbury was an equally prominent social reformer (p. 50). Besides his factory reforms, he took up the cause of numerous exploited and oppressed minorities in England, especially of young workers, and after a long struggle he secured in 1875 protection for the chimney-sweep apprentices. He was a strong advocate of slum clearance in London and for the establishment of schools for the poor. He was also a founder of the Young Men's Christian Association, and working men's institutes, and a fervent advocate of missionary work abroad.

General effects of the Evangelical Movement

The Radicals distrusted the movement because of its Tory associations. Wilberforce opposed trade unions, and Shaftesbury the mild Reform Bill of 1832 – to him, as to many others, democracy and the French Revolution of 1789 were synonymous. The Radical William Cobbett detested the Evangelicals and described the fervent religious propagandist Hannah More as that 'old bishop in petticoats'. The contemporary opponents of the Evangelicals denounced their tendency to defend the class structure and preach the doctrine that every man should be satisfied with the station to which God had called him – a doctrine convenient to the middle and upper classes, but scarcely satisfactory to others.

Nevertheless, the Evangelical movement achieved a considerable religious revival. The sale of religious literature was enormous. The British and Foreign Bible Society sold 16 million English Bibles in the period 1804–50. Religious tracts had vast sales. One by Bishop Ryle of Liverpool sold over 12 million copies. The British and Foreign Bible Society employed hawkers in the countryside to distribute religious tracts and Bibles, and earnest middle-class ladies flung tracts from railway carriages, spread them in gaols, lodging-houses, workhouses and military camps. This gave rise to sarcastic comment by Charles Dickens and other writers. Henry Mayhew, in his famous work *London Life and the London Poor*, describes how the half-starving inmates of lodging-houses lit their fires with the tracts saying 'tracts won't fill your belly'. Probably the most lasting achievements of the Evangelicals were in the various social improvements for which Shaftesbury and his supporters worked and, on the purely religious side, their greatest results were achieved among the middle class. Even there the attitude of a number of leading Evangelicals to literature restricted their influence. Shakespeare was regarded as especially dangerous to adolescents, as were the eighteenth-century novelists such as Fielding, Smollett and Sterne. One Evangelical, P. H. Gosse, wrote in 1864 concerning the tercentenary of the birth of Shakespeare: 'At this very moment there is proceeding unreproved a blasphemous celebration of the birth of Shakespeare, a lost soul now suffering for his sins in hell.'

The Oxford Movement

The Clapham Sect declined in importance after Wilberforce's death in 1833. It had stressed the importance of personal honour and morality but was very little interested in the formal position of the Church. In the 1830's, however, a High Church party group rose as the Clapham Sect declined. This group emphasized much more the importance of the priesthood, of the bishops, and of Church doctrine. From this attempt to give new authority and dignity to the Church there sprang the Oxford Movement. In 1833 a group of Oxford dons published the first of a series of *Tracts for the Times*, in which they expounded their ideas on the future of the Church. The leaders of the movement were John Henry Newman, John Keble, Hurrell Froude and Edward Pusey. They called for a revival of Church ritual, for a re-emphasis on the importance of the priesthood, and for loyalty to the practices of the original Catholic Church as it was before the Reformation in the sixteenth century. This latter idea led to a charge of 'Popery' against the Tractarians, and in Tract Ninety, issued in 1841, Newman argued that despite the Reformation, the Church of England had remained part of the universal Catholic Church. This caused an outburst of violent controversy, and Newman gave up his fellowship and his position as Vicar of St Mary's, Oxford. Newman remained in the Church of England for another four years, living in almost monastic seclusion with a number of his followers. In 1843 he withdrew all his former criticisms of the Church of Rome, and in 1845 he was received into the Catholic Church. Newman's influence in Great Britain increased as the years passed, largely due to his writings and work in education. He became involved in a sharp controversy with the novelist and Christian Socialist, Charles Kingsley, as the result of which he wrote his famous *Apologia pro vita sua* in which he described clearly and sincerely his motives for joining the Church of Rome. In 1870 he published his *Grammar of Assent* in which he argued the case for religious belief. In 1879 he was made a Cardinal. His influence on sections of the Anglican clergy was considerable, and several hundred clergymen joined the Catholic Church. On the other hand, not all the early Tractarians joined him, and Edward Pusey and some others led the Anglo-Catholic movement within the Church of England.

The Christian Socialists
Yet another demonstration of the intense interest of the Victorians in all religious matters was the mid-century movement known as Christian Socialism. Its members attempted to apply Christianity to industrial conditions and relegated the discussion of doctrines and the saving of souls to second place. It leaders were Thomas Hughes, author of *Tom Brown's Schooldays* and a former pupil of Thomas Arnold at Rugby, Charles Kingsley, the novelist, and Frederick Denison Maurice. Their aim was to bring the Church to grips with social reality, and a number of Kingsley's novels, especially *Alton Locke*, are imbued with this spirit. Above all they preached the need for industrial co-operation as opposed to competition; their pioneering work in the co-operative movement was considerable and they gained much trade union support. Although the societies they themselves established did not last long, their influence with Parliament enabled the co-operative societies to gain the privileges of friendly societies in 1852 long before the trade unions. Another achievement was to prevent a complete rift between religion and the working classes – the Labour movement in Britain never became completely anti-religious as was often the case on the Continent. The Christian Socialists recognized the duties of Christians to the working people and Kingsley denounced the use of religion to repress the masses: 'We have used the Bible,' he declared, 'as if it were a mere special constable's handbook, an opium dose for keeping beasts of burden patient while they are being overloaded!'

The Working Men's College, established in London in 1854, was a direct outcome of the work of the Christian Socialists in popular adult education. Here lecturers from the older universities, who sympathized with Christian Socialist aims, gave their lectures free to working men.

The Salvation Army
Another important religious development of the second half of the nineteenth century was the Salvation Army. Like Christian Socialism, it was not a movement of religious revival in the narrow theological sense only, but applied itself directly to the social evils of the times. Its founder, William Booth (1829–1912) experienced religious conversion in 1844 when he was fifteen and became a preacher of the Methodist New Connection. He had been apprenticed to a London pawnbroker and knew at first hand the problems of squalor and poverty in the Walworth district. In 1861 he broke away from the Methodists and founded the Christian Mission at Whitechapel. In 1878 this became the Salvation Army, with

William Booth its first General. The organization of the British Army was taken as the model and Booth issued his orders and regulations as chief of staff. Open-air meetings, bands, tents used for meeting-places – all these methods of direct appeal to the people – were used. At first there was violent opposition to the Salvation Army and groups were organized to break up its meetings and disrupt its evangelical work. Booth and his followers also suffered fines and imprisonment as breakers of the peace. However, by the end of the century the movement had spread widely both to Europe and the rest of the world, and Booth's wife, who died in 1890, had firmly established the women's ministry.

While fervently believing that the unconverted were doomed to eternal damnation, Booth devoted his immense energy to the denunciation of poverty, suffering and the exploitation of the poor. This naturally made him an unpopular figure with many of the wealthier classes. On the other hand he was highly respected by sections of the trade union movement in his attempts to improve the conditions of the unskilled workers. In 1890 he published *In Darkest England and the Way Out*, in which he argued strongly for a combination of direct religious conversion with such devices as the 'prison-gate brigade' and the 'household salvage brigade' and social action through the establishment of farm colonies, the poor man's savings bank, the poor man's lawyer and other such efforts to combat poverty, drunkenness and crime. His disclosures and constructive social ideas contributed substantially to that movement for social reform which gained fresh impetus after 1906 (see Chapter 17).

Conclusion

Despite the increasing activities of the various religious movements, it would be wrong to assume that there was a great religious revival among the mass of people during the nineteenth century. A high rate of church attendance was maintained by families of the middle class, whereas working-class church attendance was found more in those areas where direct social and charitable work was highly organized. This was the strength of Methodism and the Salvation Army. The old appeal of religion was, if anything, weakening. The advance of science and the wide acceptance of Darwinism (see Chapter 33) in part accounted for this. The Roman Catholic Church, however, did increase its influence as the century progressed and became the focal point of anti-Darwin thought.

13. Gladstone and Liberal Reform

Gladstone's career from 1841 to 1868

William Ewart Gladstone was the son of a Liverpool merchant and West Indian slave owner. He was educated at Eton and Christ Church, Oxford and like Peel had a brilliant university career. In 1832 at the age of twenty-four he was elected to Parliament. In Peel's Government of 1841–6 he was Vice-president of the Board of Trade and remained a convinced free-trader for the rest of his life. He had an intense moral fervour which expressed itself in his writings on religious and ecclesiastical questions and tinged a good deal of his political activity. Although a High Churchman he always upheld the need for religious toleration in an age when religious conflicts took on violent forms. He was an astonishing combination of classical scholar, religious controversialist, financial genius, and social and political reformer as well as one of the most powerful public speakers of the century.

Gladstone's economic and financial policy

After the resignation of Peel in 1846, Gladstone was for some years entirely outside the party system. However, although attached to neither Whigs nor Tories he accepted the post of Chancellor of the Exchequer in Lord Aberdeen's Government of 1852–5. Gladstone was one of the very few statesmen who succeeded in arousing interest in Government finance. His clear, detailed and enthusiastic exposition of financial matters held the House of Commons spellbound. Indeed, the great expansion of Britain's industry and commerce in the mid-century made the Chancellor's statements of vital interest and importance to the monied classes.

In his first budget Gladstone, as a convinced free-trader, reduced or abolished import duties on more than two hundred items of trade. This meant that 123 articles were by this time entirely freed from customs duties. These articles were mainly foodstuffs and partly-manufactured items. He also introduced new scales of death duties on inherited land and wealth, a policy which the Liberals were to follow over the next sixty years. These changes reduced the cost of living and made up the loss of income from customs duties by other forms of taxation on the wealthy. Income tax was also extended to include sections of the middle class hitherto exempted. Gladstone hoped that income tax could be abolished, for even at 4d in the pound it was still very unpopular. This aim was, however, frustrated by the costs incurred by the Crimean War and the Indian Mutiny which forced him to double the rate. He regarded wars as an expensive burden to be avoided. Personally he loathed adventurist policies which led to war, but if war came he believed it should be paid for, not by huge borrowings from the banks and the public, but from money raised by duties and direct taxation. This, he thought, would make Governments think twice before taking steps leading to war.

Gladstone as Chancellor, 1859–61

In Palmerston's second Government 1859–65, Gladstone was again Chancellor of the Exchequer. In 1859, having at length thrown in his lot with the Liberals he had the unpleasant task of once more raising the rate of income tax to pay for improvements to the army and navy. The budget of 1860 must be regarded as the most important of all Gladstone's budgets. It involved all the main principles on which his financial policies were based. Above all, it took another step towards complete free trade. Early in 1860 Richard Cobden, who fervently believed that permanent peace could be assured by free trade between the great nations, had gone to Paris and negotiated with the government of Napoleon III what became known as the Cobden Treaty. By this agreement France lowered duties on English manufactured imports, and in return Britain abolished nearly all duties on French manufactures and reduced duties on French wines. This treaty was, of course, entirely in line with Gladstone's free-trade principles.

Gladstone's aim was to abolish all duties on raw materials, food and manufactures. This would benefit every section of the community, reducing costs to manufacturers and lowering prices to the consumer. These results would lead on to further expansion of trade and industry. He therefore removed import duties on 375 articles, leaving only 48 on which any duties were charged. Thus since the beginning of Peel's second term of office in 1841 more than 1,000 items of trade had been freed from duties. These changes meant a loss of £2 million to the Government, but Gladstone made up for this by increasing income tax from 9d to 10d in the pound.

Paper duties removed

Gladstone was determined to remove the paper duties which earlier Governments had imposed to reduce the sale of Radical newspapers. The mid-nineteenth century was a period of great demand for the 'popularization' of knowledge, and Gladstone believed that the paper duties hampered this. However, Palmerston opposed Gladstone, and the House of Lords rejected his Paper Repeal Bill when it was put forward as a separate measure. His next move was to introduce, in 1861, one Finance Bill which included not only the normal provisions of the budget but also the Paper Repeal Bill itself. The House of Lords would have had to reject the whole budget in order to kill the repeal of the paper duties, and by so doing they would have challenged the right of the Commons to control the country's finances.

Rather than face a crisis which might have led to their powers being further limited, the Lords allowed the Bill to go through. It led to a vast increase in cheap, popular publications.

The philosophy of self-help
In 1861 Gladstone also established the Post Office Savings Bank. He fervently believed that thrift in private and public life would lead to a healthy economic situation both for the individual and for the country. He believed that public expenditure should be confined to the barest minimum, and that it was as immoral for a nation to spend beyond its means as it was for the individual. Hence he wished to encourage private saving, especially among the working class, whom he thought could best help themselves by this means. By the end of 1862 the newly-established Post Office Savings Bank had 180,000 accounts and a total deposit of £1¾ million.

Financial policy, 1861–65
During his years as Chancellor of the Exchequer in Palmerston's last government, Gladstone was able to move close towards complete free trade and the abolition of income tax. He reduced the duties on tea and sugar and brought income tax down to 4d. in the pound by 1864.

General comments on Gladstone's financial policy
Gladstone's financial policy was designed to free manufacturers and merchants from Government-imposed restraints and to reduce the cost of living and the cost of raw materials. If this was achieved, Britain could compete on favourable terms in the world market, exchanging manufactured goods for food and raw materials. He regarded the very slight income tax of those years as contrary to the principles of good finance as well as to the interest of private enterprise. As for the wage-earners, his views were those of contemporary Liberal economists – that wages would find their natural level, and given cheap food and the continued expansion of trade, the working classes would share in the general prosperity. For these reasons he tended to regard even the trade unions as unnatural restraining forces on the free play of industry. Later on, however, his attitude to the trade unions was modified, and in 1886 he included a trade unionist in his Government.

Results of his policies
Enormous increases in trade and industry resulted from Gladstone's free-trade policies. In 1872 British exports were four times those of 1850 and imports about three times. The value of coal exports rose five fold and that of machinery four fold. Exports of iron and steel rose by more than 250 per cent. This led to a vast increase in shipping which placed Britain securely ahead of all other countries. The working classes undoubtedly profited from

this prosperity. Their purchasing power rose by 33 per cent above the 1850 level. Thanks to Gladstone's trade policy food prices rose by only 60 per cent in twenty years, whereas wage increases had been much more. The low import duties on tea and sugar led to an increase in their consumption of 60 per cent and 75 per cent respectively.

Gladstone has been criticized for concentrating purely on the mechanics of finance and trade without any direct concern for the bad conditions in which the working classes lived. Far from considering it at all necessary for the Government to spend any money on, for example, improved housing for the people, his cardinal aim was to *reduce* Government expenditure. In this aim he had remarkable success, actually reducing Government expenditure from £72 million in 1861 to £62 million in 1866.

It would be absurd to attribute to Gladstone all the improvements mentioned here, for there were great economic movements involved, but it is clear that Gladstone had correctly estimated the needs of the country in the conditions of mid-Victorian England, and he must be considered one of the greatest Chancellors of the Exchequer that Britain has known.

Gladstone's first ministry, 1868–74

The general election of 1868 returned a clear Liberal majority and Gladstone became Prime Minister. There followed six years social and administrative reforms which were even more thorough-going than those after the first Reform Bill of 1832.

To many observers the result of the election of 1868 was a surprise. It is partly explained by the fact that although Disraeli was the author of the 1867 Reform Act, much credit had gone to Gladstone and the Liberals for progressive amendments which had swept aside the 'fancy franchises'. In the country itself the Radicals, led by Cobden and Bright, had carried on an agitation which had forced the leadership of the Liberal Party to move further forward than it had intended. The newly-enfranchised workers of the towns voted solidly for the Liberal candidates. And the Liberals had out-manœuvred the Conservatives by carrying out a series of public meetings in the constituencies to appeal to the new electorate.

Ireland, 1848–68

Gladstone had for some time taken an intense interest in Ireland. He read all the available official documents and tried to master every aspect of the problem. 'My mission,' he declared, 'is to pacify Ireland.' Over the next thirty years he was to make constant efforts to solve this problem which had grown steadily worse since the union of England and Ireland in 1800.

Since the days of the Irish Famine of 1845–6, the state of Ireland had scarcely improved. In 1848 the Young Ireland Movement, inspired by the revolutions of that year on the continent of Europe, had attempted to stage a rising against British rule under the leadership of Smith O'Brien. The leaders had, in fact, planned the insurrection to coincide with a similar

movement planned by the Chartists in Britain. By far their greatest grievance was the Irish land problem, but they believed it could only be solved
by giving Ireland political independence. O'Connell, a landlord himself,
had failed to deal with the land problem, so the leaders, especially John
Mitchel and James Finan Lalor, urged the seizure of all land by the peasants.
Their efforts only resulted in sporadic peasant outbreaks which were easily
suppressed by British troops, and the leaders were transported to Australia.

Over the next twenty years the condition of Ireland grew worse. Between
1846 and 1851 over one million persons died of starvation and disease, and
the area under corn fell from about 3 million to $1\frac{1}{2}$ million acres. Landlords
changed to cattle raising and smallholders were turned off the land in
thousands. Murder and arson became the common expression of discontent. Yet the British Government continued to ignore the basic grievances
of the Irish who consequently came to see political independence as their
only hope for social and economic reform.

The Fenians
Inevitably still more revolutionary political organizations developed,
notably the Fenian Brotherhood, set up in Paris in 1858, and later based in
New York. The driving force of the movement was a group of Irish
emigrants, but they had a considerable number of American sympathizers
who remembered their own struggle for independence against George III.
Numerous secret societies were formed in the United States and in Ireland
itself. American money helped to train and arm several thousand men in
the United States. In 1866, a Fenian force, hoping for the support of the
American Government, invaded Canada, but it was quickly defeated and
some of the leaders were executed. Others were arrested and imprisoned in
Britain. This in its turn provoked a wave of Fenian violence and terrorism.
In December 1866, the Fenians attempted to release a number of prisoners
from Clerkenwell gaol by blowing up the prison wall. Twelve people were
killed and over a hundred seriously injured. Although this and other acts
of violence hardened public opinion against the Irish, it nevertheless drew
the attention of many people including Gladstone to the desperate social
and economic conditions of the Irish people.

Disestablishment of the Irish Church
Gladstone hoped to pacify Ireland by piecemeal reform and make her a
contented part of the British Empire. At this stage his object was to
save the Union of 1800, and not in any way to modify it. One grievance,
however, he could put right. It had become widely recognized that the
position of the Anglican Church in Ireland was anomalous. In a country
whose population was four-fifths Catholic, the Anglican Church drew
extensive tithe payments from the people to supplement its generous
endowments. This caused violent resentment. Gladstone's Irish Church
Bill of 1869 deprived the Church of its established position and also of most

of its endowments. Nearly half the Church's income was allotted to the improvement of workhouses and schools. Naturally, Gladstone faced strong opposition in the House of Lords, but Queen Victoria, anxious to prevent any constitutional conflict between Lords and Commons, advised the Lords to accept the measure, and they did so.

The First Irish Land Act, 1870

Gladstone recognized that the land question was even more important than the religious problem.

Three basic features of the land system account for the Irish discontent. Firstly, the great majority of landlords were Protestants who lived as absentee landlords in England, their estates being managed by bailiffs, the most hated class in Ireland. Secondly, Ireland had few industries and the population was almost entirely dependent on the land. This led to the sub-letting of land already rented from the landlords. This in its turn, far from solving the problem of rent payments to the main landlord, led to the existence of small and uneconomic land units. In Ireland a man was regarded as fortunate to be able to cultivate as much as twenty acres. Thirdly, the landlords, unlike their English counterparts showed no interest in improving their tenants' land and methods and if the tenants set to and improved the land by new buildings and better drainage, they had their rents raised. This system discouraged any improvements and the soil yielded less and less. Land hunger, failure to pay increased rents, eviction and the workhouse, was the common cycle of Irish life. This led to violence directed against the landlords and hatred for Britain with whom they were identified. To make matters worse, by the middle of the nineteenth century there appeared a new type of landlord, the man who bought land as an investment or speculation, and had even fewer scruples about evicting tenants than the old non-resident aristocrats.

By the Land Act of 1870 Gladstone attempted to extend the 'Ulster custom' of fixity of tenure, freedom of alienation (freedom on the part of a tenant to sell his lease to another tenant), and fair rent, to the rest of Ireland. He enforced the payment of compensation to evicted tenants who had improved their land. A 'scale of damages' was established for eviction, but this did not apply when eviction was for non-payment of rent. The Act failed because it did not define what was a reasonable rent and could not therefore prevent unjust evictions. John Bright secured the insertion of a clause by which it was possible for a tenant to obtain a loan of public money to purchase the land and become an owner. He saw the answer to the Irish land problem in the creation of peasant-proprietors and the gradual abolition of landlordism. However, this and other clauses in the Act were resisted by the Irish landlords and were unsuccessful in practice. The legal profession and the magistracy in Ireland was, in any case, heavily weighted in favour of the landlords, and this made Irish legislation very difficult to enforce.

This well-intentioned Act was a failure, and violence was in no way abated. Gladstone resorted to a Coercion Act in 1870, giving the police and the Lord Lieutenant in Ireland extensive powers of arrest, trial and imprisonment, while a mild conciliatory measure, the Irish University Bill, was defeated in the Commons.

The movement for Home Rule

By this time events in Ireland were fast outpacing Gladstone's piecemeal policy. In 1870 the Home Rule League was formed to fight for the repeal of the Act of Union of 1801. The demands of the League, denounced by Gladstone, were really quite moderate – namely, the establishment of an Irish Parliament to govern the purely internal affairs of Ireland, leaving defence, imperial taxation and matters affecting external trade to the British Government. There was no demand for the separation of Ireland from the British Crown, except by the most extreme Fenians. These new developments in Irish opinion were brought home forcibly to the British Parliament by the election of 1874 in which fifty-seven supporters of Home Rule were returned under the leadership of Isaac Butt.

Elementary Education Act, 1870

Gladstone's first ministry witnessed a most important advance in education. Some changes had already occurred since the first Government grant to education in 1833. In 1839 the grant to Church of England and Nonconformist schools had been increased to £30,000 and a Committee of the Privy Council set up to supervise the administration of the funds. To meet the shortage of teachers the various religious bodies established training colleges. By 1846 the annual grant had risen to £100,000 and the pupil-teacher system was introduced. By 1858 the grant had been increased to £500,000 and the Government appointed a Parliamentary Commission under the Duke of Newcastle to inquire into the state of elementary education in Britain. This Commission reported unfavourably on the extent and nature of much of the education being given. They found huge areas of the industrial regions in which there was little if any education, and cited appalling cases of popular ignorance. They were naturally shocked to find one child who did not know that Victoria was Queen and believed George III still to be on the throne! Even more shocking to the mid-Victorian conscience was the discovery that many children had never heard of Jesus Christ.

The Commission's recommendations led to Robert Lowe's introduction in 1862 of the system of payment by results. Under this system the inspectors tested the pupils by examination and the schools received payment according to the number of children who passed. This led to more efficiency, but at the cost of artificial cramming and great strain on the teachers. Though fiercely criticized at the time of its introduction, payment by results remained until 1897.

The most powerful inducement for further educational reform was the Reform Bill of 1867, by which for the first time a section of the working class obtained the vote. Robert Lowe, having failed to stop the Bill, recognized that the education of the masses would radically affect the future of politics in Britain. He declared, 'We must compel our future masters to learn their letters'. This remark reflected strongly the fears of many of the old ruling political families who saw their activities about to be submitted to popular judgement.

Another spur to reform was the realization that European elementary education was far in advance of that in Britain, and that Britain's continued industrial superiority would depend on a better educated working class. Particularly influential was the example of Prussia, recently victorious in a series of great wars and the dominant power in Europe. Her highly organized elementary education was recognized as one cause of her military and economic superiority. Before his death in 1861, the Prince Consort had done much to promote both scientific teaching and a more widespread and popular interest in education. All these factors influenced Gladstone in his decision to introduce a complete national system of elementary schools.

The minister entrusted with the task was W. E. Forster, an ardent educationalist. He was influenced by the Education League which demanded a state system separate from the schools of the religious societies. The Act set up School Boards elected by the local ratepayers, but, as the Anglican Church especially had greatly increased its educational work, the Government decided to give the schools of the religious denominations State grants as before. The duties of the School Boards were to raise rates and build schools where those provided by the voluntary bodies were insufficient or non-existent. Violent arguments over religious education between Anglicans and Nonconformists were met by an amendment to the Bill moved by Mr Cowper-Temple, and its terms have since been known as the Cowper-Temple Clause. They remain in force to the present day. Religious teaching in the state elementary schools was restricted to the Bible and no special teaching or creed was permitted. Parents could withdraw their children from scripture lessons on religious grounds. By the Act the School Boards were to fix the school fees for their locality, with the power to excuse the payment of fees when they thought it necessary. The Boards were also to decide whether attendance in their districts should be compulsory or not. However, by an Act passed by Disraeli's Government in 1876, fines could be imposed on parents who kept their children away from school, and in 1880 the age of 13 was fixed as maximum at which the Boards could demand attendance. In 1891 the payment of fees was abandoned. In general, the Act was very successful and school attendance increased nearly fourfold between 1870 and 1890. However, bitter religious controversy bedevilled the educational question. The Anglican Church regarded Gladstone's state schools as a new and pagan development, while the

Non-conformists were dissatisfied that he had strengthened the already dominant position of the Church schools in many areas.

Army reforms

When Gladstone took office the general condition of the British Army was poor as both the Crimean War and the Indian Mutiny had shown. These campaigns had shaken British complacency, but the overwhelming defeat of France in 1870 by the efficient Prussian Army was an even greater shock. Although Gladstone himself was loath to allocate money to military purposes, even he could no longer leave the British Army with the same organization and outlook that it had had at the time of Waterloo.

The unreformed army: an army doctor, in civilian clothes, watches while a soldier is whipped. Drummer boys drown the sounds.

The minister chosen to carry through the army reforms was Edward Cardwell who had had a distinguished career since his election to Parliament in 1842. He had held the post of Secretary to the Treasury, President of the Board of Trade, Secretary for Ireland and, in 1864, Secretary for the Colonies. In this last post he had radically improved the system of colonial defence. When Gladstone appointed him Secretary for War in 1868 he was opposed by every vested interest and every prejudice which the Army establishment could muster against him, but his brilliance and determination brought into being a new military system on which the rapid expansion of British imperial power before 1914 was to be based.

Changes made by the army reforms

The Queen herself disliked Cardwell's reforms but Gladstone persuaded her to sign an Order in Council by which the Commander-in-Chief of the Army was placed directly under the control of the Secretary of War, and could no longer dictate army policy as he had done in the past. The Army was organized into three departments centralized for the first time at the War Office. Another radical change was the abolition of the practice of the purchase of commissions, an age-old Army custom by which promotions were the subject of a type of trade. An auction room existed in Charles Street, Mayfair, where commissions were bought and sold. A lieutenant-colonel's commission had a regular price of £4,500, but there were cases of them being sold for as much as £7,000. In order to circumvent the opposition of the House of Lords, Gladstone persuaded Queen Victoria to issue a Royal Warrant abolishing this trade.

Possibly the most far-reaching of the Army reforms was the fundamental change made in the conditions of enlistment. Previously men had served twelve years at overseas stations, and then entered the reserve, often with their health broken. Cardwell introduced enlistment for six years with the colours and six years with the reserve, and also arranged for the men to be taught some trade while in the army. The infantry regiments, previously known only by regimental numbers, were rearranged into 69 military districts with a name which had some local significance. The Militia and the Volunteers were also to use the same training centres as the Regulars and this began the process by which the division between the Volunteers and the Regulars was broken down. These changes led to greater administrative efficiency, a great sense of pride in the Army, and a far better type of recruit. Cardwell also based the Artillery regiments on the counties and greatly increased their strength. However, he met with the blind opposition of the Artillery officers who insisted on retaining the muzzle-loading cannon despite the German victory in 1870 which had clearly demonstrated the superiority of the breech loader.

Unfortunately, the Queen's cousin, the Duke of Cambridge, remained Commander-in-Chief until 1895, and he strenuously opposed further reform. 'I don't like Staff College officers,' declared the Duke, 'My experience of Staff College officers is that they are conceited and that they are dirty. Brains! I don't believe in brains.' The great struggle which Cardwell had to wage for his reforms, and the violence of the attacks upon him, undermined his health, and he retired from political life in 1874.

The Trade Unions

After the failure of Robert Owen's G.N.C.T.U. (see p. 47), the trade unions had been faced with great difficulties. Their legal position was difficult, and in order to cover themselves in the eyes of the law they had adopted the practice of registering themselves as friendly societies. The benefits they were thus entitled to give their members when sick were also used to maintain them when unemployed or on strike. The use of 'coercion' against an employer or, as the law phrased it, action 'in restraint of trade', made open strike action to improve their conditions extremely difficult and hazardous. The leaders and members of a striking union could be placed under arrest and transportation for life to the convict settlements of Australia was one possible penalty.

The Chartist movement of 1836–48 concentrated the efforts of the workers on direct political action, and many leading trade unionists were members of the movement. After the failure of Chartism, and the vast general unions of the thirties, there was a revival of trade unionism among the skilled trades. In 1851, for example, the Amalgamated Society of Engineers (forerunner of the present Amalgamated Engineering Union) was established. The new society began a campaign against piecework and overtime which the employers met with a lock-out in January 1852. In spite of a good deal of public sympathy, the men had to resume work on the employers' terms. The A.S.E. then concentrated on enforcing apprenticeship for its members and on providing friendly society benefits. It accumulated substantial funds from a subscription of one shilling a week – a considerable sum in those days. Its financial strength and stability increased its bargaining powers with the employers. Other skilled workers soon followed suit. In the 1860's it became customary for the London secretaries of these unions to meet together and discuss common problems, and to organize support in case of strikes or lock-outs. This group was the origin of the present Trades Union Congress which was formed in 1868. The skilled unions represented on the London Trades Council played an important part in securing a limited working-class vote by the Reform Bill of 1867.

However, the legal position of the trade unions was further weakened by a court decision of 1867. A trade union – the Boilermakers' Society – which had registered itself as a friendly society, prosecuted its secretary for having stolen £24 of its funds. The judge ruled that this was a society 'in restraint of trade', and that its funds could not therefore be protected by law. This decision caused widespread agitation by the trade unions to secure their full recognition in law. Other incidents had occurred which focused public attention on the trade union question. In 1866 some trade unionists on strike at Sheffield took violent action against other workers who would not support the strike. One man was killed and another had a canister of gunpowder lowered down his chimney. The 'Sheffield outrages', as they were called, led the Government to appoint a Royal Commission to inquire into the whole trade union question. The Commission's report led to the Trade Union Act and the Criminal Law Amendment Act of 1871.

The Trade Union Act recognized the legal right of the trade unions to hold property and to have it protected by the law. However, the Criminal

Law Amendment Act, passed at the same time, took them a step backwards. By this law a previous Act of Parliament of 1859, which had made peaceful persuasion of other workers to join in a strike perfectly legal, was repealed. It was declared illegal for trade unionists on strike to 'obstruct', 'molest', 'intimidate', or 'persistently follow', other workers. Some judges ruled that even unfriendly looks at other workers constituted 'intimidation'. The 'intimidation' of employers by merely preparing a strike led to the imprisonment of some trade union leaders. Naturally, this Act aroused fierce opposition to Gladstone among trade unionists.

Civil Service reforms

With increasing legislation and the creation of new Government departments for education, the army, factory inspection, etc., the work of the central administration was growing fast. Several European states were far ahead of Great Britain in the efficiency of their administrations.

The Civil Service in Britain had up to this time been recruited by recommendation and family influence. A Civil Servant might inherit a post from his father or receive it by recommendation from a Member of Parliament. Such posts were often regarded as 'sinecures', the salary from which would enable the holder to live independently and pursue other interests. A number of prominent novelists of the nineteenth century were holders of such posts. These practices made the Civil Service amateurish and slapdash in a country whose trade, population and administrative responsibilities were increasing daily. Naturally, the Utilitarians and other upholders of administrative efficiency campaigned for reform of Civil Service selection. There was also an urgent need for a great increase in the actual numbers of Civil Servants.

In 1870 Gladstone, by an Order in Council, introduced the system of open competitive examinations for entry to the Civil Service, except in the Foreign Office which retained the system of recommendation.

University Test Act

Another reform was the abolition of the long-standing University Test Act, by which only members of the Church of England could hold scholarships, fellowships and administrative posts at Cambridge and Oxford.

The Ballot Act, 1872

Gladstone was responsible for the introduction of the secret ballot in elections – one of the original six points of the Chartists. This was the first of several important changes Gladstone made to abolish bribery and intimidation in elections. Once the ballot was secret, bribery became pointless and intimidation ineffectual. One unforeseen result was the creation of a really independent Irish Nationalist Party.

The Licensing Act, 1872

Gladstone denounced the widespread drunkenness of the mid-Victorian era and placed the blame for it squarely on the shoulders of the brewing interests. Many politicians believed that drunkenness was preferable to any control of the trade by Government, and it was a measure of Gladstone's moral courage that he took up the question at all. His Home Secretary, Bruce, introduced a measure which fixed the closing times of public houses at twelve midnight in the towns and eleven o'clock in the country. In areas where too many public houses existed some were closed, while other regulations prevented the adulteration of drink. These mild and sensible measures aroused the violent opposition of the brewing interests. They organized themselves in the Conservative interest and spread anti-Liberal propaganda through the public houses. The Conservatives in their turn encouraged the brewers. Even the Bishop of Peterborough declared that he preferred 'England free rather than England sober'.

Foreign policy

Britain had not committed her army to any major intervention in Europe since 1815 and Gladstone's foreign policy was based on his recognition of the fact that the small British army was no match for the vast Continental military machines, especially that of Prussia. He kept the country out of the Franco–Prussian war though he did manage to secure a guarantee of the neutrality of Belgium from both Bismarck and Napoleon III. The Government were also unable to prevent Russia unilaterally denouncing the Black Sea Clauses of the Treaty of Paris of 1856 (see p. 92).

Even in the last years of Palmerston's administration it had been obvious that British influence in Europe had declined, but the apparent weakness of Gladstone's foreign policy was very unpopular. Gladstone particularly aroused public opinion in his handling of the *Alabama* dispute (see p. 85). Very sensibly he agreed to submit the question of compensation to the United States to an international tribunal, but to a nation which had only recently been applauding the jaunty jingoism of Palmerston his action seemed cowardly and unpatriotic. His reputation suffered still further when the tribunal awarded the United States £3,500,000 damages.

14. Disraeli and Tory Democracy

Reasons for Conservative victory, 1874

Gladstone's reforms had aroused vigorous opposition from many quarters. The Licensing Bills had thrown the brewing interests into the arms of the Conservative Party, with public houses themselves as centres for Conservative propaganda. The Army reforms had struck a serious blow at old family privileges in the forces, while the House of Lords had been exasperated by Gladstone's determined use of Orders in Council to get round their opposition. The Nonconformists resented the creation of state schools and the support given to the schools of the Anglican Church. The trade unions, many of whose most skilled and intelligent members had been enfranchised by the second Reform Bill of 1867, were angered by the Criminal Law Amendment Act. In foreign policy, Gladstone's opponents made capital out of the Alabama decision which went against Britain, while the defeat of France in the war of 1870 was attributed to Gladstone's policy of neutrality. A large proportion of the electorate was still upper and middle class, whereas many of those who had benefited from Gladstone's reforms had no vote. The result was that every element of the 'establishment' – Irish peers, Anglican bishops, the old military families, the brewing interests – opposed Gladstone, and the trade unionists in the towns gave the final blow. Disraeli was returned to power with a substantial majority.

Benjamin Disraeli and social reform

Disraeli was a man of great versatility both as a novelist and a politician. He hoped to combine the new democratic trends with both the virtues of the old aristocracy and the power of Empire, binding them together within the framework of British constitutional monarchy (see Chapter 8). He believed that Britain should extend her civilizing influence as widely as possible in the world, and in the race for power, Britain must not be left behind the rising empires of Germany and of Russia. At home, Disraeli saw more clearly than any other Conservative statesman of the nineteenth century the need to convince the 'masses' that progressive social reform was not only introduced by Liberals and Radicals. In this he had an able and dedicated assistant in Richard Cross, the Home Secretary.

The Artisans' Dwellings Act, 1875

The growth of population in London and the big cities had put immense

Beaconsfield Buildings in North London erected in 1879 and named afte Disraeli. At that time they seemed to be a great improvement on the o slums seen in the background.

pressure on living space. The industrial towns were crowded with insanitar back-to-back houses, built without damp courses and often with walls onl one brick thick. The housing of the people had been undertaken by privat builders out for high profits. The first real State intervention in this privat speculative building came with the Artisans' Dwellings Act. Cross had t fight opposition to it in his own party, and this accounts for some of it weaknesses. Nevertheless the Act achieved for local authorities the right t purchase and demolish insanitary property and to clear and reconstruc whole areas. However, they still did not have powers of compulsor purchase.

The Public Health Act, 1875

This Act made important new demands upon the local authorities. The were compelled to appoint Medical Officers of Health, to whom infectiou diseases had to be notified. They were also compelled to ensure adequat drainage and sewage disposal in their districts, and to collect refuse as regular service. The water supply was no longer to be left to the haphazar efforts of private concerns and water-sellers. Inspectors of nuisances wer appointed, and local authorities had to see that polluted foodstuffs wer destroyed.

In the history of the efforts to improve the health and well-being of th people, the Public Health Act of 1875 was undoubtedly of great im portance. Even so, many of its opponents, both Conservative and Libera denounced it as a serious invasion of the 'liberties' of private persons, an sneered at the work of Disraeli's administration as 'a policy of sewage'.

Conspiracy and Protection of Property Act, 1875

Disraeli had decided to improve the legal position of the trade unions, an the Conspiracy and Protection of Property Act, replacing the Criminal Law Amendment Act, went a long way to strengthen their standing in law. At last a combination of workpeople to further their interests was clearly legal. If an action by a trade union during a trade dispute could legally have been committed by *one* person then the trade union action was also legal. This implied that, just as one person could withdraw his labour from an employer, a combination of workers could do the same – in other words, they had a clear right to strike in furtherance of their own interests. Finally, by the Trade Union Amendment Act of 1876, a trade union was clearly defined and the old regulations against them acting 'in restraint of trade' were finally swept aside.

Employers and Workmen Act, 1875

This improved the legal position of a worker in relation to his employer. Employers and workmen were henceforth on equal terms in any contract of service between them. Previously, an employer's breach of contract was treated as an offence under the civil law and could be met by the payment of damages, whereas a workman who broke his contract was liable to a criminal law penalty of fine and imprisonment. Under the new law they were both liable to the penalties of civil law.

Factory Acts of 1874 and 1878

This ministry also introduced important changes in factory regulations. Since the achievement of the ten-hour day in the textile industries (see p. 63) the only advance gained by the textile workers had been by a Factory Act of 1850 which gave the Saturday half-holiday, but left the working week at sixty hours, which meant in effect a working day of ten and a half hours. By the Factory Act of 1874 this was changed to a working week of fifty-six and a half hours, which gave an actual daily rate of ten hours. By a number of Factory Acts passed between 1860 and 1864 several other trades had been brought under the same regulations as the textile factories, and in 1867 all factories employing more than fifty workers were included. Workshops employing less than fifty workers were placed under the supervision of the local authorities. The latter, however, failed to carry out their inspections regularly, and by Disraeli's Factory and Workshops Act of 1878, all such factories and workshops came under State inspection. This was an important advance in the protection given to industrial workers by the State, and showed a response to the demands of the trade unions.

The Merchant Shipping Act, 1876

The conditions of employment for sailors in the merchant service were appalling. Their living quarters were cramped and insanitary, and ships were sent to sea overloaded and unseaworthy. Attention had been drawn to this situation by a number of tragedies at sea in which crews were lost and the insurance companies had to pay out large sums. The cause of the seamen was taken up by Samuel Plimsoll, M.P. for Derby since 1868. He attempted to secure the passage of a Bill through Parliament to remedy the evils of the 'coffin ships', but failing in these efforts, he published an important work entitled *Our Seamen*, and in 1873 he circulated his book at the Trades Union Congress. As yet the seamen had no organized trade union and reform was left almost entirely to Plimsoll's own efforts. He secured the appointment of a Royal Commission which in the main proved his allegations, and in 1875 a Government Bill was introduced. In the meantime the shipowners had brought heavy pressure on the Government, and when Disraeli announced that the Bill would be dropped, Plimsoll denounced his opponents in the House as villains, and even threatened the Speaker. However, Plimsoll had considerable popular support, and Disraeli wisely introduced the Merchant Shipping Act in 1876. This act gave very wide powers of inspection of ships to the Board of Trade and laid down regulations regarding the accommodation of sailors on board ship. The principle of the load-line was also enforced, but the responsibility for its actual positioning on the ship's hull was left to the individual shipowner until 1890, when it passed to the Board of Trade. Later, Plimsoll himself became President of the Sailors' and Firemen's Union, and continued his agitation for reform throughout his life.

Other measures of great social significance were the Enclosure of Commons Act and the Education Act, 1876. By the first the enclosure of common land was prohibited unless it could be shown to be for the benefit of the community. As a result two years later Epping Forest was saved for the recreation of the people of London. By the Education Act parents became liable to fines for keeping their children away from school without permission.

General comment on Disraeli's social reforms

Disraeli had spent thirty years of his political life attempting to bring his party up-to-date. He turned it from a party of resistance to change to one which passed the 1867 Reform Bill and the great reforms of his 1874–80 ministry. He and his sympathizers, especially Cross, put the idea of 'Tory Democracy' into practice. Disraeli was alive to the great importance of the trade unions and to the rising power and significance of the working classes. The almost inexplicable phenomenon of the 'Conservative working man' was the result of his policy of social reform. Disraeli was responsible for a great extension of State activity and he resisted the pressure put upon him by reactionary vested interests in his party. Where he nearly succumbed to these influences, as in the case of the shipowners, he had the political sense to respond to popular opinion and agitation.

Disraeli's foreign and imperial policies

In 1830 Disraeli had travelled to the Near East on the proceeds of one of his novels, and from that moment the East had fascinated him. During this journey he visited Spain, the Balkans, Constantinople, Palestine and Egypt. He became convinced of the need to support Turkey against her enemies and to build a powerful British interest in the East.

It is not surprising that in 1875 Disraeli took even more interest in the exciting business of imperial and foreign affairs than in social reform. His unorthodoxy and daring were strikingly shown in the purchase of nearly a half-share in the Suez Canal for Britain, borrowing £4 million from the house of Rothschild entirely on his own responsibility without even consulting the Cabinet. Disraeli's action, entirely outside the usual methods of British politics, aroused the opposition of many Conservative and Liberal politicians but proved most popular in the country as a whole. Gladstone, who had refused to buy the Canal outright in 1870, denounced the venture as commercially and financially unsound, but in this he proved wrong, for the possession of this interest was vital to the development of the Empire. The canal reduced the cost of freight carriage by sea to Australia and New Zealand by at least three-quarters, and made communications with India and the Far East shorter and safer. It also greatly improved Britain's military and naval capacity in both the Middle and Far East.

Disraeli arranged the visit of the Prince of Wales to India in 1875–6. His purpose here was to stress the link between the British and Indian peoples, through the Royal Family, and to increase Britain's sense of

The opening of the Suez Canal in 1869; six years later Disraeli acquired a major interest in the Canal for Britain.

imperial destiny and power. This was taken a step further by the proclamation of Queen Victoria as Empress of India, a title much criticized in Britain, but of advantage in India, since it recognized India as a separate entity with its own sovereign. The proclamation was made in India by the Viceroy, Lord Lytton, at the Delhi Durbar of 1877 attended by all the ruling princes of India.

The Eastern question

By the Treaty of Paris, 1856 (see p. 92), the Sultan of Turkey had promised better treatment for his Christian subjects. His promises had meant nothing. The Turks continued to exploit and persecute their Balkan subjects. In 1875 a revolt broke out in Bosnia and Herzegovina. At once the Emperors of Austria and Germany and the Czar of Russia sent demands for reform to the Sultan; demands which once again brought forth the promises, but no action. Meanwhile the rebellion spread to Bulgaria and Macedonia. Germany, Austria and Russia then presented the Berlin Memorandum to Turkey demanding an armistice and drastic changes in Turkish methods of government.

Disraeli's policy

The Berlin Memorandum, which was also supported by Italy and France, seemed justified, but Disraeli who had not been consulted beforehand refused to support it and it was withdrawn. Disraeli distrusted both Austria and Russia, and was determined to protect the integrity of Turkey in the interests of British power in the Mediterranean. Next a reforming party headed by Midhat Pasha and encouraged by the hope of British support, seized power in Turkey and placed Abdul Hamid on the throne. There followed the 'Bulgarian Atrocities' in which Abdul Hamid let loose his bands of irregular troops, the 'Bashi-Bazouks', on the helpless civilian population of Bulgaria.

At home Gladstone issued his celebrated pamphlet 'The Bulgarian Horrors and the Question of the East', in which he violently attacked Disraeli's policy and demanded that the Turks should be expelled 'bag and baggage' from the Balkans. He also went on a political tour of Britain, during which he aroused popular hatred of the Turks, and gained wide support for his policies. But he seriously divided his own party who were not all as sympathetic towards Russian policy as Gladstone.

Still relying on British support Abdul Hamid rejected the demands for reform made by the Great Powers in the Conference of Constantinople, attended by Lord Salisbury as British representative. This refusal was followed in April 1877 by a Russian declaration of war on Turkey. Disraeli agreed that Britain should remain neutral, provided that Russia avoided any threat to Egypt or the Suez Canal and did not enter Constantinople. After a number of setbacks, including the Turkish defence of Plevna for several months, the Russians reached Adrianople within easy striking distance of Constantinople. Disraeli demanded an armistice and sent the Mediterranean Fleet to Constantinople. In Britain patriotic fervour was whipped up against Russia. The word 'Jingoism' originated in the popular song of the day:

> We don't want to fight, but by jingo if we do
> We've got the ships, we've got the men, we've got
> the money too . . .

Perhaps influenced by Disraeli's show of force and several minor military setbacks, the Russians agreed to an armistice with the Turks.

The Treaty of San Stefano, 3 March 1878

The terms imposed upon Turkey by Russia produced immediate opposition from Great Britain and Austria. By the treaty Rumania, Serbia and Montenegro were declared independent states and Russia herself gained the territory of Bessarabia from Rumania. The treaty also created a large state of Bulgaria stretching right across the Balkans from the Aegean almost to the Adriatic – a State which would apparently be able to control the whole of the Balkans in the Russian interest. Britain and Austria at once demanded another conference of the Great Powers to reconsider the whole treaty. Indian troops were sent to Malta, and Lord Salisbury succeeded the indecisive Lord Derby as Foreign Secretary. At this point Bismarck invited the Great Powers to meet at Berlin. Russia, sensing the danger of a union of the European Powers against her, agreed to the Congress, which met in Berlin from 13 June to 13 July 1878.

The Treaty of Berlin, 1878

Disraeli attended the Congress and negotiated personally with the Russians. The Treaty of San Stefano was drastically modified and the proposed 'big Bulgaria' broken up. This had, in fact, been secretly agreed with Russia before the Congress opened. Turkey recovered from Bulgaria sufficient territory to protect Constantinople. The northern part of Bulgaria became an independent principality, while a southern part, Eastern Rumelia, was put under Turkish control but with a Christian governor. Another secret agreement between Britain and Turkey gave Britain Cyprus in return for a guarantee to defend Turkey against any Russian attack. Turkey also promised to reform her administration and the treatment of her Christian subjects.

In the general conference Disraeli obtained a ratification of these preliminary secret negotiations. He gained the right for Turkey to move troops into Eastern Rumelia, and successfully resisted the Russian demand that Eastern Rumelia should be known as Southern Bulgaria. Austria was permitted to occupy Bosnia and Herzegovina, and the size of the new independent states of Montenegro and Serbia was somewhat reduced.

Disraeli dominated the Congress, but the results of his policy have always aroused controversy. He gained Cyprus which then appeared to be a most valuable naval and military base. He checked Russia's Middle Eastern and Mediterranean ambitions. He strengthened the anti-Russian front by encouraging the Austrian occupation of Bosnia and Herzegovina.

On the other hand, he had put many Bulgars and Greeks once again under ruthless Turkish rule. Nor did even the immediate future bear out his policy, for the centre of Britain's influence in the Middle East was soon to become Egypt, not Cyprus. By encouraging Austrian power in the Balkans as a counterweight to Russia, Disraeli was furthering his avowed aim 'to break up and permanently prevent the alliance of the Three Emperors'. Britain's interests would best be served by this division, but it eventually led to the clash between Austria and Russia in the Balkans which precipitated the Great War of 1914. As for the Turkish promises of good conduct to their Christian subjects, they were soon forgotten under the 'Red Sultan', Abdul Hamid.

When Disraeli returned from Berlin claiming he brought 'peace with honour' there was widespread approval and enthusiasm. However, this was not echoed by the Liberals, who denounced the whole settlement, in Gladstone's words, as 'an insane covenant'. Gladstone, who had handed over the Liberal Party leadership to Lord Hartington in 1875, emerged once more on the political scene with an electoral campaign in Scotland, starting in his own constituency of Midlothian. He not only denounced the Berlin settlement, but launched a violent attack on all Disraeli's imperialist ideas, and stressed the need for justice, national freedom for oppressed peoples, and the use of arbitration in international disputes. He condemned the empire-building of Disraeli to the great annoyance of Queen Victoria. She was particularly angered when Hartington was removed from the leadership of the Liberal Party and Gladstone resumed his old position. The powerful Midlothian campaign was a great success, however, and in part accounts for the defeat of Disraeli in the election of 1880.

Disraeli's imperial policies. (1) India

The North-West Frontier presented the main problem for Britain in India. Lord Lytton, appointed by Beaconsfield as Viceroy of India, was a supporter of his 'forward' imperial policy. He had to deal with a difficult situation in Afghanistan. For some years the Russian frontiers had moved nearer and nearer to Afghanistan, and the British determined to gain effective control of the mountain kingdom before the Russians did. To Lord Lytton this became even more urgent when a Russian mission arrived at Kabul in July 1878, and received a great welcome from the people. General Sir Frederick Roberts was sent against Afghanistan with 35,000 men and the reigning Amir was replaced by his son, who signed a treaty of friendship with Britain. However, Roberts' army later withdrew and the small British mission left in Kabul was massacred. Two British forces suffered disastrous defeats at the hands of a new claimant to the throne, the brother of the Amir who had been supported by Britain. However, General Roberts retrieved the situation by marching from Kabul to Kandahar under most difficult conditions and defeating the pretender's army outside Kandahar in August 1880. In the meantime, Gladstone had come to power in Britain. He withdrew the British army altogether from Afghanistan, which in fact remained friendly to Great Britain. British defeats in Afghanistan badly damaged Disraeli's popularity at home, and his 'forward' policy was effectively attacked by Gladstone who argued that Britain had no right whatever to attack an independent state.

(2) South Africa
In South Africa ominous difficulties arose in 1878. On the grounds that the Zulus were about to attack the Transvaal and annihilate its Boer population, Britain, with the agreement of most of the Boer leaders except Kruger, annexed the independent republic. In January 1879, the Zulus attacked and wiped out a British force under Lord Chelmsford at Isandhlwana in Zululand. In July, however, the Zulu chieftain Cetewayo was completely defeated at Ulundi. At once further complications arose when Sir Garnet Wolseley was sent out by Disraeli as High Commissioner. He gave the Transvaal the constitution of a Crown Colony, despite the fact that before the annexation of the Transvaal the Afrikaaner leaders had been promised self-government. Gladstone attacked this policy when in opposition, but once in office, he himself refused to give independence to the Transvaal, and in February 1881 the Boers attacked the British forces and defeated them at Majuba Hill. Gladstone then withdrew all British forces and in 1884 recognized the South African Republic. The whole business had been badly managed by both Conservative and Liberal Governments and the Boers gained a sense of power which was to make them more serious opponents in the future.

The Agricultural Depression
Disraeli was also faced with serious economic problems at home, especially in agriculture. By this time corn was being imported from the 'virgin lands' of Canada, the American Middle West and Australia so cheaply that arable farming was unprofitable for British farmers. A series of bad harvests between 1875 and 1879 made matters worse. The distress was severe for both farmers and farm workers and many of the latter drifted into the industrial towns and created further unemployment. All this told very much against the Government in the elections of 1880, and the Conservatives lost considerable support in the countryside.

The place of Disraeli in British politics
Disraeli, who had been created Earl of Beaconsfield in 1876, died in 1881. He has an important place in the history of Great Britain and of the Conservative Party. He was distinguished by openness of mind and was able,

Disraeli with Queen Victoria in 1877.

after a long struggle with his party's right wing, to win his party away from the old Tory attitudes and develop a political programme with a broad national appeal. Both at that time and since his policies at home and abroad have been severely criticized. His social reforms brought down on him the wrath of the old Tories in his own party who particularly opposed the extension of State power. His European policy, which was so highly praised at the time, has since been shown to have had disastrous consequences. His imperial policy was partly discredited by the unfortunate events in South Africa and Afghanistan towards the end of his ministry. Yet as a social reformer, as the creator of the modern Conservative Party and as an imperialist statesman he did have many concrete achievements to his credit and he was certainly one of the most brilliant and colourful political figures of the century.

15. Gladstone and Salisbury, 1880-95

Gladstone's second ministry, 1880–5

Although Gladstone and the Liberals obtained a substantial majority in the General Election of 1880, nothing could disguise the divisions within the Liberal Party and within the Government. Within the Liberal Party were still the remnants of the old Whig factions to some of whom Gladstone gave important Government posts. The younger and more dynamic men, such as Joseph Chamberlain, were given only junior ministries. The Whigs in the Government supported cautious and reactionary policies, while the newly enfranchised voters were demanding further social reform. In fact, the Radical voters had returned Gladstone to power, but his achievements were to be far from radical.

Perhaps the most important reason for this was that the Irish Nationalists, now eighty in number in the Commons, were strong enough to ensure that the Government was concerned with the Irish Question, to the almost total exclusion of other urgent matters. Lengthy Irish debates disrupted any legislative programme and the future of Gladstone's Government came to depend upon the way it handled the problem.

The Irish Question, 1880–5

Since Gladstone's last Irish legislation (see Chapter 13), the situation had grown worse. The economic depression which had affected Disraeli's Government had drastically reduced the price of corn and the profitability of agriculture. In Ireland there had been another famine in 1879 and the landlords tried to create larger and more profitable farm units by evicting thousands of tenants. Even so, the number of farmers in 1881 was about 600,000, and the average holding only thirty acres. This terrible pressure of population upon the land was the basic source of Ireland's troubles. Starvation, evictions, and a harsh Poor Law intensified the prevailing hatred and violence. Murder, arson, and destruction of landlords' property were common events in these years. Michael Davitt, who had been a member of the Fenian movement and its successor the Irish Republican Brotherhood founded a powerful new movement, the Land League. His aim was to unite the agitation for agrarian reform with the demand for Irish national independence. To this end he allied with Charles Stuart Parnell, leader of the Irish Nationalist Party.

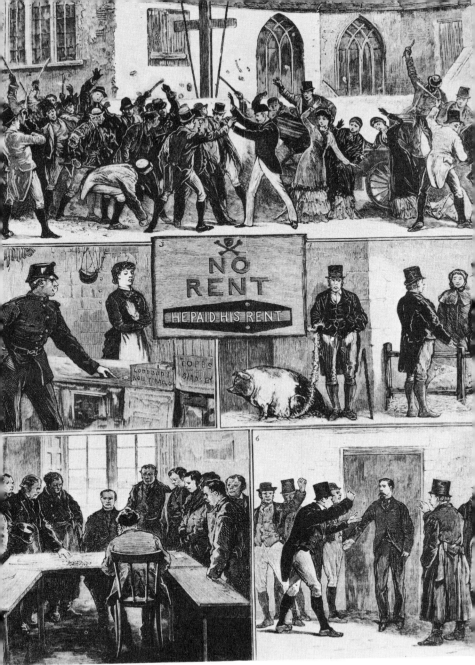

The condition of Ireland in 1881: 1. A riot at Temple Garden, Limerick County. 2. 'Boycotted' policeman. 3. A 'No Rent' placard. 4. A farmer being boycotted in the pig market in Tipperary. 5. A collection in aid of political prisoners in Tipperary. 6. Tenants refusing to pay rent.

Charles Stuart Parnell, 1846-91

Charles Stuart Parnell dominated Irish politics in the late nineteenth century. His mother was an American, and from her he inherited a considerable hatred of England, but being of English extraction, educated at Cambridge and also a Protestant landlord, he was entirely un-Irish in manners and temperament. His interest in Irish politics developed late, but the case of the Fenians executed in 1867 (see p. 122) aroused his intense interest and increased his hatred of Britain. He became a supporter of Isaac Butt, the founder of the Irish Home Rule League, and in 1875 was elected M.P. for County Meath.

Parnell and the boycott

In 1880, Gladstone introduced a Bill into the Commons to compensate evicted Irish tenants, but this was rejected by the Lords and came to nothing. Parnell reacted with what was known as the 'boycott', a method of action named after Captain Boycott, agent for the estates of the Earl in Erne in County Mayo. Captain Boycott had refused to accept rents fixed by the local supporters of the Land League, and he was immediately put under a form of siege. His servants were forced to desert him, no one would talk to him or sell him goods, much of his property was destroyed and a force of nearly a thousand soldiers had to be used at one time to protect the estates. Parnell's campaign was directed against anyone taking over a farm from which a tenant had been evicted. Such a person was to be isolated from his kind, declared Parnell, 'like a leper of old'.

In the agitated state of Ireland, boycotting was bound to lead to outrages and murder. Parnell disliked violence but could never be brought to condemn it explicitly before the House of Commons and the English people. This led to the widespread belief that he really approved of, and even directed 'moonlighters' who went out at night to burn ricks and buildings and to maim the cattle of those who would not accept the Land League's demands.

Gladstone's policy

In 1881 Gladstone passed a Coercion Act to repress violence in Ireland. This Act suspended the Habeas Corpus Act, and gave the administration the right to imprison suspected persons without trial. But he quickly followed this with a much improved Irish Land Act, by which the Irish tenants were accorded the 'three F's', that is, fair rent, fixity of tenure and free sale, for which they had long been agitating. Land courts were set up to establish fair rents, and a tenant who paid this rent could not be evicted. If he wished to give up his land, he could sell his interest in it to the highest bidder.

Parnell continues his campaigns

Parnell's response to the Second Land Act disappointed Gladstone. It was undoubtedly a great concession to the Land League, and was witness of Gladstone's sincere wish to settle the land question. But this partial success only spurred on Parnell to continue the Land League's campaigns. The League decided to have nothing to do with the new land courts, and this, of course, meant that evictions and outrages continued. Parnell was now determined to show that only by Home Rule could the Irish problem be settled. He had already ousted Isaac Butt from the leadership of the Irish Home Rule Confederation and secured his own election as President. His party of eighty Irish Members in the House of Commons came to accept the iron discipline he imposed upon them, and conducted a campaign of organized obstruction in the following years. Irish members could be ordered to speak in debates for hours on end – for example, the opposition to Gladstone's Coercion Bill had led to a debate on one stage of the Bill which lasted forty-one hours, and was only brought to a vote by a ruling of the Speaker. Eventually the Government had to amend the rules of debate in the Commons to get any business done.

The Kilmainham Treaty, 1882

Faced with this refusal to co-operate, Gladstone ordered the imprisonment of Parnell and several other Irish leaders in Kilmainham Gaol, Dublin, where they remained until April 1882. The Land League was outlawed and its treasurer fled to Paris carrying with him its records and accounts. But violence continued unabated, and the situation in Ireland grew worse rather than better. Gladstone, anxious to reach an understanding with Parnell, was himself already considering Home Rule as the solution for the Irish problem. Through the mediation of Parnell's friend and supporter, Captain O'Shea, an agreement was reached by which Parnell would call off the 'no-rent' campaign and denounce and prevent outrages if Gladstone would introduce a Bill to release Irish tenants from all arrears of rent which had accumulated during the Land League's campaign.

The Phoenix Park murders, 1882

Gladstone achieved this agreement with Parnell without consulting the Secretary and Viceroy for Ireland, who both resigned and were replaced by a new Viceroy, Lord Spencer, and a new Secretary for Ireland, Lord Frederick Cavendish, whose immediate task was to see that the Kilmainham agreement was carried out. On the evening of his arrival in Dublin, Cavendish was walking with the Under-Secretary for Ireland, Burke, in Phoenix Park, when they were both attacked and stabbed to death by a group of Irish extremists calling themselves the 'Invincibles'. They had intended to murder only Burke, and Cavendish was killed trying to protect him. Parnell was horrified and denounced 'this cowardly and unprovoked assassination of a friendly stranger'. The assassination, for which five men were hanged and three others sent to penal servitude, was a terrible setback for Parnell from which he never really recovered. English opinion became implacably hostile towards him, and many people blamed him for the crime. The anti-Irish groups in Britain were strengthened in this belief when the extremists launched a campaign of dynamite outrages in Britain itself. Gladstone introduced a Crimes Act and a further Coercion Act which gave summary powers to the magistrates, police and army in Ireland so that jury trial was abandoned in serious cases. Despite the passing of an Arrears Act by which the Government paid one-half and the landlords surrendered one-half of arrears, outrages and murder continued. Parnell refused to accept the demand of some M.P.s that he should defend himself from charges of instigating violence by appearing before an independent tribunal. He was, he declared, answerable only to the Irish people; in 1883 a subscription amounting to £37,000 known as the 'Parnell Tribute' was raised for him in Ireland to enable him to pay off his debts, and in recognition of his services to the Irish cause. When in 1885 Gladstone proposed to renew the Crimes Act of 1882, Parnell with a group of his followers voted with the Conservative opposition to defeat the budget, whereupon Gladstone resigned.

Gladstone and the problem of Empire, 1880–5

Gladstone inherited from Disraeli's Government a number of complicated imperial problems, which were made more difficult by his own ambiguous policy. In opposition he had publicly denounced Disraeli's policy and had aligned himself with the Radical and anti-imperialist wing of his own party, led by John Bright. Once in power, however, he found it more difficult to apply his anti-imperialist principles.

Gladstone and Egypt

Since Disraeli's purchase of the Khedive's shares in the Suez Canal in 1875, conditions in Egypt had gone from bad to worse. Foreign loans were subscribed to build new railways, docks and roads, but the money was grossly misused. The bulk of the taxation fell on the *fellaheen* or peasantry and, when a cattle plague broke out in 1878, the country was brought to the verge of financial and political collapse. As Britain and France were the chief creditors, an Anglo-French Dual Control Commission was set up to effect reforms and economies. Ismail Pasha, the Khedive, refused to co-operate and the Powers persuaded the Sultan to depose him in favour of his son Tewfik Pasha. This interference led to the emergence of an anti-foreign Nationalist Party led by army officers with Colonel Arabi Pasha at their head. In 1882 Arabi Pasha seized power and formed a Government pledged to oppose foreign intervention in Egypt. In 1882 some of his followers massacred Christians in Alexandria although an Anglo-French fleet had arrived to protect foreign interests. The nationalists then began to build batteries which could be used against the fleet in the harbour. At this point the French, afraid of Germany and anxious not to be deeply involved in Egypt, withdrew their fleet and left the British to decide on the action to be taken. Admiral Seymour, in command of the British fleet, bombarded Alexandria and Arabi Pasha withdrew to Cairo. The British troops under Sir Garnet Wolseley landed at Port Said and marched across the desert to Tel-el-Kebir, where Arabi was defeated and captured.

Egypt and the Suez Canal were economically important to Britain, and Gladstone could not ignore imperial and trading interests, despite his denunciation of 'forward' policies. He therefore decided to leave sufficient forces in Egypt to guarantee a sound, stable Government but not to take over the country as a colony. This policy represented a compromise between the anti-imperialism of Bright who resigned from the Cabinet in protest and the imperialism of those in Britain who considered that Gladstone should have annexed the country outright while the opportunity presented itself. In 1883 Sir Evelyn Baring, afterwards Lord Cromer, was appointed British Agent and Consul-General in Egypt; he remained there for twenty-three years as virtual ruler of the country.

Gladstone and the Sudan
Gladstone was equally uncertain in his handling of the Sudanese question. In the Sudan a religious leader, the Mahdi or Messiah, had won great popular support and his fanatical followers drove the occupying Egyptian army back into their fortresses. The British Government allowed Tewfik Pasha to send an Egyptian army under an English officer, Hicks Pasha, against the Mahdi, but this ill-equipped force was annihilated at the battle of Shekan.

General Gordon and the Siege of Khartoum
The position of the Egyptian garrisons in the Sudan was perilous. Many of them were under British officers, and every moment's delay in sending help added to their danger. For some time the Government hesitated, divided between those who advocated the complete conquest of the Sudan and those who demanded evacuation. At last Gladstone decided to send out General Gordon to evacuate the garrisons. This was a curious choice in the circumstances. Gordon was an experienced soldier and administrator both in the Far East and in the Sudan itself, but he was notorious for his obstinacy of character fortified by Christian missionary zeal. Sir Evelyn Baring was justifiably alarmed at the selection of Gordon.

Gordon arrived in Khartoum in February 1884 and decided to hold the Nile Valley against the Moslem followers of the Mahdi. He proposed to make a former slave-trader, Zobeir, Consul-General of the Sudan to rally support against the Mahdi. At home Gladstone refused to accept this sudden dictation of policy by Gordon. Divisions in the Cabinet continued. Gladstone himself, believing in the rights of nations to self-government, declared that any move against the Sudan would be against a people 'rightly struggling to be free'. But public pressure at home was against him and Baring in Egypt requested a relief force. In August 1884 Gladstone dispatched Sir Garnet Wolseley with this force, which moved up the Nile and defeated the Mahdi in two battles. An advance party arrived at Khartoum on 28 January 1885 to find that the fortress had been taken by the Mahdi's followers and Gordon murdered only two days before. There was a violent outcry against the Government at home. Gladstone's nickname of The Grand Old Man (G.O.M.) became 'Gordon's Only Murderer'. Gladstone, however, pressed ahead with the complete withdrawal from the Sudan.

The Penjdeh incident, 1885
In the meantime, there was trouble once again on the Afghan frontier with Russia. In 1884 Russia had occupied Merv, although this was contrary to the general agreement with Gladstone's Government in 1882. While a boundary commission was being formed on Russian request to settle this matter, their forces seized Penjdeh on the Afghan frontier. Gladstone called out the reserves and prepared for action. The Russians agreed to international arbitration, and Penjdeh was awarded to them.

General comment on Gladstone's foreign and imperial policy
In the years 1880–5 Gladstone had to grapple with a difficult inheritance from Disraeli and with some new imperial problems. He was anxious to avoid intervening against genuine nationalist movements, but was often strongly pressed to do so by members of his Cabinet. His hesitation to withdraw from the Transvaal seemed to many to contradict his previous denunciation of Disraeli and ended in the humiliation of Majuba Hill. In Egypt Arabi Pasha's revolt seemed to him a genuine movement of social and national revolution against a corrupt despotism. But European and British interests were at stake and he was forced by the imperialist section of his Cabinet to intervene. He regarded the Mahdi's revolt in the Sudan as another national movement, but his choice of Gordon to organize the evacuation was disastrous. In trying to continue his policy of international arbitration to settle serious disputes, he earned nearly as much criticism over the Penjdeh incident as he had done earlier over the Alabama arbitration.

Charles Bradlaugh
Another difficulty for Gladstone arose from the case of Charles Bradlaugh, Radical M.P. for Northampton, an avowed atheist, founder of the National Secular League and a pioneer propagandist, with Mrs Annie Besant, for birth-control. Bradlaugh claimed that he had a right to refuse to make the Parliamentary oath which implied a belief in God and offered to affirm his allegiance instead. The Speaker unwisely allowed a debate and the reference of the case to a select committee which ruled against Bradlaugh by a majority of one. Bradlaugh then came forward to take the normal oath,

but the Speaker again allowed the House to debate and to reject Brad-laugh's right to take either the affirmation or the oath. This example of Victorian prejudice was exploited by Gladstone's opponents to embarrass his position in the House, especially as his own cabinet was divided on the question. Gladstone himself, greatly to his personal credit in view of his strong religious convictions, argued strongly for toleration, but the majority was against him. At last in 1886, after Bradlaugh had been expelled and re-elected three times by his constituents, a new Speaker ruled in his favour. He then took the oath and remained M.P. until his death in 1891.

The Third Reform Bill, 1884

Gladstone was more interested in removing the serious voting inequalities left by the Second Reform Bill of 1867 than in dealing with Egypt, and other imperial questions. The main fault of the 1867 Act was that it granted the vote to working men in the boroughs but not in the countryside. Gladstone was determined to remove this injustice.

In 1884–5 a Reform Act and a Redistribution Act were passed. The Reform Act gave the vote in the counties to all householders and thus reduced considerably the landlord influence. About two million voters were added to the roll, making the electorate five million in a population of thirty-five million. The Redistribution Act deprived seventy-nine small towns of under 15,000 inhabitants of their separate representation in Parliament, and towns with less than 50,000 were left with one M.P. only. This meant that the great majority of constituencies had only one member and approximately 50,000 voters. It is interesting to note that the figure of 50,000 was originally put forward by the Chartists about forty years pre-viously. There were two other unforeseen consequences of the Acts. In Ireland the new voters greatly increased the strength of Parnell by voting solidly for nationalist candidates and, secondly, the Radicals increased their strength at the expense of the Whigs, who had usually shared the old two-member constituencies with them. This led in time to a decline of the aristocratic Whig faction and the emergence of the Radicals as the real driving force behind the Liberal Party in the early twentieth century.

The fall of Gladstone's second ministry

In 1885 Parnell was able to use the powerful position of his party in the Commons to force Gladstone's resignation. Joseph Chamberlain had proposed a scheme which would give Ireland at least a measure of local self government. Gladstone supported him, but they were met by powerful Whig opposition in the Cabinet and Chamberlain resigned. At this point Parnell agreed with Lord Randolph Churchill, the Conservative leader in the Commons, to vote against the Budget. The Budget was defeated, Glad-stone resigned and Lord Salisbury, Disraeli's successor as leader of the Conservative Party, became Prime Minister.

Salisbury's 'Ministry of Caretakers', 1885-6

Gladstone resigned in June 1885, but a general election had to wait for the new register of voters under the Third Reform Act. In the meantime Salisbury continued as Prime Minister relying upon Irish support. A brief period of complicated political manœuvre and intrigue began, which highlighted once again the new forces which were transforming British politics. Churchill, Leader of the House of Commons, with his small but vocal following the 'Fourth Party', was pledged to keep the Conservatives on the path of social reform and imperial expansion initiated by Disraeli. Yet Churchill was prepared to meet some of the demands made by Parnell and his Home Rule followers, and entered into negotiation with him and the new Viceroy of Ireland, Lord Caernarvon. The Conservatives also removed the Coercion Act and secured the passing of Lord Ashbourne's Land Act. There was another wave of violence in Ireland, but Ashbourne's Act enabled the peasants to claim State aid in the purchase of land, a policy which was widely adopted later.

By August 1886 Gladstone was finally convinced of the need for Home Rule for Ireland, but he feared that if he announced his conversion publicly his own party would fall apart. The unity of the Liberal Party was further endangered when Chamberlain launched his famous 'unauthorized programme' of radical social reforms (See Chapter 16). Among his proposals was that of Home Rule not only for Ireland, but also for Scotland and Wales, with a federal Parliament at Westminster.

The autumn election gave the Liberals a majority of eighty-six in the Commons, but this was the exact number of Parnell's M.P.s and the latter continued to keep the Salisbury Government precariously in power. Then suddenly Gladstone's conversion to Home Rule was announced by his son, Herbert Gladstone. Salisbury and Churchill abandoned any support for limited Home Rule, and Parnell was forced to turn to the Liberals and secure the defeat of Salisbury's Government in January 1886.

Gladstone's third ministry, 1886, and the first Home Rule Bill

Gladstone was now pledged to introduce Home Rule for Ireland, but his attempt to do so immediately began to break up the Liberal Party. The Whig section, led by Hartington, refused to join the Government at all and Chamberlain resigned as soon as Gladstone announced the details of the Home Rule Bill. In April 1886, Gladstone introduced his Bill to the House of Commons. It proposed to set up an Irish Parliament in Dublin to control most internal Irish affairs, but to leave control of the armed forces, foreign policy and trade with the British Parliament. The Bill made no arrangements for any Irish representation at Westminster. Not only was the Bill attacked by Lord Salisbury and the Conservatives, but also by the Whigs under Hartington and a number of Radicals led by Chamberlain. The latter opposed it as it differed entirely from his scheme of devolution or federation. The Bill was defeated by a majority of thirty, with no less than ninety-three Liberals voting against Gladstone.

Those Liberals who had voted against the idea of a separate Parliament for Ireland became known as the Liberal-Unionists. Some members of this group, including Chamberlain, later accepted office in the Conservative Governments. The effect of this defeat on the Liberals was profound. They remained deeply divided over Ireland and the consequent split in the party kept it out of power for all but three of the next twenty-years.

Lord Salisbury's second ministry, 1886–92

Lord Salisbury took office for the second time in August 1886. The general election gave him a majority of 118 including 78 Liberal-Unionists. After the Prime Minister, the most important figure in the new Government was Lord Randolph Churchill (father of Sir Winston). He was Chancellor of the Exchequer and Leader of the House of Commons at the age of thirty-seven. His forceful dynamic character and his restless activity as the self-appointed guardian of the principles of Tory democracy as set out by Disraeli forced the reluctant Salisbury to give him high office. At this very moment of triumph, however, Churchill threw away his political future by a serious miscalculation. He had decided that a reduction in the Army and Navy estimates was necessary and feasible, but he was strongly opposed by the War Office, who had the Prime Minister's support. Churchill resigned expecting to bring Salisbury to heel. But Churchill's shock tactics failed, for Salisbury ignored him and offered the Chancellorship to a Liberal-Unionist, Sir Edward Goschen. Salisbury was only too glad to get rid of Churchill's embarrassing challenge to his own brand of Conservatism. This serious setback affected Churchill's health, and he died at the early age of 45 in 1894.

Salisbury and Ireland

In the debate on Gladstone's Home Rule Bill, Salisbury had opposed any concessions to the Irish Nationalists. He contended that, given firm government for twenty years, Ireland would accept any reforms which the Government considered fit. Not surprisingly, therefore, Salisbury began by imposing an even harsher Crimes Act than before. It extended trial without jury to all offences against law and order. This measure was the work of the new Secretary for Ireland, Arthur James Balfour, Salisbury's nephew, later to succeed him as Prime Minister. Balfour's policy of ruthless coercion was softened a little by another Land Act giving further assistance to tenants who wished to purchase their farms. However, discontent in Ireland grew alarmingly. The Irish Nationalists, under O'Brien and Dillon, organized the 'Plan of Campaign'. By this scheme the tenants of an estate banded together and offered the landlord what they considered to be a fair rent. If the landlord refused to accept, the rent was paid into a special 'war chest' to further the anti-landlord and anti-British campaign in Ireland. Balfour's response to this campaign was the rigid application of the Crimes Act, and full military and police support for the landlords.

'The Times' and the campaign against Parnell

While these events were taking place in Ireland and earning the Secretary the epithet of 'Bloody Balfour', *The Times* published a series of articles to show that Parnell was reponsible for the violence in Ireland. Its aim was to discredit Parnell and weaken the opposition to Salisbury's policy. In April 1887 the paper published what was claimed to be a facsimile reproduction of a letter Parnell had written to a supporter after the Phoenix Park murders in which he regretted the death of Lord Frederick Cavendish but went on to say that 'Burke got no more than his deserts'. Parnell denounced the letter as a 'barefaced forgery', but public opinion was against him. In 1888 the Government was compelled by the pressure of opinion in the House and by Parnell's denials concerning further letters that *The Times* published, to appoint a Commission of Inquiry. Parnell's counsel successfully proved that the letters were forgeries by a drunken journalist named Richard Piggott, who fled the country and committed suicide in Madrid. He left behind a full confession of his crime.

Parnell's prestige even in England rose higher than it had ever been. At the same time Balfour's stringent application of the Crimes Act was beginning to turn public opinion in England against the Government. But at this very moment, when there was a clear possibility that the Liberals would win the next election and succeed in passing Home Rule with the help of Parnell, the latter was cited as co-respondent in a divorce suit brought by one of his supporters, Captain O'Shea, against his wife, Katherine O'Shea. Victorian England was shocked. Overnight Parnell became more of a social outcast than he had ever been a political one. In Ireland the Catholic Church turned against him, while Gladstone, embarrassed and frustrated by the turn of events, advised Parnell to abandon his leadership of the Irish Nationalists. Parnell refused. He clung desperately to his position, but found his own party no longer unanimous in their support of him. His supreme efforts to vindicate his leadership taxed his strength beyond endurance and he died on 6 October 1891 at the age of 45.

Parnell's disgrace weakened the whole Irish Nationalist movement and created damaging divisions among the leaders. The administration was able to gain a much firmer hold over Ireland and Salisbury continued his policy of piecemeal improvement. The Land Purchase Act of 1891 made it easier for the Irish peasant to buy land with Government help. Another law set up the Congested Districts Board. The purpose of the Board was to improve conditions in the western parts of Ireland where the pressure of population on the available land was enormous. In the meantime, Balfour's ruthless application of the Crimes Act significantly reduced the amount of violence in Ireland.

The County Councils established, 1888

Salisbury's domestic legislation included one major reform. No fundamental change had been made in local government since the Municipal Corporations Act of 1835. In the counties local administration was carried on by a multiplicity of district boards and vestries for such matters as lighting, drainage and sanitation. The members of these boards, which numbered nearly 27,000 throughout the country, were not directly elected as the members of the municipal corporations had been since 1835. In the counties the Justices of the Peace exercised wide administrative control and powers of nomination to these various bodies. This meant, of course, that the landlords' influence in the countryside had remained predominant. By the County Councils Act of 1888 new elective councils were established as in the towns, and the landlords' powers were correspondingly reduced. The Justices of the Peace, who had been the local administrators since Tudor times, retained their judicial functions but lost their old administrative powers.

The London County Council was established at the same time, covering parts of Middlesex, Surrey and Kent, but leaving the City of London with its own corporation. Since 1885, vestries for the various London districts had, in fact, been elected by the ratepayers, and a Metropolitan Board of Works had been set up to supervise the whole organization, including the City of London. But a Government commission had shown up much corruption and mismanagement. The organization of local government was completed by the London Government Act 1899, and the system then established remained unchanged until the Greater London Council Act of 1965. By the 1899 Act, towns with populations of over 50,000 could become county boroughs and enjoy the wide powers of self-government given to the county councils.

Two other important social reforms were passed in Salisbury's second administration, the Factory Act of 1891 which raised the minimum age for the employment of children in factories to eleven years, and the Education Act of 1891 which abolished fees in elementary schools.

Salisbury's foreign policy, 1886–92

England's most obvious enemies at this time were Russia and France. The former was a formidable rival in the Balkans and Asia, while France bitterly resented Britain's hold on Egypt. But Salisbury was also conscious of other dangers in Europe. Germany, now the most powerful land force in the world, was closely allied to Austria-Hungary and Italy in the Triple Alliance and would have welcomed a quarrel between France and Britain. Salisbury, however, was determined not to be a tool to serve German plans.

Faced with this delicate situation, Salisbury made a secret agreement with Italy and Austria-Hungary in 1887 by which Italy was to support Britain's position in Egypt in return for protection of Italy against a naval attack by

France. Austria and Italy were also pledged to help Britain against any move by Russia which would disturb the prevailing balance of forces in the Balkans. Bismarck gave his blessing to this agreement, which also served Germany's interests by restraining both France and Russia. Thus Salisbury, without committing Britain directly to the support of Germany, entered into a clear agreement with two members of the Triple Alliance. Although the agreement remained in force for only five years, Salisbury's policy in this case had certainly not been one of 'isolation'. However, when Bismarck suggested an Anglo-German alliance against France in 1889, Salisbury refused, on the grounds that Britain also required guarantees of assistance in the event of Russian aggression. As Bismarck was not prepared to pledge himself to move against Russia in the interests of Britain, the proposals came to nothing. To Bismarck Britain's weakness as a land power made her of doubtful value as an ally against France and Russia, while to Salisbury no German alliance without a guarantee of assistance against Russia was of any use.

The Bulgarian question, 1885–8
After the Congress of Berlin, events in the Balkans had developed in an unexpected way. In the first place, the Russians had failed to gain any real influence over the small Bulgaria which the Congress created. In 1885, Eastern Rumelia rose in revolt against Turkey and demanded union with Bulgaria, thus defying the decisions of the Congress. But Russia, seeing that such a union would strengthen a Bulgaria which had shown a surprisingly strong anti-Russian feeling, opposed the creation of the big Bulgaria, thus reversing her policy of 1877. Russia organized the kidnapping of Prince Alexander of Bulgaria and forced his abdication, but the Bulgarians themselves, supported by both Italy and Austria, chose Prince Ferdinand of Coburg as their sovereign instead of a Russian puppet. Bismarck also made it clear that under the Dual Alliance with Austria of 1879, Germany would support Bulgaria against Russia. At this Russia gave way and accepted the creation of the big Bulgaria demanded by her opponents. Salisbury gave his approval because the settlement barred the way to further Russian advances in the Balkans which suited British interests.

Salisbury and imperial expansion
The division of Africa amongst the Great Powers took place in the years 1880 to 1900. Salisbury avoided direct Government action, preferring to leave things to the private enterprise of British trading companies. Past experiences in South Africa and Egypt discouraged the Government from any further commitment, yet at the same time Salisbury was anxious to clear up difficulties with France and Germany.
    The British penetration of Nigeria began with the trading activities of the Royal Niger Company, while in Kenya and Uganda the British East Africa Company was established. Cecil Rhodes and the British South Africa

Company extended their control into what was to become Rhodesia. In 1890 the Government signed agreements (1) with Portugal which gave Britain control of Nyasaland, (2) with France which recognized Britain's control of Zanzibar and French control of Madagascar, and (3) with Germany which recognized British control of Uganda, Kenya and Zanzibar. In return for the latter recognition, Britain accepted German control of German East Africa, the Cameroons and South-West Africa and also Heligoland in the North Sea.

Salisbury's steady and unspectacular policies did not increase support for his Government either in the House of Commons or the country and, after a number of near defeats, he decided to dissolve Parliament. After the general election of July 1892 Salisbury was defeated and Gladstone formed his fourth ministry. He was, however, once more dependent for his majority in the House of Commons on the Irish Members.

Gladstone's fourth and last ministry, 1892–4

Gladstone was still determined on Home Rule for Ireland and in February 1893 he introduced his second Home Rule Bill. It was similar in detail to the first, but included the representation of Ireland at Westminster by members who could vote only on Irish or imperial matters. The House of Commons passed the Bill by a majority of 34, but the Conservative-dominated House of Lords rejected it by 378 votes. Gladstone resigned and was succeeded by Lord Rosebery, whom, contrary to the wishes of most of the Liberal Party, the Queen had insisted upon as Prime Minister. As a member of the House of Lords with only half-hearted support from many of his party, Rosebery was in an impossible position. The Conservative House of Lords blocked a number of progressive social measures accepted by the Commons and he resigned in June 1895. Salisbury formed a Conservative Government, Parliament was dissolved, and in the general election Salisbury was returned with a majority of 152, including the Liberal-Unionists under the leadership of Chamberlain. There followed ten more years of Conservative rule until 1905, years of great importance in the history of Britain and the Empire. Gladstone's last ministry was not entirely barren. It brought the important Local Government Act of 1894, usually known as the Parish Councils Act. In addition to setting up parish councils with very limited powers it filled in the framework of the County Council's Act by creating urban and rural district councils. By the Act some women were qualified not only to vote in local elections but also to sit as councillors.

Gladstone and British politics

In his farewell speech to the House of Commons in 1896 Gladstone had some harsh things to say about the House of Lords and the Establishment. He had waged a long and fairly consistent fight against those interests which he regarded as the enemies of progress and freedom, and the

Gladstone during his Second Ministry addressing a Liberal Party banquet in Leeds.

Radicals in the Liberal Party were to continue this fight in the early twentieth century. Gladstone's greatest efforts were made to solve Ireland's problems – and here too was his greatest failure. The reasons for his failure were not of his own making, and in taking up the question with his characteristic moral fervour he made clear to the public how important these issues were. It has been said that Gladstone failed to attack the real problem – landlordism, and that he attempted to preserve landlordism in Ireland by granting a half measure of political semi-independence. Ironically it was the power of the landlord class and the House of Lords which caused his downfall.

16. Conservatism and Imperialism, 1895-1905

THE NEW IMPERIALISM

Introduction

The years 1890 to 1900 saw important changes in British political life. The Liberal Party became more radical as the official policy set out in the Newcastle Programme of 1891 showed. The Radicals were strengthened when many old Whigs joined the Conservatives and were replaced by new men such as David Lloyd George. However, there was much working-class discontent with the old political parties and in 1891 Keir Hardie, the first Independent Labour Party M.P., took his seat in the House of Commons wearing a workman's cap and a red tie.

This was also the outstanding period of popular imperialism. Trade within the Empire flourished and increasing emigration from Britain made the Empire significant to working people as well as to merchants, manufacturers and politicians. Joseph Chamberlain, now in the Conservative Party, made the Colonial Office one of the most important of all the Ministries. Salisbury and Chamberlain dominated the new Government, and at critical moments Chamberlain wielded even more influence than the Prime Minister.

Joseph Chamberlain, 1836–1914

Chamberlain was the son of a London boot and shoe manufacturer who also had financial interests in the Birmingham engineering firm of Nettlefold, and was brought up in the competitive commercial atmosphere of mid-Victorian England. After serving for some time in his father's London business, he was sent to Birmingham to work in the engineering company. Here he was brilliantly successful, and was quick to adopt new inventions and business methods. He had great success in buying out or amalgamating with rival firms, and was able to retire in 1874 on the personal fortune which he had accumulated. He was then only 38, and was henceforward to play an increasingly important part in Birmingham's municipal affairs.

His political views were at this time markedly unorthodox. He was an extreme Radical and for a while a republican. He became a member of the Birmingham Liberal Association in 1869. He was enthusiastic for free undenominational education and became chairman of the National

Education League which had played a great part in securing the passage of Gladstone's Elementary Education Act of 1870. In 1873 he was elected Mayor of Birmingham after the Liberals had gained a majority on the city council.

Chamberlain's work in Birmingham

Such was the importance of Chamberlain's work that it is customary to date the beginnings of the modern city from his time as Mayor. A form of municipal Socialism was adopted, by which the gas and water supplies were owned and administered by the local authority. Chamberlain and his council also dealt with the appalling housing conditions left by the Industrial Revolution by a big programme of slum clearance, and new, planned building of working-class houses transformed the appearance of large parts of the city. Sanitation was greatly improved; Chamberlain, in fact, gave a national lead by calling a special conference in Birmingham of all sanitary authorities. His enthusiasm for popular education and the spread of culture led him to promote the Birmingham Free Library and Art Gallery, and in 1900 he founded Birmingham University.

Chamberlain's parliamentary career

In 1876 Chamberlain entered Parliament unopposed as one of the members for Birmingham. In 1877 he organized the National Liberal Federation, an association of the new constituency Liberal organizations. In discussions of policy within the Federation, Chamberlain's Radical views helped to reduce the influence of aristocratic Whigs like Lord Hartington. The Liberal Party's success in the election of 1880 can partly be ascribed to the Federation's work. Somewhat reluctantly Gladstone brought Chamberlain into the Government as President of the Board of Trade. His friend, the Radical Charles Dilke, was President of the Local Government Board, and they constantly pressed Gladstone to introduce measures for social reform. But Gladstone was distracted by Irish affairs, and the only significant measure was the Third Reform Bill of 1884 (see p. 148). Chamberlain was a severe critic of Gladstone's ineptitude in Egypt (see Chapter 13), although he recognized the need to give Egypt a national Government. In Ireland Chamberlain opposed coercion and believed that a constructive settlement was possible. Gladstone gave him the task of negotiating with the imprisoned Parnell, and the Kilmainham Treaty was the result. The Phoenix Park murders ruined this (see p. 144), but in 1885 he placed before Gladstone's Cabinet a plan for Ireland which Parnell himself was prepared to accept. This scheme would have established in Ireland an elected council for Irish affairs, with the British Government controlling matters relating to the Empire. This was a form of semi-Home Rule, but the Cabinet rejected it. As a consequence, Chamberlain and his supporters opposed Gladstone's Home Rule Bill of 1886 which made no arrangement for Irish representation at Westminster and which they believed broke the imperial connection. From this point Chamberlain and his supporters were known as the Liberal-Unionists.

Chamberlain and the 'unauthorized programme'

At this time Chamberlain ardently supported the Radical proposals known as the 'unauthorized programme' – that is, unauthorized by the Liberal Party. It was an attempt to force the 'official' Liberal Party into far-reaching social reforms. It demanded free education, and the creation of small-holdings for agricultural workers in order to break the feudal system of landlordism in England and Ireland and to ease the problems of British agriculture. This policy, popularly dubbed as 'three acres and a cow', was eventually applied in Ireland. It was no answer to England's agricultural difficulty, but at least it produced new ideas and focused attention on a very pressing problem. Among his other unorthodox proposals he demanded a policy of graduated taxation of incomes, especially those derived by the wealthy from capital investment, in order to pay for social improvements which would benefit the whole nation. He also urged that local authorities should have compulsory powers to purchase land and property for the purposes of social improvement. Gladstone and the main body of the Liberal Party, however, rejected these points as part of the Liberal programme.

During the years 1886–95, Chamberlain developed his radical ideas still further and continued to oppose Gladstone's Irish policy. He campaigned both inside and outside Parliament for such measures as compensation to workers for accidents in industry and old age pensions, both of which were to be introduced later: the first by Salisbury's Government in 1897, the second by Lloyd George in 1909. A number of Salisbury's reforms of 1886–92, such as Ashbourne's Act (Ireland), the establishment of the Congested Districts Board and the County Councils Act, 1888 (see p. 152) were in part derived from Chamberlain's ideas.

Chamberlain and the imperial idea

Unlike many Radicals, Chamberlain had never been an opponent of the Empire and in time he became its most ardent advocate. In 1889 he went to the U.S.A. on an official Government mission, and as a result of his visit he became even more convinced of the need to build up the Empire's political and trading strength. In Salisbury's Government of 1895 he deliberately chose the neglected post of Colonial Secretary. Almost at once he was faced with a fresh outbreak of trouble in South Africa.

SOUTH AFRICA

In 1806, during the Napoleonic Wars, a British fleet had seized Cape Town to safeguard the British route to India, and in 1814 the Dutch agreed to

Britain's permanent occupation of the Cape for a payment of £6,000,000. From that time increasing numbers of Britons emigrated to the Cape. Difficulties soon arose between the British and the Dutch settlers, or Boers who resented competition for land from the new settlers. The British administration at the Cape under Sir B. d'Urban gave greater political rights to the native population than the slave-owning Boers thought necessary or right. A further cause of ill-feeling was the growth of British missions, for the missionaries championed the coloured population against their Boer masters. In 1828 the right of coloured people to purchase or possess land was acknowledged. English was declared the official language of the law courts and the schools. Finally in 1833 the British Government abolished slavery and, although compensation was paid, the Dutch claimed that they had not received their due. They also claimed that Britain was giving them inadequate protection against the incursions of the Kaffir tribes, and when d'Urban seized part of the Kaffir territory as a safeguard, the British Government countermanded his annexation and returned the territory to the Kaffirs. The resentful Cape Boers began a mass exodus from the Cape in 1836 and set out on the Great Trek northwards in order to establish free communities. One section moved over the Drakensberg, packing all their belongings on covered ox-wagons, to Natal, where they suffered heavily from the attacks of the Zulus; another group moved beyond the Orange River into the territory which later became the Orange Free State; and a third force moved beyond the Vaal River into the land of the Matabele (whom they drove out) and established the Republic of the Transvaal.

The Sand River and Bloemfontein Conventions, 1852 and 1854

The Great Trek created a new and difficult situation. It had stirred up trouble with the Zulus, especially in Natal, and threatened to bring counter-attacks not only on the Boer settlements but also on the eastern parts of the Cape Colony. In view of this danger, Natal was declared a British colony in 1843. In 1848 the Orange Free State was also annexed by Sir Harry Smith, the Governor of the Cape, but in 1852 the home Government signed the Sand River Convention with the Boer leader Pretorius by which the Transvaal's independence was recognized, and two years later in 1854 the Bloemfontein Convention restored the independence of the Orange Free State. In the latter case there was considerable discontent among a number of Boers at the withdrawal of British protection, but the extreme Afrikaaners who wished to sever all connections won the day. However, not all Boers were opposed to the British and many remained in Cape Colony.

Events leading to the First Boer War, 1880–81

During the next twenty years the Government of the Cape took steps to protect the native peoples against the Boers and to safeguard their own colony from native attacks. In 1868 Basutoland was annexed to the British Crown to prevent the incessant raids and counter-raids of the Basutos and Orange Free State Boers. The Governor of the Cape was also High Commissioner for native affairs, and in a dispute over a diamond-mining area, later to become Kimberley, claimed both by the Griqua tribe and by the Orange Free State, he gave judgement in favour of the Griquas. Soon afterwards the territory was ceded by the Griquas to the British, and annexed in 1871. The Orange Free State were given some compensation, but the annexation aroused opposition among many Radicals at home, as well as increasing hostility among the Boers. The most pressing problem in the 1870's was the growth in power of the Zulu tribes under their chieftain Cetewayo, whose aim was to drive all the whites out of South Africa. In 1874, the Colonial Secretary, Lord Caernarvon, sent Sir Theophilus Shepstone to inquire into the situation in the Transvaal and to take it over for the British if necessary. He found the republic bankrupt, and the Afrikaaner President Burgers only too willing to accept annexation and British protection on the understanding that after the Zulu crisis had been resolved self-government would be restored. Significantly the violently anti-British Vice-President, Paul Kruger, was the only leading Boer who did not agree with the annexation. In 1879 a force was sent out from Britain to invade Zululand, but at Isandhwana 800 men were lost against the Zulus. However, the Zulu invasion of Natal was successfully resisted by the heroic defence of Rorke's Drift and eventually Cetewayo was defeated at Ulundi and sent as a captive to Britain. He was restored as chieftain of part of his territories in 1883, but was driven out by his opponents among the Zulus themselves, and died in a native reserve.

Disraeli's Government failed to restore independence to the Transvaal Afrikaaners. Gladstone himself hesitated and consequently involved the country in the disastrous First Boer War (see Chapter 15). By the Pretoria Convention of 1881 the independence of the Transvaal was restored, with the vague limitation that the republic was 'under the suzerainty of Her Majesty'. Subsequently a more important agreement was signed in London by which the Transvaal was allowed to call itself the South African Republic; agreed to allow free trade; promised not to impose any taxes on foreigners which were not imposed on the republic's own citizens; and undertook not to make any treaties with foreign states or native tribes without the consent of the British Government. The agreement was negotiated by the new President of the Republic, Paul Kruger.

Expansion of the Transvaal

The conflict between the British and the Boers grew steadily worse. Kruger's attempts to extend the boundaries of the Transvaal, contrary to the decisions of the London Convention, were baulked by Britain. For example, a British force compelled Kruger to give up Bechuanaland which had been occupied by raiding parties from the Transvaal. This ensured that there were no Boer territories to the north of the British-controlled diamond area of Griqualand West. Soon afterwards the British South Africa Company, whose guiding genius was Cecil Rhodes, received a charter to develop the resources of what later became Rhodesia, and the northward expansion of the Boers was frustrated. Kruger's attempt to gain a seaport for the Boers was defeated in 1895 when the British annexed Tongoland and with it Kosi Bay on the east coast.

The Rand gold discoveries and the Uitlanders

The whole position in South Africa was transformed by the gold discoveries at Baberton in 1882, and on the Witwatersrand in 1884. The former gold-field was exhausted by 1887, but the Witwatersrand fields proved to be the richest in the world, and thousands of prospectors poured in from the Cape, from Natal, from the Orange Free State, Germany and America. This transformed the Transvaal from a poor agricultural state to one of untold wealth. For Kruger the gold seemed to offer a solution to his Government's financial problems. The prospectors, nicknamed strangers or 'Uitlanders' by the Boers, were subject to heavy direct and indirect taxation. In order to benefit from the mining developments Kruger's Government adopted the policy of selling monopolies in essential utilities. For example, monopolies were granted for the import of dynamite and iron, for the building of railways and the sale of liquor, all of which raised the cost of living for the thousands of prospectors. As a result, the motley population of the new mining town of Johannesburg was bitterly opposed to Kruger and his policies. Kruger, however, stood firm. Indeed, but for the financial needs of the South African Republic, he would have kept out the British and other European speculators altogether.

The heavily taxed Uitlanders demanded a greater voice in elections. In 1882 the right to vote was restricted by law to those who had been resident at least five years in the Transvaal and later more franchise restrictions were imposed including a minimum residence qualification of 14 years. Thus the Uitlanders, who outnumbered the whole Boer population and paid nearly nine-tenths of the taxes had almost no political rights. Kruger, of course, feared his own people would be swamped if the franchise were widened, particularly since he had failed in 1887 to make an alliance with the Orange Free State which would have maintained the supremacy of the Boers. His anti-British policies also led him to cultivate close political ties not only with the Netherlands but also with Kaiser William II of Germany. This led to increasing tension between Boer and Briton in South Africa.

Cecil Rhodes, 1853–1902

The life of Cecil Rhodes was intimately bound up with the development of the British Empire in Africa and the events which led to the South African War. His parents had intended him to enter the Church but, on account of poor health, he moved to Natal in 1870 to live on his brother's farm. This was the year in which diamonds were found at Kimberley. Both Cecil Rhodes and his brother were very successful diamond prospectors, and by the age of 19 Rhodes had made a fortune. Soon after this he undertook an eight-month journey into the undeveloped lands north of the Vaal and Orange Rivers. This journey above all filled him with the ambition to make Britain the dominant power in Africa. Between 1878 and 1881 he secured the amalgamation of all the Kimberley mines in the de Beers Corporation, in which he became the leading figure. In 1881 he was elected a member of the Cape Assembly. His whole purpose was now to use his personal wealth and political influence to establish British control throughout South Africa. He visualized the domination of the whole continent by Britain and the eventual construction of a railway from the Cape to Cairo.

Rhodes and Kruger
Inevitably Rhodes and Kruger became political enemies. Rhodes feared the expansion of the Transvaal Afrikaaners under Kruger's leadership and did everything he could to frustrate it. Rhodes advocated an African Federation within the Empire, giving the Boer territories virtual independence, but Kruger detested the British and wished to have no part in their Empire. At first Rhodes was successful. In 1884 he was appointed Deputy Commissioner in Bechuanaland, where a number of Boer emigrants from the Transvaal had set up their own Government in two territories. Rhodes persuaded the reluctant Cape Government to send a military expedition to Bechuanaland, and the Boer settlers, under Kruger's instructions, withdrew. Bechuanaland up to the 22nd parallel became a British protectorate. The way for British expansion northwards was now safeguarded. The successful annexation of Bechuanaland was regarded by Rhodes as the key to the future of British Africa. He knew that Kruger had established close relations with both the Germans and Portuguese, who also had ambitions in Bechuanaland.

Establishment of Rhodesia
To the north of Bechuanaland, the Germans and Portuguese were negotiating for trading concessions from Lobengula, the native ruler, and Rhodes was determined to forestall them. He decided to establish a special chartered company to develop the British interest in the northern areas, Mashonaland and Matabeleland. He applied successfully for a charter and succeeded in spreading the company's operations to the southern end of Lake Tanganyika. In 1893 he persuaded the British Government that a war against Lobengula and his Matabele tribesmen was essential, and, when this was successful, nearly half a million square miles were added to the British Empire. Rhodes' British South Africa Company was given control of the area and distributed the land to white settlers. After further resistance from the Matabele had been suppressed, the territory

was officially named Rhodesia and by 1895 had a white population of 12,000.

Rhodes became Prime Minister of the Cape in 1890, chiefly because he had gained the support of those Cape Dutch whose ancestors had not broken their connection with the British at the time of the Great Trek. His power in South Africa was immense. He came to detest any sign of opposition and tended to appoint 'yes-men' as his advisers. At the same time he showed an attitude to the Africans which was progressive for those times, including the rapid extension of their education. However, just when his power in South Africa was at its peak, it was destroyed by the disastrous Jameson Raid in 1895.

The Jameson Raid

Relations between Boers and British grew worse between 1894 and 1896. Kruger refused any concessions to the Uitlanders, conscripted British settlers in the Transvaal for the suppression of a native rising, and increased his contacts with Germany. The British occupied Tongoland in 1895 (see p. 161), and thus finally blocked the Boer ambition for access to Kosi Bay. In 1894, the Netherlands Railway Company, mainly controlled by the Transvaal, completed the line to Delagoa Bay, and Kruger began to impose heavy rates on the Transvaal section of the Cape railway in order to divert traffic to the new line. In reply to this the Cape traders unloaded their goods at the drifts, or fords, on the Vaal River, whence they were sent on wagons to Johannesburg. To counter this move, Kruger, in defiance of earlier agreements, closed the drifts. Only the threat of action by the British home Government, in which Chamberlain was now Colonial Secretary, forced Kruger to give way and re-open the route.

In this situation Rhodes decided on a planned rising of the Uitlanders in the Transvaal aided by an invading force from Bechuanaland. He made contact with the leaders of the Uitlanders and arranged that the invading force should be under the command of Dr Starr Jameson, one of the principal administrators of Rhode's British South Africa Company. However, difficulties arose when the leaders of the Uitlanders learnt that the movement was to be under the British flag, for they had always stressed their loyalty to an independent Transvaal. Despite certain assurances from Rhodes, they decided to postpone their rising, but Jameson, apparently against the wishes of Rhodes, invaded the Transvaal on 29 December 1895 with 500 men. There was no rising in Johannesburg, and the Boer authorities had time to enrol special forces which surrounded Jameson at Doornkop and compelled him to surrender. The following day the Kaiser sent a telegram to congratulate the Transvaal President on having re-established peace and maintained the independence of his country.

The ignominious – not to say ludicrous – failure of Rhodes's conspiracy against the Transvaal Government had a disastrous effect on the relations between the Boers and the British. Rhodes had to resign the premiership of

Cape Colony and lost the hard-won support of the Cape Dutch, while Kruger's position in the Transvaal was strengthened. During the years 1896–9 all efforts made to bring about improvement in the position of the Uitlanders failed. Sir Alfred Milner, Governor of the Cape, met Kruger at Bloemfontein in May 1899, but, although Kruger offered seven years' residence as the voting qualification in the Transvaal, he attached difficult conditions to it and the Colonial Secretary, Chamberlain, supported Milner's demand for a five-year franchise. The Uitlanders petitioned Queen Victoria, complaining of the 'intolerable' burdens imposed upon them, and this aroused widespread anti-Boer hysteria in Britain. Troops were moved to the Transvaal frontiers, while the Boers themselves began military preparations. In October 1899 the Boers sent an ultimatum to the British Government, proposing the solution of all problems by arbitration, but at the same time demanding the immediate removal of British forces from the

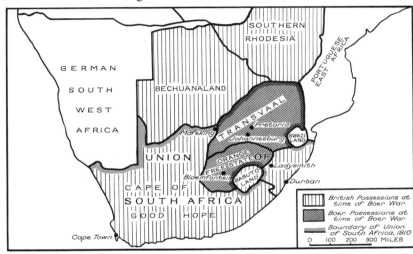

FIG. 3. Southern Africa during the Boer War.

Transvaal borders, the removal within a reasonable time of all forces which had recently arrived in South Africa, and the turning back of those forces on their way to South Africa. This ultimatum was rejected and the war between Britain and the combined Transvaal and Orange Free States began.

The South African War (The Second Boer War) 1899–1902

At the outset both sides underestimated each other. Kruger had large numbers of up-to-date German arms, and the Boers were excellent guerrilla fighters who knew their terrain well. At first they had superiority in numbers and artillery. They were also buoyed up by the considerable moral support they received in Europe, where Britain was widely regarded as a ruthless bully determined to force the Boers into the Empire against their will. In Britain itself they had a number of Radical supporters, including the young Lloyd George, who waged a vigorous campaign against the home Government, with Chamberlain as his main target. On the other hand, as the war proceeded, the British had considerable support from the new Dominions and the Colonies, and to Kruger's dismay, neither Germany nor any other power actually intervened on his side.

Main military operations
The Boers attacked immediately, invading both Natal and the Cape. Their forces laid siege to Kimberley, Mafeking and Ladysmith. In one week of December 1899, known as the 'black week' for the British, three major defeats by the Boers at Stormberg, at Magersfontein and the Tugela River, all proved that the republics were not going to be overwhelmed in a few weeks' fighting as had been widely supposed in Britain.

As a result of these early reverses, important changes were made in the British command. Lord Roberts became supreme commander and Lord Kitchener Chief-of-staff. Roberts gathered 250,000 troops under his command and was able to use them to overwhelm the regular Boer forces under Cronje. Ladysmith and Kimberley were both relieved early in 1900 and Mafeking in May, after holding out under the command of Colonel Baden-Powell for seven months. By June 1900 Roberts had decisively defeated the organized armies of the Boers and occupied Bloemfontein, Johannesburg and Pretoria. But although Kruger escaped through Portuguese territory and fled to Holland (where he died in 1904), the Boers kept

'Mafeking Night' in Piccadilly. When the news of the relief of Mafeking reached London there was a night of wild 'jingoistic' celebrations. Note the picture of Baden Powell, the commander at Mafeking, carried by a demonstrator.

up a form of guerrilla warfare for another eighteen months under their commando leaders, Botha, de Wet, Hertzog and Smuts. Kitchener countered this with special forts to protect the railways and concentration camps for all civilians who might have aided the guerrillas. Kitchener's ruthless policy also led to the widespread destruction of farms and food. In the camps about one in five of all those interned died, through bad sanitation and food. The Liberal opposition at home raised an outcry and Chamberlain was compelled to take urgent measures to improve conditions in the camps. But the name of Britain was tarnished in the war.

The superior forces of the British and the ruthlessness of Kitchener at length made it impossible for the Boers to continue the struggle, and a peace treaty was signed at Vereeniging in May 1902. By this treaty the Transvaal and the Orange Free State lost their independence, but were promised self-government and the maintenance of Afrikaans as their official language. Britain made a grant of £3 million to enable the Boers to repair the destruction which Kitchener's campaigns had caused. In this way the treaty did something to make up for the evils of a war which Britain could not justify, and which had badly damaged her prestige abroad. Rhodes died two months before the treaty which in many ways fulfilled his dreams.

The Union of South Africa
In 1906 the Liberal Government gave separate parliaments and governments once again to the Transvaal and the Orange Free State, and in 1910 the Union of South Africa was established. The separate parliaments were then abolished and one parliament established at Cape Town. A Governor-General represented the British Crown and, besides the elected Assembly, there was a Senate. Each of the four provinces had an elected council to deal with local matters. The first Prime Minister of the Union was General Botha, the former guerrilla leader. Outside the Union there remained Northern and Southern Rhodesia under British administration, and also the territories of Bechuanaland, Basutoland and Swaziland.

The peaceful functioning of the Union as a self-governing dominion in the Commonwealth and the important part which Boer leaders like Smuts were to play in imperial affairs seemed to indicate the complete success of the British policy in South Africa. However, there were always some Boers who remained anti-British and who opposed South African co-operation with Britain in the two World Wars. These men were to be responsible for the policy of apartheid after 1945 and for the secession of the Republic of South Africa from the Commonwealth in 1961.

SALISBURY'S FOREIGN AND IMPERIAL POLICY

During the years of Salisbury's ministry the Portuguese, Italians, Germans and French were all advancing on areas in which Britain had an interest and there had to be frequent adjustment of colonial frontiers to prevent a clash. The French were the most obvious rivals for colonial lands and at times disputes over remote border territories seemed in danger of embroiling the two countries in a major war.

Reconquest of the Sudan

Salisbury had decided that it was in Britain's interest to reconquer the Sudan before the French moved in from the Sahara. Sir Herbert Kitchener was given command of a strong force, and in 1898 the army of the Mahdi was overwhelmingly defeated at Omdurman. A few days after Kitchener entered Khartoum he heard that a French force under Major Marchand had reached the Upper Nile at Fashoda and had raised the French flag. The French aimed to control the Southern Sudan and with it the upper reaches of the Nile. Kitchener moved southwards and confronted the French at Fashoda. Lord Salisbury and Delcassé the French Foreign Minister adopted uncompromising positions and the English and French Press carried on violent campaigns. However, France was isolated and feared German action in Europe, and Kitchener persuaded Marchand to withdraw. By the Anglo-French Convention of 1899 French and British spheres of influence in the Nile and Congo basins were clearly defined and the continued British control of both Egypt and the Sudan ensured.

Salisbury and Turkey

In Europe, Salisbury, like Castlereagh and Canning, hoped to maintain a 'Concert of the Powers'. He believed that the Great Powers could settle problems peaceably, and in this respect Britain was prepared to play her part. The Turkish question, however, proved to be particularly difficult.

The promises of Abdul Hamid to govern his Christian subjects well proved utterly worthless. In 1896–7 his Armenian subjects demanded self-government and religious freedom within the Turkish Empire. He met this agitation with massacre and persecution. In Britain, Gladstone re-emerged to denounce the Turks and to call for action by the British Government on behalf of the Christian Armenians. Salisbury made the usual protests, but took no decisive action. However, in 1897 the Greeks supported Crete's demand for independence from Turkey. The Turks attacked and defeated Greece, but this time Salisbury threatened action against the Turks and thus won the territory for Greece. Salisbury's policy, like Disraeli's, was a restraining influence on the Turks, but not one of outright opposition. Turkey was still regarded as a bulwark against Russia, and the complete break-up of the Ottoman Empire would have been regarded by Salisbury as a disaster for British policy.

Great Britain and Germany

By 1890 Germany had become a strong rival of the other imperial Powers, especially in Africa. Bismarck, under pressure from German business men and colonizers, modified his early policy of limiting Germany's political interests to Europe alone. In 1890 Kaiser Wilhelm II succeeded and Bismarck was dismissed. The old European policy was abandoned. Wilhelm II and his Minister of Marine, Admiral von Tirpitz, began the creation of a fleet to rival Britain's by the German Naval Programme of 1898. Next a German plan appeared for a Berlin-Baghdad Railway running through the Balkans and Asia Minor to the Middle East. This, if successfully completed, would counteract Britain's naval power in the Mediterranean and Russian influence in the Middle East.

In reply Salisbury attempted to make an agreement with Russia and France to thwart German expansion. Russia, however, showed no interest, and the Fashoda incident caused strained relations between France and Britain. Salisbury turned instead to the idea of a direct alliance with Germany. This also failed, for the Kaiser was not interested in any such alliance, and pressed on with his naval programme by the 1899 Naval Bill. The Kaiser's sympathy for the Boers during the South African War was further evidence of the unbridgeable gulf between British and German imperialism. Britain's sense of diplomatic isolation at this time from France, Russia and Germany – the major continental powers – produced a new search for allies. The Foreign Secretary, Lord Lansdowne, negotiated the Anglo-Japanese Alliance of 1902, by which Britain and Japan promised mutual support if one party to the alliance were attacked by two other powers, but neutrality if attacked by one. This treaty weakened the position of Russia in the Far East and won Britain the friendship of Japan which was emerging as a powerful industrial state.

Death of Salisbury and Queen Victoria

The Anglo-Japanese treaty was one of the last acts of Salisbury's Government in international affairs. After the Boer War a general election once again returned a substantial Conservative majority in a wave of hysterical patriotism. Soon afterwards Salisbury retired, and died the following year, 1903. The premiership fell to his nephew, Arthur James Balfour. Queen Victoria died in January 1901, after a reign of 64 years and was succeeded by her son Edward VII.

The Entente Cordiale, 1904

Balfour's foreign policy was directed, with the obvious approval of the new King, to bringing Britain closer to France in order to counter the growing power of Germany. A visit of Edward VII to Paris was arranged with the

Edward VII taking the salute during his visit to France in 1903.

purpose of breaking through the old Anglo-French antagonisms. France, realizing the challenge of Germany and unable to forget the humiliation of 1870, was now more inclined towards a compromise with Britain. Delcassé, Colonial Minister at the time of Fashoda and now Foreign Minister, negotiated with Lord Lansdowne one of the most important international agreements of the age. Lansdowne agreed that Britain would support French claims in Morocco and Delcassé agreed to recognize unconditionally the British occupation of Egypt. Delcassé rightly saw the new agreement as a move by Britain away from Germany, who had previously supported the British position in Egypt against France, and an end to any possibility of an Anglo-German alliance. The agreement was an understanding and not an alliance. Later events, however, such as the continued growth of the German Navy, the defeat of Russia by Japan in 1905 and the German attempt to intervene in Morocco in 1906 (see p. 182) brought Britain and France into closer co-operation.

Thus Salisbury's and Balfour's policy brought Britain much nearer to political commitments in Europe and modified Britain's so-called isolation. Indeed Salisbury's policy never had been isolationist in the strict sense of the word. What was changing in 1904 was the *direction* of Britain's commitments away from the Triple Alliance of Germany, Austria and Italy towards the Dual Alliance of Russia and France. This shift of emphasis was to have profound effects in the next ten years.

DOMESTIC AFFAIRS UNDER SALISBURY
AND BALFOUR

Ireland

The Conservatives under Balfour were still faced with the Irish land problem. They hoped to weaken the demand for Home Rule by improving the position of the Irish peasant. The Government's most sweeping measure, introduced by the Secretary for Ireland, George Wyndham, showed how far Conservative opinion had moved towards the old Radical proposal of creating an Irish landowning peasantry. Wyndham's Land Purchase Act of 1903 accepted the principle of lending the peasantry money for purchase where the landlord had agreed on a fair price. The annual repayments of the purchase price at only $3\frac{1}{4}$ per cent interest were spread over $68\frac{1}{2}$ years. The scheme proved so popular that by 1910 more than 250,000 tenants had come into it, and to finance it the Government raised £150,000,000. Another improvement was the establishment of county councils in 1898. This greatly increased Irish participation in local administration, and fulfilled the demands that Chamberlain had repeatedly made over a number of years.

Workmen's Compensation Act, 1897

Chamberlain's Radical influence was also felt in the Workmen's Compensation Act of 1897. The trade unions had for some years been demanding drastic improvements in the law governing the relations between employer and employed. By the new act workers could claim compensation for injuries sustained at work. Although this first Compensation Act was hedged round by all kinds of legal difficulties for the worker, it at least recognized a principle that had been accepted in Bismarck's Germany as early as 1884. A scheme for old age pensions, which had the strong support of Chamberlain, was abandoned on the outbreak of the Boer War.

The Education Act, 1902

A measure which had profound effects on the future of English education was introduced by Balfour in 1902. A Royal Commission of 1895 had reported on the general backwardness of British education, especially technical education, as compared with some continental countries including Germany. In 1899 the Board of Education was set up to ensure better direction and co-ordination in the educational system. The greatest pressure for educational reform came from the Prime Minister himself and from Chamberlain. Balfour had to face violent opposition to his proposed changes from the various religious bodies who already had a strong stake in the educational system, but he persisted. The Education Act of 1902 was the foundation of the English educational system in the twentieth century. By its terms the old school boards were abolished and the county and borough councils were to appoint their own education committees to administer elementary schools and, in the case of the bigger authorities, secondary education. The schools of the Catholics and Anglicans retained their own forms of religious teaching and appointed their own teachers, but were aided by money from the rates to bring them up to a recognized standard of efficiency. In secondary education, the new committees were empowered to assist the older grammar schools and to build their own where necessary. Thus both elementary and secondary education became more the concern of the state than ever before. The Nonconformists, angered by the privileges given to Catholics and Anglicans, waged a campaign, supported by the Liberals in Parliament, to block the payment of rates for the schools. The Balfour Government faced this situation firmly and opposition gradually died down.

Chamberlain's Tariff Reform

Joseph Chamberlain had fatally split the Liberal Party in 1886 over Ireland, and nearly twenty years later he caused an equally fatal rift among the Conservatives, this time over Empire trade. He had come to believe that the Empire could be strengthened by a radical change in its trading policy. His study of Germany and the United States had convinced him that these countries had, through a system of protective tariffs, increased their trade since 1870 more rapidly than Britain, which had clung to free trade since the mid-nineteenth century. In 1903 Chamberlain founded the Tariff Reform League and resigned from the Government in order to carry on his campaign. His programme consisted of the following demands. Firstly a small import duty on food imports from foreign countries should be imposed in order to favour foods imported from the colonies. Secondly there should be an import duty of 10 per cent on manufactured imports to weaken foreign competition, expand British industries and increase employment. Thirdly to help meet a possible rise in the cost of living, duties on tea, sugar and other articles of general consumption should be reduced. These measures, he argued, would greatly increase trade with the colonies and they in their turn would be prepared to give preferences to English exports. This would help to compensate for the fact that Great Britain had for many years been exporting fewer and fewer manufactured goods owing to the tariffs imposed by such countries as Germany and the United States.

Balfour opposed Chamberlain's proposals. He felt that the Conservatives could not risk the adoption of a policy which would, as Chamberlain himself admitted, lead to a rise in the cost of living. Chamberlain summoned a general meeting of the Unionist Party at which supporters of free trade were ousted from control. Soon afterwards Balfour resigned the premiership and the Liberal leader, Campbell-Bannerman, formed a government in December 1905. Early in 1906 he dissolved Parliament and prepared to fight an election on the free trade issue.

General Election of 1906

The result of the election was a crushing defeat for the Conservative Party – one that astonished both Conservatives and their Liberal and Labour opponents. The Liberals returned 399 members, the Irish Nationalists 83, the Labour Party 29 and the Conservatives only 157. The free traders were therefore in an overwhelming majority and, perhaps even more important for the future, the Labour Party had emerged as a real political force. On the other hand, the blow to Chamberlain was disastrous. A serious illness in 1906 prevented him from speaking again in the House of Commons. He continued to be returned as M.P. by his Birmingham constituency, however, until his death in July 1914.

Working-class opposition to tariff reform had been decisive, and had been vigorously led by the Liberal and Labour Parties. Chamberlain's proposals, while receiving the support of the local Conservative Associations, had divided the Party leadership. (It was over this issue that Winston Churchill left the Conservative Party and joined the Liberals in 1904.) But other issues had also affected the result of the election. A strong popular revulsion against imperialism had told against Chamberlain. The issue had been taken up in the 1906 election very strongly by Lloyd George and his fellow Radicals. Another question which aroused fierce anti-Conservative feeling was the importation into South Africa of Chinese coolie labourers to work in the mines of the Transvaal. They were paid little and worked almost as slaves. This meant severe discrimination against working-class immigrants from Britain, and the conditions under which the Chinese were employed shocked humanitarians at home.

Moreover, Balfour and Salisbury had done little in the nature of social reform. The Workmen's Compensation Act was a weak measure, and the Unemployed Workmen's Act of 1905 which allowed the use of voluntary subscriptions to create work for the unemployed was regarded as a charitable insult to labour. Balfour had furthermore refused to change the law relating to trade unions in such a way as to counteract the results of the Taff Vale decision of 1901 (see p. 296). As long as this decision remained in force, the trade unions were powerless to use the strike weapon in disputes. Both the Liberal and Labour Parties took this up as an election issue and thus won the trade union vote. After nearly two decades of Conservatism the tide seemed to have turned against them and the country was ready for a new period of radical reform.

17. Liberalism and Reform, 1906-14

Introduction

In many ways the basis of the 'Welfare State' was laid in the years immediately before the Great War of 1914–18. The new Liberal Government headed by Henry Campbell-Bannerman was under great pressure to produce reforms which would substantially benefit the mass of the people. The rise of the Labour Party was a sign that the working man was not content with the record of the old political parties. The trade union movement was growing and becoming more militant. Within the Liberal Government the Radicals in the party itself were represented by David Lloyd George, the President of the Board of Trade, and John Burns, one of the leaders of the dock strike of 1889 (see p. 284), the new President of the Local Government Board. Campbell-Bannerman himself was generally regarded as a Radical. The ministry also included Winston Churchill, Sir Edward Grey and R. B. Haldane, all of whom were to play important parts in shaping Britain's future. Most of these men, including the Prime Minister, were not drawn from or directly connected with the old aristocracy. In this sense this was the first British Government whose composition was a distinct break from nineteenth-century tradition, and which really reflected the results of the extended franchise.

The Conservatives, badly weakened in the Commons, were forced to rely on their enormous majority in the Lords to resist the radical tide. But this was a dangerous weapon, as their leader Balfour warned, and was soon to lead to a constitutional crisis which altered the whole relationship of the two Houses of Parliament.

Campbell-Bannerman and South Africa

In 1906 the new Government, much to its credit, banned the importation of Chinese coolie labour into South Africa (see also p. 172). Campbell-Bannerman himself was far ahead of his own supporters in his views on self-determination for those who had only recently been fighting the British in South Africa. He had denounced the concentration camps (see p. 166) and gave self-government to the Transvaal and the Orange Free State in December 1906 and June 1907 respectively. This courageous action, pressed forward by the Prime Minister against much opposition even in his own party, broke down some of the old antipathy between the British and the Afrikaaners and led to the formation of the new Dominion of the

Union of South Africa in 1909 (see p. 166) which strengthened the Empire as the challenge from Germany became more pressing.

Trades Disputes Act, 1906
One of the first actions of the Liberal Government was to bring in an act to protect trade unions from the effects of the Taff Vale decision (see p. 296). By this Act the trade unions were no longer held liable for the payment of damages as a consequence of organizing strike action. Even in the House of Lords, the Conservatives led by Lord Lansdowne, dared not oppose this change. However, legislation designed to improve the Education Act of 1902 and to stop plural voting in elections (by which many people could vote both in their home constituency and where they carried on business), were rejected by the Lords. In 1907, when the Lords had rejected other Government measures, Campbell-Bannerman counter-attacked, demanding limitations on the powers of the House of Lords to reject Bills passed by the Commons.

The rise of Lloyd George
One of the most successful new ministers was David Lloyd George, whose first ministry was the Board of Trade. Among many other achievements he set up the Port of London Authority to improve the efficiency of the London docks and the working conditions in them. Another Act controlled the living conditions of seamen in English vessels. Campbell-Bannerman resigned in 1908 and Asquith became Prime Minister with Lloyd George as Chancellor of the Exchequer. Lloyd George was therefore largely responsible for the People's Budget of 1909 and for the constitutional changes that resulted from it.

The People's Budget of 1909
The Liberal Government were determined to increase Government expenditure on social benefits. In 1908 the first old age pension (long ago advocated by Chamberlain) was introduced. This gave 5s a week at the age of 70 if other earnings were not more than 10s. a week. The size of the pension and the 'means test' attached to it were heavily criticized by many Radicals and by the Labour Party. The measure was partly prompted by the reports of the Royal Commission on the Poor Law set up by the Conservatives in 1905; both the majority and minority reports criticized the Poor Law and the workhouse system. The introduction of an old age pension was regarded as a means of reducing the reliance of the aged on poor relief in the workhouse.

The pension scheme cost money, as did a new naval building programme undertaken by the Government as a reply to German rearmament. More than £15 million were needed as additional expenditure, a large sum at that time, and Lloyd George's problem was to find this money. He made no secret of his intention. 'Make the rich pay,' was his slogan. In the Budget of

1909 death duties were increased and 2d. was added to the rate of income tax. A super tax was levied on incomes over £3,000. In addition to this, Lloyd George proposed a national survey of land with an imposition of a land tax on all increases in value due to development.

The land tax proposal aroused the fury of the landowners, whose main defence was still the House of Lords. The House of Commons passed the Budget by 379 votes to 149, but the Lords rejected it by 350 to 75. A head-on collision thus occurred between Lords and Commons, over which House should have final power in such important matters as finance.

Two days later, the Prime Minister, Herbert Asquith, secured the passage in the Commons of a resolution declaring the action of the House of Lords in rejecting the financial side of the Budget to be a 'breach of the constitution'. Parliament was then dissolved and an election held. The result was the return of 275 Liberals, 273 Conservatives, 40 Labour Party and Lib-Lab supporters and 82 Irish Nationalists. This return disappointed both Liberals and Conservatives; the Irish members could now control the parliamentary balance, and their leader Redmond occupied almost the same position of power as Parnell had done in the 1880's. He secured from the Liberals an undertaking that they would support Home Rule for Ireland in return for Irish Nationalist support in the House of Commons in the struggle over Lloyd George's Budget.

The Parliament Bill, 1911

A Parliament Bill was now introduced into the Commons, to deprive the House of Lords of any powers of amending or rejecting money Bills, to give the Speaker of the House of Commons the authority to decide which Bills were money Bills; to enact that a Bill passed by the Commons in three successive sessions and rejected in each by the Lords should become law; and to reduce the maximum life of Parliament from seven to five years.

Before this Bill was introduced the new King, George V (Edward VII had died in May 1910), attempted to settle the whole matter by a conference between the Liberal and Conservative leaders, but six months of discussion proved futile. George V then agreed to create enough Liberal peers to enable the Bill to be passed through the House of Lords provided that another election gave a clear indication of the will of the people. The election followed in December 1910, and the result was almost exactly the same as before.

When the Bill was presented to the House of Lords, amendments were made but the Commons refused to accept them. In the Lords, Lansdowne and his supporters were prepared to pass the Bill rather than see the Conservative majority swamped by the creation of 250 Liberal peers. The old, diehard aristocratic section held out for some time, but eventually the compromisers won the day and the Bill was passed by the narrow margin of 131 votes to 114.

Importance of the Parliament Bill, 1911

From this time, the House of Lords had no power over the financial proposals of the Commons, and had only a suspensory veto of two years in other legislation. However, this did mean that the House of Lords could prevent the passage of Bills, apart from finance Bills, during the last two years of a five-year Parliament. The passage of the Act was undoubtedly a victory for parliamentary democracy against the deeply entrenched privileges of the nineteenth-century political system. The radical Liberals, the Labour Party, and the trade union movement were all pressing for important reforms – social, political and religious – which collided with powerful and reactionary vested interests.

Haldane's army reforms

An important Liberal achievement was the further reform of the British Army, implementing, at last, many of Cardwell's early ideas. Haldane, the Secretary for War, wanted to expand the Army, foreseeing Britain's possible involvement in a continental war. Because of financial restraints, he could not achieve this, but he was responsible for producing a small highly efficient army. He created a General Staff, and fostered the closest co-ordination between the Regulars and the new Territorials. The Territorial Army was organized in 14 divisions and 14 mounted brigades. It provided a force of 300,000 men vastly better trained than the old Volunteers and yeomanry which it superseded. An Expeditionary Force was formed of Regular units – six infantry divisions and one cavalry division with all the necessary services, and reserves to provide drafts. Haldane brought the volunteer officer corps at the public schools under the supervision of the War Office and created the Officers' Training Corps which, in the crisis of 1914, was to provide leaders for the new force. In 1911 he also produced the 'War Book' compiled by the Committee of Imperial Defence, which laid down clear instructions for every department of State in case war broke out.

Liberal social reforms

In the same year as the first old-age pension scheme (see p. 174), the Coal Mines Act introduced an eight-hour day in the mines in answer to pressure from the militant miners' trade union. Action had also to be taken on the railways as the Amalgamated Society of Railway Servants, predecessor of the present National Union of Railwaymen, threatened strike action in 1907 to improve their wages and working conditions. Lloyd George, then at the Board of Trade, supervised the creation of conciliation boards for the railways to settle disputes peacefully between the men and the railway companies. Another measure was the setting up of trade boards for four sweated industries. On these boards both employers and workers were represented. This resulted in the introduction of minimum wages for a number of underpaid and sweated trades, especially those employing women. This was the first legislation to interfere directly with the wages of adults. The experiment was successful and trade boards were extended to a large number of industries in the next twenty years.

In 1909 Labour Exchanges were set up to enable unemployed men and women to register and to be found other work in a more systematic way than hitherto. This reduced the waiting period between one job and another and made labour more mobile. In 1907 the medical inspection of children was introduced, and the provision of school meals by the local authorities for those urgently in need was encouraged, though not made compulsory. This latter measure was very much the result of agitation by the Labour Party, the pioneer city being Bradford, where the Labour Party under the local leadership of Arthur Henderson was already strongly entrenched. The Education Act of 1907 which brought about these important changes also increased educational opportunity by introducing the scholarship system. By this system all secondary schools receiving aid from the rates were to reserve 25 per cent of their places for the pupils of elementary schools who were proved to be of the required standard by examination (see also p. 352).

National Insurance Act, 1911

In 1909 the Poor Law Commission which had been set up under the Conservatives issued its Majority and Minority Reports. In the main these recommended an end to the old Boards of Guardians set up by the Poor Law Act of 1834 and the relief of the poor by the local councils instead. But the Minority Report wanted the Poor Law system, with its taint of charity, pauperism and the workhouse, to be completely abolished and a wide social welfare service instituted, including a national public health system and a scheme of unemployment insurance.

Lloyd George was given the task of producing a National Insurance system. He copied many features of the German system, and both employers and workers were made to contribute to a national insurance fund. He instituted a system of Approved Societies (such as trade unions, friendly societies, insurance companies) which were allowed to administer benefits to their members. On the medical side, he set up the panel system by which doctors received fixed annual payments for each patient getting medical attention under the National Insurance Act. The Act was passed in 1911, and in spite of a good deal of dishonest and undignified opposition by the Conservative 'diehards', proved an immediate success. Part I of the Act, which enforced payment of contributions by worker, employer and the State, gave the insured worker sickness, disablement and maternity benefits, and created the 'panel' system by which the medical profession, very reluctantly in many cases, now had a fee payment from the State for its services to the insured. The scheme was compulsory for all persons with incomes below £160 per annum. This minimum was raised in future years as the cost of living rose. Part II of the Act introduced unemployment insurance for certain industries only, such as building, where employment was very insecure. It included workers' contributions, which really meant that the employed and healthy worker was contributing out of his wages to support those in need. A number of socialists denounced this scheme as unjust – it was really making the worker pay. They demanded a complete non-contributory system run by the state and financed by the incomes of the wealthy, taking to its natural conclusion Lloyd George's own earlier slogan of 'make the rich pay'. However, Lloyd George won the support of the trade unions and the official Labour Party for the scheme which enabled the unions to qualify as 'approved societies' and thus to help in administering the new system.

Payment of M.P.s.

In 1911 the Liberal Government enacted a measure which had been one of the demands of the Chartists sixty years before. This was largely a result of a legal ruling of the House of Lords in 1909 known as the Osborne Judgement (see also p. 297). This stated that it was illegal for a trade union to put aside part of a member's subscription for the purpose of financing parliamentary candidates. This, of course, mainly affected Labour Party candidates, and their M.P.s lost the salaries which various unions had provided. The judgment led to considerable labour unrest. The Liberal Government responded to this pressure by introducing the payment of M.P.s at the rate of £400 and then went on to protect the unions from the effects of the Osborne Judgement. By the Trade Union Amendment Act, 1913, a trade union could use its funds for political purposes if this was agreed by a majority decision arrived at by a secret ballot of its members. Furthermore, any member of a trade union could 'contract out' of paying into the special political fund, and would not lose his general trade union rights by doing so.

Social unrest in the period 1906–14

Although valuable social work had been accomplished by the Governments of Campbell-Bannerman and Asquith, this was a period of sharp conflict between employers and workers. Such reforms as National Insurance and Old Age Pensions could not disguise the fact that there had been a rise in the cost of living. Wages fell behind prices, and Britain's foreign competitors were rapidly increasing their share of world trade. Britain's industrial supremacy was coming to an end and this was reflected at home in increased unemployment. Lloyd George's policy of conciliation through the trade board system could not alter the basic economic facts. In the trade unions the revolutionary wing, led by such militants as Tom Mann and A. J. Cook, the miners' leader, were attempting to turn the Labour Party away from its support for the Liberal Government. Many union leaders were attracted by Syndicalism, a movement which was powerful in Europe at this time. They hoped to form single unions for each of the great industries and use the weapon of the general strike to end capitalism and secure the revolutionary overthrow of the old system of society. Their influence in the trade unions was considerable before 1914, and there were widespread strikes by miners, railwaymen and other key workers. The employers responded by using the lock-out against the workers – 120,000 were locked out in the cotton industry in 1910. The Syndicalists despised the Labour Party and directed much of their anger against its secretary, J. Ramsay MacDonald, the future Labour Prime Minister, whom they did not regard as a socialist at all (see Chapter 28).

Another important political group were the suffragettes, who demanded the vote for women. This, of course, was only one aspect of the campaign which militant women were fighting for equal rights in law, work, and

The Suffragettes: Mrs Pethwick Lawrence and a male sympathizer, the novelist Israel Zangwill, in a great rally in Hyde Park, June 1908.

education. In 1897 a Bill to give women the vote had reached a second reading in the House of Commons, but had been 'talked out' by one of its opponents. In 1903 Mrs Emmeline Pankhurst founded the Women's Social and Political Union. When its members discovered that the Liberal victory of 1906 did not result in the acceptance of their demands, they took to more violent methods of protest. Campbell-Bannerman had encouraged them during the election, but upon gaining power he edged away from his promises, except for one relatively small measure, the Qualification of Women Act, 1907, which enabled women to become councillors, chairmen or mayors of county or borough councils. The suffragettes sought to force the Government to act by organized lawlessness. They chained themselves to the railings of ministers' houses, set fire to pillar boxes, attacked policemen and slashed pictures in the National Gallery. In return the police, and some of the public, treated them roughly, and in prison they were forcibly fed when they went on hunger strike. The Government secured the passing by Parliament of the 'Cat and Mouse' Act, as it was called, by which suffragettes who were almost dying in prison could be released and rearrested on recovery, released again, and so on. The most shocking event occurred on Derby Day, 1913, when a suffragette, Emily Davidson, threw herself under the King's horse and died as the result of her injuries. In general, their tactics did little to further their cause. They exasperated many people and discouraged many of their sympathizers. Above all, they annoyed and embarrassed the Government whose support they had to win for legislative action.

Irish affairs, 1906–14

John Redmond, the leader of the Irish Nationalists, had secured from the Liberals a promise of Home Rule for Ireland in return for his support in the 1911 Budget conflict. In return, in April 1912, the Third Home Rule Bill was introduced by the Prime Minister Asquith himself.

The situation had changed considerably since the time of Parnell. Asquith's Bill, passed by the Commons, was rejected by the Lords, but under the Parliament Act, it was bound to become law automatically in 1914. The interval of two years was used by the Conservatives and their Unionist supporters in northern Ireland to organize the opposition there to the Home Rule policy. This movement, led by a Protestant lawyer and M.P., Sir Edward Carson, resulted in the formation in northern Ireland of the Ulster Volunteers (partly armed with imported German guns) to resist Home Rule by violent means. In April 1911, on the eve of the passing of the Home Rule Bill, Carson was able to hold a review of 80,000 men of the Ulster Volunteer Force. The strength of this movement in the north was due to the rapid growth there of British industries, financed by British capital and the fear that the Protestant population which formed a majority in several counties would suffer from the predominance of the Catholics in the rest of Ireland. The Ulster movement was essentially an alliance of the Protestant and industrial interests against the Catholic and agricultural south.

Asquith at first attempted to meet the Ulster movement by a compromise which would have left Ulster out of the provisions of the Home Rule Bill. But Redmond remained adamant. He was under pressure not only from his supporters in Parliament, but from more extreme nationalist movements in Ireland, especially the Sinn Fein, who demanded a complete break from Britain and did not regard even the Home Rule Bill as adequate. Redmond therefore was unable to agree to any solution which would have left

The Ulster Volunteers: Ulstermen drilling in September 1912, ready to resist the operation of Irish Home Rule.

northern Ireland or even part of northern Ireland out of Home Rule. Yet Asquith himself knew that Ulster could not be coerced, led as it was by Carson and backed by the Conservative opposition.

In Ireland the position became more tense as the months passed. The Nationalists formed the Irish Volunteers in readiness for civil war. Asquith should have acted with vigour to put down both the private armies but there were few people in Ireland who were not committed to one or the other.

The Curragh 'Mutiny'

Another serious complication arose as the date for Home Rule drew near. The British officers stationed in southern Ireland, with their headquarters at the Curragh in Dublin, openly declared that they would rather be dismissed from the service than lead the British armed force in Ireland against the north. This came near to an open rebellion against the Government at Westminster, but Asquith and the War Office eventually assured them that they would not be required to use force against the Ulster movement. To the great indignation of many Liberal supporters in Britain, the mutinous officers had gained the day against the decisions of the House of Commons. Asquith was widely criticized for timidity, but the main feeling was against his Conservative and Unionist opponents who had encouraged near-mutiny and rebellion.

When the war against Germany broke out in 1914 the Home Rule Act was suspended for the duration of the war. However, the Sinn Fein ('We ourselves') Party were not prepared to accept this situation, and there was to be further trouble in Ireland before the end of the war in 1918.

Developments leading to the outbreak of the First World War, 1914–18
From 1906 to 1914 relations between Britain and Germany steadily deteriorated. The task of conducting British foreign policy during this critical period fell to Sir Edward Grey who became Foreign Secretary in 1905 in Campbell-Bannerman's Government. It would be wrong to assume that Grey saw Germany as the inevitable enemy of Britain, and France and Russia as her natural allies. Right up to 1914 he devoted his efforts to settle outstanding causes of disagreement with Germany. However, the general situation did not depend solely on British and German relations. There was serious conflict of interests between Germany and Russia, between France and Germany and between Austria and Russia.

Britain and France had entered into the *Entente Cordiale* in 1904. This was not an alliance by which either Power was bound to support the other in case of attack but an effort to eliminate the state of tension which had existed for many years between them. Delcassé, the French Foreign Minister, had rightly calculated that the *entente* would make British policy less friendly towards Germany, though there was as yet no open quarrel between them.

Morocco and the Algeciras Conference, 1905–06
Anglo-German relations deteriorated still further over Morocco. In 1905 the Kaiser and von Bülow, his Chancellor, visited Tangier and assured the Sultan of his support for the continued independence of the state. His statements were clearly directed against France, which had considerable financial interests in Morocco and was in the process of turning it into a French protectorate. Delcassé, with British support, stood up to German demands and although he was forced to resign by his more timid colleagues, he did achieve the calling of an international conference at Algeciras in January 1906. In general, the results of the Conference went against Germany. France and Spain agreed to undertake the policing of Moroccan ports, while France was to have control of the customs and arms supply. The only concession to Germany was an equal control with France and Britain of the State Bank of Morocco, which at least guaranteed Germany's trading rights in the country. Even so France was allowed the dominant capital investment in the bank. However, while the Conference was proceeding, Germany obtained a concession for the building of the port of Tangier – a concession previously promised to the French.

The Anglo-Russian agreement and the formation of the Triple Entente, 1907
Russia had supported Britain and France over Morocco and during the two years previous to Algeciras Delcassé had been attempting to persuade the Czar Nicholas II to settle the outstanding differences between Russia and Britain. The French and British Governments had been seriously alarmed at the first attempted revolution in Russia in 1905. Both Governments, and especially the French, were anxious to bolster up the Czarist

régime not only to counterbalance Germany but to protect the considerable French and British investment in Russia. After 1905 French supplies of armaments to Russia greatly increased and further French loans were negotiated. Thus the French had every reason to strengthen the international position of Russia by bringing her into closer relations with the *Entente Cordiale*.

Conditions were certainly more favourable for agreement between Russia and Britain than for many years past. The British fear of Russian aims in the Middle and Far East had greatly diminished. The catastrophic defeat of Russia by Japan in 1905 had shown that Britain's ally, Japan, was strong enough to protect Anglo-Japanese interests there. In the Balkan Peninsula, the small nations established since 1878 were maintaining their independence of Russia. On the other hand Germany posed a greater political and military threat in Turkey and the Middle East. The German plan for the Berlin-Baghdad Railway was a danger to both Russian and British interests in the Middle East. All these factors made possible the agreement achieved by Sir Edward Grey with Russia in August 1907. By this settlement, Britain gained control of the foreign policy of Afghanistan and shared trading rights in that country with Russia. In Tibet, both powers bound themselves not to interfere, and to negotiate through China, Tibet's suzerain. In Persia, Russia gained control of the northern part of the country and Britain of the southern half, where oil-prospecting was already in progress; a neutral zone kept the two Powers apart. Once again, however, as in the case of the *Entente Cordiale*, this agreement was not an alliance, and in fact very shortly afterwards Grey again approached Germany with the offer of a disarmament agreement. His offer was rejected.

German and British naval policy

In 1906 Britain produced a new battleship, the Dreadnought, which by its speed and armour outclassed all existing capital ships. The ship, 18,000 tons and capable of 21 knots, had been developed by Lord Cawdor, the previous Conservative First Lord of the Admiralty, and Sir John Fisher, the aggressive and eccentric First Sea Lord. The Dreadnought provoked a new naval arms race between Britain and Germany. Von Tirpitz and the Kaiser had already built up their conventional fleet by the Navy Laws of 1897 and 1900 and were now determined to overtake Britain in the production of Dreadnoughts. This in turn provoked a public outcry in Britain for the building of at least eight new ships of this class. At the same time the Atlantic, Mediterranean and Channel Fleets were reorganized and under Winston Churchill, First Lord of the Admiralty from 1911, an efficient Naval Staff was created.

The Agadir Incident, 1911

The naval and military programmes of Fisher and Haldane had been

The Arms Race: H.M.S. Dreadnought *at Portsmouth in 1906. In the background is Nelson's* Victory.

prompted not only by the German programme, but also by the tension arising from the Moroccan situation which caused further difficulties in 1911. In that year French forces occupied the capital Fez, in order to suppress a rising against the reigning pro-French Sultan, and proceeded to take complete control of the country. The Kaiser replied by sending the German gunboat *Panther* to Agadir ostensibly to protect German interests. Preparations for war were made in Germany, Britain and France. The situation looked very black indeed and Britain was alarmed both by the threat to France and by the possibility of the Germans obtaining a Mediterranean naval base. After a long period of international tension, the Kaiser drew back and abandoned his claims in Morocco in exchange for half the French Congo. During this period of crisis Britain had refused to remain neutral as the Kaiser demanded and before the German withdrawal Lloyd George gave an emphatic warning to Germany that her policy could lead to war with Britain.

Even at this stage Grey and his colleagues wished to find some basis of agreement with Germany, and Haldane was sent to Berlin for negotiations. However, the Kaiser insisted that Britain must first undertake not to intervene in conflicts between Germany and another Power. This Britain would not accept and almost at the same time reached a naval agreement with France whereby the British Navy was concentrated in the North Sea while the French took care of the Mediterranean.

The Balkan Wars and the outbreak of World War I

The Great War of 1914–18 really began in the Balkans. In 1912, Bulgaria, Serbia, Greece and Montenegro united against Turkey and, in the ensuing conflict, won considerable territory from her. This was the First Balkan War, soon to be followed by the Second in 1913 when the victors quarrelled over their gains. Rumania entered the Second Balkan War in alliance with Serbia, Greece and Montenegro against the Bulgarians, who claimed part of Macedonia which the Serbs refused to give up. The outcome of the war was the defeat of Bulgaria and the strengthening of Serbia, Rumania and Greece, while the Turks took the chance to regain some of the territory lost in the First Balkan War.

Serbia

The Balkan state which had profited most was Serbia. Her gains in Macedonia had encouraged the Serbian nationalists to demand more strongly than ever a port on the Adriatic Sea, so that their land-locked peasant state could develop trade and industry. It was clear that Austria was determined to block Serbian ambitions which were so dangerous to the unity of her multi-national empire. The Serbians were equally determined to stir up the 17,000,000 Serbs and Croats controlled by Austria and used secret terrorist societies like the Black Hand to this end. Serbia was able to act so boldly largely because she could rely on the protection of the greatest Slav power and Austria's rival, Russia.

The Sarajevo assassination

On 28 June 1914 the Archduke Franz Ferdinand of Austria, heir of the Emperor, was murdered with his wife by a student member of the Black Hand society in the Bosnian capital, Sarajevo. On 23 July, nearly a month after the assassination, the Austrian Government sent a 48–hour ultimatum to Serbia demanding the suppression of all anti-Austrian societies, the dismissal of officials hostile to Austria, and the right of Austrian officials and police to enter Serbia to supervise the carrying out of these demands. Germany had given Austria a free hand to frame the ultimatum as strongly as she wished. The Serb reply was conciliatory; it accepted most of the Austrian demands and offered to refer the remaining points to the Hague Court for arbitration. The Serbs, however, could not agree to the entry of Austrian officials and police without surrendering their national independence. Austria declared war on Serbia on 28 July 1914. This action, too, had the agreement of Germany. Russia now mobilized and Germany declared war on Russia on 1 August 1914. This was soon followed by a German declaration of war on France, who had mobilized on 31 July. On 2 August the Germans demanded free passage for German troops through Belgium and, when this was refused, invaded Belgium on 4 August.

British policy
Sir Edward Grey attempted to call a conference of ambassadors in London to settle the Serbian question, but Germany would not accept this. The Cabinet was divided on the question of assisting Russia and France. Sir Edward Grey had, in fact, told the Russian Ambassador on 30 July that Britain might remain neutral. In Britain there was no enthusiasm for war – Serbia meant very little to the British public. However, Sir Edward Grey knew, although the House of Commons did not, that Britain was pledged to protect the north coast of France from naval attack. The attack on Belgium enabled the section of the Government in favour of intervention to win the day. To overcome any popular opposition to British intervention, the dastardly nature of the German invasion was emphasized. In the debate of 3 August, Grey took the line that the treaty of 1839 pledged Britain to defend Belgium and that she must do so. There were, however, resignations from the Government, including those of John Burns and John Morley. Bonar Law pledged Conservative support and John Redmond courageously gave his. J. Ramsay MacDonald, the elected leader of the Parliamentary Labour Party, opposed Britain's entry into the war, but the Labour Party itself disagreed with him, and MacDonald was removed from the leadership. MacDonald and a small socialist minority continued to lead a pacifist opposition to the war.

The British Government sent an ultimatum to Germany demanding her respect for Belgian neutrality. When no answer was received by 11 p.m. on 4 August, Britain declared war on Germany. Largely through the vigour of Lord Haldane, orders for the mobilization of the Army, the reserves and the territorials had gone out on the morning of 3 August.

Some further considerations on the origin of the First World War
It is not very easy or constructive to try to apportion blame for the war. Undoubtedly the Kaiser's policy was dangerously arrogant and aggressive. On the other hand, there were many leaders in France and England such as Lord Fisher who believed in a 'preventive war' against Germany and welcomed the chance to deal with the German menace before it got any stronger. In France many thirsted for revenge for the defeat of 1870 and hoped to regain Alsace-Lorraine. There were apparently powerful forces opposed to the war, for instance the Socialist International Movement, but when war came patriotism proved to be stronger than the international brotherhood of workers. In all countries the majority of the Socialist or Labour Parties voted in favour of the war.

It is now widely accepted that the invasion of Belgium was not a basic reason for Britain's entry. The treaty of neutrality of 1839 had long ceased to have much meaning, for Belgium had been drawn more and more into the diplomatic camp of Britain and France. Both Britain and France had plans to use Belgium as a base in case of war against Germany. These facts were not, however, generally known in 1914 and Parliament was unaware of some of the most vital undertakings to which successive British Governments had committed the nation.

There were also important economic motives for the war. One of these was the rise of the economic power of Germany after the creation of the German Empire in 1870. By 1900 German trade and industry had left French efforts far behind, and Germany was becoming a strong competitor of Great Britain for the world's carrying trade. These facts, combined with the Kaiser's aggressive policy and the highly nationalistic and Pan-German teaching of history in the German schools, alarmed France and led to the efforts of Delcassé to settle old disputes with Britain. In Germany there were already racialists who argued that the German nation was superior to all others, an idea later carried to further extremes by the Nazis. On the other hand, nineteenth-century imperialism produced Britons with equal faith in Anglo-Saxon racial superiority.

Austrian imperialism lay behind the violence in the Balkans which the Germans could have checked but chose to encourage. The Sarajevo murder was regarded as a godsend by a number of Austrian statesmen, for it gave an excuse for the realization of their long-cherished aim to wipe Serbia off the Balkan map altogether. Russia, tied by sentiment to Serbia, may have encouraged the latter to reject the ultimatum. Certainly her decision to mobilize set in motion a chain of events which politicians could do nothing to arrest.

Britain must also bear her share of responsibility. Germany was Britain's principal competitor for world trade and influence. The British Government engaged in open rivalry with the Germans in naval armaments, and gave secret undertakings to the French. Yet Grey never made it clear either to Parliament or to the Germans that Britain would join France. Had her commitment been more explicit it might have checked the Germans and helped to avert the most terrible war men had yet known.

18. The First World War and the Post-War Settlement

The German offensive

The German plan was to strike westward, overrun France in six weeks and then turn eastward against Russia. Its whole success depended on speed. The weight of the German offensive was therefore concentrated on the right wing, which was to move through Belgium, seize the Channel ports, envelop Paris from the north and then turn against the French armies thus isolated on the frontiers of Alsace-Lorraine. The French were aware of this plan, but based their whole strategy on attack – especially the attack through Alsace-Lorraine. However the French attacks against Alsace-Lorraine and in the Ardennes were halted in August, and the offensive was abandoned.

Meanwhile Moltke, the German commander, launched his forces through Belgium. Stubborn resistance at Liège held him up for four days, but thereafter everything was swept before him, despite the resistance of the British Expeditionary Force under Sir John French at Mons. The Germans reached the River Marne and shells began to fall in Paris itself. At this critical point the German command made a radical change of tactics. Moltke suddenly abandoned the sweep round Paris for an attempt to encircle the French centre, and for this purpose the direction of the German advance had to be changed over a wide front. At the same time substantial forces had been diverted to the Eastern Front, where the Russians had moved with unexpected speed. A reserve French army under General Joffre was brought into action from Paris and the British Expeditionary Force, which had been retreating with the French, moved into the gap created by the withdrawal of the German forces across the Marne.

The Battle of the Marne was of great strategic importance in the war. The Germans were pressed back to the River Aisne, both Britain and Russia gained time to muster their forces, and the German hope of a quick victory in the west, on which their whole plan depended, was decisively frustrated. A combination of dogged and heroic defence by the French and British, with the sudden change of German tactics, produced this unexpected result.

Trench warfare

However, attempts by the French and British to turn the German right flank failed, and the Western Front remained almost static for the next four

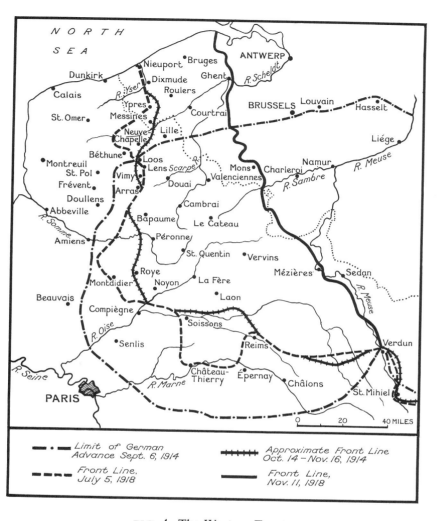

FIG. 4. The Western Front

appalling years. Trenches, barbed wire and concrete emplacements ran across Europe from the Belgian Coast down to Switzerland. Numerous offensives were launched from these positions during the next four years, preceded by intensive artillery bombardments to 'soften up' the opposition. The mass attacks of infantry that followed faced devastating fire from machine-gun emplacements. Later the Germans tried poison gas attacks which were quickly countered by the introduction of the gas-mask. Aircraft first used for reconnaissance began bombing attacks and by 1916 tanks were used in increasing numbers in the efforts to break the deadly stalemate.

The desolation of war:
(above) *machine gunners advance through the remnants of a wood in Flanders;* (below) *front line troops relax in the trenches.*

This trench warfare of the Western Front was the most ghastly and nerve-shattering warfare that men had ever been called upon to endure. The commanders on both sides were slow to realize that little could be achieved by frontal offensives which turned into massacres. The politicians, however, from early in the war sought to open up new fronts and break the deadlock.

The Eastern Front, 1914

On the Eastern Front the Russians invaded East Prussia in early August, but were heavily defeated by the German armies at the Battle of Tannenberg. On the other hand, the Russian armies operating in Galicia scored important successes against the Austrians, while the Serbs managed to recapture their capital, Belgrade.

However, serious political developments made the tasks of the Western Allies even more difficult. In November 1914, Turkey joined the war on the side of Germany, as also did Bulgaria in October 1915. This made the Allied task of maintaining contact with the Russians increasingly difficult, although the decision of Italy to enter the war in May 1915 on the side of Britain, Russia and France was some compensation.

The entry of Turkey on the side of Germany was extremely serious for the Allies. Germany now had on its side an empire of 21,000,000 people whose armed forces had been trained by German officers, and which held critical areas of the Middle East – Mesopotamia, Syria, Palestine and Arabia. Russian ports and shipping in the Black Sea were now open to attack.

The naval war, 1914

From the beginning of the war the British navy went into action against German naval units stationed abroad. Britain's naval superiority was soon proved. The Battle of the Falkland Islands disposed of one of the main German squadrons and very soon no German units of any importance were active outside home waters. This enabled the Allies to transport troops without much interference in the first two years of the war. In the Far East the Japanese completed Britain's work by capturing the German base of Kiaochau.

The year 1915

On the Western Front 1915 opened with a position of stalemate, but in March the British launched an offensive against the German positions at Neuve Chapelle. They advanced about one mile with heavy casualties. An offensive at Festubert in May had similar results. In April the Germans had launched a counter offensive at Ypres with the aid of poison gas. They broke through the French lines but were held by the Canadians. The tactics of Sir John French, the British Commander, had failed, and he was heavily criticized for having held on to an exposed salient at Ypres before the German attack. But the British army in France grew rapidly, numbering twenty-one divisions in France by July 1915. The distractions of the Germans on the Russian front encouraged the Allies to launch another offensive in September. In the British sector the Battle of Loos resulted in appalling casualties and no real success. In December 1915 Sir John French was replaced as British commander by Sir Douglas Haig. During 1915, thanks to the organizing ability and vision of Lord Kitchener who had become Secretary for War, steps were taken to build up a formidable British army of millions of men and to organize labour so that industry could be directed towards the supply of munitions. To this end the National Registration Act was passed in July 1915, and the Ministry of Munitions established in June 1915, but the full effects of these measures were not felt for some time.

The Eastern Front, 1915
On the Eastern Front the year 1915 was equally gloomy for the Allies. The Germans defeated the Russians in February at the Battle of the Masurian Lakes in East Prussia, inflicting a quarter of a million casualties. The Germans then drove the Russians out of Poland and captured Warsaw in August. However, the Russian lines remained intact, and the German hope of knocking them out of the war and concentrating all their forces in the west was not achieved. Nevertheless, the Russian casualties amounted to nearly two million men. The Austrians were also relieved of Russian pressure and, with Bulgaria's help re-captured Belgrade.

The Gallipoli Campaign
The entry of Turkey into the war and the stalemate on the Western Front convinced the British Cabinet, urged on particularly by Lloyd George and Winston Churchill, that an attempt should be made to force a way through the Dardanelles Straits and capture Constantinople.
   The aim was to relieve Russia and to bring the Balkan states over to the Allied side. The plan appeared to be good, but the methods adopted to carry it out proved calamitous. The first bombardment in February was a naval attack only and the attempt of the fleet to force a way through the Straits into the Black Sea was frustrated by mines. Thus forewarned, the Turks and Germans strengthened their shore defences during the next six or seven weeks. In April the Allied force of 75,000 men, including a large contingent of Australians and New Zealanders (the 'Anzacs') landed at Gallipoli. The British force could only hang on to its exposed beach positions, and found it impossible to advance. In December the whole force was evacuated. The campaign had been an extremely costly failure. Simultaneously disaster overtook the British army in Mesopotamia which was forced to surrender at Kut-el-Amara.

The year 1916. The siege of Verdun and the battle of the Somme
In 1916 the Germans decided to attack heavily in the west. The first stage of

the German plan was to attack the key French fortress of Verdun, draw into it the best French forces and destroy them. The purpose of the attack on Verdun was to 'bleed the French army to death' and then to launch a decisive offensive to end the war. In February the attack began. With French casualties in the war already over two million and the British over half a million, the German plan came near to success. But, through the heroic resistance under Pétain, the fortress of Verdun, battered by German artillery and under constant attack, was still held by the French in July. The German attack weakened and was finally broken off. The German casualties had been far greater than their command had expected, and the French had won a great defensive victory.

The greatly enlarged British forces were now ready to relieve the pressure on the French by launching their own offensive. This would also prevent the Germans from sending reinforcements to the Eastern Front where the Russians were having considerable success against the Austrians, and where the Rumanians had now entered the war against Germany. The British offensive on the River Somme began on 1 July 1916, and British casualties on that day alone amounted to 60,000. The artillery bombardment had failed to destroy the German machine-gun posts, and the British soldiers were expected to climb out of their trenches with over 60lbs of equipment on their backs, which reduced their movements to a slow walk. The British tanks were too few to have any decisive effect. However, the offensive was continued by Haig during the autumn at a cost of 450,000 British casualties. The French casualties were 340,000 and the German, 530,000. The Allies gained about seven miles on a thirty-mile front. During the winter the Germans withdrew into the concrete emplacements and

The new weapons of war: infantry advance under cover of a tank and a smoke screen; above, a German bi-plane.

underground defences which made up the Hindenburg Line. The failure of the Allies to break through enabled the Germans to send reinforcements to the Eastern Front to assist Austria, and Rumania was completely overrun.

The Battle of Jutland, 1916

At last, in May 1916, the German High Seas Fleet emerged into the North Sea under the command of Admiral von Scheer, at a time when the British Grand Fleet was sailing through the North Sea. The battle of Jutland on 31 May was indecisive. The British Fleet under Admiral Jellicoe lost 14 vessels and 6,274 men as against the German loss of 11 vessels and 2,545 men. The British public were dismayed and bewildered at the failure to achieved a Trafalgar-like victory, and Jellicoe was heavily criticized for allowing the Germans to escape back to their base. However, he knew that if he lost the Grand Fleet, he would also lose the war, and the German fleet made only one more brief appearance in the North Sea war.

Asquith's resignation, December 1916

The slaughter at the Somme, the stalemate in the west, Gallipoli, the disappointment of Jutland and the death of Lord Kitchener (see p. 198) in whom the British public had great confidence, brought increasing discontent with Asquith's direction of the war. As the result of a series of political intrigues he was succeeded in December 1916 by David Lloyd George. Lloyd George had been successful at the Ministry of Munitions, and his oratory and energy contrasted with the seeming lethargy of Asquith. An inner War Cabinet was set up to direct and co-ordinate the war effort more effectively.

The war in 1917

However, the war in 1917 continued on much the same lines as the previous year, with limited Allied advances on the Western Front at the cost of enormous casualties. In April, Haig launched a British offensive at Arras and succeeded in capturing Vimy Ridge which was part of the Hindenburg Line. Altogether, however, only a few miles had been won. The French offensive, aimed at breaking through the Hindenburg Line and devised by the new French commander-in-chief, Nivelle, failed completely. Nivelle was then replaced by Pétain, whose first task was to suppress the mutinies which broke out in the French Army from sheer war-weariness. Haig's new offensive at Passchendaele (July-November), by which he aimed to reach the Channel ports, ended in a sea of mud with a loss of 300,000 British soldiers. Serious discontent was evident now among the men of the British Army as well as their French comrades and the ghastly failure of Passchendaele had serious political repercussions at home.

In the east the Russian Revolution broke out in March and by November the Russian army was completely ineffective. A British offensive at Cambrai had some success thanks to a better use of tanks, but the Third Battle of Ypres failed to achieve a break-through.

In Italy the Italian armies suffered a severe defeat at the hands of the Austrians at Caporetto, and Allied troops had to be rushed from the Western Front to help them establish a new line on the River Piave fifteen miles from Venice.

Unrestricted submarine warfare, February, 1917

Despite the failure of the Allies to break through on the Western Front, Germany's position was becoming desperate. The British blockade, became tighter. German food supplies dwindled, and the people faced starvation. This situation led to harsher and more desperate efforts by the Germans in their submarine warfare. Up to this time German submarines had usually respected neutral shipping, but in February 1917 they began unrestricted submarine warfare.

The rapid starvation of Britain into surrender was now considered more important than the risk of United States intervention. In April 1917, the toll of Allied shipping had risen to 875,000 tons. During the year two million tons more shipping was sunk than was constructed.

The entry of the United States into the war, April 1917

In April 1917 the United States entered the war, but Germany still hoped to achieve the surrender of Britain before American forces could reach Europe in any effective numbers. They almost succeeded and were only prevented by the aid given to the Allies by the American navy, by the development of anti-submarine devices and by the use of the convoy system in the Atlantic.

Altogether the year 1917 was as black as 1914 for the Allies, but in the long run the German unrestricted submarine warfare proved to be a great mistake.

The war in the Middle East, 1917

There was one gleam of light for the Allies. The Turks were being beaten. In Mesopotamia, General Maude captured Baghdad, and avenged Kut. In Arabia, Colonel Lawrence was uniting the Arabs against the Turkish overlords. In December 1917, General Allenby entered Jerusalem.

The Treaty of Brest-Litovsk, 3 March 1918

Following the collapse of the Russian front and the Bolshevik revolution of 7 November 1917, an armistice between the Central Powers and Russia was negotiated in December 1917. The Treaty of Brest-Litovsk, which was virtually a dictated peace and showed clearly how Germany would treat a defeated enemy, was signed on 3 March 1918. By this Russia abandoned Poland, the Baltic Provinces, Lithuania, the Ukraine and Transcaucasia. Of these, the European provinces remained under German domination until the collapse of the Central Powers. A similar Treaty, the Treaty of Bucharest 7 May 1918 despoiled Rumania, a tardy entrant into the war on the side of the Allies. She lost the Dobrudja to Bulgaria and the Carpathian Passes to Austria. These she regained in the peace treaties of 1918–19.

1918 and the end of the war

At the beginning of 1918 the German position was seriously weakened, not through military failure, but through economic privation, and the need to support allies who were already in difficulty. Social unrest was spreading in Austria-Hungary whose economic resources were insufficient and whose food supplies were largely being directed into Germany. The Turks were facing defeat in the Middle East. However, the defeat of Russia had freed half a million German troops for the Western Front and it was here that Ludendorf planned to launch what was to prove to be the last German offensive of the war.

The Allies, led by Lloyd George and Clemenceau, the French Prime Minister, had secured the appointment of a supreme commander, Marshal Foch, for all Allied forces on the Western Front and preparations were made to meet the impending German effort. Ludendorf's plan was to strike at the junction of the British and French armies at Arras. The German offensive began on March 21, spreading along the whole Allied front. It continued until July. The British army on the Somme was almost annihilated, but the Germans failed to capture Arras and a second offensive in Flanders failed to capture Ypres. Yet the impetus of the German attack carried them to the Marne within fifty miles of Paris. In the course of the offensive the Germans took 250,000 prisoners and shells were fired into Paris. Marshal Foch held back the counter-offensive until the German drive was exhausted; the Germans had lost more than 500,000 men by the time their forces reached the Marne, and at no period in their advance did they achieve an actual break-through. By the end of June 700,000 American troops had arrived in France, and by August the American army was ready for action. The Germans had lost their best reserves and their new troops were young and inexperienced. The acute food shortage and an appalling influenza epidemic were weakening their effort even more than that of the Allies.

The Allied counter-offensive and the collapse of the Central Powers

On 21 August Marshal Foch launched the Allied counter-offensive beginning with an attack by the British forces under Haig at Amiens, where hundreds of tanks were now decisively used. The British attack drove deep into the Hindenburg Line in the north and the Americans successfully attacked near Verdun. In September these partial offensives developed into one general advance. The Americans successfully drove through the Argonne Forest and the British once again took Cambrai. A great French offensive now began and the German position quickly became desperate. Firstly, the Bulgarians, defeated by the British army from Salonika, capitulated on 30 September. Secondly, the Turks doubly defeated in Syria and Mesopotamia gave in on 31 October. Then the crumbling Hapsburg monarchy collapsed after defeat in Venetia and the Trentino. In Germany itself mutinies broke out in the German army and at the naval base at Kiel. Revolution smouldered in the major cities. The Kaiser fled to neutral Holland and an armistice was signed with the Allies on 11 November 1918 with Germany itself still almost free from invasion.

THE HOME FRONT

At the outbreak of the war Britain was reasonably well prepared thanks to the work of Fisher, Haldane and Churchill. Some members of Asquith's Cabinet thought that the war would end in six months but Lord Kitchener, who became Secretary for War on the outbreak of war, foresaw a protracted struggle. His forceful recruiting drive had enrolled a million volunteers by December 1914. Three men were above all responsible for the war effort in its early stages – Lord Kitchener, Winston Churchill, the First Lord of the Admiralty, and Asquith. Lloyd George was still Chancellor of the Exchequer, and one of his first tasks was to increase income tax from 9d to 1s. 6d in the pound.

The complacency with which many viewed the prospect of war was soon shattered by the reverses and terrible casualties on all fronts. The first political crisis arose over the shell shortage on the Western Front, and was soon followed by the resignation of Lord Fisher, the First Sea Lord, because he disagreed with the Gallipoli strategy, a disagreement which was

The Home Front: women workers in an engineering shop.

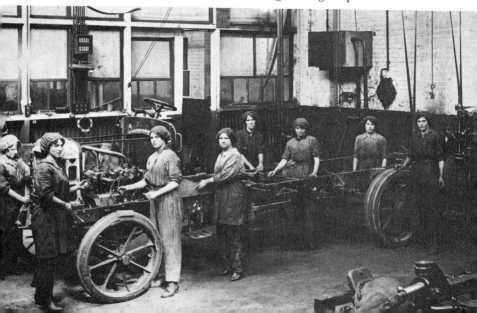

tragically justified. The Conservative Party was generally in favour of the Western Front policy while Lloyd George and others wanted to open up another front farther east. Asquith's reply to these criticisms was to form a Coalition Government containing twelve Liberals, eight Conservatives and one Labour Minister (Arthur Henderson at the Board of Education). Kitchener, who was in favour of the western strategy, remained Secretary for War and Lloyd George was given the newly created Ministry of Munitions. In this key post Lloyd George showed outstanding drive and initiative, forcing employers to speed up their efforts and persuading the reluctant trade unions to accept women workers in the factories, in transport and on the land.

Conscription
As the war progressed in 1915 the serious losses of the British Expeditionary Force, most of which was destroyed by mid-1915, forced the Government to face the problem of conscription. Kitchener was opposed to it and placed his faith in the voluntary principle, but the new Chief of the Imperial General Staff, Sir William Robertson, was strongly in favour of conscription and was supported in this by Lloyd George. After attempts to devise other schemes had failed, full conscription was introduced in January 1916. In June 1916, Lord Kitchener was drowned at sea on his way to visit the Russian front. This was a serious blow to British morale, for Kitchener was highly esteemed by the general public, though not by the leading politicians. His place as Secretary for War was taken by Lloyd George.

Criticism of Asquith. Lloyd George becomes Prime Minister
The year 1916 was another very bleak one for Britain and there was ever increasing criticism of Asquith's conduct of the war. The main complaint was that he was indecisive. He had made little change in the old peace-time methods of government, beyond the creation of a Coalition, and continued to put all important questions for discussion before the whole Cabinet, which led to long discussions, personal feuds and dangerous delays. The leading public critics of Asquith were Lloyd George, Sir Edward Carson (of Ulster fame) and the newspaper magnates Max Aitken (*Daily Express*) and Lord Northcliffe (*The Times* and the *Daily Mail*). After much discussion and political intrigue, Lloyd George became Prime Minister of a new Coalition.

The Easter Rebellion in Dublin, 24–28 April 1916
Ireland was a serious problem throughout the war and particularly in 1916. The Germans promised support for a rebellion and on 20 April 1916 Sir Roger Casement, a former British Consul who was a fervent Irish Republican, landed in southern Ireland from Germany where he had been endeavouring to form an Irish Brigade to fight the British. He was immediately arrested, and later brought to trial for treason and executed on

Curious Dubliners inspect the damage in Sackville Street after the Easter Rebellion.

3 August 1916. Casement's arrival was timed to coincide with a country-wide rebellion, but owing to lack of German support this was called off. However, there was a rising on Easter Monday 24 April in Dublin. The General Post Office was seized and an Irish Republic proclaimed. After four days of bitter fighting in which 100 British soldiers and 450 Irish were killed, the Provisional Government of the Irish Republic surrendered. Sixteen of the leaders were court-martialled. These, with Casement, were the martyrs for Irish freedom; though they failed in 1916, the rising and their deaths hastened the coming of the Irish Free State.

That Ireland could not be treated in all respects as was the rest of the United Kingdom was shown by the fact that conscription was not applied to Ireland until 1918, and then was soon withdrawn as it was a failure owing to nationalist opposition.

Lloyd George as war-time Prime Minister

Lloyd George was outstanding in his new role. The vigour he infused into the war effort contributed fundamentally to the defeat of Germany. He introduced new ideas when they were urgently needed and ruthlessly axed colleagues who opposed him or were inefficient. He, like Churchill in the Second World War, could rally the nation with compelling oratory and was at the same time a brilliant administrator.

Organizational changes

Lloyd George immediately created a small War Cabinet consisting of himself, Bonar Law, Lords Milner and Curzon, Sir Edward Carson and (mainly to sustain the support of the trade union and Labour movement) Arthur Henderson. He also kept in closer touch with the Dominion Prime

Ministers. Faced with labour unrest in South Wales, he promised to nationalize the coal mines. No longer relying on purely political appointments, he chose leading business men to deal with food supplies, the naval blockade and other aspects of the war effort. He himself was the driving force behind the new convoy system (see p. 195) aimed at defeating the German submarines. He also took unpopular measures which were essential for the war effort. For example, he reduced the consumption of alcohol by increasing taxation and cutting licensing hours of public houses. In 1917 he introduced restrictions on restaurant meals, controlled the distribution of basic foods, and in 1918 introduced rationing. On the wealthier classes he imposed higher super tax and an excess profits tax. National Savings and War Bonds were introduced with great success. He established the important new ministries of Air, of Pensions, of Labour and of Food. In 1918, by the Representation of the People Act, he gave the vote to all men of 21 and over, and he recognized and rewarded the great services of women in the war effort by giving the vote to most women over the age of thirty.

Lloyd George and military strategy
The main decisions on military strategy were in the hands of Haig and Robertson, and Lloyd George's powers were limited. Both Haig and Robertson believed in the possibility of victory on the Western Front, but Lloyd George was sceptical. After the ghastly failure of Passchendaele, he was even more convinced of the basic error of the policies of the higher command, and at times withheld supplies of ammunition and reinforcements from Haig. In order to reduce Haig's influence, Lloyd George pressed for the creation of one Supreme Commander on the Western Front. In February 1918 Lloyd George succeeded in replacing Robertson by Sir Henry Wilson as Chief of the Imperial General Staff. Wilson was in favour of the eastern strategy, but before any radical re-direction of British forces could take place, the last German offensive made concentration on the Western Front imperative. However, Haig was forced to accept Marshal Foch as Supreme Commander there.

The general importance of Lloyd George during the Great War
There can be little doubt of Lloyd George's greatness as a war Prime Minister. His personal failings were considerable, but his tendency to intrigue, his ruthlessness, lack of loyalty to his friends and rash and demagogic promises were less significant than his great abilities. Indeed, it could be argued that these critical times demanded ruthless efficiency and the abandonment of political and personal loyalties where necessary. It was precisely this flexibility which enabled Lloyd George to cut through official obstruction and conservative attitudes. He greatly extended state control, despite opposition from Conservatives in his Government. He advocated or introduced harsh and unpopular measures of regimentation –

price control, rationing and conscription. As Minister of Munitions in the earlier years he overcame opposition to his methods from manufacturers, the trade unions and from the War Office. In introducing the convoy system (see p. 195) he had to overcome serious obstruction by the Admiralty. He had an astute awareness of the importance of the trade unions and the Labour Party and maintained Labour representation in the Coalition Government. At the end of the war he was willing, also, under pressure from the Labour Party, to make promises of radical post-war reforms.

Above all, Lloyd George was keenly aware of the new political and social forces at work in the terrible conditions created in Europe by the war. 'Europe,' he said 'is filled with revolutionary ideas. A feeling not of depression but of passion and revolt reigns in the breasts of the working class against the conditions that prevailed before the war.' This understanding led him to hold the 'Khaki Election' of 1918 and to cash in on the goodwill created by victory before it vanished in the inevitable disillusionment with the post-war world.

The Treaty of Versailles, 1919

The state of Europe at the end of 1918 was appalling. Besides the vast physical damage which had completely ruined huge areas of eastern France and Belgium and a deathroll of at least 13,000,000 men, famine was widespread in Germany, Russia and the Central European states. In Russia the Communist Government of Lenin had gained control and Communist Parties were attempting to seize power all over Europe. Against this background the Versailles Peace Conference opened in January 1919.

The main terms of the peace settlement with Germany were devised by Lloyd George (Britain), Georges Clemenceau (France), Woodrow Wilson (President of the U.S.A.) and Orlando (Italy) – the Council of Four. President Wilson had formulated his own ideas in the famous Fourteen Points, of which the most important was national self-determination but his democratic principles found little favour with Clemenceau who cynically remarked that Christ had ten commandments but Wilson fourteen. Clemenceau, whose political career went back to the Franco-Prussian War and the Paris Commune of 1871, was mainly concerned to maintain the complete and permanent subjection of Germany and the extraction of every possible penny in reparations. The problem for Lloyd George was to strike some happier mean between the idealism of Wilson and the anti-German ferocity of Clemenceau (appropriately named 'the Tiger').

The main settlements

Clemenceau demanded that Germany should lose not only Alsace-Lorraine, but the Rhineland, the Saar, Upper Silesia, Danzig and East Prussia. This would have deprived Germany not only of territory but also of her most important sources of coal and iron. Both Lloyd George and

FIG. 5. The Versailles Settlement in Central Europe, 1919

Wilson considered these demands too extreme, and eventually a compromise was reached. The Saar was placed under international control for fifteen years, after which a plebiscite would decide its future. In the meantime the control of the Saar coal mines went to France. Danzig became a Free City under the control of the newly created League of Nations. A plebiscite in Upper Silesia showed a majority in favour of Germany, but a substantial minority in favour of Poland. Eventually about a third of the territory was incorporated in Poland, as well as the province of Posen. Poland was recreated as an independent State, and now had a 'corridor' running to the sea and dividing East Prussia from the remainder of Germany. This was to create much future difficulty. The plebiscite was used again to determine the wishes of the people of Schleswig, and the predominantly Danish part voted to return to Denmark.

Germany was declared guilty of provoking the war. She lost all her colonies, which were handed over to the League of Nations, and distributed to the conquering powers as mandates. She was required to pay the Allies a vast, indeed impossible, sum in reparations – part of which was to be delivered in the form of ships, coal, chemicals, etc. The total reparations were fixed at £6,500,000,000. Germany was also disarmed except for a force of 100,000 without heavy artillery or aircraft.

In eastern Europe Austria was reduced to a small country of 6,500,000 inhabitants, all that remained of the old Austro-Hungarian Empire. Out of this empire were formed the independent states of Hungary, Czechoslovakia and Yugoslavia. The Turks were allowed to retain Constantinople and a small area around it, but otherwise were confined to Asia Minor. The whole of the Turkish territory in Thrace was given to Greece, and Rumania gained Transylvania, Bukovina and Bessarabia. In northern Europe the small new States of Esthonia, Latvia and Lithuania were formed along the Baltic coast from the old Czarist Empire, and Finland gained complete independence from Russia.

Although an effort was made to give 'natural' frontiers to the new states created, the settlement also left a problem of 'minorities' within certain states, and this was to cause great difficulties in the future; for instance Italy gained the Lower Tyrol containing some 200,000 Germans and the Istrian Peninsula containing 360,000 Yugoslavs. In the new Poland there were 10,000,000 people who were not Polish, including 2,500,000, Germans. In Czechoslovakia there was a powerful minority of Germans.

The League of Nations

An integral part of the Versailles settlement was the creation of the League of Nations with its headquarters at Geneva in Switzerland. This had been the cherished aim of President Wilson, and for the first time an organization was created whose main purpose was to prevent war and secure the peaceful settlement of international disputes. At the same time it aimed at the steady reduction of armaments. The Peace Treaty had disarmed

Germany, but the disarming of the Allies proved more difficult. France prevented any scheme for disarmament on land, but the Washington Conference of 1921 produced a formula for naval disarmament by which Britain, America, Japan, France and Italy agreed to the ratio of capital ships $5 : 5 : 3 : 1\frac{3}{4} : 1\frac{3}{4}$. It was at least a sign that Britain was prepared to reduce her armaments where she was particularly strong and accept a new role in international affairs.

The Council of the League was to consist of the representatives of five Great Powers and four lesser ones. The Council was to meet at least once yearly and more frequently if necessary. The Assembly of the League consisted of representatives of all the member states. The two main Powers excluded from the League were Germany and Russia. The first Secretary General was an Englishman, Sir Eric Drummond.

The Covenant of the League, besides binding its members not to resort to war to settle international disputes, contained the 'sanctions' clause by which other members were to impose economic and, if necessary, military sanctions, upon any member guilty of aggression.

On his return to U.S.A., Wilson was met by a hostile Congress which refused both to guarantee the European peace treaties and to enter the League of Nations. This was a crushing blow to Wilson's ideals and he died soon afterwards, a broken-hearted man. The United States returned to political isolation, a bad beginning to the post-war era and to the League of Nations on which Wilson and many others had pinned their hopes for the future.

19. Post-War Britain and the First Labour Government, 1918–24

Effects of the war on Britain

British war casualties were very heavy. About 750,000 men from the United Kingdom were killed, and about 200,000 from the Empire. Air-raid casualties and coastal bombardment resulted in 1,500 civilian casualties. Owing to the high rate of casualties among officers, many potential leaders in all walks of life were lost, and it took another generation to make up for it. There were great material losses too. Forty per cent of British shipping had been sunk. House-building had been held up by the demands of war, and in 1919 about 600,000 new houses were needed. The National Debt had increased enormously, and the interest on it to be paid by the Government accounted for at least 50 per cent of income from taxation, whereas before the war it had accounted for only 14 per cent. Post-war Governments continued to be saddled with this enormous debt which reduced the funds available for the social services. However, Government control had been widely extended and the new Ministries of Transport, Labour, Pensions and Air remained a permanent part of the life of the country, although some other wartime departments were abandoned.

The 'General Election', 1918

Lloyd George immediately held an election. At the height of his popularity as the man who had 'won the war', he was determined to cash in on the emotions the war had created. A member of his wartime Government, George Barnes, produced the slogan 'Hang the Kaiser' and Lloyd George promised 'A land fit for heroes to live in'. In the anti-German atmosphere of 1918 and the hopes raised by the 'war to end war' these slogans and promises were effective vote-winners. Although doubtful about the wisdom of exacting the maximum reparations from Germany, Lloyd George himself did not repudiate the extreme anti-German demands of some of his followers. Moreover, although the Labour Party had left the Coalition, Lloyd George had the support of the Conservatives under Bonar Law and of his own section of the Liberal Party. Between them they drew up a joint list of candidates so that Conservatives and Lloyd George Liberals would not be fighting each other.

It is not surprising therefore that the Coalition won an overwhelming victory, with 484 members, of whom 338 were Conservatives, 136 Lloyd George Liberals and 10 other Coalition supporters. The Asquith Liberals gained only 26 seats, but the Labour Party increased its representation from 39 to 59. There were 48 non-Coalition Conservatives, 9 Independents and 7 Irish Nationalists. The 73 Sinn Fein candidates elected for Ireland refused to take their seats and set up their own Parliament in Dublin. In fact the Conservatives had a majority without the help of Lloyd George Liberals so that although he remained Prime Minister he was forced to modify his policies to please his powerful allies. Lloyd George wished for a conciliatory policy abroad towards Germany and Soviet Russia, and at home towards the demands of the trade unions, but Conservative opposition to this policy was determined. It was mainly Conservative pressure which resulted in the disappearance by 1921 of the wartime ministries of National Service, Reconstruction, Munitions, Food and Shipping.

Lloyd George and the peace treaties
Lloyd George played a major part at the Versailles Peace Conference, and a number of important settlements were the direct result of his influence. His policy of moderation was seen most clearly when he was faced by Clemenceau's demands that Germany should lose the Rhineland, the Saar, Upper Silesia, Danzig and East Prussia (see p. 203). Lloyd George also did something to soften the demand for excessive reparations. He distrusted the French proposals for an immediate assessment of Germany's liabilities and secured the appointment of a special Reparations Commission which eventually reported its findings in 1921. By this delay he modified what could have been a policy of mere revenge against Germany in the heated atmosphere immediately after the war. Although the Commission fixed the total liabilities of Germany at the colossal sum of £6,500,000,000, in 1919 it would have been even more. In fact a committee of British advisers appointed by Lloyd George in 1918 had suggested a payment of £24,000,000,000. Lloyd George was later blamed for the bad economic results of reparations, but in fact he sought a reasonable settlement and faced heavy criticism in the House of Commons as a result.

Lloyd George and Soviet Russia
The policy to be adopted towards Soviet Russia was a matter of great controversy. Several governments were determined to destroy Communism before it could make further headway. This was the official policy of France, of the U.S.A. and of Japan, all of whom sent expeditions to different parts of Russia. Lloyd George himself criticized the French policy and was reluctant to involve Britain, but here again he was unwilling openly to resist the anti-Bolshevik elements in his Government, of whom Winston Churchill, Secretary for War, was the most forceful spokesman. Eventually over £100 million worth of arms were supplied to the anti-Bolshevik or White leaders Denikin and Kolchak, and British expeditions were sent to

Archangel, Murmansk and Baku. But things went badly for the interventionist forces, and there was considerable Labour opposition in Britain. There was similar unrest in France and a mutiny on French warships in the Black Sea. By the end of 1919 all British troops were withdrawn, with nothing to show but the waste of many millions of pounds at a time when Britain was struggling to recover from the effects of war. Although failure was the result of Conservative pressure, Lloyd George lost much personal prestige as a result. The advance of the Labour Party (they won thirteen by-elections between 1918 and 1922) was partly attributable to their strong campaign against the Coalition's Russian policy and the increasing feeling in the country that Lloyd George was tied to Conservative policies.

Social unrest after 1918

Immediately after the end of the war serious trouble arose over demobilization. The Government's first plan was to release all those who held key civilian posts – that is, skilled men and those having important executive posts. Unfortunately, these men had been the last to be called up, and were now to be the first out. This caused such discontent that there were mutinies in the army both in Britain and in France, and in one demonstration that really alarmed the Government, 3,000 men occupied the Horse Guards Parade in protest. Rather than use force to repress this discontent, Churchill as Secretary for War, agreed to the principle of 'first in, first out'. By the middle of 1919 about 4,000,000 men were demobilized, and at that time, in the post-war industrial boom, they were quickly absorbed into jobs. Women war workers were everywhere displaced, and by 1921 there were in fact fewer women employed in industry than in 1913.

Further social discontent arose from the Government's policy of removing wartime controls on prices, profits and wages. Lloyd George himself supported this policy of a return to the uncontrolled economy of pre-1914 but it resulted in a vicious spiral of inflation – higher prices, higher profits and higher wages. The trade unions in this situation were determined to defend and improve the workers' position at all costs, and in 1919 the old 'triple alliance' of the miners, railwaymen and transport workers was re-formed. Lloyd George was faced with serious industrial unrest, and during 1919–20 there were over 2,000 strikes. Lloyd George staved off a miners' strike by appointing a special commission under Sir Sankey to inquire into the mines. When its members could not agree (some demanded nationalization, others complete private ownership and the removal of Government control), Lloyd George maintained Government control of the mines and guaranteed the seven hour day by Act of Parliament. A national railway strike occurred in September 1919, and Lloyd George once again intervened to give the railwaymen their demands. A special Commission of Inquiry was set up by Lloyd George, and as a result dockers' wages and working conditions were greatly improved. In general, Lloyd George had recognized the power of the 'triple alliance' and was prepared to oppose the 'die-hard' employers rather than force a national strike. These policies were disliked by many of his Coalition colleagues. The miners were led by the militant A. J. Cook, and there was a continuous and bitter dispute between workers and owners. Even the 'die-hard' Lord Birkenhead, while condemning the miners, held no brief for the mine-owners. 'I should,' he declared, 'call them [the miners] the stupidest men in England if I had not previously had to deal with the owners.' The problems of the miners grew suddenly worse when the post-war boom in British industry collapsed (see Chapter 20). Prices fell and trade stagnated, producing a million unemployed by February 1921 and two million by June of the same year. At this point Lloyd George handed back both the railways and the mines to private control. The miners wanted a national wage-rate, but the mine-owners demanded what was known as the 'district rate', which would have meant a drastic reduction of wages in some mining areas. The owners began a lock-out of the miners on 1 April, 1921. On 15 April, the 'triple alliance' partners of the miners, the railwaymen and transport workers, called off the strike they had threatened in support of the miners. This left the miners isolated, their wages fell, and many other workers suffered wage reductions. Lloyd George had failed to bring industrial peace on terms favourable to the workers, and the credit he had earned with trade unionists in the earlier years was lost. He was bitterly attacked for not having supported the nationalization of both the railways and the mines. The conditions which produced the General Strike of 1926 had already been created.

Social reform under the Lloyd George Coalition
In a number of directions there was considerable social advance. The Minister of Health, Christopher Addison (later to join the Labour Party), carried through a building programme of over 200,000 new houses in three years – a considerable achievement for that period, for he had to stir the local authorities into action and find the money to assist them. But even then the shortage of houses in 1922 was worse than in 1918 on account of the high post-war marriage rate. This was another factor in the increasing influence of the Labour Party, which in by-elections continued to win votes from the Liberals. Lloyd George improved the social conditions of the workers in another important direction by a new National Insurance Act in 1920. In the face of mass unemployment the insurance system proved totally inadequate. The great weakness of the 1911 system was its very limited range of benefit. For example, unemployment benefit could only be paid to a worker for a total of fifteen weeks in any one year, and six weeks' contributions only guaranteed benefit for one week. In the new Act the benefits of sickness and unemployment insurance were extended to 12 million workers, whereas the Social Insurance Act of 1911 had covered only 3 million workers in building, engineering and shipbuilding. The 1920

Act also allowed a period of unemployment benefit for which no contributions had been paid, and this benefit was then extended to wives and families. By this process the mass of workers were supposed to be freed from their dependence on the old Poor Law in periods of unemployment, but many found this benefit inadequate and still had to apply for Poor Relief.

Lloyd George was particularly concerned with this problem of unemployment. He stressed the need for a healthy economic recovery of Europe, and especially of Germany. If Europe was prosperous, then Britain was sure to benefit. For this reason he was opposed to the extreme demands for reparations from Germany made by the French Prime Minister Poincaré, and at the important international conference at Genoa in April, 1922, he tried, though unsuccessfully, to reduce the French demands. At the same conference he tried to secure the British and European recognition of Soviet Russia and to bring that country into the 'comity of nations'. However, to this recognition he attached the condition that Russia should pay her debts to her former Allies. The Russian delegation retorted that the Powers who had intervened in support of the Whites should pay compensation for the damage done by their forces in Russia. In the midst of all this, the Russians and Germans signed the Treaty of Rapallo by which Germany recognized the Soviet Government as the legal Government of Russia and all claims and counter-claims between them were wiped out. The Russo-German treaty, which alarmed the anti-German and anti-Communist elements in Britain, was blamed on both Lloyd George and the French, although in fact the Russians and Germans had been negotiating since the beginning of the year. Nevertheless, it was true that Lloyd George had failed to achieve his avowed aims at the conference. Instead, the 'nightmare' of a Russian-German alliance faced the other Western Powers.

Lloyd George and Ireland

Irish problems more than any other issue undermined Lloyd George's position as leader of a Coalition containing Unionists, many of whom opposed even mild Home Rule, let alone to the independence which the Irish eventually gained.

In 1918 the Sinn Fein members elected to the British Parliament refused to take their seats, set up the Dail in Dublin and proclaimed the Republic of Ireland. De Valera, the only surviving leader of the 1916 rebellion, was the first President. Throughout Ireland the republicans established their own courts and administration alongside the British, and gradually they were recognized by most of the people. This left the British administration with its centre at the Castle in Dublin increasingly isolated. In general, this peaceful take-over was what the Sinn Fein party wanted, but inevitably there were clashes between the Irish Republican Army, whose most able leader was Michael Collins, and the Royal Irish Constabulary. Collins was also at this time Minister of Finance in De Valera's Government, and had built up for himself a reputation for energy and daring, and for miraculous escapes from the English authorities. Fighting broke out in earnest in January 1919, when the I.R.A. ambushed a cart containing gelignite and escorted by two policemen, who were shot dead. From that point guerrilla warfare went on without much pause for two years. In March 1919 the Lord Mayor of Cork, who also commanded the Cork Brigade of the I.R.A. was murdered by the police, and a verdict of 'wilful murder' was returned against Lloyd George himself and the British administration in Ireland. Violence and bitterness spread on both sides. Michael Collins was particularly effective in running what was called his 'Irish Mail'. Arms and ammunition, obtained in Britain and Germany, were brought into Ireland, and Collins would ride on his bicycle down to Kingstown Harbour, supervise loading on lorries and take the lot openly into Dublin – to such an extent was the Customs Service penetrated by I.R.A. agents.

The British Government soon reinforced the Royal Irish Constabulary with recently demobilized soldiers wearing Khaki uniforms and black belts who were known as the 'Black and Tans', and a further force of Auxiliaries – ex-officers. The Black and Tans and Auxiliaries killed prisoners, burnt Irish farmsteads and massacred their inhabitants in reprisal for Irish acts of terrorism. Brigadier-General Crozier, appointed to command the Auxiliaries in July 1920, found them, in his own words, 'employed to murder, rob, loot and burn up the innocent because they could not catch a few guilty men on the run'.

This horrifying situation told heavily against Lloyd George and the Coalition, and the Labour Party denounced the whole Irish policy of the Government. Lloyd George wanted Dominion status for Ireland and at one point in negotiations with De Valera was prepared to see Ulster incorporated into an Irish Free State, but the Ulstermen and their Unionist allies would never have allowed that. When a treaty was eventually settled, De Valera repudiated it and walked out of the Dail with a large minority of its members. He was succeeded as President by Arthur Griffith, who had negotiated the treaty between Great Britain and Ireland with the help of Collins in December 1921. The Irish Free State officially came into existence exactly one year later when the British Parliament approved her new constitution. By the treaty Ireland received full independence in twenty-six counties, while six of the counties of Ulster remained under the British Crown, with M.P.s at Westminster and their own Parliament for local affairs. Southern Ireland became completely independent with something very like dominion status. The British Government held three 'treaty ports' for the use of the navy – Queenstown, Berehaven and Lough Swilly. The members of the Dail took an oath acknowledging the 'common citizenship of Ireland with Great Britain' and her membership of the British Commonwealth of Nations and a Governor-General was appointed by the King. This form of Dominion status was repudiated at a later date by the Free State, which became in the 1930's virtually an independent republic only loosely bound to the Commonwealth. The treaty was not accepted by De Valera's followers who began a civil war against its supporters, a war which continued after the last British troops were withdrawn in December 1922. Before the end of this struggle in April 1923 Michael Collins, who stood by the treaty, was shot by the breakaway I.R.A. and Griffiths died of overwork. However, it was the supporters of the treaty under a new leader, Cosgrave, who eventually won the civil war.

It has been said that Ireland ruined Lloyd George. He never entirely recovered his reputation amongst the Liberals after the horrors of the Black and Tan period when he appeared to be pursuing methods dictated by the extreme Unionists. On the other hand, many Unionists deplored the Treaty which he negotiated in the end. The Irish question produced great strains within the Coalition Government, with opinions as divided and violent as in the days of Gladstone.

The end of the economic boom and growing difficulties for the Coalition

The short period of post-war prosperity ended in 1922, and there was large-scale unemployment in the old basic industries. This, of course, reduced the revenue of the Government, and there were demands for economy in public expenditure. In any case, the prevailing fiscal theory was that heavy taxation hindered the growth of investment and purchasing power. This nineteenth-century belief dominated economic thinking right into the 1930's. Lloyd George appointed a special economy committee under the chairmanship of Sir Eric Geddes, and this committee recommended drastic cuts in public services. The 'Geddes axe', as it was nicknamed, descended with special force on education. One of the most progressive Acts of the Coalition Government had been the Education Act of 1918 introduced by the President of the Board of Education, H. A. L. Fisher. By this Act the school-leaving age was raised to fourteen and free places were assigned in the secondary grammar schools for 'scholarship' pupils. By 1922 about 34 per cent of grammar school places were taken by these pupils. Fisher also planned a system of continuation schools for pupils up to sixteen. At the same time the Act introduced a national and uniform scale of teachers' salaries, and the Burnham Committee was set up as the negotiating body. However, the 'Geddes axe' reduced the number of free places, cut down salaries and halted educational building.

Lloyd George's difficulties mounted month by month. His unpopular economy measures strengthened the Labour Party, his main competitor for the votes of the working class. Trouble in the mines, in transport and at the docks flared up again with the depression, and he was far less successful in dealing with it than in the previous years. The fact that civil war continued in Ireland, even after the treaty, weighed heavily against him in the eyes of the Coalition Conservatives, for it appeared that his policy of conciliation was failing. The Genoa Conference (see p. 209) witnessed the failure of other policies on which he staked much of his own reputation. To both

Socialist and Liberal opinion in the country it became increasingly clear that he was completely dependent on the Conservatives. At the same time many Coalition Conservatives feared that he would divide their own party as he had already divided the Liberals. Finally the Chanak incident put an end to his leadership of the Coalition.

The Chanak incident

This crisis arose as the result of events in Turkey stemming from the Treaty of Sèvres (1920) which was part of the general Versailles settlement. In Turkey a national leader had arisen in the person of Mustapha Kemal, or Kemal Ataturk, who had deposed the Sultan and declared a republic of which he was President. His aim was to modernize Turkey and to undo the Treaty of Sèvres which had placed the forces of France, Italy and Greece in control of much of Asia Minor. As a result of nationalist pressure, France and Italy withdrew from their zones, but the Greeks remained in control of Smyrna. Kemal defeated the Greeks, occupied Smyrna (the scene of an atrocious massacre of the Greeks), and moved towards the Straits at Chanak which was part of a neutral zone held by British forces under General Harington. Lloyd George failed to gain French or even Dominion help against the Turks, but fortunately neither the Turks nor Harington started fighting. Eventually British troops were withdrawn and the new Turkey was recognized by the Treaty of Lausanne in 1923.

Lloyd George found himself under fire from all sides. He was criticized for giving in to the Turks and abandoning Britain's Greek allies; he was also attacked for a dangerous and irresponsible policy which had nearly led to an unnecessary war and one in which Britain would have been completely isolated. Coming as it did on top of so many other grievances, the crisis finally persuaded many Conservatives that Lloyd George was a dangerous and unnecessary political ally and that the Coalition should end.

Among the Conservatives who felt this way was Stanley Baldwin. Baldwin was only a junior member of the party, but he persuaded the highly respected Bonar Law, who had resigned from the Ministry and his party leadership because of ill-health, to come out against the continuation of the Coalition. However, the new leader Austen Chamberlain and many senior Conservatives such as Lord Birkenhead remained loyal to Lloyd George. On 19 October 1922, a vital meeting of Conservative M.P.s was held at the Carlton Club. The vote was 187–87 in favour of ending the Coalition. Lloyd George at once resigned. Austen Chamberlain gave up the leadership of the Conservative Party to Bonar Law and with it all hopes of becoming Prime Minister. The General Election of 1922 which followed showed the change in party strengths very clearly. The Lloyd George Liberals won only 57 seats, the Asquith Liberals 60, the Labour Party 142 and two Communists also won seats. The Conservatives held 347 seats and thus had a clear overall majority. They formed a

Government under Bonar Law and for the first time in its history the Labour Party became the official opposition in Parliament. James Ramsay MacDonald, who had been in the political wilderness during the war, was elected leader of the Parliamentary Labour Party.

Stanley Baldwin

Bonar Law resigned in 1923 and was succeeded by the industrialist Stanley Baldwin, to the acute disappointment and surprise of Lord Curzon, the senior member of the Government. Baldwin, whose bowler hat and pipe came to typify the popular conception of the sane, balanced, common-sense Englishman, averse to extremes of both Right and Left, was to play a significant part in the development of the Conservative Party over the next fourteen years. His industrial interests led him to sympathize with the idea of protective tariffs, and to move away from Britain's long established Free Trade policies. Significantly he appointed Neville Chamberlain, son of Joseph and half-brother of Austen, as Chancellor of the Exchequer. Their new trade policy represented such a radical change in economic thinking that a general election was fought mainly on this issue in December 1923. Both the Liberal factions and the Labour Party campaigned, as they had done in 1905, for the maintenance of Free Trade as a protection against inflated prices and the lowering of the workers' standard of living. The election was fought in an atmosphere of bitterness among the unemployed working people, and especially among the miners and textile workers. The result was a serious setback for the Conservatives, and a great advance for the Labour Party. It gave 258 seats to the Conservatives, 158 to the two groups of Liberals and 191 for Labour.

The first Labour Government. Ramsay MacDonald Prime Minister, January 1924

The Conservatives, having lost their over-all majority, gave way to Labour, who depended on Liberal support to maintain themselves in power. MacDonald appointed old Labour campaigners to the key Government posts (Philip Snowden, Chancellor of the Exchequer, Arthur Henderson, Home Secretary, J. H. Thomas, Colonial Secretary) but included a number of former Liberals in his administration. For the most part it was a Cabinet of moderates. The situation made it impossible for the Labour Party to bring in measures of nationalization (which had been adopted as official policy), and they were confined to the introduction of moderate liberal reforms. The most important of the first Labour Ministry's enactments was a Housing Act introduced by the Minister of Health, John Wheatley, one of the party's extreme left, designed to speed up the clearance of slums and the rebuilding of houses promised by Lloyd George in 1918. This Act greatly increased the direct financial assistance of the central Government to local authorities for housing, and was the motive force behind a great drive in municipal house-building. The Act also strengthened the building industry

The Labour Party on the brink of its first period in power: Ramsay MacDonald (seated at desk) *surrounded by party workers in January 1924. Also in this picture are Sidney Webb the prominent Fabian Society leader* (bearded) *and the young Herbert Morrison* (standing in front of the picture), *a most important figure in the Labour Party in the 1940s.*

by providing a 15 year programme and, in fact, the housing shortage was overcome by 1932.

The first Labour Government was also responsible for further important advances in education. The Minister of Education, C. P. Trevelyan, repealed the educational economies of the 'Geddes' axe', and appointed Sir Henry Hadow to report on the further needs of education. Although the Hadow Report which established the break between the primary and the secondary school at the age of eleven did not appear until 1926, when Labour was out of office, it reflected in the main the policies advocated by Trevelyan.

The financial policies of the Chancellor of the Exchequer, Philip Snowden, were neither original nor distinctly socialist. They represented a free trade orthodoxy which commended itself to the Liberals as much as to Labour. He repealed the wartime McKenna duties which had imposed duties on a number of 'luxury' imports. He was also quite unoriginal in his attempt to secure a balanced budget even at the cost of blocking increased expenditure by the central and local governments.

The Government had considerable difficulty with the trade unions, especially when they prepared to use the wartime Emergency Powers Act in industrial disputes (see also p. 291). MacDonald himself condemned militant unionism. 'Strikes,' he declared, 'for increased wages, limitation of output, not only are not Socialism, but may mislead the spirit and policy of the Socialist movement.'

MacDonald's foreign policy

Macdonald was a strong believer in the League of Nations and in the real power of goodwill and persuasion. Above all, he sought to reconcile France and Germany. In Britain itself at this time there was considerable sympathy for Germany in view of the extreme demands by France for reparations, demands which MacDonald now, in contrast to Lloyd George, succeeded in moderating. MacDonald's policy resulted in the acceptance by France and Germany of the Dawes Plan in 1924 by which German payments were considerably reduced and an American loan to Germany was arranged. This policy of reconciliation played a great part in easing international tensions in the years 1924 to 1929, and MacDonald was its initiator. In general he believed the League of Nations would make the use of military sanctions unnecessary, for with the triumph of goodwill there would be no call for them.

Relations with Russia and the fall of the first Labour Government

Diplomatic relations between Britain and Soviet Russia had been severed since the Revolution and the intervention of the Coalition Government against the Bolsheviks. Under strong pressure from sections of the Labour movement, MacDonald recognized the Soviet Government as the *de jure* ruler of the former Russian Empire and resumed diplomatic relations. He also signed important trade agreements, which were strongly condemned by the Conservatives, who saw in them only a strengthening of the forces of the Communist International. Another complication arose from the Campbell case. Before Parliament rose for the summer recess J. R. Campbell, editor of the *Workers' Weekly*, had been charged in the courts with inciting the troops to mutiny, but during the recess the Attorney-General withdrew the prosecution. The Conservatives contended that the withdrawal of the prosecution by the Labour Attorney-General was a purely political move. When Parliament reassembled the Conservatives moved a vote of censure in the Commons. Eventually the Liberals voted with the Conservatives and defeated MacDonald. As the Prime Minister had made it a matter of confidence, he resigned and another general election followed.

Polling day was 29 October and on the 25th the *Daily Mail* published a letter reputed to be from the Russian Communist leader Zinoviev, President of the Comintern – the Moscow-based International Socialist organization – to the Communist Party in Britain, containing instructions for the preparation of armed rebellion. This letter might have been dismissed as an obvious forgery and an election trick, but it was made to appear serious and genuine by the publication by the Foreign Office of a letter to the Soviet *chargé d'affaires* protesting against such propaganda and interference in British domestic affairs. Disgraceful though the publication of the alleged letter was, it did its work, and the Conservative Party under Baldwin was returned with 419 seats. The Liberals sank to only 42 and Labour 151. However, it is worth noting that the Labour vote actually increased by a million. The Conservatives increased still more and it was the Liberals who suffered most heavily. The notorious Zinoviev letter itself has since been conclusively proved to be a forgery.

20. Baldwin and the General Strike

ONCE again the man who, in his own words, typified 'safety first', was in power. This time his Government included four important members of the Coalition who had not served in 1922 – Austen Chamberlain as Foreign Secretary, Balfour as Lord President of the Council, Lord Birkenhead as Secretary of State for India, and Winston Churchill, amazingly, as Chancellor of the Exchequer. Churchill had not even been a Conservative candidate at the election, but was elected as a Constitutionalist. Baldwin personally occupied a middle place in the Conservative ranks, anxious to avoid anti-Labour legislation which might create further industrial strife, and hoping to preserve peace abroad as well as at home. Most of his Cabinet were astute educated business men who disagreed with the old aggressive, imperialist policies of the Unionist Party. They were also prepared to carry through social reforms at home. In 1925 the Widows, Orphans and Old Age Contributory Pensions Act was passed. Under the Old Age Pensions Act of 1908 the old age pension was non-contributory, but the Act of 1925 introduced a contributory system for the first time. This extended its scope and provided more funds. Later, supplementary pensions were added in cases of need by the Public Assistance Boards.

Foreign affairs

In November 1924 Austen Chamberlain announced that the Government would not proceed with the Russian treaties. In March 1925 the Government also killed the Geneva Protocol for the Pacific Settlement of International Disputes, for which the Labour Government had worked so hard. With the ending of the Protocol went all hope of a universal organization for peace. But the Conservatives hoped to gain a more limited objective, in the Locarno Pact signed in December 1925. By this agreement the western frontiers of Germany were guaranteed, the Rhineland demilitarized, and a Franco-German pact of non-aggression was backed by Great Britain, Italy and Belgium. Germany was to apply for membership of the League of Nations with the support of Britain and France. The pact was a triumph for the statesmanship of Briand (France), Stresemann (Germany) and Austen Chamberlain.

Locarno appeared to be an important step in the establishment of peace in Europe and an extension of Macdonald's policy of reconciliation. Yet it also marked the progressive abandonment of the Versailles settlement.

Austen Chamberlain openly stated that no British government would fight to maintain the Polish corridor and so to some extent it was also a fore-taste of the appeasement policy of British governments in the 1930's.

The period 1925–9 was the 'golden age' of the inter-war years, when there seemed real hope in Europe that a permanent peace had been achieved. The French and Germans were on better terms, while Soviet Russia was too involved in the huge task of reconstruction to present any danger, even in the eyes of the most violent anti-Communists. The U.S.A. stepped in to assist European recovery, and arbitrated in disputes. In these circumstances the Baldwin Government and its opponents agreed to what was known as the 'ten-year rule' – that is, British defence arrangements were based on the supposition that no great war was likely within ten years, and this policy was renewed annually for several years to come. British expenditure on armaments was steadily reduced from 1922 onwards, until in 1933 armaments expenditure accounted for a smaller proportion of the national income than in 1913. Even the naval power in the Far East given to Japan by the Washington Naval Treaty of 1921 (see p. 204) was not regarded as dangerous. Baldwin's Government began to build an impor-tant naval base at Singapore in 1926, but it proceeded very slowly and the programme was stopped by the Labour Government in 1929. The Army was most affected by these arms economies and was reduced to the position of a force for colonial defence, especially for Britain's new interests in the Middle East. The Air Force also failed to get much support – it certainly got nothing like the fifty-two squadrons its commanders demanded. The only force which remained at a high level of effectiveness was the Navy, which the Government was pledged by the Washington Treaty to keep on a par with that of the U.S.A. There was considerable jealousy and competition between the three services, which thought more of their own independence than of the need of a truly co-ordinated defence system.

The return to the gold standard

Since the end of the war, there had been a steady deflation with a fall in prices and more slowly in wages. Winston Churchill in his budget (April 1925) announced a return to the gold standard and a return also to the pre-war parity with the American dollar. This measure was demanded by the City magnates who wanted to see London restored to its pre-war position as the world's money market. However, it was badly misjudged and crippled exports, hampered trade and forced down wages. The burden of the vast National Debt with its fixed rates of interest became increasingly great with the overvaluation of the pound in relation to the dollar.

One of the industries heavily hit was coal mining, in urgent need of reorganization and unable to compete with the more highly mechanized foreign mines on the existing wage structure. In June 1925 therefore, the Mining Association gave notice to terminate existing wage agreements and proposed lower wages for longer hours. The miners naturally reacted violently but the crisis was postponed till April 1926 by a Government subsidy to maintain miners' wages, while a Royal Commission under Sir Herbert Samuel sought a solution to the problem.

The Samuel Commission's Report and the General Strike

The Samuel Commission, reporting in March 1926, advocated the nation-alization of mining royalties, the reorganization of the coal-mining industry under private ownership, better relations between employers and men, and better pit, social and housing conditions. But, in view of the condition of the industry, the Commission believed that wages must be lowered or hours increased. The miners' leaders, A. J. Cook and Herbert Smith, refused to consider a wage reduction while the most the Mining Association would do was to offer a 13 per cent reduction with a return to an eight-hour day. The miners began a nationwide strike and it soon became clear that other major unions might strike in sympathy. The Trades Union Congress through its Negotiating or Industrial Committee was preparing to call out the so-called 'front line' – the railwaymen, transport workers, engineers, iron and steel workers, electricians, shipbuilders and printers – in support of the miners, but the T.U.C. never really believed the Government would face a paralysis of the nation's life and therefore made no adequate pre-parations. Meanwhile, the Government was prepared to use to the full the powers given it by the Emergency Powers Act 1920, and to accept the offer of help from a private body, the Organization for the Maintenance of Supplies.

The General Strike: a food convoy in the East India Dock Road, May 1926

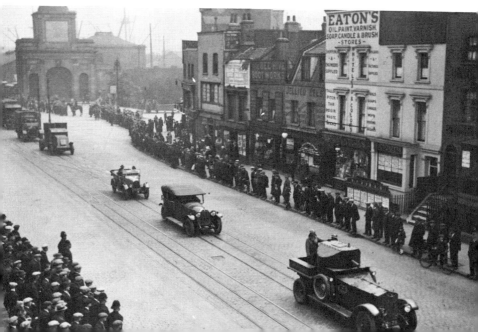

Negotiations still had not been broken off between the Negotiating Committee and the Government, when printers of the *Daily Mail* refused to print an editorial strongly critical of the trade unions. This stiffened the Cabinet, who demanded the withdrawal of the instructions for a general strike. The T.U.C. refused, and on 4 May 1926 the strike began. The support among 'front line' workers was amazing; they all believed that victory would soon be theirs. There was at first little violence on the part of the workers who gave permits to vehicles carrying essential supplies, but it was clear that the contest would be stern and bitter. The Government's emergency measures became increasingly efficient. Food supplies were maintained by volunteers, ships were unloaded and even a skeleton train service began. The Press was muzzled by the printers' strike and the *British Gazette* run by Churchill and the B.B.C. radio service which was monopolized by the Government were almost the only means of getting news. The financial resources of the unions were soon nearly exhausted, but the T.U.C., staggered at the public's reaction to the strike, prepared to call out the 'second line' unions. Then, with the threat of violent clashes over the Government's decision to make more use of troops and the T.U.C.'s withdrawal of permits to vehicles carrying food, came Sir John Simon's declaration that the General Strike was not a strike but an illegal proceeding, and that the men involved were liable to be sued for damages. On the eighth day of the strike Sir Herbert Samuel offered to mediate on the basis of the Commission's report and the T.U.C. were glad of the opportunity to call off the strike on 12 May. The Prime Minister urged employers to take back the strikers, but there were many reprisals. The railwaymen, for instance, had to promise not to enter into such a strike again, and some actions of the Government's agents seemed like insulting provocation, though King George V and Baldwin himself intervened to smooth things over. Within a few days resistance ended. The miners were left to fight on. They held out until December, when, bitter against the Government, the public and their fellow trade unionists, they gave in and the strike petered out, with wages reduced and hours increased, and the settlement on a regional, not national, basis.

The Trade Disputes Act, 1927

The Government followed their victory with the Trade Disputes Act in 1927. This measure reflected the pressure from the extreme right of the Conservative Party, and was the cause of bitter feeling in the Labour Party until its repeal by Attlee's Labour Government in 1946. By this Act 'any strike having any object beyond the furtherance of a trade dispute within a trade or industry in which the strikers are engaged is an illegal strike if it is designed to coerce the Government or to intimidate the community or any substantial part of it'. No member of a union was to be expelled for refusing to take part in a strike; there was to be no intimidation by pickets; members wishing to contribute to a political levy were to give written notice that they wanted to do so; established Civil Servants were not to belong to unions affiliated to the T.U.C., for their loyalty was to be to the Crown only.

The Act reflected the mood of the Government and a large part of the public at the time, but it had not the long-term effects its supporters hoped for. It is true that the general strike resulted in the depletion of union funds and a reduction in membership of unions, but the events of May 1926 turned the leaders of the Labour Party and of many of the trade unions towards parliamentary action. By May 1929 enough Labour Members were returned to enable Ramsay MacDonald to form the second Labour Ministry, again without an overall majority, but at least at the head of the largest party in Parliament.

Social and economic reforms

The Conservative Government gave some consideration to social legislation as well as to anti-labour policies. The leaders in this movement for social reform were Neville Chamberlain and Winston Churchill, both of whom were particularly vigorous in the opposition to the general strike. The first measure was the Widows, Orphans and Old Age Contributory Pensions Bill which provided pensions of 10s. a week for widows and allowances for their dependent children, 7s. 6d. a week for orphans, and 10s. a week for workers covered by the National Health Insurance scheme and their wives. The non-contributory old age pension at 70 continued at 10s. The Unemployment Insurance Bill, which included some restrictions and limitations of benefit, was strongly contested by the Labour opposition, while the Government's action against certain Boards of Guardians which, it was held, were too generous with their poor relief also aroused protests.

The Representation of the People (Equal Franchise) Act of 1928 gave the vote to those women not enfranchised in 1919, but it still did not deal with the question of plural voting, by which a man could vote both in the constituency where he resided and in that in which he owned business premises.

The most comprehensive reform was the Local Government Act, 1929, the chief work of Neville Chamberlain as Minister of Health. It was for the most part a codifying Act drawing together the provisions of earlier Acts and recommendations for reforms proposed by Royal Commissions and other bodies. By this Act the Poor Law Unions and their Boards of Guardians were abolished, and their duties transferred to the Public Assistance Committees of counties and county boroughs; rural and urban district councils were reviewed and regrouped; agricultural land and farm buildings were completely derated, and the rates on industrial buildings, railways, etc. reduced by three quarters. Block grants to local authorities were substituted for the percentage grants, which were held to favour the wealthier authorities. The grants for the most important functions – education, police and housing – were, however, not affected.

London's East End in the mid 1920's. Areas like this only gradually felt any benefit from reforms in Local Government and new housing schemes.

Two other important measures were passed in December 1926. The distribution of electricity became the responsibility of a national body, the Central Electricity Board, and the British Broadcasting Company was turned into a public corporation.

The decline of Baldwin's Second Ministry and the General Election of 1929
After the success of the Locarno Pact nothing of consequence was achieved in the field of foreign affairs. The naval disarmament conference to re-settle the relative naval strengths of the United States, Britain and Japan broke down. No progress was made with general disarmament proposals.

The Government itself was unimaginative and lacking in energy. Baldwin seemed ineffective, yet he held the Government and the party together. A group of young Conservatives (including Harold Macmillan) agitated for more state interference and more sympathy for the working man, but the general atmosphere was one of stagnation. Meanwhile, the Liberals were stirring to action under a rejuvenated Lloyd George, putting forward plans which were in part accepted twenty years later, and the Labour Party produced *Labour and the Nation*, a manifesto for a Socialist programme to end the 'capitalist dictatorship'.

The general election which took place on 30 May 1929 evoked little excitement or interest. The new electorate included a large number of new women voters. Labour won 287 seats, the Conservatives 261 and the Liberals 59. Nevertheless, the Labour Party polled fewer votes than the Conservatives, and were still dependent on the co-operation of the Liberals. Once again they were incapable of decisive action and this time at a moment when it was even more urgently needed.

21. MacDonald and the Economic Crisis

BALDWIN did not wait for defeat in the Commons but resigned on 4 June 1929, advising the King to send for MacDonald. MacDonald soon announced his Cabinet which was composed once again of moderates. He appointed Arthur Henderson to the Foreign Office, Snowden to the Exchequer, J. H. Thomas as Lord Privy Seal, J. R. Clynes as Home Secretary and Sir John Sankey as Lord Chancellor. The omission of the left-wing John Wheatley, one of the successes of the 1924 Cabinet seemed to indicate that the Government would follow a policy of which the Liberals would approve. For the first time a woman, Miss Margaret Bondfield, entered the Cabinet as Minister of Labour.

The new Labour Government was in a difficult position. Liberal support was uncertain and intermittent, and Conservative opposition determined. The Ministry was unable to proceed with genuinely socialist measures and it could do nothing constructive to solve the unemployment problem. In 1930 the numbers of unemployed rose alarmingly from 1,750,000 in January to 2,500,000 in December.

Foreign and imperial policy

The earlier policies of the conciliation of Germany were maintained by the Foreign Secretary, Arthur Henderson. He strongly favoured the Young Plan, named after the American financier who was responsible for the detailed proposals. In 1929 this new system of reparations payments by Germany was devised, by which the annual payments were further reduced, although Germany was still expected to pay £50,000,000 a year for the next fifty-nine years. The world economic crisis of 1929–31 frustrated this plan, and the rise of the Nazis in Germany put an end to it. Henderson also secured the withdrawal of Allied troops from the Rhineland five years ahead of the time originally agreed. In general, Arthur Henderson's belief in, and support of, the League of Nations was as fervent as MacDonald's, and he succeeded in gaining the confidence of both Germany and France – a remarkable achievement. He also arranged for a Disarmament Conference to meet in February 1932, and was himself named as its president. Ramsay MacDonald was a strong advocate of closer Anglo-American co-operation and he was criticized by the extreme Left for playing into the hands of American capitalism. However, his efforts to achieve agreement with the U.S.A. on naval strengths bore fruit, and, in the circumstances of immense

American power, this was no mean achievement. In the first place, the London naval conference of 1930 secured the agreement of the U.S.A. and Japan to the ratio. of 5 : 5 : 3, with no capital ships to be built for five years. At the same time MacDonald agreed to a British limit of fifty cruisers.

MacDonald made considerable efforts to tackle the situation in India, where Gandhi was leading his people in a campaign for independence. Lord Irwin, the Viceroy in 1929, promised Dominion status to India, but Gandhi was not satisfied. In 1930 the Simon Commission promised responsible government to the Indians in the provinces and a system of consultation in the central Government (see also p. 343). MacDonald then called a Round Table Conference for London in 1930, but the Indian National Congress refused to attend and when Gandhi had at last agreed to attend the second session of the conference, the Labour Government had fallen in the crisis of 1931.

Henderson attempted to improve Britain's relations with Egypt and, as a token of good faith, removed the imperialist Lord Lloyd from his post as High Commissioner. He promised to give up Britain's control of Egypt's internal affairs and withdraw British forces to the Canal Zone. Negotiations broke down when the Egyptians demanded more control over the Sudan. Nevertheless, Henderson's proposals anticipated the Anglo-Egyptian Treaty of 1936. In Palestine the Labour policy of conciliation was, however, unsuccessful, as the extraordinary complexity of the problem produced great strains between Arabs and Jews. The latter were now entering Palestine with the avowed intention of setting up a Jewish National State, and, in an attempt to reduce tension the Colonial Secretary, Lord Passfield, halted Jewish immigration. This was unpopular, not only with the Jews, but with a wide section of the British public.

By the Statute of Westminster, 1931, the right of the Dominions to complete independence was recognized. In the future, they were to all intents and purposes sovereign independent states. This statute put an end to many remnants of nineteenth-century British imperialism and, in fact, enabled both India and Pakistan to remain within the Commonwealth after 1947 without compromising their independence.

The Great Depression

In October 1929 a sudden collapse of stock prices on the New York Stock Exchange marked the beginning of the greatest economic disaster the modern world has yet seen. With falling prices of basic commodities and the rapid spread of unemployment in the United States, other states (most of whom were dependent in one way or another on American trade and financial loans) began to feel its effects. American money had been lent to Germany to help pay war reparations. German payments made to Britain were intended to help her to pay her debts to the United States, and thus the great states of Europe were linked in a complicated circle of payment

Police move in to quell disorders in Wall Street after the crash on the Stock Exchange, 24 October, 1929.

and re-payment which made it certain that any economic disaster in the U.S.A. would react directly on Europe. But in the hopeful, optimistic years of the twenties, few had thought such a disaster possible.

Continental investors who had placed their money in the London money market now withdrew their funds in order to meet their commitments in Europe. Gold began to move rapidly from Britain to the continent, the value of the English pound fell, and unemployment spread to all the major industries.

Home policies

The dependence on Liberal support prevented the introduction of any measures of nationalization, and in place of this the Government encouraged various industries to control and regulate their own affairs on a national basis – a kind of 'controlled capitalism'. Examples of this were the introduction of the Agricultural Marketing Act of 1931 by the Minister of Agriculture, Christopher Addison. By this Act boards of producers were established to fix prices and to organize efficient marketing of a number of commodities. Another example of this was the London Passenger Transport

Board, which, although finally established by the National Government in 1933, was first mooted by Herbert Morrison. In the field of social improvement the Government had much to its credit. The Minister of Health, Arthur Greenwood, renewed Wheatley's subsidies to local authorities for house-building which had been removed by Baldwin's second Government. The Housing Act of 1930 also specifically included measures for speeding slum clearance. The application of Greenwood's Act by the National Governments after 1934 led to the clearance of more slums in the years 1934–39 than in all the previous fifty years, and the credit for initiating this policy lay with the second Labour ministry.

The Chancellor of the Exchequer, Philip Snowden, continued to apply orthodox financial policies. His budget of 1930 raised income tax to 4s. 6d. in the pound and also increased surtax. He aimed above all at a balanced budget, which he hoped would maintain national and international confidence in Britain. This in turn would offset the effects of the Great Depression which was spreading from the United States to the rest of the world.

J. H. Thomas, who was responsible for measures to combat unemployment, struggled with schemes for road building, railway improvements, the transfer of industries to depressed areas and for colonial development. But this had little effect, and Thomas retired to the Dominions Office. The Unemployment Insurance Bill of November 1929, extended 'transitional benefit', that is benefit to which insured persons were not entitled by the number of their contributions. It also made some provision for training unemployed persons. But differences within the Labour movement were made worse by the crisis. The I.L.P. led by James Maxton (to which Ramsay MacDonald had belonged since 1894) was acting almost as a separate party, and MacDonald felt obliged to resign his membership. The Coal Prices Act of 1929 which provided for a $7\frac{1}{2}$-hour shift instead of 8 hours aroused no enthusiasm amongst Labour members. The attempt to repeal clauses of the Trade Disputes Act, 1927, was wrecked by amendments, as was an Electoral Reform Bill which would have done away with plural voting. Sir Charles Trevelyan's Education Bill, another praiseworthy measure, which would have raised the school-leaving age to fifteen, was rejected by the Lords.

The Conservatives had their difficulties too; they were divided on tariffs, especially preferential duties on foodstuffs and other products from the Empire; they were split on Dominion status for India, a question on which Winston Churchill withdrew from the Opposition Front Bench. Led by the Press Lords, Beaverbrook and Rothermere, the Conservatives campaigned for 'Home and Empire', and there was an unsuccessful attempt to shake Baldwin from the leadership and put Neville Chamberlain in his place.

The economic crisis, the Macmillan and May Reports
It became increasingly clear that the second Labour Ministry could not last

long. In February 1931 the Conservative Opposition moved a vote of censure on wasteful expenditure, and a Liberal amendment led to the setting up of the May Committee on National Expenditure. Even before the May Committee had reported, the unemployment problem was getting out of hand; by July 1931 the total of unemployed had reached 2,750,000

The alarm had already been sounded by the report of Lord Macmillan's committee on Trade and Industry, which drew attention to the adverse balance of payments now afflicting Britain through the loss of her shipping and banking business which the depression had brought about. This was producing a serious drain on British gold reserves and threatening the

The National Government in the garden of 10 Downing Street. Standing *left to right: Sir Philip Cunliffe Lister (Con.); J. H. Thomas (Lab.); Lord Reading (Lib.); Neville Chamberlain (Con.); Sir Samuel Hoare (Con.)*
Sitting *left to right: Philip Snowden (Lab.); Stanley Baldwin (Con.); Ramsay MacDonald (Lab.); Sir Herbert Samuel (Lib.); Lord Sankey (Lab.).*

value of the pound. The May Report forecast a Government deficit of £120 million, and recommended cuts in pay for Civil Servants, teachers and even judges as well as a 20 per cent reduction in unemployment benefits. The drain on gold was temporarily arrested by credit from Paris and New

York, but the crisis continued, and the Government was warned by banks at home and abroad that the country was on the edge of a precipice. The raising of the Bank Rate to 4½ per cent failed to attract foreign money to London and conditions for American aid included drastic public economies on the lines of those recommended by the May Committee.

The Labour Government was faced with a painful decision. Could it really advocate and carry out economies which included a reduction in unemployment benefit? MacDonald himself wanted to save the pound, even at the expense of harsh economies. The rift in the Cabinet widened as attempts were made to work these out. No agreement could be reached on the level of unemployment benefit, which MacDonald reduced by 10 per cent. On 24 August 1931 MacDonald tendered the resignation of the Labour Government. On the same day he formed a National Government in which both Baldwin and Samuel, the Liberal leader, agreed to serve.

The formation of the National Government, August 1931
It seemed that Ramsay MacDonald had been anxious to end the Labour Government and assume the leadership of a National Government into which he took only a handful of his former colleagues. King George V, largely on the advice of Herbert Samuel, asked MacDonald to lead the new Ministry and Baldwin readily agreed that this was the correct action. From August to November 1931 the Cabinet had only ten members, four former members of the Labour Cabinet (MacDonald, Snowden, J. H. Thomas and Lord Sankey) four Conservatives, including Baldwin and Neville Chamberlain, and two Liberals, Sir Herbert Samuel and Lord Reading.

MacDonald was branded as a traitor by his former party. For his part he might have claimed that by risking his political future he saved his country and made possible the eventual recovery. The partnership of Ramsay MacDonald and Stanley Baldwin continued until May 1937, with Baldwin taking over as Prime Minister in June 1935.

22. Depression and Recovery, 1931-9

Snowden's budget

The Government turned first to the financial and economic situation. The economies proposed by the May Committee were, in the main, accepted as the basis for recovery. Snowden's budget increased taxation by about £76 million with income tax at 5s. in the pound. Cuts in the salaries of all state servants were introduced – few escaped the net which enveloped Cabinet ministers, judges, most grades of civil servants, the armed forces, teachers and the unemployed. A general reduction of 10 per cent was imposed, with 15 per cent for the teaching profession. In the ensuing debate, both the Conservatives and Liberals supported the Budget, but only twelve Labour members did so. However, the Government had a majority of fifty. This drastic and unprecedented policy had an immediate effect on the international money market, and the United States gave Britain a credit of £80 million, which temporarily stopped the decline in the value of the pound. But this was indeed only temporary, and foreign creditors of Britain, fearing that Britain would get no more reparations from Germany, showed little confidence in the pound. Funds continued to be withdrawn from Britain at an alarming rate and there was a danger that Britain's credit would be completely exhausted. The Government suspended the gold standard, the value of the pound fell by one quarter on the foreign exchanges, and Britain was thrown back on a paper and credit currency.

The General Election of October 1931

At this time the Labour Opposition was in complete disarray. It had few men capable of producing a convincing and constructive socialist solution to the crisis. The Labour Party itself was forced into a very unconvincing position, opposing economies without offering a real alternative. This allowed MacDonald to gain the electorate's support for a national, non-party approach, and to claim that, by taking the measures he had, the pound had been saved from complete collapse. In the election the Conservatives, National Labour and National Liberals gained 60 per cent of the votes and 521 seats. Although the Labour Party gained a third of the total vote it was reduced to 52 members. The Liberals won 33 seats.

MacDonald now made some important Cabinet changes. Snowden was removed to the House of Lords and Neville Chamberlain became Chancellor of the Exchequer. Sir John Simon (National Liberal) became Foreign

Secretary. The appointment of Chamberlain was a sign of the Government's intention to move towards protection. The first instalment was made under the Abnormal Importation Act in November 1931, which placed restrictions on a number of imports, and in February 1932 a more far-reaching change was made under the Import Duties Bill. This imposed an immediate general tariff of 10 per cent, and a special advisory committee under Sir George May was to make further recommendations for the restriction of trade. The policy of Empire Preference meant that the Empire was not affected, and duties were not imposed on raw materials and foodstuffs, for the fate of Joseph Chamberlain's scheme of 1905 had shown how unpopular a so-called 'stomach tax' could be. About half Britain's imports were eventually placed under 10–20 per cent duties.

Chamberlain's budget of April 1932
The budget of 1932 was memorable for proposing the lowest expenditure on armaments between 1918 and 1939. At the same time the income from the new import duties enabled Chamberlain to avoid increasing income tax. He also saved £23 million by reducing interest on War Loans – a measure which, in so far as it reduced the incomes of middle and upper-class bondholders, would have been denounced only a few years before as outright socialism. But the Government's position was so powerful that it could risk sacrificing the interests of some of its supporters.

Empire Free Trade was another of Chamberlain's cherished aims, and the Ottawa Imperial Conference of July-August, 1932, was summoned to promote this policy. However, it did not succeed in producing the powerful 'closed Empire' which the advocates of the idea wanted. In fact, the Dominions had also suffered severely in the depression of 1929–31 and were themselves imposing high duties on their imports from foreign countries. The only preference they gave to Britain was in the form of lower duties than those charged against foreigners. In other words, even within the Commonwealth itself national protectionist policies were applied. The Empire was not the neat, cohesive trading unit which the imperial idealists wanted. The same difficulties arose at the World Economic Conference in London in 1933 over which Ramsay MacDonald presided. His attempt to apply his policies of conciliation and agreement in the economic field as in the political achieved very little. All the Great Powers were now involved in protectionist policies based on the purest national self-interest. International trade was being reduced rather than increased and MacDonald was unable to reverse the trend.

The 'Means Test' and the problem of unemployment
Another basic problem facing Chamberlain as Chancellor of the Exchequer was that of long-term unemployment, which afflicted above all the old industrial areas of the country – for example the North East, where in the

town of Jarrow at least two-thirds of the workers were permanently unemployed, and from which protesting 'hunger marchers' in their thousands
moved upon London in powerful demonstrations in the early thirties. The
Government in 1934 at last declared certain regions Special Areas – namely,
Scotland, South Wales, West Cumberland and Tyneside – and provided
about £2,000,000 to help their revival. When this policy failed, money
was put aside in 1937 to attract new industries, and some industrial
estates were created. These, however, provided new work for only a
few thousands. This was the least effective of the policies of the National
Governments.

A new approach was made to the problem of the long-term unemployed
who had exhausted their benefits based on their contributions. The relief
they received came directly from the Exchequer, and in 1931 the policy of
the May Report led to the introduction of the 'means test'. By this test an
unemployed man's total resources were taken into account in assessing his
entitlement to relief. The Labour opposition to this was violent, for it
appeared that the man who had been thrifty and saved was to be penalized
because of it. The 'hunger marches' to London, led by such Labour stalwarts
of the extreme left as James Maxton and Ellen Wilkinson, were above all
protests against this system, and many Labour-controlled councils refused

*The Jarrow Marchers, with a harmonica band, pass through Bedford on
the final stages of their journey to London.*

Victims of unemployment sing in the streets of London, while the more fortunate queue for theatre tickets.

to allow their Public Assistance Committees to follow the Government's rules.

Chamberlain's Unemployment Act of 1934 was intended to remove some of the strains produced by these policies. The Public Assistance Committees were replaced, for the purposes of unemployment relief, by the Unemployment Assistance Board with branches in every part of the country. This attempt to take relief out of the area of local politics was nearly wrecked by the fact that the new assistance rates were less than those under the old 'means test' system, and there was a renewal of the 'hunger marches'. Chamberlain stepped in and forbade the payment of any rates below the old ones. Nevertheless, Chamberlain was the main target for Labour attacks during his Chancellorship, and constant conflict arose over rates of assistance to the unemployed. All the same, the Act of 1934 was an important step towards taking unemployment assistance out of the hands of the local committees which were also administering the Poor Law, a change which was complete by 1940.

An important fact, for which the National Government of MacDonald took considerable credit, was that unemployment fell by over one million in 1933. Again, by 1934, Chamberlain had reduced income tax, which was back at 4s. 6d. in the pound. At the same time he repealed the economy cuts in unemployment benefits, and by 1935 the salaries of all public servants were back at their former level. Wages had fallen, but the cost of living had fallen much more. For those in employment, the years 1935 to

1939 were years of prosperity. However, the national picture was darkened by the intractable problem of mass unemployment in the Special Areas. Only by moving out of them, which many did, was there hope of personal improvement, but the majority remained in the vain hope of revival.

The abdication of Edward VIII

Amidst the tortuous problems of economic policy and unemployment an event of an unusual kind stirred Britain and the world – the abdication of King Edward VIII. He had succeeded his father, King George V, on 20 January 1935. The new King was lively, popular and unconventional. He wished to play a wider part in the affairs of the nation than was usual for the monarch. As Prince of Wales he had shown genuine concern for the conditions of the working people, and particularly the unemployed. On a visit to South Wales he had promised that 'something must be done' about unemployment in the coalfields – a statement for which he was criticized in some quarters. His life was unconventional in other respects, and he had formed a strong attachment to Mrs Simpson, an American divorcee, whom he wished to marry. Mrs Simpson did not find favour with the Establishment, represented most strongly by Dr Lang, Archbishop of Canterbury, Dawson, editor of *The Times*, and Baldwin himself. The King, however, had his supporters, especially the 'Press lords' Beaverbrook and Rothermere. Suggestions were also put forward for the creation of a King's Party, which could have caused serious national division and have thrown the monarchy into the political arena. The King himself was anxious to avoid this and, under pressure from Baldwin, he abdicated on 11 December 1936. His brother, the Duke of York, became King as George VI. Besides the great bulk of the Conservative Party, the Labour Party at this time also officially supported the abdication. Mr Baldwin's action helped him to regain some of the prestige he had lost through failures in foreign policy. However, after the coronation of George VI in 1937, he retired from politics, followed shortly afterwards by Ramsay MacDonald. Neville Chamberlain succeeded Baldwin as Prime Minister.

General comment on National Government policies

The various devices employed by the Governments of 1931 to 1939 in their efforts to revive the economic life of the country were a mixture of success and failure.

The abandonment of the gold standard lowered British export prices and enabled foreign buyers to buy more cheaply. This increased exports until both France and the United States left the gold standard in 1936. The Government's response was a fairly successful attempt to reach agreement with these countries to maintain a steady international rate of currency exchange. The protectionist policies of the Government, while assisting manufacturers concerned with the home market, tended to reduce exports more than they reduced imports, for the foreign countries who were kept out of the home market by the tariffs became strong competitors in the export markets. Thus the protectionist policies produced unforeseen difficulties. Another aim of high tariffs was to protect the basic industries until they had been modernized. This was a period of 'rationalization', when methods of production were improved and surplus plant and machinery was deliberately destroyed, but only by maintaining high prices under the protective shield could the costs of this process be borne. The shipbuilding and cotton industries, which were 'over-capitalized', were given this economic trimming, but the coalowners were unwilling to combine and reorganize. There was some fairly successful reorganization of agriculture, and the Government granted subsidies of up to £40 million a year to help farmers introduce new methods without raising prices to the consumers. Yet, despite increased output and reasonable prices, workers were still leaving the land in 1939 at the rate of 10,000 annually (see also Chapter 28).

With wages stationary but prices of food either steady or falling, people had more money to spend on home produced goods of all kinds. In the case of the building industry, the Governments tried to reduce expenditure by local authorities, but many local councils took advantage of the low Bank Rate of 2 per cent to borrow and to build, while 3 million houses were built for private individuals between 1930 and 1940, incidentally creating the hideous 'ribbon development' to be seen around many towns. This building boom, which the Government had not intended, accounted for nearly one-third of the increase in employment in the years 1932 to 1935. Whether intended or not, this improvement counted for a great deal with the electorate and largely explained the popularity of the Conservative Party in the years 1931 to 1939. Another criticism that can be made of the Government policies of this period was that, while they provided credit for reorganizing industry and agriculture, they only nibbled ineffectively at the problem of the Special Areas – they were still hoping to revive the old industries and failed to develop enough new ones to replace them. The idea that Britain could return to the economic structure of 1914 or even of mid-Victorian prosperity died very hard.

23. Crisis and Appeasement, 1931-9

Ireland

In 1932 De Valera succeeded the moderate Cosgrave as Prime Minister of the Irish Free State. He quickly took advantage of the Statute of Westminster to abolish the oath of allegiance to the Crown and to do away with the Governor-General as the representative of the King. The treaty of 1922 ceased to be the basis of the Irish Constitution and an Irish citizenship was substituted for the common British citizenship, although at this time Ireland remained nominally a member of the Commonwealth. The first British reaction under the guidance of the Dominions Secretary, J. H. Thomas, was to impose restrictions on Irish agricultural exports to Britain, and the Irish replied with restrictions on British exports to them. However, in 1934 a new trade agreement was arrived at as between equals. De Valera's next move was in 1937 when he declared Ireland a Republic in 'external association with the Commonwealth' – a solution which only Ireland and Britain could have thought of or made workable. But the incorporation of the six counties of Ulster in the Irish Free State was still a declared purpose of the Irish leaders, and occasional violent activities of the I.R.A. on the borders have continued since 1937.

Foreign policy under MacDonald's National Government, 1931–5. Anti-war opinion

Since the First World War a spate of poems, novels and films had depicted the ghastly and apparently futile side of war. Remarque's *All Quiet on the Western Front*, a powerful indictment of war from the German side, became an equally powerful film which gained an international reputation. In Britain R. C. Sherriff's *Journey's End*, *Death of a Hero* by Richard Aldington, and *Goodbye to All That* by Robert Graves all denounced war and the generals and politicians who brought it about. By 1931 most people believed that it was not German aggression which started the 1914 war, but human weakness. Many also believed (and there was considerable truth in it) that the great armaments firms had a vested interest in war and directly intriqued with governments. Thus the climate of opinion in Britain turned to constructive efforts to maintain and strengthen peace.

The World Disarmament Conference, February 1932 – April 1934

The National Government of MacDonald steadily resisted the efforts of the Chiefs of Staff to increase British armaments, though the pressure upon the Government became greater after the Japanese attack on Manchuria in 1931 and after Hitler became German Chancellor in 1933. In 1932 the Government gave way a little by cancelling the old ten-year rule (see p. 218), but in fact Chamberlain's budget of 1932 involved the lowest expenditure on arms since 1919. It was during the years 1932 to 1934, when this pressure from the Army, Navy and Air Force chiefs was increasing, that the World Disarmament Conference, on which MacDonald had pinned all his hopes for peace, met.

This Conference, the most important international meeting since 1919, was a complete failure. Above all it failed to reduce the old mistrust and animosity between France and Germany. Germany demanded military equality with France and France would only accept this demand if Britain would rearm and guarantee to come to her aid if she was attacked. But opinion in Britain was strongly against any such commitment, as Mac-Donald was well aware. He was prepared to stake everything on his efforts to reconcile France and Germany, to avoid any action which committed Britain to military intervention on the continent. Moreover, there was far more sympathy with the German complaints against the Versailles Treaty than with French fears of German aggression; indeed, the French were widely regarded in Britain as the vindictive perpetrators of the Versailles injustices against Germany. Eventually, the French offered Germany equality in armaments at the end of four years. Many Germans considered this insulting, and it gave Hitler a clear excuse for withdrawing from the League of Nations. This outcome of the Disarmament Conference was a shattering blow to MacDonald's attempts at moral persuasion and conciliation, and he never recovered from it.

British policy and the League of Nations
The British public and the Government wished to see international security achieved not by rearmament, but by disarmament. Britain's refusal to guarantee the security of France at the Disarmament Conference stemmed from this attitude. The Labour Opposition followed this policy, and could only criticize the MacDonald Government for their failure to carry it to success. The policy of moral persuasion without 'teeth' was clearly shown when, on 18 September 1931, Japan seized control of Manchuria. This became at once a matter for the League of Nations, of which Japan was a founder member. Sir John Simon, Foreign Secretary, tried to reconcile China and Japan. It could be claimed that, as the Japanese Navy had supremacy over Britain in Far Eastern waters, and as the U.S.A. was not prepared for action against Japan, it was in any case impossible for Britain to carry out armed sanctions, even if the League had demanded them. British policy secured the appointment of the Lytton Commission to inquire into the Manchurian affair. In the meantime the League Assembly voted unanimously not to recognize any changes brought about by force.

When the Lytton Commission reported, it condemned Japan's methods, but agreed that she had grievances against the Chinese. Sir J. Simon secured the acceptance of this report by the League, but no sanctions of any kind were imposed. Japan left the League, which was weakened by the ineffectiveness which the British Government had done nothing to redress. The Manchurian affair led opponents to condemn the National Government's role in the League of Nations, for not even economic sanctions had been employed. On the other hand, many defenders of Britain's policy were convinced that any sanctions against Japan would have led to a war by Japan against the League members with every factor in favour of Japan. It was certain that the powerful non-League nation, the U.S.A., which had an extensive trade with Japan, would not have supported the League. The Manchurian affair was a victory of the strong over the weak, a defeat for the League of Nations and for British foreign policy. From this point it became clear that the future of the League as an effective international force was in doubt.

Foreign policy and the rise of Hitler

Japanese success in the Far East cast a black cloud over the Disarmament Conference, but the rise of Hitler in Germany was even more threatening. This time, the problem was nearer home. In Britain the Labour Party wanted an anti-Hitler crusade because he was a fascist, but they wanted action, not by rearmament, but by collective action with other Powers through the League. The National Government, however, was apparently not worried by Hitler's fascism and was certainly not prepared for an ideological war. Indeed, it was not until 1936, after serious disturbances in the East End of London, that the Government forbade the wearing of uniforms by Oswald Mosley's British Union of Fascists. But it was Hitler's increasing persecution of the Jews that turned many Conservatives strongly against him. The Chiefs of Staff were also worrying the Government. They saw Hitler in simple terms as a threat to Britain's security, which could only be safeguarded by air parity with Germany, by strengthening the Navy still further and, above all, by a drastic increase in British land forces. These pressures began slowly to modify the Government's defence and foreign policies. In 1935 Chamberlain's budget showed an armaments expenditure only slightly above that of 1925. However, in March 1935 the Government published an important White Paper entitled 'Statement Relating to Defence'. This document made it clear that Britain could no longer rely on collective security through the League and that her own armed forces must be her main protection. This was the beginning of a new policy, which did not, however, receive great publicity in Britain. Hitler's reply to the White Paper was to restore conscription in Germany – again in defiance of the Versailles Treaty.

In answer to this move MacDonald met Mussolini and the French Foreign Minister, Laval, at Stresa. The Stresa Conference secured the approval of the League Council to a resolution condemning Hitler's repudiation of the Versailles Treaty. Before the Conference ended the three powers stated their opposition to 'any unilateral repudiation of treaties which may endanger the peace of Europe'. The word 'Europe' was significant, for Mussolini was already preparing action against Abyssinia. MacDonald was here exploiting the dislike which Mussolini showed at this time to the rise of a rival dictator in Germany. However, this was followed in June of the same year by the Anglo-German Naval Agreement by which Hitler limited the Germany Navy to 35 per cent of the British fleet. This contradicted the declaration of the Stresa Front, for it accepted Hitler's repudiation of the naval clauses of the Treaty of Versailles. It also went entirely against the previous aims of disarmament by international agreement. This agreement caused bewilderment in France, in Italy and in the Soviet Union, and considerable controversy in Britain. But there were many in Britain, both in the Government and outside, who considered German grievances over Versailles justified and the Anglo-German Naval Agreement was even regarded as a contribution to peace. There was still wide conviction that Germany would pursue a peaceful and co-operative path once her grievances were redressed.

At this point, June 1935, Ramsay MacDonald, whose health was failing, retired from the premiership in favour of Stanley Baldwin and became Lord President of the Council. He played a decreasing part in national affairs and died in 1937. Sir Samuel Hoare now became Foreign Secretary in place of Sir John Simon and Anthony Eden became Minister for League of Nations Affairs.

The Peace Ballot of the League of Nations Union

To test the public's attitude to disarmament and the League of Nations, the League of Nations Union organized a house-to-house canvass, and the results were announced in June 1935. To the important question: 'Should an aggressor be stopped by armed action?', 6,750,000 answered Yes, 2,000,000 No and 2,000,000 abstained. Clearly a majority favoured armed action against an aggressor, and the vast majority of householders favoured collective security by economic sanctions. This showed a clear public support for the League of Nations at a time when the Government was beginning to abandon collective security in favour of national armaments. It was at this moment that Mussolini's attack on Abyssinia dominated the international scene.

The Abyssinian problem

The National Government once again tried to arbitrate in this dispute. Anthony Eden was sent to Mussolini with the proposal that Italy should have the Abyssinian lowlands and Britain would compensate Abyssinia with British Somaliland, but Mussolini rejected this offer – which in any case would have had to be forced on Abyssinia. The Government were obviously anxious to placate Mussolini, whom they valued as a member of the newly-formed Stresa Front. The Foreign Secretary, Sir Samuel Hoare, announced his Government's support for collective security at Geneva, and when Mussolini attacked Abyssinia at the beginning of October, economic sanctions were immediately applied by nearly all League members, causing Italy severe economic difficulties. Thus the National Government had taken the initiative at this point in support of the League, and all who had supported sanctions short of war in the Peace Ballot saw their ideas being applied. The Labour Opposition, while giving official support to the Covenant of the League, was in fact divided on the question of the type of sanction to be applied. The pacifist leader of the party, George Lansbury, openly opposed any aggressive measures, and was soon afterwards replaced by Clement Attlee. At this point Baldwin decided upon a general election to be held on 14 November. The time was well chosen, and it was during this election that Baldwin made his promise: 'I give you my word that there will be no great armaments.' Although he was later accused of having thus exploited the Peace Ballot sentiments of the public, it is likely that he sincerely thought that collective security could be recreated and thus make big national armaments expenditure unnecessary. At the same time he asked for a mandate for rearmament to make up for weaknesses in British defence. The election gave the Conservatives the same vote as in 1931, but the Labour Party gained about one hundred seats, to bring them up to 154 in the House of Commons. The decline of the Liberal Party continued with a fall from 33 to 20 seats. Supporters of the National Government still had an overwhelming majority with 432 seats.

Baldwin had skilfully asked the electorate to approve some British rearmament while at the same time supporting collective security – a support which the sanctions against Mussolini seemed to justify. But, with the election over, and with the Italians moving forward relentlessly against the Abyssinians, he still faced major decisions of foreign policy. There was widespread public demand for the use of oil sanctions against Italy, but the Government claimed that this would lead to war which the majority in Britain did not want. Official British policy was still to use Mussolini as an ally against Hitler and once again the British policy of compromise and appeasement seemed to predominate. Sir Samuel Hoare visited Laval in Paris and together they worked out the Hoare-Laval plan which would have given the Italians the most valuable part of Abyssinia, leaving the remainder to the Emperor. But, before this plan could be presented to the League of Nations, its terms appeared in the French Press. At once a storm of indignation broke out in Britain. Protests were made from all quarters. Sir Samuel Hoare resigned and was hastily replaced as Foreign Secretary by Anthony Eden. The Hoare-Laval plan was pilloried as the betrayal of a small country to a bully, and Baldwin's stock fell sharply. However, oil sanctions were still not imposed. By May 1936 the Italians were victorious and Haile Selassie, having made a moving protest to the League of Nations

Assembly at Geneva, was in exile in Britain. In June all sanctions against Italy were withdrawn. As in Manchuria, the powerful had conquered the weak and the League of Nations had failed. To this failure British policy had made a most discreditable contribution. Would the British public have supported war against Italy? This was unlikely. But would Italy have dared to challenge Britain in the Mediterranean? Did not the Government exploit the fear of war in order to preserve the Stresa Front? At almost the same time Hitler reoccupied the Rhineland with troops on 7 March 1936 This was a flagrant breach of the Versailles Treaty and of the Locarno Pact but Baldwin argued, probably correctly, that public opinion in Britain would not have tolerated British military action. The Rhineland was to most people in Britain a natural German territory. Nevertheless, this mean the League was falling to pieces, and all it could do at this time was to register the fact that both the Versailles Treaty and the Locarno Treaty had been broken by Hitler. After 1936 the League ceased to play any effective part in the mounting crisis.

Baldwin won the election of 1935 on the promise of collective security but failed to carry it out in Abyssinia and the Rhineland. Soon the Government began to edge towards rearmament, although the public knew little about it at the time. During the next few years the R.A.F.'s bomber force was greatly increased. At the same time eminent scientists were working on the development of radar, which was to be of inestimable value to Britain in World War II.

Baldwin's Government survived and recovered from the failures of foreign policy in 1935 and 1936. This was partly due to general improvement in economic conditions, but also to the division among its opponents. Until 1937 the Labour Party remained opposed to rearmament and clung to the aim of collective security, but clearly without arms there could be no collective security and after 1936 there was already open war in Western Europe.

The Spanish Civil War, 1936-9

In July 1936 General Franco led a military revolt from Morocco against the Spanish Republican Government. He hoped to gain a rapid victory, but the desperate Republican defence of Madrid checked him and from then on a ferocious civil war raged in Spain until 1939.

The Spanish Civil War became one of the outstanding political issues in Britain in these years. The anti-Fascists in Britain saw Franco as the dangerous spearhead of international fascism supported by Hitler and Mussolini. Among the Left there was a powerful demand for the formation of a Popular Front Government in Britain which would give direct aid to the Spanish Republicans. The strongest propagandists for this policy were the Socialist League led by Sir Stafford Cripps, the Independent Labour Party and the Communist Party. Lloyd George also appeared on the Popular Front platform. However, the Labour Party under Attlee refused to have anything to do with this alignment, especially with the Communist Party, which had kept up a running fire against the Labour Party for the previous fifteen years. The official Labour Party view was that Communism, like Fascism, meant dictatorship, to which democratic Socialism was opposed. Sir Stafford Cripps was expelled from the Labour Party for his support of the Popular Front campaign.

Baldwin's position was strengthened by these divisions. Moreover, the Popular Front Government of the Socialist Leon Blum in France pursued the same policy as Baldwin towards Spain – namely, non-intervention. The contradictions and inconsistencies in Socialist policy made a united opposition to the National Government extremely difficult.

Non-intervention

From the beginning the Spanish Civil War was widely regarded as a danger to European peace. 'Volunteers' from Italy (about 100,000 before the war ended) and Germany fought on the side of Franco, while the International Brigade (containing at least 2,000 English volunteers) fought for the Republicans, Russia also intervened with technical aid, arms and a certain number of 'volunteers'. Baldwin was unwilling to intervene in such a struggle, for his party contained many Conservatives who disliked the Republican régime, which was anti-capitalist, anti-monarchical and anti-clerical. In Britain and France there was a safe majority support for non-intervention. In 1936 a Non-Intervention Agreement was signed by most European states, including France, Britain, Germany and Italy. A special Non-Intervention Committee was set up in London to supervise this agreement. It was flagrantly broken at once by both Hitler and Mussolini and this became generally known to the British public. From the beginning non-intervention was a farce, yet Baldwin, and later Chamberlain, kept rigidly to Britain's side of the bargain, while the dictators flouted it.

The problem of rearmament

The threat of German aggression had become more real by 1936. Hitler boasted in March, 1935, that German air power equalled Britain's and Churchill's warnings in the House of Commons echoed the alarm of the Chiefs of Staff. It is now known that Hitler's claim was exaggerated. He was speaking for home consumption as well as to browbeat potential opponents. He deliberately aimed in these years to frighten Britain into neutrality. All the same, in 1936 Germany was rearming fast. Chamberlain replied with a new defence programme. In 1938 Britain was spending 25 per cent of Government expenditure on armaments – about the same as Germany, and in 1939 British aircraft production surpassed that of Germany, while the number of trained pilots was about equal. There was, however, a relative neglect of the Army in favour of the RAF, for Government policy was influenced by the prevailing idea that a war could be won by air power alone – a fallacy which only the experience of 1939–45 was to discredit. The strength of the Royal Navy was also well sustained in these years – something for which Britain was to be thankful in 1939–40.

This increasing tempo of rearmament resulted from the worsening situation in Europe and the world, and in 1937 the Labour Party in Parliament abandoned its tactics of directly opposing the defence estimates. Yet Chamberlain himself was reluctant to see the country's resources go into armaments, and right up to 1939 he clung to the idea that Hitler and his confederates were open to a reasoned and peaceful settlement of European problems.

Chamberlain's foreign policy, 1937–9

The shocking sufferings of the Jews and other inmates of the Nazi concentration camps produced revulsion in all parties in Britain. They were not, however, sufficient to deter Chamberlain from his efforts at agreement with the Nazi régime. Churchill's warning that German policy was really planned aggression received little attention, for he was politically isolated at this time and without great influence. The Labour Party, which had recognized German grievances over the Versailles Treaty, was scarcely in a position to condemn Chamberlain's efforts outright. Leading Conservatives sympathized with Hitler's condemnation of Versailles.

The Left was also suspicious of Chamberlain's attitude to Soviet Russia. Since her entry into the League of Nations in 1934, Russia, represented by Litvinoff, had been a consistent advocate of collective security and a consistent critic of French and British policy. This had gained Russia much prestige amongst the Left in Britain, who suspected that Chamberlain wanted a Soviet-German war. Chamberlain's policy towards Soviet Russia was conditioned by three main considerations: (1) extreme dislike of any alliance with a Communist state, (2) the belief, strongly held by the British Chiefs of Staff, that the Red Army would prove of little use, especially after the purges of 1937–9, (3) the belief that Germany must control the Balkans and that nobody could stop her.

At the Imperial Conference of 1937 Chamberlain's European policies had strong support, for the Dominions, especially Australia and New Zealand, wished to see European problems settled in order that the menace of Japan in the Far East could be more effectively faced by Britain. Japan's renewed attack upon China in 1937 reinforced Dominion fears for their security.

Anthony Eden, Foreign Secretary, 1937

There were, however, differences of opinion within the Government and the Conservative Party. Anthony Eden was by no means completely in agreement with Chamberlain's policies. Lord Halifax, Chamberlain's principal supporter at this time, had already assured Hitler that the Polish Corridor, Danzig, and Austria could all be settled to Germany's satisfaction. Eden

FIG. 6. The Expansion of Germany 1935–9.

represented those who wanted a firmer stand against Hitler, although he himself had failed to rally opposition to Mussolini, had advised the French to accept the Rhineland occupation by Germany, and continued to support the farcical Non-Intervention Agreement over Spain. However, he was convinced that Hitler and Mussolini could both be restrained by an adequate show of opposition. In one respect at this time Eden's policies proved successful. In the summer of 1937 Italian submarines were sinking food vessels destined for Republican Spain, and many captains, like the British hero 'Potato Jones', were attempting to run the dangerous gauntlet. Eden succeeded in calling a conference of the Mediterranean Powers at Nyon. An anti-submarine patrol was established, and Italian attacks ceased.

In 1938 President Roosevelt proposed the calling of a world conference to attempt the settlement of all outstanding issues. Eden considered it an important proposal – especially if Britain was to gain adequate backing from the U.S.A. in the Far East and Europe – but Chamberlain preferred to continue direct dealings with the dictators. Chamberlain and Halifax believed that Mussolini could be persuaded to resist Hitler's Austrian ambitions. Eden was opposed to this policy, and resigned. Lord Halifax succeeded him as Foreign Secretary, and at once brought about the Anglo-Italian agreement of April 1938. Britain agreed to recognize the Italian Empire in Abyssinia, on condition that Italian volunteers were withdrawn from Spain. In November, however, even this condition was abandoned by Halifax. This attempt to woo Mussolini by accepting the results of his aggression against Abyssinia was a betrayal of all League of Nations principles. Moreover, Halifax's policy proved signally unsuccessful, as subsequent events were to show. Even during the negotiations for the Anglo-Italian agreement, Hitler had occupied Austria on 13 March, and both Hitler and Mussolini expressed pleasure that Eden had fallen.

Chamberlain and Czechoslovakia
The fall of Austria was viewed with dismay in Britain by all who believed like Churchill that Hitler's aggression could not be halted by concessions. On the other hand, Chamberlain and Halifax still believed that peace could be achieved by resolving German grievances arising from Versailles.

In Czechoslovakia President Benes was determined to resist Hitler's demands for self-determination for the Sudeten Germans in the north-west of Czechoslovakia. Any arrangement by which the Sudeten mountain frontier was abandoned or weakened would open Czechoslovakia to attack with little hope of effective resistance. The Czechs saw that to concede German demands would destroy the country, but this view was not accepted by Chamberlain. Both Britain and France put pressure on Benes to reach an agreement. Lord Runciman was sent out in July 1938, to mediate but his mission failed. Neither side was prepared to make concessions. The policies pursued by Britain and France made it obvious to Hitler that they were not prepared to declare war over the Czech question. (It is now known that Hitler told his closest associates at this time that he would not act if Britain and France were united against him.)

Berchtesgaden and Godesberg
On 13 September 1938 the Sudeten Germans attempted to force the pace by an open rebellion against the Czech Government. This rebellion was suppressed, but it had a most alarming effect in Britain and France. There was a real danger that Hitler would march in. Chamberlain decided to meet Hitler personally, and on 18 September he flew to Germany and saw Hitler at Berchtesgaden in Bavaria. It was here that Chamberlain agreed to Hitler's demand for the separation of the Sudeten area from Czechoslovakia.

The agreement caused an outburst of anger from the Left, but the idea of self-determination for the Sudeten Germans had considerable support in

Britain – after all, Czechoslovakia was a creation of Versailles and it was logical to clear up German grievances. The French Government, however, disagreed, seeing in Hitler's Sudeten policy another move towards complete German domination of Europe. In view of these fears Chamberlain agreed with France to guarantee the reduced Czechoslovakia. He clearly thought that Hitler would respect the force of this guarantee, even when the main Czech defences had gone. On 21 September, under pressure from Britain and France, Benes agreed to the Berchtesgaden arrangements, realizing that neither Britain nor France would support him if he refused. On the following day, however, at another meeting with Chamberlain at Godesberg, Hitler demanded the immediate occupation of the Sudetenland by German troops, though at Berchtesgaden it had been understood that this would only take place after all negotiations with the Czechs and the other Powers involved had been completed. Chamberlain persuaded Hitler to defer occupation until 1 October.

Hitler's demands at Godesberg gave the impression that he was now forcing the pace and that the Czech settlement was a German victory rather than an international agreement. This attitude was ominous, and a number of Chamberlain's supporters began to waver. Churchill's warnings had received dramatic proof. Chamberlain now found that his Foreign Secretary, Lord Halifax, as well as two former Foreign Secretaries, Sir J. Simon and Sir Samuel Hoare, were all opposed to Hitler's Godesberg demands. The Labour Party and the trade unions also demanded resistance to Hitler. National opinion appeared to be hardening against Chamberlain's policy, and he sanctioned preparations for war. Air raid shelters were prepared, gas-masks issued and arrangements made for the evacuation of schoolchildren from the main cities to country areas. On 26 September the fleet was mobilized for action on orders from Chamberlain himself. Whether these were serious preparations for war or a gesture of warning to Hitler hoping to deter him, is a matter of controversy.

Chamberlain at last attempted to use his trump card. He announced in the House of Commons on 28 September, that Mussolini had, on Chamberlain's request, persuaded Hitler to agree to a Four-Power Conference of Britain, France, Germany and Italy at Munich. This dramatic announcement was received with obvious relief by the vast majority of the House of Commons, and the Labour and Liberal leaders gave Chamberlain their blessing. All rose from their seats and cheered. Only four members showed disapproval or doubt – the sole Communist M.P., W. Gallacher, Winston Churchill, L. S. Amery and Anthony Eden. The immense relief that war had been avoided swept all other considerations aside, both in Parliament and the country.

The Munich Agreement and after

On 29 September Chamberlain, Daladier, Mussolini and Hitler met at Munich. In the outcome there was very little improvement on the position reached at Godesberg, except that Hitler's occupation of the Sudetenland was to take place over ten days instead of at one fell swoop. It was also agreed that Czechoslovakia should be guaranteed by the four Powers after the claims of Poland and Hungary in respect of their minorities in Czechoslovakia had been settled. Before leaving Munich Chamberlain secured the signature of Hitler to a statement which read as follows: 'We regard the agreement signed last night and the Anglo-German Naval Agreement as symbolic of the desire of our two peoples never to go to war with one another again. We are resolved that the method of consultation shall be the

'Peace with Honour': Neville Chamberlain holding the Munich agreement in his hand soon after landing at Heston airport in September 1938.

method adopted to deal with any other questions that may concern our two countries.' On returning home, Chamberlain declared: 'I believe it is peace for our time.'

The general public relief in Britain that war had been averted and Britain and Germany were pledged to settle their future differences by consultation overcame all other considerations, except in the minds of that minority who wished for no compromise with Hitler. This relief was natural to a people who had been constantly told that German military power was overwhelming and that Britain was not prepared for war. The Labour Party's motion in Parliament condemning the Munich Agreement seemed to make no impact on the Government and not much on the country. True, Duff Cooper, First Lord of the Admiralty, who wanted armed action against Hitler, resigned, but the vast majority of the Conservative Party supported Chamberlain, who declared that a war over Czechoslovakia would have been fought 'because of a quarrel in a far-away country between people of whom we knew nothing'.

All the same, in the year after Munich, British rearmament was speeded up. Sir John Anderson, an energetic administrator, was put in charge of Air Raid Precautions (A R P) and plans were made to evacuate to safe areas all school-children and mothers with children under five years of age. Staff talks were held with the French and a British Expeditionary Force planned in case of need. At the same time both Chamberlain and Halifax visited Mussolini, whom they still considered a moderating influence upon Hitler.

The fall of Czechoslovakia and changes in British policy

After Munich Hacha succeeded Benes as President of Czechoslovakia. Slovakia became independent and Hungary took over part of the south. Hacha was forced to declare Bohemia, the old heart of Czechoslovakia, a German protectorate, and on 15 March 1939 German forces entered Prague.

Thus in a very short time Chamberlain's Munich peace plan had collapsed. The Four-Power guarantee was worthless and the heel of Nazi tyranny had completely crushed the Czechs. Munich was now seen to have been not a settlement, but a capitulation to Hitler.

Chamberlain was genuinely shocked by Hitler's betrayal and began to take a different stand. On 17 March, two days after the fall of Czechoslovakia, Chamberlain asserted the need to resist any attempt by Germany at world domination. Rumours of German troop movements towards the Polish frontiers pointed to Poland as the next victim. Chamberlain and the French offered the Poles a guarantee which they accepted. The alliance was not confirmed until as late as 25 August and, despite many requests, neither money nor arms reached the Poles from Britain. Hitler's answer was to repudiate the German-Polish non-aggression pact of 1934 and the Anglo-German Naval Treaty of 1935. In Britain a new Ministry of Supply was created and compulsory military service introduced for men as they reached the age of twenty.

Anglo-Russian negotiations, 1939

Stalin's army purges 1937–8 had led the West to doubt the effective military power of Russia. On the other hand, the failure of Munich had emphasized the weakness of the Western Powers without an ally on

Germany's eastern flank. Churchill, Lloyd George and the Labour Party all pressed for an alliance with Russia without which the Polish guarantee was useless. Despite Chamberlain's dislike of Soviet Russia, negotiations were opened in April 1939.

The negotiations did not go well. Britain feared that Stalin would take over the Baltic states of Latvia and Esthonia on the plea of 'indirect aggression' by Hitler, who had sympathizers in those states. Britain would only co-operate with Russia if Poland were attacked and requested Russian help, while Stalin wanted to be allowed to move Russian troops across northern Poland. To this the Poles would not agree, for they feared the Russians as much as the Germans. Chamberlain wished to frighten Hitler by these negotiations, but it is doubtful whether he intended to go further. Chamberlain still toyed with the idea of a form of 'economic appeasement' of Hitler consisting of a gigantic loan to Germany and the joint development of Africa by Britain and Germany. These ideas strengthened Hitler's contempt for Britain and weakened the negotiations with Russia.

The Soviet-Nazi Pact and the outbreak of war

During early 1939 German pressure on the states of eastern Europe increased. Hitler had already forced Lithuania to cede to him the port of Memel, Mussolini had sent troops into Albania on 7 April and King Zog was forced to flee. The year seemed to promise more and more Axis conquests whether there was open war or not.

On 23 August, Hitler's Foreign Minister, Ribbentrop, and his Russian counterpart Molotov, signed the Soviet-German Pact, one of the most startling and controversial developments of this tragic year. By this pact the Soviet Union would stay neutral if Germany went to war, and eastern Europe would be partitioned between them. Chamberlain promised that the pact would make no difference to Britain's attitude to Poland, and the Anglo-Polish Treaty was signed on 25 August. Yet, both Chamberlain and Halifax continued to put pressure on the Polish Government to negotiate with Hitler over the Corridor and Danzig. On 1 September German troops crossed the Polish frontier and Warsaw was bombed. Even at this point Chamberlain decided that if Hitler would halt hostilities and withdraw, then a conference might well settle the matters in dispute. On 2 September Chamberlain put forward his proposal for Hitler's withdrawal and an international conference. However, such was the disquiet in the House of Commons and in his own Cabinet that Chamberlain sanctioned the dispatch of an ultimatum to expire at 11 a.m. on 3 September. No reply was received from Germany and Chamberlain announced that Britain was at war. On the same day France also declared war.

Why was there a war in 1939? The reasons were even more complex than in 1914. The blame could be put on the weakness of the Versailles settlement, the failure of the League of Nations, on the effects of the great economic crisis of the thirties. The ruthless ambition of the dictators and the complacent short-sightedness of the democratic leaders led to a fatal situation. Equally fatal were the divisions between the United States, the European democracies and Soviet Russia. So long as they remained divided, the Axis powers were triumphant.

24. The Second World War

From September 1939 to April 1940

Within a month the vastly superior German forces had completely over-whelmed Polish resistance. Under the terms of the Nazi-Soviet pact the Germans occupied the western part of the country while the Russians took over the rest. Officially the war had begun and yet for several months everything outside Poland remained strangely peaceful. The French waited defensively behind the Maginot Line while the British Expeditionary Force took up their position on the French left flank. Both sides bombarded each other more with propaganda material than shells during these early months.

The Russo-Finnish War

The Western Allies seemed more concerned with a war which broke out between Russia and Finland in November 1939. The Russians were deter-mined to strengthen their frontier in the north-west, but the Red Armies were brilliantly resisted by the tiny Finnish force under General Manner-heim. Plans to send help to the Finns proved quite impracticable and they had to agree to most of the Russian demands in March 1940.

Blitzkrieg in the west

Directly after the Russo-Finnish Treaty, Hitler began the war in the west in earnest. In April he rapidly overran Denmark and began his invasion of Norway. The Norwegians did not succumb so easily and the French and British were able to send troops to help them. However, the Allies were totally unprepared for this sort of campaign and Hitler had complete control of the air. In a few weeks the Allies were forced to withdraw and the Germans set up a puppet government under Vidkund Quisling, a Nazi sympathizer.

The downfall of Chamberlain

The complete failure of the Norwegian campaign shook the confidence which many Conservatives still had in Neville Chamberlain and, after a dramatic debate in the House of Commons in which the Prime Minister was attacked by members of all parties, he resigned. On 10 May his successor Winston Churchill formed a Coalition Government which included prominent Labour Party leaders such as Clement Attlee and

British troops wait to be evacuated from the beaches of Dunkirk, June 1940.

Ernest Bevin and the Liberal leader, Sir Archibald Sinclair. On the very day that the Coalition was formed Hitler launched a new attack in the west. His armoured divisions smashed through Belgium and the Netherlands, completely by-passing the Maginot Line and drove the British and French troops back to the Channel. With the greatest difficulty 320,000 men of the British Expeditionary Force and the French 1st Army were rescued from the beaches at Dunkirk. The survival of this force was to be of great importance in the long run, but for the moment the situation in France appeared hopeless. The French Government fled from Paris and under the leadership of Marshal Pétain, the hero of the First World War, they signed an armistice with Hitler and with Mussolini, who had now joined the war against the Western Allies. The Pétain Government were allowed to rule south and central France from their new capital at Vichy but the north and the whole Atlantic coastline came under direct German control. The Vichy Republic was officially neutral in the war between Germany and Britain but a few Frenchmen who had escaped to Britain set up a Free French Government under their self-appointed leader General de Gaulle, determined to continue the fight against the Nazis.

Operation Sealion

Hitler's only surviving enemy in the west was Britain and in the summer of 1940 he drew up his plans for operation Sealion, the invasion of the British Isles. Britain's Regular Army was still very small and ill-equipped and at first some of the Local Defence Volunteers or 'Home Guard' were armed with sticks and pitch-forks for want of guns and ammunition. However, Hitler had first to cross the Channel. Therefore in the late summer the German Air Force sought to destroy the Royal Air Force bases in southern England. During the Battle of Britain that followed in August and September the British Spitfires and Hurricanes succeeded in inflicting such heavy casualties on the Germans that Hitler was forced to abandon daylight raids and postpone the whole invasion plan. The Germans switched to heavy night bombing of the big cities during the winter of 1940–1, but although the civilian population suffered severely, these raids had little military significance and hardly affected British war production.

The Middle East and Mediterranean

In the meantime the British had also won some encouraging victories against the Italians. The Italian Navy was decisively defeated at Taranto, in November 1940 and at Cape Matapan in March 1941. The British Army in North Africa also defeated the Italians in Somaliland and threw them back from the Egyptian frontier into Tripoli. In the summer of 1941 Mussolini had to seek German help both in North Africa and in the Balkans, where he had got involved in an unsuccessful invasion of Yugoslavia and Greece. The Germans proved much more effective. Rommel, one of their ablest generals, was sent to North Africa and a German army overran Yugoslavia and Greece. A British force sent to help the Greeks was driven out and the Germans seized Crete in a brilliant airborne attack. The British were able to take Syria and the Lebanon from the Vichy French and to install a pro-British régime in Iraq, but their Balkan campaign had severely weakened their forces in the Middle East and the vital line of communications through Suez was soon in danger.

Operation Barbarossa

However, for Hitler the war in the Middle East was really a sideshow. With the situation in the west under control, he turned to that part of his plan which interested him most, the subjugation of Soviet Russia. Operation Barbarossa, the conquest of Russia, should have been launched early in 1941 but the Balkan campaign delayed it. It was therefore not till June that the Germans began an invasion along the whole length of the Russian front. Stalin had been warned by the British that such an attack was imminent, but there was, at first, nothing the Red Armies could do to prevent the rapid advance of the technically superior Germans. The war in the east was fought with unparalleled ruthlessness. The Germans committed appalling atrocities against prisoners and civilians and the Russians fought back from defeat with amazing tenacity. Although they lost thousands of square miles of territory including major areas of industrial and agricultural production, the Russians rallied to Stalin's call for a Great Patriotic War against the invaders and the German advance was halted on the outskirts of Moscow and Leningrad.

The Russian campaign not only gave some respite to the British in North Africa, it also meant that Britain was no longer alone. Although the Russians were for the moment in almost total defeat they had enormous resources of manpower and materials and they were eventually to play the major part in the defeat of Hitler.

The attack on Pearl Harbor

Within a few months the nature of the war was changed even more dramatically. The Japanese had already used the war in the west as an opportunity to extend their control in China and to occupy French Indo-China. Neither the British nor the Dutch were in any position to prevent the Japanese domination of the rest of East Asia, despite the vast empires they each controlled there. The United States alone had the resources to do this and in December 1941 the Japanese sought to destroy the great American naval and air base at Pearl Harbor in a surprise attack launched without any declaration of war. At once Hitler also declared war on the United States, for although he had no direct cause for conflict he hoped that he would be able to prevent American supplies reaching Britain more effectively if he was at war with both nations.

Pearl Harbor and Operation Barbarossa transformed the war. The Axis powers won immediate victories and in the years 1941–2 their empires reached their greatest extent, but these very victories turned the strategical balance of the war against them. Once Russia and the United States could bring their enormous resources to bear in the war the Axis nations would be almost inevitably crushed.

North Africa, 1942

Yet it was bound to be some time before the British could receive effective help from America and in the meantime there was a crisis in North Africa. The German and Italian forces under Rommel had not only driven the British from Tripoli but advanced into Egypt within sixty miles of Alexandria. However, in a great desert battle at El Alamein the British commander General Montgomery won a decisive victory and from November 1942 the Germans were driven steadily back through North Africa. Meanwhile the Americans under Eisenhower landed in Morocco and Rommel was caught between two armies. By May 1943 the Anglo-American armies had complete control of North Africa and over 300,000 German and Italian soldiers were forced to surrender.

Stalingrad

The victory at El Alamein was one of the most important of the war for the British, but the battle of Stalingrad was even more momentous, In June 1942 the Germans attempted to break through the Russian lines in the south and capture the great city of Stalingrad, the gateway to the Cauacasian oil fields. After a terrible bombardment which reduced the city to rubble the Germans succeeded in occupying most of Stalingrad but before they could wipe out the remaining Russian defenders another Russian army surrounded them. 300,000 German troops were besieged in the most appalling conditions. Their communications were broken and they fought on in the largest battle in the history of mankind, short of food and ammunition but forbidden to surrender by Hitler. Eventually in January

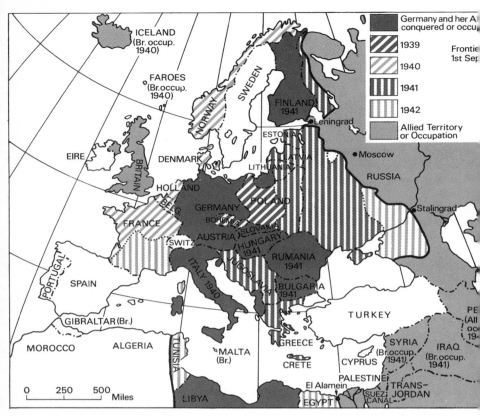

FIG. 7. German Conquests at their greatest, 1942.

1943 their commander Field Marshal von Paulus defied Hitler's orders and capitulated to prevent further slaughter. Stalingrad was a real turning-point in the war. From this time onwards the Germans were slowly but surely driven back through Russia and eastern Europe by the overwhelming weight of the Red Armies.

However, the Russians did not find this task an easy one and ever since the original invasion in 1941 they had been appealing to the Western Powers to open up a second front in Europe. This the Allies had been slow to do. Although they had already mounted heavy bombing attacks on Germany their own trans-Atlantic lines of communication were constantly threatened by German submarines and they were unable to mount any invasion in Europe until North Africa was in their hands. By the time this was achieved in 1943 it was too late in the year to start an invasion of North Europe, which was very strongly defended, and they had to be content with an attack on Italy.

The Italian campaign and the fall of Mussolini
In July 1943 Allied forces landed in Sicily and soon overran the island.

Almost immediately the King of Italy, backed by many leading Fascists, dismissed Mussolini and ordered his successor Marshal Badoglio to seek peace with the Allies. Mussolini was rescued by the Germans, who took over from the Italians and continued to resist the Anglo-American advance up through the mainland. Italy was a difficult country to overrun and it was not until June 1944 that the Allies took Rome. The Germans held a large part of north Italy until the very end of the war under the nominal control of the discredited Mussolini. In the spring of 1945, however, the Italian dictator was captured by Italian resistance fighters and shot.

The invasion of northern Europe

Clearly western Europe could not be liberated through Italy and in 1944 the British, Americans and Free French prepared for a massive invasion of France. The whole of northern France was heavily defended, but the Allies picked on the coast of Normandy, east of the Cherbourg peninsula, as the best point on which to open a beach-head. Supreme command was given to General Eisenhower and General Montgomery was given command of all land forces.

The invasion was launched on D-day, 6 June 1944. A huge force of planes, battleships and landing-craft crossed the Channel in extremely rough weather. Specially constructed floating harbours were towed across to allow the rapid debarkation of men and materials and a pipeline was run under the sea to keep up supplies of petrol. After very heavy fighting the Allies advanced from the beach-head and soon spread out over northern France. The Germans retreated from Paris and de Gaulle's Free French Army were allowed to liberate the capital ahead of the English and Americans. By this time the Allies had complete control of the air and despite a desperate counter-attack in the Ardennes at the end of 1944 the Germans were beaten. In the spring of 1945 the Western armies began the invasion of Germany itself while the Russians were already in the suburbs of Berlin. On 30 April Hitler committed suicide in his bunker under the Berlin Chancellery and his successor, Admiral Doenitz, surrendered unconditionally on 7 May.

The war in the Far East

All this time a very different sort of war was being fought in the Far East. Here the Americans bore the brunt of the fighting although the British were campaigning in north-east India and Burma from 1943 and captured Rangoon in May 1945. The Americans had already advanced into the Philippines after their decisive naval victory at the Battle of Midway in 1942 and were launching heavy bombing raids on mainland Japan. Once the war in Europe was over the other Allies turned their resources to the Far East, though at this time Russia and Japan were not yet at war.

However, despite the defeat of her allies and her own heavy casualties, Japan refused to surrender and it seemed that a long and bloody campaign would have to be fought before mainland Japan could be conquered. This situation was revolutionized by the successful explosion of an atomic bomb in New Mexico during the summer of 1945. The Japanese were warned that the next bomb would be dropped on one of their cities unless they surrendered unconditionally. No reply was received. On 6 August a bomb was dropped on the town of Hiroshima; on 9 August another was dropped on Nagasaki. Both towns were devastated and thousands of people killed. Many of those who survived suffered terrible burns and radiation poisoning and twenty years later victims were still dying from the effects of the bomb. The nuclear attack finally convinced the Japanese militarists that they must surrender unconditionally. Almost exactly six years after it had begun, the Second World War was over.

THE HOME FRONT

1939–43

At home the war began with a great flurry of activity. Air-raid shelters were dug, gas masks distributed and children evacuated from the towns. However, the months of the 'phoney war' in which the German attack never came lulled people into a sense of security. Even members of the Government thought the war would soon be over and only a few days before the western blitzkreig Chamberlain was saying 'Hitler has missed the bus'. By the spring of 1940, however, the war had begun in earnest. Churchill introduced food rationing and compulsory military service for all, except those in key civilian positions. The Emergency Powers Act of May 1940

Winston Churchill inspects the damage in the City of London. With him are his wife and Brendan Bracken, one of his senior advisers.

Londoners seek shelter from the blitz in the underground stations, October 1940.

gave the Government unprecedented powers over almost every aspect of life in Britain.

Churchill created a small War Cabinet which could deal more effectively with the most important aspects of national policy, but he also set up many new ministries to deal with the exceptional problems of the war – for instance the Ministries of Shipping, the Blockade, Economic Warfare, Food, and Home Security. Ernest Bevin became Minister of Labour and National Service. As a successful trade union leader he was especially well qualified to mobilize the nation's manpower effectively. Churchill was both Prime Minister and Minister of Defence and was thus able to keep a close control over the prosecution of the war. He brought in men from all ranks of life if they had some special talent which would be of use. Thus the great newspaper owner Lord Beaverbrook took over the newly created Ministry of Aircraft Production and threw his enormous energies into this vital part of the war effort.

However, victory was a matter of men and women as well as materials and in the critical years of 1941–3 the Government did all it could to keep the morale of the country high. Despite the defeats in Europe and the hardships of the blitz and rationing at home, Churchill had the whole-hearted support of the country behind him. People accepted the new controls and even the rigid censorship of the Press and radio as a necessary part of the defeat of Nazism.

The great increase in the power of the central Government over many aspects of the life of the individual was very significant, for these controls were slow to disappear after the war and indeed some of them have become a permanent part of British government and society. Food and clothes rationing, for example, lasted for years after the war as a part of economic policy. However, these controls were both necessary and highly effective. For instance, by controlling expenditure and by syphoning off spending power by heavy taxes the Chancellor of the Exchequer, Kingsley Wood, was able to prevent the raging inflation which had usually been a feature of wartime economics.

1943–5

After 1943 the danger of invasion and defeat seemed much less real and it soon became clear that the Axis Powers would be overcome sooner or later. However, the hardships of the war were not over. In the last months of the war Germany developed new rocket bombs, the V1s and V2s, which began to wreak terrible damage in south-east England. Fortunately, the rocket bases were overrun by the Allies, but the attacks had proved that in a future war the Channel would be no defence against destruction.

However, once the worst pressures of the war had been removed people began to make plans for a new post-war Britain and political discussion which had been muted during the worst days of the war became much more open. The Labour members of the Coalition began to press for a clear statement of post-war aims and the trade unions became less willing to subject their claims to the general interest.

Lord Woolton who had been Minister of Food became Minister of Reconstruction charged with drawing up post-war plans. Between 1942 and 1945 a number of commissions brought out reports which were to be the basis of a great deal of post-war legislation. In 1942 the Scott Report recommended State control of development in the countryside and the 1943 Uthwatt Report recommended control of all new building. This led directly to the Town and Country Planning Act of 1944. The Barlow Report led to the Location of Industry Act by which the Government had the powers to redevelop depressed areas. Most important of all was the Beveridge Report which recommended an enormous extension of the Welfare State to include free medical treatment, large sickness and unemployment benefits and a children's allowance. All these things were provided in the years after 1945. Even before the end of the war the way was opened for a great expansion of secondary education by the Butler Education Act of 1944.

Britain in 1945

In 1945 the country began to be aware of the cost of victory. Nearly all Britain's overseas assets had been sold; the country was deeply in debt to the United States and other countries. The merchant fleet had been reduced by a third and exports were less than half what they had been in 1938. Five million houses had been destroyed and resources to the value of £1,700 million lost. In 1919 Britain had been faced with the problem of rebuilding her old industries but in 1945 the problem was much more radical. In order to exist Britain had to build totally new industries and increase the level of her exports far beyond that of the thirties. With her international prestige overshadowed by Russia and America, and her old economy shaken to its foundations, Britain had clearly to be prepared for great changes.

The problems of reconstruction: St. Paul's survives but a large area of the City has been flattened in the blitz.

The General Election, 1945

In the spring of 1945 Churchill proposed that the Coalition Government should continue till the end of the war with Japan. The Labour Party, however, would only agree to continue as partners for a further six months. Churchill decided therefore to try to form a Government on his own and called for an election in July 1945. The result was an overwhelming victory for the Labour Party. They won 393 seats against 213 to the Conservatives, 12 to the Liberals and 21 to Independents and the other small parties.

Clement Attlee succeeded Churchill as Prime Minister immediately and for the first time the Labour Party had a clear majority in the House of Commons. The reasons for their victory are now fairly clear. The Conservatives had been in power for the worst years of the thirties and were held to be largely responsible for the mismanagement of foreign affairs up to 1940. Unlike the Labour Party they would not pledge themselves wholeheartedly to implement the Beveridge Report and in their election campaign they relied very largely on the emotional appeal of Churchill as the man who had 'won the war'. On the other hand the Labour Party could not be held responsible for the bad old days for they had never had a majority government. In the war the Labour leaders like Attlee, Bevin and Morrison had proved themselves quite capable of running most important ministries and they were committed to long overdue reforms in British society. For these reasons the British people felt that the Labour Party should be given a chance to put its policies into action.

25. Post-War Britain under Labour Government, 1945-51

The first Attlee Government, 1945-51

Attlee's first Government contained an outstanding group of Labour politicians who were to leave their mark on post-war Britain. Herbert Morrison was made Lord President of the Council with special responsibility for the Government's nationalization plans; Aneurin Bevan as Minister of Health and Arthur Greenwood as Lord Privy Seal were responsible for the next great advance in the development of the Welfare State. Hugh Dalton, the Chancellor of the Exchequer, and Stafford Cripps, the President of the Board of Trade, held vital posts during a critical period in the country's economic development and Ernest Bevin controlled the nation's foreign policy at a time when the statesmen of the world were struggling with the aftermath of the Second World War. Many of these men had already had distinguished careers in the trade unions or the development of the Labour Party and all of them had held important posts during the war.

The problems

The task facing the administration was enormous and the expectations of the British people high. First the economy had to be rebuilt after the strains of the war. Exports had to be encouraged and imports limited to regain a favourable balance of trade. The pound sterling had to be strengthened and investment won from foreign governments and financiers. At the same time the Government had pledged itself to implement the Beveridge Report, to maintain full employment and to undertake a vast programme of house building. These formidable tasks were undertaken with great energy under the quiet but firm leadership of Clement Attlee. However, it was inevitable that the Government's major policies should provoke considerable controversy.

Nationalization

The Labour Party had always contended, on grounds of both social justice and efficiency, that the basic industries should be removed from private control. They believed that home and overseas markets would be better served, profiteering prevented and the conditions created for a planned development of Britain's economy. In 1946 the Government nationalized the Bank of England, claiming that it would be impossible to plan the nation's future without control over its financial nerve centre. In the same year the coal mines were placed under control of the National Coal Board. The Board was ultimately responsible to the Ministry of Fuel and Power, but it was free to undertake its own organization of production. The Government also took control of various transport and communications services. British Overseas Airways Corporation (B.O.A.C.), which had been set up as a nationalized corporation before the war, was joined by British European Airways (B.E.A.). Road haulage, except that run by manufacturers themselves, was placed under the British Road Services organization. Overseas radio and telegraph services were also placed under Government control. In the same way the supply of electricity was nationalized under the Central Electricity Board in 1948 and of gas under the British Gas Council in the next year.

Steel and the House of Lords

The Labour Party had also decided to nationalize the iron and steel industries, but they soon ran into difficulties which they had not experienced elsewhere. In the first place, the capital of the industry was interlocked with that of a number of outside industries so that nationalization was bound to be very complicated. In the second place, the industry was reviving fast under private ownership and the case for nationalization was therefore harder to justify. As a result there was fierce Conservative opposition to the bill. Eventually the Iron and Steel Bill passed through its three readings in the Commons, but the Lords opposed it and this delayed its application until February 1951. By that time the Labour Party majority in the Commons had been cut dramatically and the Bill only came into operation after a heated debate in which over 600 of the 626 members of the Commons were present.

The opposition of the Conservative majority in the Lords to steel nationalization led the Government to amend the power of the Upper House as Asquith had done under similar circumstances in 1911. In 1949 a bill was passed which reduced the time the Lords might delay a bill from three consecutive sittings to two – that is to say from two years to one. At the same time the act abolished double votes under which a business man residing in one area but owning a business in another had two votes. It also abolished the special seats for the Universities. A Boundary Commission was set up to ensure a greater equality in the size of constituencies.

The measures of nationalization had their critics to the Left as well as the Right. Many Left-wingers felt that the acts which placed the nationalized industries under the control of Boards staffed with highly paid business men and a few trade union officials fell far short of the 'worker control' demanded by the Labour pioneers, and, in fact, 80 per cent of British industry remained under entirely private ownership.

Industrial controls

Although most areas of the economy remained in private hands, almost everyone was affected by the Government's overall controls. In order to revive the basic industries and help the balance of trade, all sorts of restrictions and priorities were introduced. Government licences were needed for building, so that, for instance, factories would take preference over dancehalls. Rents, interest rates and profits were also subject to controls. Similarly all dealings in foreign currency came under Government supervision. Rationing continued for clothing and most foodstuffs and the last ration cards did not disappear until 1954. The Government also kept a firm hand on labour; the war-time Arbitration Order was maintained so that the unions had to submit any wage claim to an arbitration tribunal. However, the Trade Disputes Act of 1927 (see page 302) was repealed so that the unions could once more affiliate their members to the Labour Party on a contracting-out basis.

Quite apart from these general controls the Government set up a number of special commissions. Thus the Raw Cotton Commission controlled imports for the cotton industry. The Board of Trade controlled the import of paper, chemicals, timber and other materials, while the Ministry of Supply supervised the import of iron, manganese and radio-active materials.

This planning and control did a great deal to rebuild the country's export trade in the period 1945–51. It gave an impetus to newer industries such as chemicals, electrical apparatus and motor-cars while some of the older industries like steel also made rapid strides. The nation's industry gained at least a temporary benefit from the devaluation of the pound in 1949 by Sir Stafford Cripps which made British exports cheaper on the foreign market and foreign goods more expensive on the home market. This devaluation was forced on the Government because of the drain of Britain's foreign currency and dollar reserves. It was quite a drastic revaluation from £1 : 4·08 dollars to £1 : 2·87 dollars.

On top of the economic difficulties came the English weather. The winter of 1947 was one of the worst of the century. Deep snowfalls blocked roads and ice closed ports and rivers. There was drastic fuel rationing and constant power cuts for both homes and industry. The closing down of industries left over 2,000,000 unemployed in March 1947. For the first time in British history bread was rationed and it was not until well into the summer that the economy got on its feet again.

The rationing system

These post-war years were austere ones for almost everybody. The Board of Trade controlled the import of all foodstuffs and luxuries and supervised their distribution to retailers. In any case the amount of food that each individual could buy was limited by his ration card and the Government made the prices of commodities like tobacco unnaturally high to restrain purchasers. These measures were supposed to give fair shares to all, but a

Queuing for food in East London 1946.

'black market' soon developed through which those who had the money and were prepared to break the law could buy the luxuries that most other people had to learn to do without.

There were good reasons for rationing and the Government prevented a general rise in prices such as that which had occurred after the First World War. However, people naturally found controls irksome and the Government's popularity had waned a good deal by 1950.

Social reform under Labour, 1945–51

Despite the nation's economic difficulties the Government embarked on a substantial programme of social reform which extended the work of the wartime Coalition and did something to compensate for the post-war austerities.

The National Health Service Act, 1946, was introduced by the fiery Minister of Health, Aneurin Bevan. It came into effect in 1948 and proved to be one of the most important foundations of the Welfare State. The Act gave free medical treatment to everyone, while the doctors and dentists were paid by the State according to the number of patients on their lists. The hospital and specialist services were organized into fourteen regions and each was associated with a university possessing a school of medicine. The regional boards decided general policy while the day-to-day running of the hospitals remained in the hands of management committees. The great majority of the old independent hospitals joined the scheme which proved to be an administrative success. The greatest drawback to the system was the number of old hospital buildings and the lack of money to develop the service.

Many doctors feared that their close relationship with their patients would disappear in a State-controlled service and they resented the loss of the right to set up practice wherever they pleased. Their fears were partly allayed by an amending act which prevented the Minister of Health making doctors merely salaried Civil Servants.

The provision of free medical service, including free spectacles, dentures and medicine was very costly. In its first year alone the scheme cost £400 million and in 1951 the Government re-instituted some minor charges. Even so the service still had to struggle with the high price of drugs, the shortage of doctors and the lack of modern buildings.

The National Insurance Act, passed in 1946 and implemented in 1948, had equally far-reaching consequences for British society. All working people were to be insured from the time they left school till they retired. Both employees and employers contributed to this scheme every week and in return the individual was entitled to a weekly payment if he was ill or unemployed. In addition there were maternity benefits, funeral grants, and pensions for women at the age of sixty and men at sixty-five.

The National Insurance (Industrial Injuries) Act, 1946, was closely connected with the National Insurance Act. Under the old system it was often very difficult and expensive to claim compensation for an industrial injury. The new Act made provision for grants to injured workers and in the case of severe injuries special Medical Boards could grant disablement pensions.

The National Assistance Act, 1948, was designed to meet any failures in the national insurance schemes. The Act put an end to the last traces of the 1834 Poor Law Amendment Act. Local authorities were given the duty of providing accommodation and welfare services for the aged and handicapped and a large number of local National Assistance Boards were empowered to make grants to all those who failed to qualify under the ordinary insurance schemes or whose insurance benefits proved inadequate for their particular circumstances.

The Welfare State
Apart from these important Acts there were a number of others which dealt with the welfare of children, youth employment, and school meals and medical services. The Government also extended its powers over town and country planning and the development of new towns, which closely affected the well-being of the people.

Even within the first few years all these reforms had a favourable effect. The Rowntree Report on the City of York, for example, showed a massive reduction in poverty as compared with conditions in the pre-war decade. It is true that there were many, including Lord Beveridge, who felt that the grants under the new legislation did not go far enough towards a system of complete social security. In this sense the new acts did fall short of Beveridge's Report on which they were based. All the same an enormous amount had been achieved considering the economic difficulties of the Government.

Financial and economic policy

To finance social welfare and economic reconstruction the Government had had to call heavily on Canadian and American financial assistance and at the same time to impose heavier taxation, especially on the higher income groups. Moreover, until 1947 the Chancellor of the Exchequer, Hugh Dalton, had sought to stimulate the economy and the activities of local authorities in such things as building schemes by a policy of easy credit. This led to a rapid rise in prices and his successor, Sir Stafford Cripps, imposed a rigid policy of restraint and austerity. Under a partial 'freeze' wages rose only 5 per cent between 1948 and 1950 and the great majority of companies imposed limits on their dividends. The result was that the Cripps years seemed to be ones of perpetual shortages and restrictions. However, his strict measures gradually had the desired effect. During these years imports rose by 7 per cent compared with a 25 per cent rise in exports; there was almost full employment and, although rationing remained in basic foodstuffs, furniture, clothing, soap and petrol were all freed.

Foreign policy under the Labour Governments

Ernest Bevin, the Foreign Secretary, came to office at a peculiarly difficult time for British foreign policy. On the one hand Britain's power had drastically declined; on the other hand Britain and the other Western European nations found themselves inevitably involved in difficult relations with Soviet Russia and her allies in the East.

The Labour Government's first important task in foreign affairs was the completion of the Potsdam Conference during which the election had taken place. Attlee replaced Churchill as the leader of the British delegation but there was no major change of policy. The conference put into effect the previous Yalta agreements on the division of Germany into four zones and the division of Berlin into four sectors. The conference also agreed upon the demilitarization of Germany and the trial of the Nazi leaders as war criminals. Although Germany was divided for the purposes of occupation, all the Powers agreed that the country was to be treated as a single unit – there was still no official idea of its permanent division into two states.

In the same way it was still not clear that Europe itself would be divided between the Communist and non-Communist states by a hard and fast line. Soviet Russia appeared to be adopting a friendly policy, particularly towards the Americans, and agreed that the Allied Control Council in Berlin should be in the American sector. When Churchill spoke of an iron curtain coming down through Europe many people believed he was just a war-mongering old imperialist. However, this optimism was soon dissipated.

FIG 8. The Resettlement of Eastern Europe, 1945.

It became increasingly clear that Russia and the Western Powers had quite different plans for the development of Europe and the treatment of the defeated states. Eventually the Western Powers, despairing of a democratic settlement in the Russian-controlled Danubian states, recognized the new Communist-dominated governments of Rumania, Bulgaria and Hungary. On the other hand they took increasing care to protect the democratic development of areas like western Germany which lay within their sphere of influence.

Britain and Russia

The eastern Mediterranean was traditionally an area of rivalry between British and Russian Governments and this remained true after 1945. In Greece a civil war broke out between the Communists and the Royalists in which the latter eventually won, thanks to British and later American aid. Russia also put pressure on Turkey to grant her bases in the Dardenelles and here too first the British and then the Americans warded off the Russians. These incidents were significant for two reasons. In the first place they showed that the areas of discord between Communist and non-Communist forces was spreading all round the world and in the second place they demonstrated that Britain was no longer able to maintain an independent foreign policy in the face of Communist aggression, without American help. The same was true in Germany where the British could not afford the enormous costs of maintaining their own zone of occupation and had to seek American aid. The British and Americans unified their zones in January 1947, not only for greater efficiency but also to help revive the economy of western Germany.

The Marshall Plan

The process by which the United States formally took responsibility for the defence of the democratic states was known as the 'Truman Doctrine', and it came to be a central part of American foreign policy after 1946. However, the Americans realized that military alliances would not keep western Europe free from Communism unless the economies of the European states were revived. In June 1947 the American Secretary of State, George Marshall, announced that the United States would make vast sums of American capital available for this purpose and Bevin was the first to welcome this move. 'When the Marshall proposals were announced,' he wrote, 'I seized them with both hands.' Bevin took a leading part in the founding of the Organization for European Economic Co-operation (O.E.E.C.) through which the Marshall aid was to be administered, and the new body was brought into operation by June 1948. Before this time, however, two events had divided Europe more deeply than before into two camps. First the Russian Foreign Secretary, Molotov, had refused to join the O.E.E.C. and had prevented the other states of Eastern Europe from becoming members. Secondly the Communists in Czechoslovakia, with

Russian help, had staged a *coup d'état* which replaced the democratically elected Socialist-Communist coalition which had ruled the country since the war.

The origins of N.A.T.O.
The first military alliance Britain signed after the war was the treaty of Dunkirk (March 1947) by which Britain and France united against any revival of German military power. However, Bevin and other European leaders soon came to feel that they had more to fear from Russia than a revived Germany. Russia and her satellites still had enormous armies and air forces under arms and after 1948 the lesson of Czechoslovakia seemed to show how dangerous any sort of compromise with Communism could be. The Western European Powers were naturally anxious to have American military aid to offset this threat, but the Americans insisted that the Europeans should take the initiative in the creation of collective security. Thus in March 1948 the Dunkirk Powers were joined by Belgium, the Netherlands and Luxemburg in the Treaty of Brussels, a joint defensive system with its military headquarters at Fontainebleau under the chairmanship of Field Marshal Montgomery.

The next step was even more important. In April 1949 the Brussels Pact nations were joined by the United States, Canada, Iceland, Denmark, Norway, Portugal and Italy in the Atlantic Pact. In 1951 Greece and Turkey also became members and in 1954 West Germany was admitted. The Pact created the North Atlantic Treaty Organization, the largest peacetime military organization in European history. In 1949 alone the United States granted a billion dollars to the organization and in 1950 N.A.T.O. military forces were united under the supreme command of General Eisenhower with a military headquarters in Paris. In all these changes Bevin played a leading part and it appeared that Britain was finding a new role in foreign affairs as a leading member of European co-operative ventures like O.E.E.C. and N.A.T.O.

The Berlin blockade
The strength of the new alliances were immediately put to the test by the Berlin blockade. During 1947 and 1948 Britain, France and the United States made great efforts to revive their zones of Germany. A new currency was introduced and the Germans themselves were given more and more control over their own development. The Russians opposed these moves for many reasons and in March 1948 closed all surface routes to the western sectors of Berlin in an attempt to make the Western Powers withdraw. The Western Powers had either to defeat the blockade or abandon their position in Berlin to the Communists. In fact, they maintained the beleaguered city of 2,000,000 people by an enormous air-lift which lasted until the end of the blockade in May 1949. The blockade had speeded up the development of Western defences from the Brussels Pact to

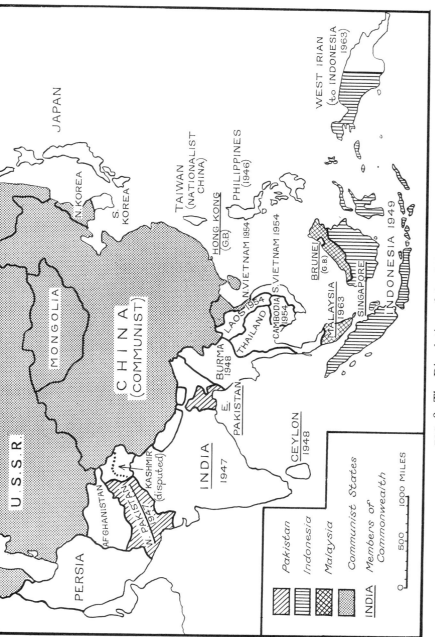

FIG. 9. The Dissolution of the Asian Empires.

the N.A.T.O. alliance and greatly strengthened those like Bevin who believed in a close alliance with the United States. His arguments became even more convincing when, in 1949, the first atomic explosion in the U.S.S R. was detected by Western scientists.

Britain and Asia

The clash between the Western Powers and the Communists was not restricted to Europe and the Middle East. By 1949 the Chinese Communists led by Mao Tse-tung had defeated the Nationalists under Chiang Kai-shek despite the enormous amounts of American aid the latter received. Chiang was forced to retire to the island of Formosa under United States protection. The next year the Communist North Koreans invaded South Korea. Thanks to Russia's absence from the United Nations at the time, the Security Council was able to denounce the North Koreans as aggressors and send a force made up mainly of Americans to defend the south. The British also sent an important contingent while the North Koreans were soon backed by thousands of Communist Chinese. At one point the American commander General Macarthur wished to use atomic weapons in the war but President Truman, with the full support of Attlee, resisted this temptation which would undoubtedly have led to a head-on clash between Russia and America. In 1954 after several years' negotiations the frontiers of North and South Korea were fixed along the 38th parallel. The war in Korea seemed of little importance to many in Britain, for the main weight of the U.N. effort was born by the United States. Yet apart from its serious effects in the Far East it also checked British economic recovery just as the country seemed to be reviving from the worst of its post-war setbacks.

Palestine

Britain had committed her troops to the war in Korea but she had played only a secondary role there. In other non-European spheres her responsibility was much greater. One of the Government's most difficult overseas problems was Palestine. The area had been administered as a mandate since the end of the First World War. Even in the thirties the situation had been difficult as more and more European Jews sought to migrate from Europe to this area which had previously been predominantly Arab. The problem was held in suspension after 1939 but in 1945 the Jews were once more anxious to return to their historic homeland, while the Arabs were equally anxious not to be overwhelmed by a flood of new-comers of a different religion and culture. The British sought to restrict immigration but this policy pleased neither side and there was soon three-way fighting between the British and terrorist organizations from the two communities. On top of this the Americans made it clear that they favoured a less restrictive policy towards the Jews. The British Government felt unable to cope any longer and abdicated its responsibilities to the United

Nations in 1947. Eventually, after a war between the Jews and the neighbouring Arab states, Palestine was divided between the new Jewish state of Israel and the Arab state of Jordan (previously Transjordan). However, the settlement only intensified the hostility between the two communities as thousands of Arabs fled from Israel and Britain's position in her remaining Middle Eastern territories was weakened.

The dissolution of the Empire

In 1947 Britain withdrew from a much larger and equally strife-torn area of her empire. During the war the Indian nationalist leaders had continued to agitate for independence. Gandhi and Nehru had spent part of the war in prison after mounting their 'Quit India' campaign against the British Raj, and a small number of Indians had supported the Japanese who they believed would free their country from European rule. The British for their part promised some form of independence after the war, for it was quite apparent that they would not be able to hold down the whole sub-continent under a constitution which pleased nobody.

However, the form under which India was to become independent was not so easy to settle. During the war the hostility between the Muslim League and the Congress movement increased and the League declared it would be satisfied with nothing less than a separate Muslim state. The Congress leaders and indeed most British administrators and soldiers in India, were opposed to the idea of partition. However, Attlee was determined to leave India as quickly as possible and when negotiations between the leaders of the two communities broke down he announced that the

*The end of the years of austerity: the Festival of Britain in May 1951.
In the centre is the Dome of Discovery and to the right the Royal
Festival Hall.*

British would withdraw, whatever the situation, in 1947. There were terrible communal killings in many parts of India in which Muslims and Hindus died in their tens of thousands. Against this background Gandhi and Nehru were forced to agree to the creation of the state of Pakistan for the two areas where Muslims predominated. The rest of British India together with the associated princely states formed the Union of India. Both states remained members of the Commonwealth, but Britain's withdrawal left enormous problems unresolved so that the sub-continent has remained under the threat of war ever since (see p. 345).

The dissolution of the empire had also been speeded up elsewhere. Ceylon became an independent member of the Commonwealth and Burma not only won its independence but left the Commonwealth as well. On the other hand the British re-established their authority in Malaya and after a long jungle-war crushed a Communist rebellion there. This rapid decolonization which gathered momentum in the fifties was all part of the readjustment of Britain to a new and more limited role in the post-war world.

The General Elections of 1950 and 1951
In February 1950 the enormous majority which the Government had enjoyed since 1945 was reduced to no more than six. There were many reasons for this drop in popularity. The people were irked by the continuation of rationing and the shortage of new houses so many years after the war. The Conservatives had launched a massive and effective campaign against the nationalization of steel. Peacetime military service which had been introduced in 1947 and had been increased from eighteen months to two years by 1950 was also unpopular. The Government seemed tired after its five years of intensive activity and the Conservatives produced an appealing programme which promised more houses and lower taxation but did not threaten to reverse any of the Labour Government's popular social reforms.

Attlee's second Government, with its tiny majority, was even more vulnerable. Two leading ministers, Ernest Bevin and Sir Stafford Cripps, died. Two more, Aneurin Bevan and Harold Wilson, resigned when the new Chancellor of the Exchequer, Hugh Gaitskell, reimposed some charges for spectacles and dentures to contribute towards the costs of the Korean War. Prices continued to rise and the Conservatives harassed the Government as it struggled to push through the controversial Steel Bill. In October 1951 Attlee appealed to the electorate again in the hope of strengthening his position. The Labour Party once more polled a majority of the popular vote, but, because of the way in which this was distributed, the Conservatives led by Churchill were able to form a Government with a majority of seventeen. It was a slender margin, but it was to be the start of thirteen years of Conservative government.

26. Conservative Government, 1951-64

The Churchill administration

Winston Churchill headed his first peacetime Government at the age of seventy-six. It was also his first real experience at the head of a purely Conservative Government, but, with such a small majority, he clearly did not have a mandate to reverse the major trends of the Attlee administrations. However, there were some concessions to the private enterprise interests for which the Conservatives stood. Steel and much of the road haulage industry were denationalized, rationing was ended by 1954 and food subsidies reduced. In 1954 the Government also broke the monopoly of the B.B.C. by allowing commercial television under the control of the I.T.A. (Independent Television Authority), a move hotly attacked by the Labour Opposition.

The economic crisis

These were all signs of the end of the years of austerity, but in 1951 the Government was immediately faced with a serious economic crisis. The Economic Commission for Europe reported on Britain that 'the economy is showing every sign of suffering from severe strain. Inflation is rampant, exports are wavering, and this, combined with the high cost of imports, has created a new balance of payments problem which will have to be countered by a new export drive or cuts in imports.'

It was a crisis situation which was to be all too common in post-war Britain. The trade deficit for the first seven months of 1951 was £679,000,000 and in June alone £151,000,000, twice as much as the worst month in the 1947 crisis. The new Chancellor, R. A. Butler, had to place drastic curbs on spending. Imports were reduced by £600,000,000 or 6 per cent, with a consequent easing of the drain on gold and dollar reserves. In 1953 there was also a general revival in world trade which led to a gradual improvement in export figures. Butler had been amongst the first of the Conservative leaders to realize that any Government had to plan the economy rather than leave everything to the workings of free enterprise. He had been the principal force behind the Conservative Industrial Charter, a policy statement drawn up in 1947, and he now put his ideas for a managed economy into practice. In particular he manipulated the Bank Rate to reduce or increase investment and personal spending, a device which was to become very common in subsequent years.

By 1955 Butler's measures had taken effect and the country was enjoying its first period of real affluence since the war. Standards of living had risen and the Chancellor was able to reduce income tax by sixpence in the pound. Moreover, the Conservatives continued to develop the welfare services which the Labour Government had founded, though with some important modifications. Thus on the one hand they placed more charges on patients for dental services and prescriptions but the Government's own spending on National Health rose from just over £400,000,000 in 1952–3 to £626,000,000 in 1957–8. By 1958 a million more patients were being treated in hospitals and the waiting lists for hospital places had been reduced by 90,000.

The Government also continued Labour's rearmament programme but spread the expenditure over five years rather than three so that money was released for other public services. The most important of these was housing. Harold Macmillan, the Minister for Housing and Local Government, began a great programme which led to over a million new houses between 1952 and 1955. In 1954 alone there were 309,000 new houses in England and Wales compared with 172,000 in the last year of the Labour Government. The Conservatives naturally placed great emphasis on this at the 1955 election. The Government also passed the 1952 Town Development Act which gave Government aid to small towns which would take overspill population from the overcrowded cities.

In 1952 King George VI died and was succeeded by his eldest daughter, Elizabeth. Her coronation the next year was hailed as the beginning of a new 'Elizabethan age'. The political scene was also changing; in 1955 Sir Winston Churchill resigned and was succeeded by the Foreign Minister, Sir Anthony Eden. Churchill had been in poor health for some years and had suffered from a stroke in 1953. Many younger Conservatives believed that this change of leadership would allow the introduction of radical changes into the Conservative programme.

The Eden ministry, 1955–7

The new Prime Minister held a general election in May 1955 at a time when everything was in the Government's favour. The balance of payments crisis had receded, employment levels were high and the opposition was rent by internal dissension. As a result Eden was able to form a Government with a comfortable majority of sixty. His most important colleagues were Butler, who became Lord Privy Seal and Leader of the House of Commons, Macmillan, the new Chancellor, and Selwyn Lloyd, the Foreign Secretary. At home the Conservative Industrial Charter of 1947 continued to guide Government policy. Every effort was made to encourage workers to buy their own houses and to develop their interest in productivity through profit-sharing schemes in industry. Macmillan encouraged saving by increasing the interest rates on defence bonds and National Savings Certificates. He also introduced Premium Bonds, an astute exploitation of the gambling instinct which rising prosperity had previously channelled into the football pools, horse-racing and bingo. His measures did something to check the withdrawal of savings and the vast increase in personal spending which threatened to throw the country once more into a spiral of inflation.

Foreign affairs and the Suez crisis

In 1953 Stalin died and the Korean War drew to an end. At last it seemed that there might be an easing of the Cold War. Eden, whose interests had always been primarily in foreign affairs, took part in a number of important meetings both as Foreign Secretary and as Prime Minister. Perhaps the most important of these was the Paris meeting in 1955 which brought West Germany and Italy into the Western European Union and allowed West Germany to rearm as a full member of N.A.T.O.

However, Eden's successes in Europe were soon jeopardized by a crisis in the Middle East. Britain's position in this area had grown increasingly difficult from the time of the Palestine crisis onwards. The Arabs blamed Britain for the creation of Israel and the problem was kept alive by the existence of thousands of Palestinian Arab refugees in the neighbouring Arab lands. In the early fifties Britain began to experience increasing difficulty in her relations with King Farouk of Egypt, who sought to recoup some of his dwindling popularity in Egypt by adopting an aggressive attitude towards the British occupation of the Suez Canal zone. In 1952 Farouk was overthrown and Eden was able to establish much better relations with his successors led by Colonel Nasser. Under the Anglo-Egyptian Treaty of 1954 Britain withdrew her troops from the canal base altogether and it seemed that Britain would be able to rebuild her relations with the Arab world on a new footing. However, two factors seemed to stand in the way of an easing of tension in this area. In the first place the enmity between Israel and the Arabs showed no sign of abating, and in the second place the influence of the Western Powers in this region was increasingly challenged by that of Russia and her allies. Soviet trade with Egypt increased very rapidly and the Czechoslovak government supplied Nasser with modern armaments in return for Egyptian rice and cotton.

Nasser for his own part welcomed aid from any source, for he was engaged in building the Aswan High Dam which he hoped would revolutionize Egypt's backward economy. An offer of aid for this project from the Soviet Union was immediately capped by one from Britain, the United States and the World Bank in 1955. However, by the next year the Western Powers felt that Nasser was becoming increasingly pro-Communist despite their aid and the offer was withdrawn. Nasser's reaction was to nationalize the Suez Canal in July 1956. The Canal Company, owned mainly by the British Government and a number of French shareholders, was promised compensation, but this did not satisfy Eden. He believed that Nasser was as untrustworthy as Hitler in the thirties and that it would be equally dangerous to appease him. He also believed the Egyptians' real aim was to undermine Britain's whole position in the Middle East in alliance with the Communist Powers. At first Britain sought to reverse the nationalization by peaceful means. The British Government called an international conference of the major shipping nations called the Canal Users' Association, but the United States did not support the Association and it achieved nothing. An appeal to the U.N. Security Council was blocked by the Russian veto. Then in October events took a dramatic turn.

First Eden and Selwyn Lloyd held meetings with their French opposite numbers in Paris. Then, on 29 October, Israeli forces crossed the border and rapidly drove back Egyptian troops across the Sinai peninsula. It now seems clear that there was some collusion between the Israelis and the French and British Governments. On 30 October the British and French ordered the Israelis and Egyptians to withdraw to positions ten miles either side of the Suez canal and when the ultimatum was rejected they launched a joint attack which captured Port Said and a section of the Canal.

The British, French and Israeli Governments were immediately condemned by the General Assembly of the United Nations, the Russians threatened military action and the United States dissociated itself entirely from the British policy. As a result military action ceased by 6 November and the Franco-British forces withdrew.

The results of Suez

Eden and his supporters claimed that, although the Suez campaign had failed in its immediate purpose, it had at least forced the United States to play a greater part in the defence of the Middle East against Communist encroachment. However, many people in Britain and outside saw it as an unmitigated disaster for British foreign policy. It certainly marked a watershed both for British policy and for British public opinion. The Suez crisis demonstrated once and for all that Britain could no longer apply the methods of nineteenth-century imperialism in a world in which both her prestige and power had rapidly declined.

Conversely the affair had very deep effects in the Afro-Asian world. Despite his defeat at the hands of the Israelis, Nasser's position had been immensely strengthened. A small emergent nation had successfully defied two of the Great Powers and this certainly encouraged the other new nations to adopt an independent line in the United Nations and elsewhere. Moreover, Western warnings that the Egyptians would be unable to run the canal properly proved utterly wrong. In 1956 the canal could not take ships of over 40,000 tons. After ten years of Egyptian control the maximum was 60,000 tons.

The affair naturally had important political repercussions in Britain. Hugh Gaitskell, the leader of the Opposition, had roundly condemned British action as a contravention of the principles of the United Nations and even within the Conservative Party the Prime Minister's position was weakened. Late in 1956 Eden's health gave way under the strain and he resigned in January 1957.

Britain adjusts to a new role in World Affairs: a British soldier stands guard at Port Said while United Nations troops move in after the 1956 Suez War.

The Macmillan administration, 1957–63
Eden's successor, Harold Macmillan, was faced with the difficult task of restoring the popularity and morale of the Conservative Party. In this he was remarkably successful, for in the 1959 elections his majority rose to over a hundred. Never before in modern British history had a party in power increased its lead on two successive occasions.

Finance and trade
However, the immediate situation was very difficult. The new Chancellor of the Exchequer, Peter Thorneycroft, was soon grappling with the endemic problem of inflation. Private spending, encouraged by easy hire purchase,

was increasing in leaps and bounds, especially on cars, household appliances, betting and foreign holidays. Once again exports were failing to keep pace with imports and the Chancellor had to stave off a balance of payments crisis by severe deflationary methods. Government spending was cut back, the Bank Rate increased from 5 per cent to 7 per cent and every effort was made to discourage over-spending and stop the rise in prices. This in turn would encourage manufacturers to turn to the export market. By the end of 1957 gold and dollar reserves had improved, so the measures had been reasonably successful, but in 1958 Thorneycroft resigned when his opposition to Government spending was ignored. His successor, Heathcote Amory, reversed his policy and reduced the Bank Rate to 4 per cent. The economy was once more encouraged to expand rapidly but this in its turn led to a new period of inflation and balance of payments crisis. By 1960 a new Chancellor, Selwyn Lloyd, was applying the brakes harder than ever. The Bank Rate rose to 6 per cent, hire purchase was restricted and on top of this the Government tried to enforce a very unpopular 'pay freeze'. This alternation of rapid expansion and rapid deflation led Labour critics to label Conservative policy as 'stop-go' economics and to complain that the country was being run under a series of temporary measures rather than constructive planning.

The planning phase

All the same Macmillan showed much more interest in state planning and control than any of his Conservative predecessors. Even before 1960 there was a very great increase in spending on the Welfare Services, especially the National Health Service. Yet even this did not keep pace with changing conditions. There were no new hospitals built in the fifties and there was a great shortage of doctors, teachers and police. Many highly trained young men, notably doctors and scientists, went abroad, especially to the United States, where salaries and research facilities were so much better. The economic policies of the Government met considerable opposition from the trade union movement and by 1960 there was mounting industrial unrest over wage claims.

The Prime Minister was not slow to react to the decline in Conservative popularity shown in the opinion polls. After 1960 the old short-term policies gave way to a new interest in long-term Government planning. Dr Beeching was brought in to investigate the organization of British Railways; the Newsom and Robbins Committees were set up to advise on the future of education and the Buchanan Inquiry investigated the problems of road traffic. By 1962 the Government had introduced several long-term plans, including a programme for building ninety new hospitals over ten years and a six-year scheme for the development of roads and motorways costing £1,000,000,000.

Yet another sign of Government planning was the creation of the National Economic Development Council which came into full operation

CONSERVATIVE GOVERNMENT, 1951–64 279

in February 1962. On it economists, employers and union leaders joined to advise the Government on the major problems in the long-term development of British industry. Another of the Government's creations, the National Incomes Commission, was less successful. Its purpose was to advise the Government on an incomes policy which would keep wages in line with the growth of production and prevent the inflationary spiral. Unlike the N.E.D.C. this body did not win the approval of the T.U.C.

All these changes were made to overcome the recurrent problems of the British economy. Events in 1962 showed just how necessary this was for, as the deflationary measures of Selwyn Lloyd took effect, unemployment figures rose to half a million. Even before this peak was reached the Prime Minister was making drastic changes to overhaul his administration. In July seven ministers, including Selwyn Lloyd, were replaced and younger men such as Maudling, the new Chancellor of the Exchequer, were brought in to lend their weight to Macmillan's policies. Yet this was not enough to check the steady decline in Conservative popularity between 1961 and 1964.

Defence under the Conservative Governments

The development of the hydrogen bomb and of long-range missiles led to a great controversy in British defence policy during the fifties. The first point in dispute was whether Britain should possess a nuclear defence system at all. The second was whether such a system could be entirely in British hands or must be run in co-operation with the United States. On the first point both the major parties were broadly in agreement. The production of a British atomic bomb in 1952 was the fulfilment of a policy initiated by Attlee, though the Conservatives extended this by their efforts to build a British rocket that could carry a nuclear warhead.

They soon found the missile race was an expensive one in which the British could hardly keep pace with Russia or America. Macmillan's decision to rely increasingly on nuclear weapons in the late fifties led to the rapid reduction of the armed forces. Conscription ended and the Government sought to replace the large conscript army with a small but highly trained and mobile force of regulars. At the same time the Government's decolonization policy meant a considerable reduction in the number of overseas bases. Britain did succeed in exploding her first hydrogen bomb in 1957 but the Blue Streak rocket which was to carry the nuclear warhead proved to be a very costly failure. The Government turned instead to an American missile, the air-to-ground Skybolt, but this too had to be abandoned when the Americans gave up their Skybolt programme. In the end, after a meeting at Nassau in 1962 with President Kennedy, Macmillan persuaded the Americans to supply Britain with the Polaris missile which was fired from submarines. At the same time the two heads of Government agreed to try to set up a joint nuclear force with their N.A.T.O. partners. Thus Britain had found a modern nuclear delivery system but in the process she had demonstrated her dependence on the United States.

This concentration on defence policy was a reflection of the continued tension in world affairs. A long awaited summit meeting in Paris in May 1960 broke up almost before it had begun when Krushchev walked out after an American spy plane had been shot down over Russia. The next year the continued division of Europe into two camps was emphasized by the building of the Berlin Wall between the eastern and western sectors of the city.

In October 1962 the world seemed closer than ever before to a nuclear conflict. American reconnaissance planes photographed rocket sites in Cuba which were supplied and manned by the Russians. President Kennedy gave a stern warning that any attack on the United States would be met by immediate retaliation against the Soviet Union and at the same time he set up a naval blockade to prevent further supplies reaching Cuba. In the face of this resolute action Krushchev ordered Soviet ships on their way to Cuba to turn back and agreed to dismantle the existing sites. Although Kennedy had not consulted him, Macmillan gave his full support to the United States, and he and his Foreign Secretary Lord Home played an important part in arranging the 1963 Nuclear Test Ban Treaty by which Britain, the United States and the Soviet Union agreed to suspend the testing of nuclear weapons in the atmosphere.

Britain and Europe

The Cuban crisis was just one example of the way in which the two Great Powers could come close to nuclear war without reference to the other nations of the world. However, during these years there was a powerful movement towards the unification of the states of Western Europe as a third great political and economic force. In 1957 France, West Germany, Italy, the Netherlands, Belgium and Luxembourg had signed the Treaty of Rome which created the European Economic Community (or Common Market). Many of its supporters saw this as the first step towards the creation of a political union in western Europe and were anxious that Britain should join. But the British Government was reluctant to see Britain's political sovereignty submerged in a united Europe; they were also concerned to safeguard the economic interests of her Commonwealth trading partners who enjoyed considerable advantages on the British market. The Common Market members were unwilling to agree to the looser arrangement which Britain wished to create and so the Government took the initiative in creating another trading system, the European Free Trade Association (E.F.T.A.) comprising Britain, Austria, Denmark, Norway, Portugal, Sweden and Switzerland. These countries began to free their trading relationships by 1962, but E.E.C. was a much more natural grouping and it made rapid economic progress. In 1962 the British Government sought once more to gain entry and Edward Heath, then President of the Board of Trade, led the British delegation in the lengthy negotiations.

As he commented at the time, 'We see opposite us on the mainland of Europe a large group comparable in size only to the United States and the Soviet Union, and as its power increases so will its political influence'. However, his efforts were unsuccessful. In January 1963 the negotiations were brought to an end on the insistence of President de Gaulle, though against the wishes of many leaders in the other five member States.

The dissolution of the Empire

The first round of decolonization came very soon after the war with the granting of independence to India, Pakistan, Ceylon and Burma. However, the desire for self-government could not be restricted to the colonies in Asia. Soon the British and indeed all the colonial Powers had to face the demands of nationalism in Africa too. The Conservative Government was not blindly opposed to granting independence and in 1957 Ghana (formerly the Gold Coast), and the state of Malaya became self-governing members of the Commonwealth. Thereafter the pace speeded up with the full support of Macmillan and his progressive Colonial Secretary, Iain Macleod. In 1960, Nigeria, a country of over 50,000,000 people followed in the path of Ghana and over the next four years all but one of Britain's major colonial possessions in Africa were granted independence. It seemed that Britain was going to succeed in turning her vast empire into a multi-racial Commonwealth of freely associated states.

Freedom was not always granted without bloodshed. For instance Cyprus only became free after several years of guerrilla fighting between Greek nationalists and British forces and communal clashes between the Greek and Turkish communities. Nor have the new states all had peaceful histories since independence. Cyprus, Nigeria, Ghana and Zanzibar, to name just a few, have all suffered from revolution or communal strife in the last few years.

Both these things have jeopardized the future of the Commonwealth; it has also had to face a grave problem of race relations between or within its component members. As the African and Asian membership of the Commonwealth increased it was natural that these issues should be increasingly under discussion. One of the first results was that South Africa, where racial discrimination was an official policy, quitted the Commonwealth in 1961. However, this did not resolve the problem; in the early sixties attention was turned to Rhodesia, a self-governing colony where all political power was effectively in the hands of the white minority. The Rhodesian Government resisted attempts by the British Government to widen its electoral base to include the African population, and the unilateral declaration of independence of 1965 was a direct consequence of this disagreement. The Labour Party were back in power by this time and they refused to recognize the legality of this step, but they disagreed with many of the African members of the Commonwealth on the use of force against the rebel régime. By the end of 1966 this issue seemed likely to cause a fundamental split within the Commonwealth.

Another cause for ill-feeling between the members of the Commonwealth and Britain has been immigration. Until 1962 migrants from Commonwealth countries were free to come and work in Britain without any restriction. In that year, however, the Government introduced a Bill which limited entry. The Macmillan Government was disturbed by evidence that Britain was not absorbing the mounting tide of immigrants without considerable inter-racial strain and, although the Labour Government opposed the Act at the time, they continued to practise restriction after they came to power in 1964. Both the restrictions and the signs of racial conflict which produced them have strained the goodwill of many Commonwealth countries in spite of measures designed to prohibit racial discrimination brought in by the Labour Government after 1945.

The Labour Party in opposition
The Conservative Party enjoyed strong electoral support throughout the fifties, while the Labour Party lost seats in four successive elections from 1950 to 1959. Such a sustained political swing in one direction was without precedent in modern British electoral history and was due partly to the success with which the Conservatives won the credit for the growing affluence of British society. The Conservatives also profited from the deep internal dissensions within the Labour movement.

Revisionists and fundamentalists
In the early fifties the split was between the fundamentalists who wished to stick to the main principles laid down in the party constitution in the early twentieth century and the revisionists who wished to see a modification of Labour policy over such issues as nationalization. The latter group were led by first Herbert Morrison and then by Hugh Gaitskell. It was thanks to Morrison that the party manifesto of 1950 dropped the old practice of including a list of the industries to be nationalized under Labour. The other group contained such prominent politicians as Aneurin Bevan, Harold Wilson and Barbara Castle. They stood firm on Clause IV of the constitution which declared that the party would fight for 'the common ownership of the means of production, distribution and exchange'. Bevan roundly declared that Socialism without nationalization was an impossibility and in this he had the support of a large part of the Parliamentary Party and the trade unions.

There was an even deeper division on defence policy. In 1954 the Parliamentary Party only agreed to support German rearmament within the European Defence Community by four votes. Bevan and 62 M.P.s opposed the manufacture of a British hydrogen bomb and kept up a constant attack on the Conservative rearmament policy, although this was merely an extension of a policy initiated by Attlee. At one point attempts were made to expel Bevan from the Party but a formal split was prevented by Attlee. In 1955 Gaitskell succeeded Attlee as Party Leader and he began to campaign for the repeal of Clause IV. His position seemed to be strengthened when Bevan accepted the party line on defence and became shadow Foreign Secretary. However, Gaitskell met stern opposition over Clause IV even after the disastrous defeat in 1959 and he gave up his efforts. In 1960 he suffered a further setback when Frank Cousins won the support of the Party Conference against the leadership's policy on defence. A year later, however, Gaitskell reversed this decision after a vigorous campaign in favour of Britain's nuclear deterrent.

By 1963 Gaitskell had finally welded the party into a strong and unified force and then, at the moment of his highest prestige, he died. His successor was one of his former Left-wing critics, Harold Wilson.

The election of 1964

After 1961 the tide began to turn against the Conservatives. In 1961 the pay pause, the poor trading figures and the slow rise in national productivity all added to the Government's difficulties. In the next year this brought its first electoral effect when the Conservatives lost the apparently safe seat at Orpington to a Liberal. In 1963 the Macmillan administration, which had thrown itself heavily behind Britain's entry into the Common Market, was sharply rebuffed by de Gaulle, who also refused to have any part in the plans for a multilateral nuclear force which Macmillan and Kennedy had discussed at Nassau. A bad winter started a sharp rise in the unemployment figures; at one time the figures reached 7 per cent in the North East and the ghost of the depression years seemed about to rise again.

On top of this the government ran into several highly publicized security scandals. First an Admiralty clerk was convicted of spying for Russia and subsequent inquiries revealed serious weaknesses in the security system. Then came the Profumo scandal, in which the Secretary of State for War at first denied, and then admitted, an association with a young woman who was also a friend of a former Soviet diplomat. The subsequent inquiry sharply criticized the way in which the Prime Minister and his colleagues dealt with the situation, and a number of Conservative M.P.s began to show their dissatisfaction with the leadership.

In October Macmillan was taken ill and resigned. After an involved struggle for the leadership the Foreign Secretary, Lord Home, resigned his peerage and took over despite the very strong claims of R. A. Butler, the pioneer of post-war Conservatism.

In October of the next year, after an intense election struggle, the Labour party returned to power on an overall majority of five seats.

27. Labour Government, 1964-70

THE Labour Party returned to power with many long-term plans for the development of the economy and of social services such as education, housing and pensions. However, these were frustrated by the old problems which had dominated the period 1945-64. The basic obstacle remained the instability of the economy. This instability was closely related to the heavy balance of payments deficit in Britain's international trade – the tendency for imports to far exceed exports, thus producing an outflow of funds and constant pressure on the value of the pound sterling. In 1964 disaster was only averted by the success of the Bank of England in borrowing 3,000 million dollars from the European central banks.

Constructive work of the Labour Government
Despite the difficulties produced by the economic instability of the country, the Government introduced important changes in the period between the election of 1964 and that of 1966. These included the setting up of the National Board for Prices and Incomes – a special body whose function was to advise the Government on the justice or otherwise of claims for higher wages or higher prices. The Government also established the Regional Economic Planning Committees to co-ordinate and supervise the work of special development urgently needed in some of the relatively depressed areas of the country. They also established bodies such as the Science Research Council and the Economic Research Council, thus showing a determination to bring the full weight of the latest scientific advances to bear on the modernization of British industry. In line with this, the Government in 1966 established the Industrial Reorganization Corporation. The main idea of which was worked out by the Ministry of Technology. The Corporation was responsible for considerable achievement in aiding the reorganization and technical re-equipment of British industry during the period of the Labour Government to 1970. The great increase of Government grants to industry to aid this process was also a feature of the period. This policy undoubtedly had direct results in improving the flow of British exports and making them competitive in the international market, and thus contributed substantially to the favourable balance of trade which was achieved at last by 1970. Provision was also made for the system of redundancy payments for workers forced to retire before the normal retiring age. Funds were also increased in aid of schemes of re-training.

1966–1970: The struggle to stabilize the economy
The Government's slender majority in 1964 was unsatisfactory to them, and the Prime Minister sought, and obtained, a more substantial majority (97 over-all) in the general election of March, 1966. However, the basic economic problems of the country seemed to be getting worse rather than better and gave the Government an extremely tough, uphill task. In order to reduce the amount of internal consumption and to reduce the rate of inflation, the Government introduced a number of inevitably unpopular measures in 1966. A compulsory prices and wages freeze was introduced to extend over six months – a measure unpopular both with trade unionists and industrialists. The Government faced difficulties and frustrations elsewhere. In December 1966, Harold Wilson met the Rhodesian Prime Minister, Ian Smith, with the aim of achieving a settlement of the differences between the two governments over the future constitution of the former colony which had declared Unilateral Independence from Britain. The talks failed, mainly on the question of guarantees for the future progress of Rhodesia to majority rule, which would mean the eventual control of the country by the indigenous inhabitants. Another problem was that of the Common Market. In May 1967, Wilson announced the Government's intention to apply for membership of the Common Market – provided the terms were right. This announcement produced an opposition group within the Labour Party, comprising, within the Parliamentary Party, about one-third of its back-bench members. Seven Parliamentary private secretaries were desired to resign. However, in November, President de Gaulle came out in opposition to British entry once more. The Government had been forced in the meantime to devalue the pound in an effort to stimulate exports, and the President cited this as a sign of British economic weakness which would be a handicap to the Common Market system. What amounted to a French veto thus frustrated the Government's efforts in this direction.

The economic situation continues to be unsatisfactory
It appeared that the stringent economic measures of the previous year were not being effective. The trade deficit remained high and unemployment rose to just below 500,000 in July, 1967. Further difficulties were created by world events over which the Government had no control. The closure of the Suez Canal after the Arab–Israeli Six-Day War; a temporary ban by the Arab states on oil shipments to Britain and the U.S.A.; the struggle between the breakaway Biafra and the Nigerian constitutional government – all these events resulted in a reduction of oil supplies (Biafra contributed normally ten per cent of all British oil imports), with the result of rising costs in industry and rising prices. An unofficial strike of Liverpool dockers and of men in the Port of London was also affecting Britain's external trade. Further attempts to reach a settlement with Rhodesia also failed. The Government now reserved its powers to delay price and wage increases for another year.

All these circumstances resulted in decreasing support for the Government in the country, and at a by-election at Walthamstow in September a Labour majority of 8,725 was turned into a Conservative majority of 62.

In an attempt to take further purchasing power out of the economy and thus reduce inflation and at the same time concentrate the attention of industry on the need for exports, the budget of 1968, introduced by the Chancellor of the Exchequer, Roy Jenkins, increased taxation by more than £900 million. New charges were also imposed on National Health prescriptions. A drastic change also took place in Labour's attitude to the social services with the acceptance of the principle of selectivity instead of universality (the original Beveridge idea). The social services were now as a matter of principle to take into account in various directions the actual means of individuals and groups. This change was a blow to the Prime Minister himself, who in the past had clung to the Beveridge principle. To achieve substantial economies, the Government also announced its policy of withdrawal of British forces east of Suez, except in the case of Hong Kong. This was to be achieved by the end of 1971, except in the case of the Persian Gulf, where phasing-out would occur by stages after 1971. This was the end of the old British Imperialism and emphasized that Britain was now essentially a European rather than a world power.

The Race Relations Bill, 1968
This important legislation arose essentially from the new problems which the influx of Kenyan Asians into Britain created. The Kenyan Government refused to give work permits to Asians who had not taken out Kenyan citizenship – about 100,000 in all, mainly Indians and Pakistanis. (In the early 1970s this influx was to be further increased by the expulsions of Asians from Uganda.) In the first three months of 1968 over 7,000 Asians holding British passports had entered Britain. This immediately gave rise to widespread controversy. The extreme opposition to immigration was expressed by Enoch Powell who pointed out the dangers of future racial strife in Britain on the American model and to the drastic change in character of areas where Asian settlement was intense. The Labour Government opposed strongly the anti-immigration views expressed by those on the 'right' in English politics, but nevertheless were compelled to place some restraint on the rate of immigration in view of the severe social problems, particularly in the field of housing, to which it would give rise. The first step was to make the same rules apply to Kenyan Asians as to colonists and other members of the Commonwealth. By the Commonwealth Immigration Act of 1968 a British citizen of the United Kingdom colonies holding a British passport could only enter Britain if he had connections, especially family ones, already established here.

The Race Relations Act of April 1968 was introduced to make easier the assimilation of the newcomers into British society and to safeguard them against discrimination. The Act made it a civil offence to discriminate against anyone on grounds of race in such matters as employment, membership of trade unions or employers' associations or in the provision of houses and other services. The Race Relations Board was established to administer the Act and to assist in the removal of difficulties by persuasion rather than immediate resort to law.

The Labour Government and the trade unions

The period of the Labour Government had seen a great increase of unofficial strikes. In 1968 the Prices and Incomes Act of 1967 was extended for a further period with the imposition of a ceiling of $3\frac{1}{2}$ per cent on wage rises.

The year 1969 was critical for the relations between the Government and the trade unions. The Government had appointed a Royal Commission on Industrial Relations and received its report in June 1968. In 1969 the Government published a White Paper, *In Place of Strife*, which outlined its proposals for new methods of dealing with industrial disputes. Its principal spokesman was Barbara Castle, Minister of Employment and Productivity. The main proposals were (1) the Minister could order a twenty-eight day delay of an unofficial strike; (2) the Minister could order a union to ballot its members before calling an official strike; (3) an Industrial Board would impose penalties on unions or employers for refusal to carry out the Minister's orders; (4) an Industrial Commission was to be set up to advise employers and trade unions on ways of improving industrial relations. In the event these proposals received so much opposition from the trade unions and from within the Labour Party itself that they were abandoned after long consultations between the Government and the T.U.C. The Government accepted the latter's assurance that it would be able to play a direct and effective role by intervening in industrial disputes and in its advice to member unions.

In 1969 the Government's difficulties were further increased by the failure of the economy to respond to taxational and other measures taken previously. There was strong international speculation against sterling. The April budget imposed a further £340 million in taxation, although income tax was entirely abolished for about a million low-paid workers. Then a glimmer of light appeared on the international trade horizon – for the first time for many years a small trading surplus for the first six months of the year was announced. By December the surplus had risen to £350 million. Thus in 1970 the Government was able to make much of the improving trade surplus and public opinion in the country began to turn in its favour. This was a very considerable change from, for example, the year 1968 when amidst widespread student unrest and unofficial strikes, the Labour Party lost control of the G.L.C., and by-elections showed a swing against the Government of over 17 per cent. Now the opinion polls showed a very definite swing in its favour. The Prime Minister announced a General Election for 18 June and, against almost every prediction of the opinion polls, the Conservatives won a substantial majority and a Government was formed under Edward Heath.

Some reasons for the Conservative victory of 1970
(1) There is little doubt that many former Labour supporters abstained. This reflected above all dissatisfaction over the policies of wages control and rising prices of basic foodstuffs. (2) A few days before the election a small trade deficit was announced. (3) The Conservatives made telling capital out of Labour's failure to bring the trade unions under some form of control. (4) Rising prices and heavy taxation affected all members of the community, and the Conservatives promised to reduce the rate of inflation and lessen taxation. (5) In the first half of the year there had been very substantial gains by the big trade unions, and it was possible to make out a case for the argument that the Government was now giving in to the trade unions and thus making inflation more likely. (6) There was high unemployment and no significant increase in total national production.

Conclusion
While by no means an exhaustive account of the work of the Labour Government, these brief references will have given some idea of the enormous economic problems facing the country. These problems were not always within the Government's control – such as rising world prices and international speculation against the pound sterling. There was a baffling combination of problems both internal and external – Northern Ireland, the Common Market, Rhodesia, the Middle East conflict, Vietnam, widespread unofficial strikes, student unrest (especially in 1968), and the problem of immigration with all its dangerous potential of racial strife. The Conservatives offered dramatically new solutions to many of these difficulties, though subsequent events were to show just how intractable they were.

PART TWO

Special Studies

28. The Development of the Trade Unions and the Rise of the Labour Party, 1848-1970

Introduction

After the decline of Chartism, the trade union movement entered a more cautious phase. The unions accepted the essentially capitalist idea of self-help. They concentrated, not on transforming society as Owen had intended, but on obtaining the best possible conditions for their members within the framework of society as it existed. The journal of one trade union in 1845 urged its members to 'keep from it [the strike] as you would from a ferocious animal'. After 1848 this attitude became even more firmly entrenched in the trade union movement. Self-help and self-education were the aims of vast numbers of workers at this time. This was the age when the twopenny encyclopedia issued in monthly or weekly parts came into its own, when Samuel Smiles's *Self-help* became the bible of the self-improver, when the 'Society for the Diffusion of Useful Knowledge' had more influence with the British working class than Karl Marx.

The craft unions

A new type of trade union developed composed of men of a single craft. One of the earliest of these was the Amalgamated Society of Engineers (1851) whose weekly subscription was one shilling. This was very high for those days and could only be afforded by men of the skilled trades. The Amalgamated Society of Carpenters and Joiners was another powerful craft union which was founded at this time. These 'new model' trade unions employed full-time officials with headquarters mainly in London. The leading officials of these unions were in the habit of meeting together to discuss labour problems, and they became known as the 'Clique' or the 'Junta'. They were the backbone of the powerful London Trades Council (see p. 97) which was founded in 1860. The trades council movement developed rapidly in all the main industrial towns and took an important part in local affairs from the mid-century onwards.

The Trades Union Congress, 1868

A number of national conferences were held in the 1860's to co-ordinate the whole labour movement in Britain, but the London 'Junta' clung rather

BE UNITED AND INDUSTRIOUS

AMALGAMATED SOCIETY OF ENGINEERS, MACHINISTS, MILLWRIGHTS, SMITHS, AND PATTERN MAKERS.

This is to Certify *that* *was admitted a Member of the* *Branch, on the* *day of* *18* *In witness whereof, we have subscribed our names and affixed the Society's Seal*

PRESIDENT   SECRETARY

A membership card for one of the oldest craft unions, The Amalgamated Society of Engineers.

jealously to its own leading position. Attempts to establish a Trade Union Labour Party also failed through differences of policy and local organization. However, in 1868 the first conference fully recognized by the powerful London Junta was held at Manchester. This was the official origin of the present-day Trades Union Congress and the London trade unions remained the real force behind the Trades Union Congress for the next twenty years at least. The London Trades Council also played an important part in securing the franchise for a section of the working class for the first time in 1867. Through the National Reform League they had allies among the radical middle class, including John Bright and Richard Cobden.

The Trade Union Acts of 1871 and 1875

The evidence given by the leaders of the new trade unions to the Royal Commission on Trade Unions led to Gladstone's Trade Union Act of 1871 and to the further improvements achieved for the trade unions in Disraeli's Conspiracy and Protection of Property Act, 1875. However, trade union anger with the attack on picketing and strike action by Gladstone's Government played an important part in securing Disraeli's victory in 1874 (for details see Chapter 13).

Thus in the thirty years or more after the decline of Chartism the new craft unions accumulated large funds and exercised considerable political influence. In general they avoided the strike weapon, but succeeded in securing clearer legal recognition of trade union rights. Their funds were frequently used to assist fellow trade unionists, for example, the engineers contributed £3,000 in three weeks in 1859 to the London building workers who had been 'locked out' by the employer. This development of mutual help and co-operation in the trade union movement was the real basis of the Trades Union Congress.

The new unionism

This cautious phase in trade union history was increasingly challenged from the 1880's onwards. The attitude of the younger and more militant trade unionists was expressed forcibly by Tom Mann in a pamphlet he wrote in 1886. He agreed that the trade unions had done good work in the past, but were now concerned with little more than keeping up wage-rates. 'The true unionist policy of *aggression* seems entirely lost sight of; in fact the average unionist of today is a man with a fossilized intellect, either hopelessly apathetic, or supporting a policy which plays directly into the hands of the capitalist exploiter.'

These new trends developed after the period of 'mid-Victorian prosperity'. The latter part of the century saw rather more rapid swings of slump and recovery in industry, with more frequent periods of unemployment. Agriculture also declined, and Britain's trading position became increasingly challenged by other nations whose industries had now caught up with, and in some cases passed, those of Britain. This militancy developed earlier on the continent, and European labour movements had a strong influence on the British trade unions.

The influence of Marxism

The most important continental influence was the teaching of Karl Marx, the founder of modern Communism. His close collaborator, Friedrich Engels, had been in contact with some of the earlier Chartist leaders, especially Harney (see p. 70). His study of English working-class conditions in the 'hungry forties', *The Condition of the English Working Class in 1844*, is still regarded as an important work of reference for that period. In 1848 Marx and Engels had issued the Communist Manifesto. This was an analysis of history in terms of the class struggle and the replacement of one ruling class by another. Eventually the revolt of the wage-earning class would destroy the old societies of exploited and exploiters and would replace them first by the dictatorship of the proletariat and finally by the classless society of Communism. Marx developed in great detail the economic theory on which these ideas were based in his work *Das Kapital*, published in 1867.

The influence of Marxism on the British trade union movement

In 1848 Marx was expelled from Germany and lived for the remainder of his life in London. In 1864 he established the International Working Men's Association with its headquarters in London. British trade union officials were represented on this body, but not for long. As Marx gained more and more influence in the organization, the respectable English 'Junta' withdrew. Socialism by revolution was not their aim.

Despite this official trade union break with the First International, attempts to popularize Marx's ideas in Britain continued. One of the most influential popularizers of Marxism in Britain was Henry Mayers Hyndman, author of *England for All*, who founded the Social Democratic Federation in 1881. The Federation was the first outright Socialist organization to exist in Britain since the days of Robert Owen. The trade recession and unemployment after 1875 (see Chapter 14) seemed to favour revolution, but in 1885 the candidates of the Social Democratic Federation who stood for Parliament gained very little electoral support, and the influence of Hyndman's organization declined as trade revived. Nevertheless the Social Democratic Federation did much to develop Socialist thought and action in Britain. Such men as John Burns, Tom Mann, Will Thorne, George Lansbury and Ernest Bevin were members at some time.

The Social Democratic Federation had a more powerful rival in the Fabian Society established in 1884. This was an influential group of Socialist intellectuals and included Sydney and Beatrice Webb, George Bernard Shaw and H. G. Wells. The Fabians did not believe in violent revolution, but argued that Socialism could be achieved gradually through parliamentary reform. They were pioneers of the Welfare State and advocated the local and national ownership of the basic industries of the country, a demand which later became one of the basic creeds of the Labour Party. In the meantime, the leaders of the craft unions continued in their support for Liberalism and Radicalism rather than Marxism. Even some of the militant young trade unionists such as John Burns who had led the

Social Democratic Federation's agitation in London, resigned from it and returned to purely trade union activity. Thus, at that time, the specifically Marxist organizations made little impact on the trade union and Labour movement, although a number of the younger leaders had undoubtedly absorbed Marxist ideas.

Beginnings of the Labour Party

The leading part in the formation of a new Labour Party was undertaken by a Scottish miner, Keir Hardie. After years as a Liberal Party member he became convinced that it could not work consistently in the interests of the wage-earners. In 1888 he founded the Scottish Labour Party, which included in its policy a demand for the nationalization of the railways and the banks. The first independent Labour M.P.s were elected in 1892 in Battersea, Middlesbrough and West Ham (Keir Hardie himself). In the same year a new and influential Socialist newspaper was established, the *Clarion*, under the editorship of Robert Blatchford.

At Bradford in 1893 a special conference of working-class delegates met with Keir Hardie as chairman. The result was the foundation of the Independent Labour Party, whose policy included the nationalization of basic industries, the establishment of an eight-hour day in industry and the creation of a National Unemployment and Sickness Insurance system. This in its turn provoked local Socialist activity in Britain, and by the end of 1893 there were nearly three hundred branches of the I.L.P. However, progress was slow and in the election of 1895 all twenty-five candidates of the I.L.P. were defeated, including Hardie himself. In 1900 Hardie returned to Parliament as M.P. for Merthyr. Other prominent members of the I.L.P. at the end of the century were the future Labour Prime Minister, Ramsay MacDonald, and the future Labour Chancellor of the Exchequer, Philip Snowden.

The dockers' strike, 1889

A landmark in Trade Union growth was the dockers' strike of August–September 1889. Unlike the skilled craft workers, the unskilled and casual labourers endured very bad conditions in Victorian England, and lacked trade union organization. However, the great economic depression of 1875–95 (see Chapter 29), with continuously high unemployment amongst the unskilled trades, produced new leadership and determination. Thanks to the activities of a woman socialist, Annie Besant, the girls employed in Bryant and May's match factory, where illness caused by phosphorus poisoning was rife, came out on strike in 1888 and managed to obtain better conditions. The gas workers and general labourers were the next to organize their own union and in 1889 won an eight-hour day. The climax to these stirrings among unskilled labour came in August 1889. Trouble began in the South-West India Dock in the Thames, where Ben Tillett brought the small Dockers' Union out on strike over the bonus on one cargo, and soon with the assistance of John Burns and Tom Mann the strike spread to all the London docks, involving 10,000 men. A new Dockers' Union was formed and the whole of the London docks closed. The dockers' demand was for a rate of 6d. an hour, the 'dockers' tanner'. At first the employers refused, but events forced them to give way. Great demonstrations were organized by the leaders in Hyde Park, with processions through London in which dockers carried pieces of rotten bread and foul meat which was all their families could afford to eat. Great public sympathy was aroused and

The Great London Dock Strike, 1889: John Burns addressing a meeting of dockers on Tower Hill.

subscriptions poured in, including £30,000 from the Australian dockers. Cardinal Manning of Westminster and the Lord Mayor joined in as mediators, and the employers gave way to the dockers' main demands.

An immediate outburst of union activity by other sections of the unskilled workers followed. The Agricultural Workers Union, which had collapsed in the 1870's despite the efforts of their leader Joseph Arch, was now re-formed, but counter-attacks by landlords and farmers caused it to fail again in the 1890's. The General Railway Workers Union, the General Union of Textile Workers and many others were organized at this time. In the two years 1888–90 trade union membership throughout Great Britain doubled, and membership of the Miners' Federation rose from 36,000 in 1888 to 147,000 in 1890. Another important leader at the time was Will Thorne, whose Gas Workers' Union won their demand for an eight-hour day in 1889 – a great victory for the union, whose main centre of activity was the Beckton gasworks at East Ham. It is significant that the gas workers' campaign had the assistance of Eleanor Marx, the daughter of Karl Marx.

Naturally the employers did not tamely accept the rise of militant trade unionism. A number of the unions' early gains were soon lost, but at the same time their activities tended to improve the organization of the older unions which they criticized. Even the very 'close' craft union, the Amalgamated Engineering Union, reduced its entrance fees in 1892 in order to recruit from the less highly paid workers.

The leaders of the new trade unions, such as Tom Mann, John Burns, Will Thorne and Ben Tillett were quite unlike the cautious, respectable leaders of the craft unions, and gradually they came to dominate the Trades Union Congress. They demanded improvements in wages and hours and Socialism through parliamentary means, and they urged the use of the strike weapon when other methods failed.

The new unions and the Labour Party

In 1899 the T.U.C. called a special conference to put forward Labour candidates for election to Parliament. At this conference there were representatives of the trade unions, co-operative societies, the Fabian Society, the Independent Labour Party and the Social Democratic Federation. Out of this combination of forces (differing widely in their ideas on Socialism) was formed the Labour Representation Committee (L.R.C.). The first secretary was J. Ramsay MacDonald. The committee's aim was to obtain the support of the trade unions for the election of Labour men to Parliament, and this campaign, ably organized by MacDonald, made rapid headway.

The Taff Vale decision and the Labour Party

In 1900 an unofficial railway strike took place on the Taff Vale Railway in South Wales. This was later supported by the Amalgamated Society of Railway Servants which distributed strike pay to the men. The management of the Taff Vale Railway Company then sued the union for the losses sustained by the company through the strike. The case went to the House of Lords, where judgment was given against the Amalgamated Society of Railway Servants and damages of £23,000 were awarded to the company. This was a disastrous decision for the trade unions, for it meant that any unions which might undertake strike action were liable to pay damages to the employers, and this would soon ruin the unions.

However, the Taff Vale decision strengthened the Labour Representation Committee, for even those trade unionists (and there were many) who were not Socialists now saw more clearly the need for independent Labour members in Parliament to fight for the restoration of trade union rights. It was this which led to the return of Keir Hardie to Parliament as M.P. for Merthyr, and another Labour M.P. for Derby at by-elections. Three more Labour men were elected during 1902–3, including Arthur Henderson who was to hold important office in the Coalition Government during the First World War and in the Labour Governments of the 1920's. Attempts to persuade Balfour's Government to reverse the Taff Vale decision failed, and it became a major issue in the 1906 election. In that election the Labour Representation Committee gained 29 seats, and there were another 24 'Lib-Lab' M.P.s elected, thus making a combined Labour representation of at least 53 in the House of Commons. The L.R.C then changed its name to the Labour Party. The Liberals, who gained an overwhelming victory (see Chapter 17), had promised to reverse the Taff Vale decision, and this was done by the Trades Disputes Act of 1906, which clearly ruled that a trade union could not be sued for damages in respect of acts committed by the union or on its behalf.

The leadership of the Labour Party was now in the hands of J. Ramsay MacDonald. In general MacDonald supported Liberal measures which benefited the cause of labour and this policy commended itself to the leadership of the big 'craft' unions. John Burns accepted a post in Campbell-Bannerman's administration but the 'left wing' of the party, represented by Tom Mann and others, demanded a more independent Socialist line in Parliament and elsewhere.

The Osborne case
In 1908 a railwayman named Osborne, a member of the Amalgamated Society of Railway Servants, took legal action to restrain his trade union from using any of its funds to support a political party. This case, like the Taff Vale case, went to the House of Lords as the final Court of Appeal, and judgment was given in favour of Osborne. The Lords ruled that it was illegal for a trade union to spend money either in supporting candidates for elections or on any other political object.

This judgment was a serious setback for the Labour M.P.s, who lost the salaries which the trade unions had, in many cases, paid them. However, they raised sufficient public funds to maintain their position in the elections of 1910 which were concerned with the People's Budget and the Parliament Bill. The payment of M.P.s in 1911 relieved the position for the Labour Party considerably, and in 1913 the Trade Union Amendment Act legalized the use by trade unions of part of their funds for political purposes if a majority vote of its members by ballot supported this. The Act also allowed any trade unionist to 'contract out' of payment to the political funds of the union without any loss of his trade union rights.

Militant trade unionism. Syndicalism
The new trade unions of the 1880's were frequently under the leadership of

men of a more militant or revolutionary outlook than those of the craft unions. These differences of outlook continued to divide both the trade unions and the Labour Party for many years. In the years before the war a movement known as Syndicalism gained influence in the trade unions. The syndicalists, of whom Tom Mann was probably the most influential, demanded the incorporation of the numerous small unions covering the same industries in larger industrial unions, which would have much greater power against the employers and much more influence in bringing about a socialist state. Naturally, many leaders of the older trade unions strongly opposed these aims, especially as the syndicalists wanted to reduce the total number of trade unions to not more than two dozen. Moreover, such a move would undoubtedly have strengthened the influence of the Marxists.

The social legislation passed by the Liberal ministry in 1908–10 was disappointing to trade unionists. The Conciliation Boards and the Trade Boards have already been mentioned. (p. 176). In 1908 the Eight Hours Act for miners was passed. The introduction of old age pensions brought some relief to the funds of unions, and the National Insurance Act of 1911 allowed them to undertake important duties as friendly societies.

In the years 1911–14 the movement for syndicalism and big unions and against parliamentary methods gathered strength. In August 1911, a serious railway strike was quickly brought to an end by the negotiation of a national agreement. This was followed in 1912 by the formation of the National Union of Railwaymen, embracing all railway workers except salaried staff and locomotive engineers and firemen. A strike of miners in February 1912 was settled by parliamentary action, the passing of the Minimum Wage Act, 1912. In 1913 the Triple Alliance of miners, railwaymen and transport workers was formed and there was a threat of further demands including a six-hour day for the miners.

Reasons for the militancy of the trade unions before 1914

There were several reasons for increased union aggressiveness before 1914. Firstly, the rise in prices affected the working class most severely. Secondly, the more militant workers were disillusioned by the policies of the Labour Party in Parliament. Labour Party socialism was not the socialism of many of the trade unions influenced by the agitation of Tom Mann and his supporters. Mann's influence was strongest in the important South Wales Miners' Federation. The establishment of the left-wing newspaper, the *Daily Herald*, strengthened the new militants. It was a reply to the Labour Party's tamer and more 'constitutional' newspaper, the *Daily Citizen*. The latter soon failed, while the *Daily Herald* maintained its position for many years. Lastly, the Taff Vale and Osborne cases had led many trade unionists and Socialists to distrust the British judicial system and arbitration in disputes by men who lacked real knowledge of industry.

Nevertheless, despite setbacks such as the Taff Vale and Osborne decisions, both the unions and the Labour Party had increased their influence and secured a number of important legal rights by 1914.

The Labour and trade union movement during the First World War
The outbreak of war in 1914 found the greater part of the trade union movement and the Labour Party prepared to support the war effort. However, the Independent Labour Party members, including MacDonald, the Chairman of the Parliamentary Labour Party, opposed this policy. MacDonald was removed from his position and succeeded by Arthur Henderson. The unions accepted the 'dilution' of labour, which meant, for instance, the use of more unskilled workers in the engineering industry. The Government gave a guarantee, however, that this policy would be abandoned at the end of the war.

Lloyd George, the new Minister of Munitions, faced with the serious munitions shortage of 1915, saw the importance of gaining the co-operation of the trade union leaders. He secured the suspension of many pre-war practices which would hinder production, and the armaments industry came completely under Government control. All disputes were to be settled by compulsory arbitration, munitions workers were unable to move into another industry and (as a concession to trade union and Labour demands) armaments firms were permitted to make only one-fifth more than their pre-war profits.

When Lloyd George became Prime Minister in 1916 he immediately tried to gain more co-operation from the Labour Party. He was compelled to concede the Socialist demands for the state control of the mines, of shipping, of food supplies and for the establishment of a Ministry of Labour. Three Labour men then joined the Coalition Government – Arthur Henderson became Minister of Education, John Hodge (a trade union leader in the steel industry) became Minister of Labour, and George Barnes Minister of Pensions. The official Labour and trade union movements were drawn fully into the war effort, but were powerful enough to lay down a number of socialist conditions. The war strengthened the arguments for nationalization and state control of the major industries in the post-war period, for if nationalization could lead to greater efficiency in war, then why not in peace?

However, not all sections of the trade union movement were prepared to follow the official line. When the South Wales miners came out on strike in 1915 after refusing arbitration, Lloyd George was compelled to give in to their demands. Another centre of unrest was the Clyde shipbuilding industry, where the shop stewards were particularly strong. Another complication for Labour arose after the first Russian Revolution of February, 1917, when Kerensky gained power. Arthur Henderson went on an official visit to Russia, returned as an advocate of a negotiated peace with Germany, and resigned his Cabinet post. He gained the support of the T.U.C. and the Labour Party outside Parliament for the policy of a negotiated peace.

Thus at a critical point in the war, the anti-war Socialists, represented most strongly by the Independent Labour Party, were fast gaining ground. Only the allied victory in November 1918, saved the Government from the possibility of a complete rift between itself and the trade union and Labour movements.

The post-war trade union and Labour movement

In the election of 1918 the Labour Party won fifty-seven seats. The war was followed by industrial unrest and in 1919 the Miners' Federation demanded a six-hour day, a 30 per cent increase in wages and the nationalization of of the mines. In order to avoid a strike, Lloyd George appointed a Special Commission on the Mines, under the chairmanship of Sir J. Sankey and with a 50 per cent representation of the miners. The Commission recommended wage increases for the miners and, most important of all, the nationalization of the mines. The Conservative-dominated Coalition Government refused to accept the Commission's findings and this decision was to account for much industrial conflict in the coming years. The immediate reaction of the Labour Party and the T.U.C., which was now in the unusual position of having the support of a Government-appointed Commission, was to launch an official campaign for the nationalization of the mines. More unrest arose when the railway companies attempted to reduce wages. The National Union of Railwaymen conducted a seven-day national strike, and the Government intervened with the railway companies to prevent the wages reduction. In the London docks Ernest Bevin was beginning his great union work. Not only did he gain an increase in the dockers' wages, but called an important strike at the East India Dock to prevent the loading of ammunition on the *Jolly George* for use against the Red Army in Russia. However, the trade unions lost over two million members during the slump and unemployment between 1920 and 1922, and this led the smaller unions to amalgamate. One of the most powerful of the new unions that emerged was the Transport and General Workers Union, of which Ernest Bevin became the secretary.

The trade unions and the first Labour Government

After the break-up of the post-war Coalition in 1922 (see Chapter 19) the Labour Party ran 414 candidates in the election and won 142 seats. Since 1918 individual membership of the party had been allowed in addition to the old membership by organization, and many active workers in the constituencies had been recruited. Ramsay MacDonald was elected Chairman of the Party and became the first Labour Leader of the Opposition. In 1924 the Party's position improved still further and 191 Labour members were returned. With Liberal support MacDonald formed the first Labour Government. From the trade union point of view the first Labour Government was unsatisfactory. It was too dependent on Liberal support and many of its actions were no different from those which would have been taken by a Conservative Government. The Government prepared to meet a dock workers' strike by bringing in troops to safeguard essential supplies. This was regarded as nothing less than an anti-trade union policy, and both the Labour Party outside Parliament and the T.U.C. protested to MacDonald against this action.

This experience had shown the trade unions that great differences could arise between themselves and the Labour Party, and after the defeat of Labour in 1924 they concentrated on strengthening still further their organization and prepared for direct industrial action against the employers on a wider scale.

Improvements of T.U.C. organization

The new secretary of the T.U.C. was Walter Citrine, under whom important organizational changes were made. Hitherto the administrative staffs of the Labour Party and the T.U.C. had worked together, but Citrine now achieved the separation of the two staffs, and a new Organization Department of the T.U.C. was formed to advise and assist the trade unions. The T.U.C. was to play a major role in the events leading up to the General Strike of 1926. When the Royal Commission on the Mines, under the chairmanship of Sir H. Samuel, proposed wages reductions in this industry, the Miners' Federation, led by a former syndicalist, A. J. Cook, refused to accept the findings of the Commission. At this point the T.U.C. was given powers by the unions to go far beyond a mere advisory capacity, and its General Council not only undertook direct negotiations with Baldwin's Government, but also prepared thorough and elaborate plans for strike action. In fact, the General Council took control of the negotiations on behalf of the unions. When no progress was made and the government broke off negotiations, the General Strike began on 4 May, 1926.

The General Strike

A million miners and a million and a half other workers were called out, and the response was almost one hundred per cent. It involved workers in transport, engineering and shipbuilding, iron and steel, the printing trades and the power industries. Some grades of workers continued at work – in textiles, in the post office and the distributive trades. In this respect the strike was not 'general' and the T.U.C. itself never employed this term in its official statements. The Government produced its own newspaper, the *British Gazette* and in reply the T.U.C. produced the *British Worker*. In the provinces local strike committees were formed, and on the Government side Sir John Anderson recruited volunteers to try to keep essential services running. The greatest difficulty for the Government was the railways, where inexperienced volunteers were of little use. As a consequence the railway system came almost to a standstill, for only one per cent of engine drivers refused to strike.

Collapse of the General Strike

This, the greatest conflict between Government and workers and between employers and workers which Britain had ever seen, ended in complete collapse on the trade union side. Much bitter controversy followed in the trade union and Labour movement, and the miners particularly regarded themselves as the victims of treachery by a number of other union leaders. The first signs of wavering appeared at the end of the first week of the strike. Some of the trade union leaders appeared to be alarmed lest the strike committees took on a more political and revolutionary character under the influence of the Communist Party and other Marxist movements. J. H. Thomas, of the National Union of Railwaymen, played a prominent part in the ending of the strike. Sir Herbert Samuel suggested to him that a negotiating committee of the General Council of the T.U.C. should meet him, Sir Herbert Samuel, for discussions. Thomas agreed, and the committee was formed without a single representative of the miners on whose behalf the strike had been originally called. After discussions the committee accepted the original proposals of the Samuel Commission on the mines. A deputation from the T.U.C., including Thomas and Bevin, then met the Prime Minister, Stanley Baldwin. They appear to have accepted the Government's terms without any guarantee that strikers would be reinstated – a guarantee which, from the trade union side, was the least that should have been expected. On 12 May, after eight days, the General Strike was called off. The miners who considered that their interests had been betrayed remained on strike till November, when they were forced to return to work on the coalowners' terms.

Results of the General Strike

The failure of the General Strike had a profound effect on the future of the trade union movement. The immediate disillusionment of many trade unionists with their leaders led to a considerable increase in the influence of the left-wing, especially the Communist Party. But by the following year trade union opinion had come to see that a general strike, unless for outright revolutionary purposes, was likely to lead nowhere. For the trade union movement in general the most serious outcome was the Conservative Government's Trade Disputes and Trade Union Act of 1927 (see Chapter 19). As well as the restrictions on strike action already mentioned the Act declared that any trade unionist wishing to pay a Labour Party levy must sign to this effect, that is, he must make the positive step of 'contracting in' in place of the old system of 'contracting out' if he did not wish to pay. The immediate result of this Act was a loss to the Labour Party of a third of their income from the trade unions.

The trade union leaders now attempted to achieve closer contact and consultation with the employers, despite the violent opposition to this policy by the 'left-wing' led by A. J. Cook of the Miners' Federation. These consultations were known as the Mond-Turner talks. Sir Alfred Mond,

Chairman of Imperial Chemicals, had broached the idea of talks between the two sides of industry in order to improve relations between them. Ben Turner was the Chairman of the T.U.C. in 1928, but the strongest advocate of this policy on the trade union side was Ernest Bevin. At this time Bevin achieved one of his cherished plans – the building of Transport House as both T.U.C. and Labour Party headquarters. He took a leading part in saving the *Daily Herald* from bankruptcy by arranging for Odhams Press to take it over. By 1933 the *Daily Herald* became the first popular newspaper to reach a circulation of two million. The policies of Bevin and Citrine at this time created an aura of 'respectability' for the trade union movement. The extreme left, of course, disliked both of them and did not hesitate in the 1930's to call them 'social fascists'.

The trade unions and the second Labour Government, 1929–1931

As in 1924, the relations of the trade unions and the Labour Government were by no means happy. The Chancellor of the Exchequer, Philip Snowden, met the terrible economic slump of 1929–31 (see also Chapter 21) by traditional methods. The trade unions were indignant that they were not even represented on the Royal Commission on Unemployment Insurance set up in 1930. In 1931, when the May Committee on National Expenditure proposed drastic cuts in Government expenditure and unemployment benefits, both Bevin and Citrine, together with Arthur Henderson and some other members of the Cabinet, opposed this policy strongly. When MacDonald resigned and formed a National Government, the Labour Party split into the anti-MacDonald and the pro-MacDonald factions. On the trade union side, Bevin, through his platform of the *Daily Herald*, attacked MacDonald's policies vigorously. Bevin and his many supporters opposed the National Government's policy of restriction and economy – and proposed the exact opposite – an increase in industrial investment and Government expenditure. These were policies advocated by the economist John Maynard Keynes and they were to receive practical application in the U.S.A. during the presidencies of Franklin D. Roosevelt and in Great Britain after the Second World War. The T.U.C. officially adopted this policy of expansion in 1931. But the split over economic policies so weakened the Labour Party that it was overwhelmingly defeated in the General election of October 1931, only one former Labour Cabinet Minister, George Lansbury, being returned to Parliament. This was its lowest ebb in the post-1919 period.

The trade union movement and the Labour Party in the period 1931–9

The stand taken by Bevin, Citrine and their supporters was to give the T.U.C. a powerful influence in re-shaping Labour's official policies. In 1934 a National Council of Labour was set up with equal representation of the T.U.C. and the Labour Party. In the 1930's the Communist Party advocated and worked for the United Front of all anti-Fascist groups and attempted to bring the Labour Party over to this policy. Within the Labour Party they had the support of Sir Stafford Cripps, but faced the determined opposition of both Bevin and Citrine, promoting the official Labour Party line that Fascism and Communism, being forms of dictatorship, should both be resisted. On the question of resistance to international Fascism by the League of Nations, the official Labour policy was to support any measures by the Government to impose sanctions which the League demanded. On this question in 1935 the pacifist George Lansbury lost his leadership of the party to Clement Attlee. In the general election of that year the Labour Party began to recover ground and returned 154 M.P.s.

Over rearmament, the T.U.C. influenced the Labour Party to adopt the policy of rearmament when the policy of collective security through the League of Nations failed. In 1937 the Labour Party officially accepted the need for national rearmament. Once again a major influence in all these decisions was Ernest Bevin, who was to become Minister of Labour in World War II and Foreign Secretary in Attlee's post-war Labour Government.

The moderate, anti-communist policies pursued jointly by the T.U.C. and the Labour Party in the years 1931–1939 provoked violent disagreement on the extreme left, but raised the status of the unions in the eyes of the general public. Both Baldwin and Chamberlain brought the trade unions into consultation even before the outbreak of war in 1939. This was a far cry from the days of the persecuted Tolpuddle Martyrs and even from the General Strike only thirteen years earlier. During the war this was even more true. A trade unionist was Minister of Labour and the unions co-operated with the Coalition Government in wage restraint and the prevention of industrial disputes.

Labour and the unions since 1945

After 1945 the history of the Labour Party either in power or in opposition became more than ever before central to the whole political development of the country. This new phase is described in Chapters 25 and 26. The electoral victory of Labour in 1945 also brought considerable changes for the union movement. For the first time they were faced with a Labour Government which exercised real power and which began to implement some of the long-term ends of the trade union movement both in nationalization and social reform.

However, neither this fact nor the presence of many unionists in the Government prevented labour disputes even in the nationalized industries. The T.U.C. continued to criticize many of the Government's actions and the unions were divided in the same way as the Labour Party between the revisionists and fundamentalists. On the other hand this was a period in which the union movement as a whole won increasing respect under the leadership of men such as Lord Citrine and Arthur Deakin, the General Secretary of the Transport and General Workers' Union.

Under the Conservative administrations relations with the Government were naturally more strained, even though the Conservatives recognized the importance of good relations with the Labour movement as a whole. For instance, Harold Macmillan appointed Lord Robens, a former Labour minister, to the Chairmanship of the National Coal Board in 1961. The Government also sought T.U.C. co-operation in their economic plans but although union leaders joined the National Economic Development Council, they refused to have anything to do with Selwyn Lloyd's National Incomes Commission.

The unions themselves were changing during these years. There was a growth of the large general unions like the Transport and General Workers' Union which came under the dynamic leadership of Frank Cousins in 1956 and the General and Municipal Workers Union which also had more than a million members. The T.U.C. was strengthened by the growth of the 'white collar' unions like the Draughtsmen's Union which produced highly trained and often very radical leaders. Throughout these years there was a good deal of activity by comparatively small groups of Communists within the unions who wielded disproportionate power because of their close organization and willingness to attend meetings. In 1961 the Communist President and Secretary of the Electrical Trades Union were ousted from office after a trial had shown that they had been involved in rigging elections for union positions. The unions have also been troubled by 'wild cat' or unofficial strikes which have been carried out against the advice of union officials themselves.

It has been a difficult task for the unions to evolve a new role and structure in the changed conditions of the 1960's. Many of them developed as craft unions in the nineteenth and early twentieth centuries and there are still a host of very small unions for individual crafts. This has meant that in one factory the employers have had to deal with a number of different union officials to get a general wage settlement. All the unions have also had to adapt themselves to a world in which automation is replacing many old crafts and in which changes in the economy (for instance the closing of coal mines) demand that workers must be prepared to change the sort of job they do and even the area in which they do it.

One of the biggest tests for the union movement since the war came at the Trade Union Congress in 1966 when the assembled union delegates had to decide whether or not to support the Government's plans for a wage freeze. To support such a policy was to adopt quite a new role for union leadership and in the end the motion was passed by a narrow majority. On the other hand the movement was not prepared to accept the Labour Government's proposals in *In Place of Strife* (see p. 287) and their attitude contributed to the Conservative victory in 1970. Subsequently the unions had to face an even more direct challenge in the Conservatives' industrial relations legislation.

29. The British Economy, 1815-1970

Introduction

The end of the Napoleonic Wars left Britain with a severely disrupted economy. Although the Corn Laws were passed in 1815 to protect landlords and farmers from an influx of cheap foreign corn, prices remained low and many farmers were ruined. Low wages in all industries led to

Cottage industry: this photograph shows a crofter in the Hebrides at work on a handloom; in most of the textile industry this form of production was driven out by powered factory machinery in the first half of the nineteenth century.

hardship for the working people, in town and country. As a result of the Enclosure Acts, especially the large number passed during the wars, a great part of the old English peasantry who had farmed the open, unenclosed fields had given way to new landlords and farmers who hedged their farms and developed the modern compact holding. The dispossessed farmers either worked as labourers or sought jobs in the towns. In industry itself, many of the skilled weavers of the old domestic system were made redundant by the factories. This occurred especially rapidly in the cotton industry, while in the woollen industry the process was not complete until the middle of the century. In general, however, the old domestic system of production was on the way out as the Industrial Revolution entered a new phase. These drastic changes helped to produce the suffering and the social and political disturbances of the period 1815–30.

The wars had created an enormous National Debt, rising from £250 million in 1790 to more than £700 million in 1815. In order to meet the heavy interest payments to its bondholders, the Government of the day retained taxation on many consumable commodities, to the great distress of the working classes.

The growth of towns

The industrial towns were growing fast. They lacked adequate housing and sanitation and conditions were made worse by the increase in the population. Towns such as Sheffield, which in 1750 had been a collection of cottages surrounded by green countryside, now contained factories and row upon row of cheap hovels erected for the new factory population. Manchester, Bradford, Leeds and Birmingham suffered the same rapid development.

The houses in these towns were built by speculative builders whose only purpose was to rush up as many dwellings as possible in the quickest time to meet the demands of the factory owners. Back-to-back houses were built in their thousands, without proper light and sanitation. They were com-

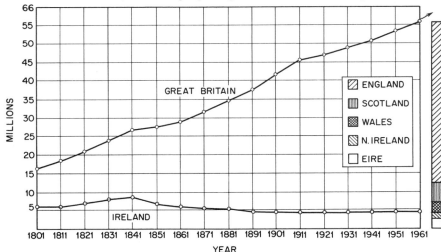

FIG. 10. Population Growth 1801–1961.

monly built with walls of single brick thickness, without damp-proof courses. Water-supply was by pump in a courtyard next to the privy which served a number of dwellings. These conditions caused the widespread cholera epidemics of the 1830's and 1840's. The middle class, although living in their own residential districts away from the centres of contamination, could not escape it and, especially after the serious cholera epidemic in 1831, began to give ear to the urgent proposals of reformers such as Edwin Chadwick. The first Board of Health was set up in 1848, and the importance of sanitation reform was emphasized by another epidemic in the following year, which killed more than 50,000 people. Even then the preachers of *laissez faire*, who opposed state action, secured the abolition of the Board of Health in 1854 However, another cholera epidemic in London in 1866 which killed at least 10,000 people persuaded Parliament to pass a series of Acts which compelled local authorities to clean up their areas and enforce stricter rules for the notification and isolation of infectious diseases. As a result, by the 1870's, cholera was no longer a menace. Nevertheless, the history of this disease alone illustrates the scale of the problems created by the Industrial Revolution.

Technical advances and industrial development

On the brighter side, the Industrial Revolution saw an immense number of British inventions and scientific discoveries, and their rapid application to industry. In 1800 James Watt's patent on the steam engine lapsed and thereafter other firms manufactured the new machines themselves. Some factories had their own machine-making and maintenance establishments. The cotton industry was one of the first to benefit from the application of the steam engine. Cotton was a newer industry than wool and was less hampered by rules and restrictions dating from the Middle Ages. The earlier inventions of such men as Arkwright and Cartwright were now more fully exploited with the use of steam.

From 1815 onwards important scientific discoveries speeded up progress in industry and communications. In 1800 an Italian scientist named Volta invented an electric cell. The Englishman Humphrey Davy went on from this to produce the first electric arc which was to become the basis in the late nineteenth century of the electric arc light and the electric furnace.

One of the most important inventions affecting the iron and steel industry was that of the hot-blast for furnaces by Neilson in 1831. This process saved about 20 per cent in fuel. This helped the vast expansion of iron production – in 1806 there were only 161 furnaces producing 243,000 tons of iron, whereas by 1852 there were 497 producing 2,700,000 tons. In 1913 the total production was 10 million tons.

The Bessemer process

In 1856 the inventor Henry Bessemer announced his discovery of a new and more effective way of refining iron into steel by a hot air-blast forced through the molten metal to remove impurities. This provided fresh impetus to British steel production and was vital in the rapid growth of railways and shipping. The process was much cheaper than the old ones and produced a steel far stronger than the old wrought iron previously used. Gradually, however, the Siemens-Martin process of the open-hearth furnace replaced the Bessemer process and by 1914 most British steel was produced by the latter method. One great technical problem had remained to be solved, however. Neither the Bessemer process nor the open hearth could be used for iron ore with a high phosphorus content. In 1879, however, the Gilchrist-Thomas process solved this problem, and thus made possible the use of ores with high phosphorus content. This discovery gave more advantage to Germany than Britain, however, for the German steel industry was now able to use the phosphoric ores of Lorraine which had come into German possession after the defeat of France in the Franco-Prussian War of 1870. By 1914 both Germany and the U.S.A., which had rich fields of phosphoric ore, were ahead of Britain in steel production.

Development of the British railway system

All these inventions affected the development of the British railways. By the end of the Napoleonic Wars the canals were too slow, cumbersome and expensive for the growing needs of industry. George Stephenson's

Locomotion No. 1, the engine which drew the world's first passenger train. It was built in 1825 for the Stockton and Darlington Railway by George Stephenson.

work on the locomotive provided the solution. In 1825 the Stockton to Darlington Railway was opened, and the Manchester and Liverpool in 1830. Stephenson's locomotives achieved a speed of 30 miles per hour, a great improvement on both road and canal traffic. In 1832 the Leicester-Leamington Railway was opened, followed by the London to Birmingham in 1838. Both were great feats of engineering. Land was extremely costly to purchase from reluctant landowners, and the canal and turnpike trusts determined to obstruct development. Each company had secured an Act of Parliament to authorize construction, and this cost huge sums before the line could be begun. However, the new lines, at first intended almost purely for goods traffic, prospered and the new middle class poured money into railway projects. Between 1830 and 1850 over 6,000 miles of railway were built.

The heavy capital costs soon caused many small companies to pool their resources, and amalgamate. The result was the formation of the Midland Railway and the London and North-western in the 1840's. Later, in 1873, the Railway Commission was set up to regulate amalgamations and passenger and goods charges. The general principle on which the Commission operated was that competing lines should not amalgamate, though lines should join up in one through system using the same gauge.

George Hudson and the 'Railway Mania'

The decade from 1840 to 1850 witnessed a massive investment of money in railways known as the 'Railway Mania'. In 1843 Parliament sanctioned 24 railway Bills; in 1845 the number was 248. There was a vast mobilization of middle-class capital for railway investment – a movement stimulated in 1844 by the decision to reduce interest on Government loans from 4 per cent to $3\frac{1}{2}$ per cent which made railway investment much more attractive. The greatest railway promoter of the age was George Hudson, the 'Railway King'. He organized and stimulated the speculators of the age to invest their capital in railways. Although many of his promotions failed and brought ruin to the investors, he was a man of vision and enterprise. He worked with George Stephenson to extend the Midland Railway to Newcastle, and by 1844 over a thousand miles of railway were directly under his control. He achieved immense popularity at the peak of his success, was elected Lord Mayor of York three times, and Conservative M.P. for Sunderland in 1845. Unfortunately, the Eastern Railway was involved in fraudulent finance, and this brought about Hudson's decline and fall; it is said that Hudson himself embezzled £500,000.

Railway progress, 1850–1914

By 1850 the main lines were almost completed with 6,000 miles of track. In 1870 there were 15,000 miles, in 1890, 20,000 miles and in 1914, 23,000 miles. The increase after 1850 was mainly accounted for by the construction of lines linking up with the main network. This vast mileage was opened up to the mass of the people by Gladstone's Railway Act of 1844. This stated that every company must provide at least one train a day in each direction along its lines with accommodation for third class passengers at a penny a mile and at an overall speed of at least 12 m.p.h.

During the First World War of 1914–18 the railways came under direct Government control and, for the first time, were run as a co-ordinated whole. The advantages were so obvious that it strengthened the case, put forward by the Labour Party after the war, for nationalization of the railways – a change which had to wait till after the Second World War. However, by the Railway Act of 1921, promoted by Lloyd George's Coalition Government, the railways were organized into four groups – the Great Western, the Southern, the London, Midland and Scottish, and the London and North Eastern. The Railway Rates Tribunal was set up to safeguard the public against unjustified charges and to control wages.

Beneficial effects of railway development

In breaking down the monopolies of the old canals and the turnpike trusts, the railways did a great service both for industrialists whose goods they carried and for passengers. All classes felt the benefits of cheaper and quicker travel, and in the 1850's the cheap excursion to the seaside, previously enjoyed only by the upper classes, added to the health and enjoyment of the people. This was even more important when the Saturday half-day became a regular feature of the working week in the 1870's. The railways provided work for many of the country's industries – iron and later steel, glass, textiles, civil engineering, and coachbuilding. They speeded the passage of goods to the ports, and this, combined with the parallel development of the steamship, helped to boost Britain's foreign trade. Better communications provided the newly-enfranchised voters with more substantial and up-to-date news of the activities of Parliament and policies of the political parties. The Liberals and Conservatives had to develop a wider political organization outside London and to take account of 'national opinion'. The railways also increased the mobility of labour needed for industrial expansion, playing a vital part in the transformation of Britain from an agrarian to an industrial society.

Shipping

Improvements in iron and steel production and the use of steam power produced a boom in British shipping in the early nineteenth century. In 1803, the *Charlotte Dundas* steamed along the nineteen miles of the Forth-Clyde canal. In 1807 Robert Fulton took one of Watt's engines to America and navigated his steamship, the *Clermont*, on the Hudson River. In 1812 Henry Bell sailed the *Comet* on the Clyde from Glasgow to Dumbarton. In 1819 the *Savannah* crossed the Atlantic from New York to Liverpool, partly under sail, taking four weeks, followed in 1833 by *Royal William*, a Canadian ship, which made the first crossing wholly under

From sail to steam: the Royal Yacht Victoria and Albert *enters Plymouth Sound in 1843, past warships which have hardly changed since Nelson's day.*

steam in twenty days. By 1869, when the screw propeller had replaced the paddle wheel, the crossing was made in eight and a half days by the liner *City of Brussels* and the invention of the steam turbine by Parsons in 1894 enabled the *Mauretania* to make her record crossing of four and a half days in 1907.

This application of steam-power to shipping after 1850 was a result not only of the improvement of Watt's engine, but the invention of more powerful, fuel-saving engines such as the compound engine designed by Elder in 1854. This in its turn speeded up the change-over from wood to metal. In 1879 the tonnage of steel-constructed steamers launched on the Clyde was only 10 per cent of the total; only ten years later in 1889 it was 97 per cent, one of the most rapid changes recorded in industrial history.

During the nineteenth century Britain was ahead of other nations in steam shipbuilding, and her supremacy in the world's carrying trade was greatly helped by the existence of numerous coaling stations throughout her empire.

Industry needed new materials after 1850 and the new ships could bring them in speedily. This applied especially to such commodities as tin for the new tinplate works of Wales, cocoa, tea, coffee, palm oil (for soap and margarine) and rubber. The invention of the refrigeration process also enabled the shipping companies, from 1880 onwards, to bring food to Britain in good condition over greater distances.

A combination of factors gave Britain an economic superiority in the nineteenth century – great home resources of coal, an empire providing raw materials in vast quantities, high engineering and scientific ability, and the rapid development of an efficient railway and shipping system. It was, too, an age when much British capital was invested in enterprises overseas, especially in railways; British companies and capital and British railway engineers were to be found in many parts of the world, from France to South America.

Economic growth by the mid-century

Between 1815 and 1850 the basic British industries increased their output enormously. Coal production rose from 10 to 50 million tons, the importation of wool for the Yorkshire cloth industry rose from about 10,000 tons in 1815 to 33,000 tons in 1850, while the cotton industry centred on Manchester developed even faster. In 1815 cotton cloth exports accounted for 15 per cent of all British exports, but in 1850 they represented more than 50 per cent. This expansion was encouraged by the gradual adoption of free trade policies (see Chapter 7). A low rate of direct taxation also helped to stimulate British business, and created the mid-Victorian prosperity. Yet in 1851 agriculture still employed more labour than all the other industries put together, and there were more domestic servants than workers in the cotton and woollen industries. Britain was not yet a country completely dominated by industry.

The Great Exhibition, 1851

The Great Exhibition of 1851 in Hyde Park was intended both to demonstrate the great growth of British trade and science, and to attract the foreign purchaser. This exhibition, strongly encouraged by the Prince Consort as its President and designed by the former gardener of the Duke of Devonshire, Joseph Paxton, was housed under acres of glass houses in Hyde Park. It attracted visitors and exhibitors from all over the world and was, for its day, a stupendous feat of organization. Half the space was taken by over 7,000 British exhibitors, the other half by foreign exhibitors from all over the world. In one of his last public appearances, the aged Duke of Wellington, who had lived to see the changes from the post-war sufferings of 1815 to the relative plenty of 1851, accompanied Queen Victoria at the opening ceremony. The exhibition ranged from iron-framed and papier-mâché pianos to the latest steam hammers for heavy industry; from the crankish exhibit of a chair carved out of a block of coal to the latest railway locomotives. The exhibition showed that British industry was still organized on a craft basis, and consisted of small family concerns. Altogether the Exhibition expressed solidity, a sense of security and unbounded optimism. The great concentration of capital and the amalgamation of separate firms into greater units was to be the main feature of the period after 1851, when the laws relating to limited liability, passed in 1856, allowed the further development of business enterprise by reducing individual risks. The profits from the Exhibition were used to develop various forms of scientific education – projects in which the Prince Consort was the prime mover.

The Great Exhibition, 1851. Guests in the main hall of the Crystal Palace await the arrival of the Queen.

Agriculture, 1815–51

From 1815 to 1851 British agriculture did not develop in the same dynamic way as industry. Widespread distress among the labourers of the southern counties caused the serious labourers' revolt of 1830, harshly suppressed by Lord Melbourne. But during the 1830's there was some improvement in farming conditions. The rapid development of industry and population expanded the market for agricultural produce, while the railways broke down the isolation of many farming areas and enabled their produce to reach new markets. In 1836 the Tithe Commutation Act (see p. 56) reduced the charges on the farmers, while the Poor Law Amendment Act of 1834 (see p. 51) reduced the burden of rates by over £3,000,000 in three years. The farmer thus had more funds to spare for the development of his farm. The repeal of the Corn Laws in 1846, far from handicapping agriculture, encouraged the farmer to rely on his own improvements and not on protection. The repeal encouraged the development of 'high farming' – that is, the increased use of machinery, modern drainage, and artificial manures such as were being produced by the pioneer of chemical farming, John Lawes of Rothampstead. The repeal also encouraged farmers to rely less on corn and to diversify their crops. By 1854 about half Britain's agricultural land was under pasture.

The Royal Agricultural Society, founded in 1838, developed a valuable information service for farmers, and the Government itself loaned over £4,000,000 between 1846 and 1850 to help farmers with the expenses of drainage. There was an increase in the average size of farms, though farms of just a few acres remained common. Britain was fortunate that her aristocracy and gentry remained interested in their estates and felt a responsibility for their tenants. A French commentator of about 1850 remarked: 'In France, when a proprietor is ambitious of playing a part, he must come away from his estates; in England he must remain upon them.'

Mid-Victorian prosperity

Between 1846 and 1873 Britain enjoyed a great business boom. In 1854 exports were £97 million, but twenty years later had risen to £200 million. Imports in 1854 were £152 million, and in 1873 were £370 million. All the basic industries expanded as never before. For instance, the output of coal on which so much of this expansion depended, rose from 65 million tons in 1854 to 130 million tons in 1873. The railways especially made a great leap forward and passenger traffic increased sevenfold in these decades.

Some reasons for mid-Victorian prosperity

There were a number of reasons for this economic expansion. By 1860 all the old restrictions on trade had been abolished – including the last remnants of the Navigation Laws. The old laws of settlement, restricting the movement of labour from one parish to another, had also been abandoned. The laws of limited liability gave a positive encouragement to capital investment and, as a counterpart to the mobility of labour, also increased the 'mobility of capital'. Every circumstance was therefore favourable for the development of London as the investment and banking centre of the world, which it undoubtedly became in this period. These circumstances, combined with the great lead established in railways and shipping, made Britain the greatest trading nation of the world.

Another favourable factor in the mid-Victorian period was the actual needs of Britain's main customers. The United States, where industrial development was set back seriously by the Civil War of 1861–5, could not keep pace with the growth of her own population. She therefore drew considerable imports from Britain. American shipbuilding, for instance, had almost ceased during the Civil War, and this gave British shipbuilding an enormous advantage. After the defeat of France in 1870 the German Empire received a huge war indemnity which increased the German power to purchase abroad, particularly from Britain. The discovery of gold in Australia led to the further development of that country, and resulted in increased exports. The investment of British money abroad was another cause of trade expansion. By 1875 over £1,200,000,000 of British money was invested abroad, and much of this investment was used by the countries concerned to purchase their needs from Britain. A good example of this was the Argentine railway system, developed by British capital, constructed by British labour and supplied with its permanent way from Britain.

Although prices of agricultural products fell somewhat in this period, the farmers were compensated by increased efficiency. The working classes consumed more meat, and pasture land for cattle was increased. The high rate of employment in industry therefore had a directly beneficial effect on farming, and the market for farm products was further widened by improvements in transport.

Working-class standards in the mid-Victorian period

Many wage-earners shared this prosperity. Those who benefited least were the agricultural workers and those in the unskilled trades. Agricultural wages rose from an average of 9s. 6d. a day in 1850 to about 12s. in 1875 and did not keep pace with the wage increases in the towns. The position of the agricultural worker was weakened by the fact that there was less demand for his labour – due to mechanization, especially in harvesting and threshing. This reduced the bargaining power of the rural worker and Joseph Arch's agricultural union encountered so much opposition from landlords that it collapsed after a few years.

The working-class share of mid-Victorian prosperity is well illustrated by the increased consumption of meat by 10 per cent in the period 1850–75, of tea by 60 per cent and sugar by 75 per cent. The skilled workers' wage-rates also rose steeply in the same period – the engineers' by 30 per cent and the miners' by as much as 75 per cent. In general, wages increased by 50 per cent between 1850 and 1875 and outpaced the rise in prices, making the rise in *real* (i.e. in terms of what the money would buy) wages as much as 30 per cent over those of 1850.

Thus almost all classes experienced an increase of real income but, of course, other conditions for the wage-earners, especially housing and sanitation in the industrial towns, were still extremely bad. Nevertheless, no previous period of English history saw such astonishing improvement in incomes and consumption in such a short time.

Economic conditions in the period 1874–1914

Mid-Victorian prosperity continued until 1873, when a difficult period began for English trade and industry. The term 'depression' has been used to describe this period, but this gives a misleading idea of what happened. The actual level of production of the main industries such as textiles, coal, steel continued to rise, as also did the standard of living except in agriculture. The real problem was the fall in prices and profits and in the value of British exports. In the years 1873–83 the price of iron fell by two-thirds. The value of all British exports fell sharply and in 1885 was £50 million less than ten years previously. It was not until 1900 that their value finally passed that of 1872. In the years 1873–1900 the wealthy classes found their returns disappointing compared with the boom and prosperity of the mid-Victorian period. But some classes actually benefited – namely, the working class who gained from the low prices of foodstuffs, and those professional people with fixed incomes. On the other hand, uncertainties of trade and profit caused employers to lay off labour more frequently than in the previous period, and therefore some sections of the working class, especially the unskilled workers, suffered from unemployment (see Chapter 28).

It was during this period that Britain's economic position in relation to other countries began to decline with an alarming speed. For example, German coal production in the years 1873 to 1883 increased by 53 per cent, compared with 29 per cent in Britain. Shipbuilding was also heavily affected, largely because the increasing employment of steel in shipbuilding led to a longer life-span for ships, reducing the demand for replacements. Foreign governments subsidized their own shipbuilding and shipping industries to undercut the rates charged by British firms. Thus both British shipbuilding and overseas carrying trade declined in relation to other competitors – especially Germany and the United States.

The iron and steel industry was similarly affected. France, Germany and the United States in particular were producing their own steel for railways and ships and British exports of rolling stock declined sharply. At the same time British railway development had now reached its limit and there was a falling-off of home demand. As with shipping, the increasing use of steel meant longer life for railway equipment. Both the iron and steel industries suffered from a decline in demand in the overseas and home market. This in turn lowered the demand for British coal. The very newness of the steel industries of Germany and the United States enabled them to use the latest technology, whereas Britain was still basing much of her production on the technical methods of the first Industrial Revolution. There was a vast amount of old equipment needing to be scrapped before Britain could move forward again at the old pace, and she was actually suffering from having been the pioneer industrial nation. In the twenty years between 1870 and 1890 her iron and steel exports only increased from 2,600,000 tons to 3,800,000 tons.

Some further reasons for the depression of 1873-1900

The economic depression was world-wide, yet Britain still did less well than other countries. The general crisis worried the economists of the time, for many had assumed that free trade would usher in an age of constant and steady improvement. Karl Marx and his followers claimed that the capitalist system inevitably led to over-production, a fall in prices and unemployment – a tendency they attributed to the uncontrolled play of the profit-motive. Others pointed out that the new German Empire, far from following Britain's lead and adopting free trade, swung round to a policy of high tariffs to protect its own industries, and this restricted the German demand for British goods as the century went on. In the same way the U.S.A. became protectionist from 1861, and even more so after 1893, and this hit British-American trade. Important currency changes also affected production and trade. The U.S.A. went on to a gold standard and abandoned silver, France restricted the coinage of silver, and in 1873 the German Empire also went on the gold standard. All these changes tended to increase the demand for gold and to cancel out the advantages which Britain had gained by basing her currency on gold. The amount of precious metal which could serve as a backing to credit and paper currencies was being restricted, and this prevented the proper expansion of trade and industry. The tendency for nations to seek their own self-interest by currency manipulation and tariffs had an unsteadying effect on trade and employment both in Britain and elsewhere. After 1900, however, in Britain prices began to rise slightly, but wages remained stationary. This caused a falling off in the consumption of commodities in common use and led to much social unrest before the First World War (see also p. 178).

Proposed remedies and partial revival

As early as 1860 there was criticism of Britain's industrial methods, especially her failure to apply the latest discoveries to industry and to produce managers and workers with a good technical education. The Royal Commission on Trade and Industry (1886) brought these facts to the notice of Parliament and industry. The report praised the efforts of the Germans to find new overseas markets for their products, and urged Britain to do the same. The Commission advised more commercial and technical education. The Report stimulated technical education in Britain (see p. 365), and the New Imperialism fostered by Disraeli and Chamberlain created new openings for British trade. In Africa Britain had a clear lead over other countries, and by 1900 she was expanding her trade with India, Canada, Australia, China and Latin America. Her industrialists and traders were helped by the rise in prices between 1900 and 1914 which was a result of new gold discoveries in South Africa and in Australia.

Between 1900 and 1914 there was, therefore, a partial recovery in Britain's overseas trade and investments, but even then Germany and the U.S.A. outstripped her in coal and steel production. Britain lagged behind the U.S.A. and Germany in applying new methods to steel production and to mining. In the cotton industry she was still employing one operative to four looms, whereas in the U.S.A. one operative worked twenty looms. Britain was also far behind the U.S.A. and Germany in making use of the new power, electricity. In 1914 the British output of electrical equipment was only one-third that of Germany. As the pioneer user of steam-power she continued to use it beyond the point at which it was really profitable. Thus at the outbreak of the Great War Britain had made a partial recovery from the relative stagnation of the years 1873–1900, but was still falling behind in the world race for industrial power.

British agriculture, 1873–1914

The depression in this period was far more severe in agriculture than in industry. A number of incidental factors greatly increased the problems of farming, especially the very bad harvests of 1873, 1875, 1876 and 1879. The price of farm produce fell catastrophically. Wheat dropped from 44s. a quarter in 1875 to an all-time low of 17s. 6d. in 1894. Land went out of cultivation and farm labourers drifted to the towns. The corn-growing southern and eastern counties were the worst hit.

Reasons for agricultural decline

The bad weather was not a basic cause of farming difficulties, for when the weather was favourable, prices remained low and farming remain unprofitable. Foreign competition was the principal cause. The great wheat surpluses which the prairie lands produced could be sent to Britain very cheaply. The American transcontinental railway system was developed and the refrigeration and canning processes (see p. 385), soon meant that stock breeding was unprofitable in Britain as well. In the same way imports of dairy produce increased in this period, and those farmers who had turned from wheat to dairy farming during the mid-Victorian period were also hard hit.

The Eversley Commission, 1893–7

The Eversley Commission produced a number of suggestions for improving British farming. It suggested a further diversifying of agriculture by market gardening, fruit and flower growing, potato growing and poultry farming. During the gradual increase in prices after 1900 many farmers adopted the Commission's suggestions, and there was some recovery. The cattle-farmer was also helped by the fact that the wealthier classes still preferred British meat.

One very bad result of the agricultural depression was the serious plight of the agricultural worker. Those who did not drift to the towns found themselves at the mercy of low wages and bad housing. Many suffered the evils of the Poor Law and the workhouse. In these circumstances the Radicals resorted to the 'two acres and a cow' policy, and attempted to revive smallholdings on which the agricultural worker could live with his family and become self-sufficient. Gladstone's Act of 1892 by which county councils were to provide land and houses to suitable applicants assisted by loans on easy terms was only permissive, and failed to achieve much. The Liberal Smallholdings and Allotments Act of 1908 gave the Board of Agriculture powers to compel the county councils to provide land for smallholdings. Unfortunately many of those who applied had little experience of the land and dreamed of escape from town life into a rural arcadia; once again little progress was made. Smallholding policies were a failure before 1914, and the farm workers continued to leave the country for the towns or for the countries of the Empire. Although there was some recovery, British agriculture was still in a precarious state at the outbreak of war.

Agriculture revived in the war. The German submarine blockade emphasized as never before the importance of Britain's own food supplies. Food production came completely under Government control. County War Agricultural Committees were set up, which supervised drastic changes in agricultural practice. Non-essentials such as flower-growing were abandoned and as much land as possible re-converted to arable farming. For the first time minimum prices were guaranteed to farmers, and the workers had the protection of the Wages Boards which established a minimum guaranteed wage. By 1918 Britain was producing 58 per cent more wheat than she averaged in the ten years before the war.

The post-war economic problems of Britain, 1918–39

The First World War had deep and lasting effects on Britain's economic power. In the first place Britain lost many export markets, especially in the Far East. This change was particularly disastrous for the British cotton industry. Japan and China were now producing more than twice their pre-war output of cotton cloth. By 1935 Japan was producing more cotton cloth for export than Great Britain, and much of this was going to India, where most of the old demand for British cloth disappeared. The Lancashire cotton industry's exports in 1935 were half those of 1914 and cotton became one of the 'depressed industries'. In the same way the iron and steel industries suffered a decline, for every one of Britain's pre-1914 customers were either producing more themselves or importing from countries where production costs and prices were lower.

The worst affected industry was coal-mining. The Royal Commission of 1926 made a general survey of the industry, and showed that coal production had fallen below that of 1914, and the proportion of coal exported had also drastically declined. As in the other basic industries, Britain's overseas customers had been lost. Germany was attempting to pay a proportion of her heavy war reparations in coal and naturally reduced her imports to a minimum. Much of Germany's coal exports was now going to Italy, previously one of Britain's principal customers. Changing consumption habits played a part. World shipping was now using an increasing amount of fuel-oil in place of coal. The British coal industry was unable to compensate for this loss by supplying more home demand, for the basic industries which used coal were contracting. The British coal industry was partly to blame for its own post-war difficulties. Neither its prices nor its costs of production could compete with other coal-mining countries. Between 1913 and 1934 the output per man-shift in Britain rose by 7 per cent, but in Belgium by 63 per cent, and in the Ruhr district of Germany by 77 per cent. This was a poor showing, even allowing for the fact that in competing countries, especially in the United States, it was easier to introduce mechanization than in the older British mines. The mines also suffered from bad financial organization and wasteful royalty payments to land-owners. In these circumstances it was difficult to produce coal for export at a competitive price. Other British industries, for example, cotton, did attempt to 'rationalize' by combining into larger units, but little on these lines was done in the coal industry. Before the Second World War there were about 2,000 mines operated by over 1,000 separate companies. Only compulsory reorganization following nationalization after 1945 was to improve the industry.

British shipping was also severely hit by post-war conditions. The general contraction of world trade reduced the demand both for British ships and for shipping services. Between the wars there was a high rate of permanent unemployment on the Clyde. The decline of Britain's coal exports affected the tramp steamers above all. All this resulted in a further decline in Britain's share of the world carrying trade. In 1890 Britain had still controlled 60 per cent of this trade. In 1914 the proportion was 46 per cent, in 1937 it was down to 31 per cent, and by 1955 19 per cent.

Britain's export trade was adversely affected by the return to the gold standard in 1925. During the war Britain had abandoned the gold standard and the Treasury had issued its own notes which were not convertible to gold. By 1925 most other countries had returned to a gold standard in an effort to halt inflation and maintain a stable value for their currencies. Unfortunately, when Britain returned to gold in 1925 the pound was overvalued. This made British goods appear expensive abroad and foreign imports seem cheap in Britain.

Britain's efforts to overcome the post-war economic problem

There were two main directions in which Britain attempted to overcome her industrial and export problems – (1) rationalization and (2) the abandonment of free trade.

Rationalization meant reducing costs of production by scrapping outdated machinery and installing new, by economies in the use of labour and by better general organization, frequently involving the amalgamation of small firms of the same industry into larger units. This type of reorganization was undertaken in the cotton industry, where there were machines still in use which had been installed as early as 1850. But reorganization was slow, and meanwhile the cotton industry was fast losing the remnants of its overseas market. The trade unions were suspicious of rationalization under private ownership, for it tended to increase unemployment.

The abandonment of free trade was a reversal of the trade policy of Britain since the abolition of the Corn Laws in 1846, and Peel's free trade budgets. Joseph Chamberlain had unsuccessfully challenged free trade in the pre-war years, but after 1919 more insistent demands for protection of British trade and industry arose. During the war itself Britain had already abandoned free trade in a number of luxury articles in order to reduce imports and save shipping space. This applied to such things as motor-cars, watches, films, etc. After 1919 the duties imposed on these imports were maintained, but reduced by one-third for imports from the Empire.

The economic crisis of 1929–31, when unemployment rose to more than 2,000,000, ended free trade. In order to boost exports by lowering prices, the National Government took Britain off the gold standard. In 1932, the Imports Duties Act was passed. This imposed a 10 per cent tariff on most imports, and an Imports Duties Advisory Committee was set up to advise the Government to raise duties when necessary. During the period 1932 to 1939 this was frequently done and import duties on a number of commodities rose to 20 per cent. This did not, however, apply to the Empire, which could export foodstuffs to Britain at the old tariff levels and receive British manufactures in return. This system of Imperial Preference was the result of an important Imperial Economic Conference held at Ottawa in 1932.

Effects of the new policies

The policies of the pre-1939 National Governments were only partly successful and in 1939 the total of unemployed was still as high as 1,500,000. However, the highest unemployment was to be found in those parts of the country dependent on coal and steel. In other parts of Britain the standard of living was much higher, especially in London and the South-East. Population moved into these areas between the wars, and again after 1945.

The industries which moved into the London area and the South-East were attracted by the advantages of a good supply of electricity, which removed their direct dependence on coal. London itself was an important home market as well as a great railway centre, so that both for sales and wider distribution it had great advantages. There was a continuous development on the fringes of London of light industries, such as electrical equipment, radios, canned food and sweets, and metalwork of all kinds. Between the wars this led to a great increase of employment in subsidiary and luxury industries in the South-East, and the London suburbs grew rapidly.

British agriculture between the wars
For a brief period after the war agriculture continued to prosper, and by the Agricultural Act of 1920 the tenant-farmer was given rights of compensation for improvements of his land which were uncompleted when his tenancy ended, and he was also entitled to a year's notice of the termination of his tenancy.

In 1921, however, farm prices began to fall rapidly. The price of wheat was more than halved in the period from 1920 to 1922, falling from about 80s. a quarter to about 40s. The Government's policy was to return to the uncontrolled conditions which had existed before 1914. The Wages Boards and the system of guaranteed prices were abolished by the Coalition Government, so that both workers and farmers were thrown back to an almost completely *laissez-faire* situation. As in the depression of 1873–1900 many farmers now returned to pasture farming.

However, this complete relapse to a 'free for all' agriculture was only temporary, and the first Labour Government initiated new measures. In 1924 Agricultural Wages Boards were established for the counties and the principle of the minimum wage was again recognized. This was necessary because of the drastic fall in farmworkers' wages from 42s. in 1921 to about 28s. in the following year. In 1929 the Derating Act relieved farm land and buildings from the rates. Direct Government aid was undertaken by the re-introduction of the war-time policy of subsidies. By 1937 wheat, oats and barley were all receiving a Government subsidy. The Governments of the 1930's also encouraged the development of the sugar-beet industry and in 1935 the new sugar-beet factories were formed into the British Sugar Corporation in which the Government had its own representatives. In 1931 and 1933 Agricultural Marketing Acts were passed by the National Government which encouraged producers to combine to market such produce as milk and potatoes. Attempts to encourage the growth of small-holdings, as in the pre-war period, achieved very little. The small farm was unable to benefit from up-to-date methods involving expensive machinery. The old policy of attempting to increase smallholdings has since been abandoned and the reverse policy of encouraging and assisting the amalgamation of farms, was announced by the Labour Government in 1965.

Agricultural wages and working conditions were not good enough to prevent the drift from the land, and between 1919 and 1939 up to 10,000 men left every year. In 1931 there were only about half the number of agricultural workers employed in 1870.

The economy, 1939–45

At the outbreak of war in 1939 the British economy was weak in those very industries on which British prosperity had depended in the past – especially in coal, iron and steel, cotton, shipbuilding and the shipping industry, as well as agriculture. While the conditions of the working people had undoubtedly advanced, there were appalling centres of unemployment and suffering in the 'depressed areas' of Britain. The 'hunger marches' of the 1930's and the fierce agitation against the Means Test for the chronically unemployed had produced serious social and political conflict in the 1930's, and these were all expressions of the basic economic weaknesses.

The war itself obviously placed enormous strains on the economy. Once more Britain diverted a major part of her industrial effort into war goods and once again millions of pounds of equipment, millions of tons of shipping and incalculable amounts of raw material were produced only to be destroyed. Before Pearl Harbor and even more afterwards Britain came to rely on American credit and American goods to supplement her own enormous efforts.

Problems of post war development

When the war ended the task of reconstruction was even greater than in 1918. However, both in the years of Labour Government from 1945 to 1951 and in the three subsequent Conservative Governments more and more elements of the economy came within the Government's planning activities so the main developments from the Labour nationalizations to the creation of the Department of Economic Affairs and the Prices and Incomes Board are best dealt with in the context of the political history of the period (see Chapters 25, 26, 27).

There are some other aspects of the economy, nevertheless, which deserve separate attention. In the first place the balance of the economy continued to change. Britain imported more than she exported throughout the period 1815–1966. Before 1914 the balance was rectified first by the enormous revenue from British investments overseas and secondly by invisible exports or services such as shipping charges, banking and insurance which foreigners often bought from British firms. The First World War reduced both of these sources of income. Investments, especially, were sold off to pay for the war effort. The war of 1939–45 made it even harder to achieve a favourable balance of payments. Many of the remaining investments were sold and other countries began to compete with Britain in the field of invisible exports. It therefore became more and more important that the difference between the visible exports and imports was kept to a minimum. During the same period the pattern of exports was also changing. Before 1914 the main exports were textiles, iron and steel, ships, machinery and coal. These products of heavy industry remained very important after the First World War but they suffered more and more from the effects of foreign competition. There were new light industries to compensate for this

(1) Average annual rate of growth of production,
    1950 – 1960 (Gross National Product)

		%
France	–	4·3
Western Germany	–	7·3
Italy	–	5·9
Britain	–	2·6
Japan	–	8·4
U.S.S.R.	–	6·7
U.S.A.	–	3·3

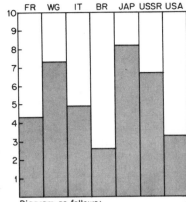

(2) Productivity per man–year, 1950–1960
    increase %

France	–	3·9
Western Germany	–	5·2
Italy	–	4·3
Britain	–	2·0
Japan	–	6·7
U.S.S.R.	–	4·7
U.S.A.	–	2·1

Diagram as follows:

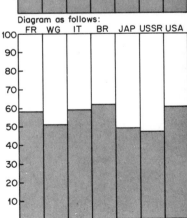

(3) Proportion of Gross National Product entering
    private consumption, 1960

		%
France	–	58·3
Western Germany	–	50·4
Italy	–	58·7
Britain	–	61·3
Japan	–	48·9
U.S.S.R.	–	47·1
U.S.A.	–	60·4

Diagram as follows:

FIG. 11. Economic Development 1950–60.

in part but the appalling effects of the depression in the North-East and North-West where the heavy industries remained predominant showed how far the country was still dependent on her traditional products in the inter-war years.

Since 1945 British industry and British exports have changed enormously. The country now earns more and more of its foreign currency from such

'Sea Quest', a new rig for drilling for natural gas, moves out of Belfast Lough on its way to the North Sea.

things as motor-cars, chemicals, electrical goods, synthetic fibres and even whisky. At the same time great efforts have been made to exploit another invisible export – tourism. However, the recurrent balance of payments crises show only too clearly that the struggle to pay for imports by exports has not yet been won.

In the struggle for exports it has become increasingly important that British industry should be rationally organized and equipped with the most modern machinery. But this is a very slow business and all too often British firms have found themselves under-priced by more efficient Japanese or Swedish or American competitors. This has been particularly noticeable in the shipbuilding industry. By the 1960's the Governments were taking both direct and indirect action to bring about rationalization not only in the old industries like shipbuilding and steel but in the newer ones like aircraft construction.

British agriculture was naturally stimulated by the war as every available acre was turned over to food production. With the resumption of normal trade relations after 1945 British farms were once more unable to compete with overseas sources of food. However, the Governments did not want agriculture to revert to its depressed pre-war state and so encouraged British farmers with very large subsidies. In 1964–5 these amounted to no less than £380 million. The farmers for their part have gradually adopted some of the most modern features of mechanized and concentrated farming practised in countries like Denmark and the Netherlands. Yet most British farms have remained very small units producing a diversity of crops rather than specializing. In any case agriculture plays a minor part in the economy as a whole. In fact a smaller proportion of the population works on the land in this country than anywhere else in the world.

Britain is, then, overwhelmingly an industrial nation and to exist she must buy her food and raw material abroad and pay for them by a growing stream of exports. This in its turn makes it imperative that there is an efficient system of internal transport, that British industries are re-equipped and reorganized so that they are competitive on the world markets, that industry is redeployed so that the old depressed areas such as the North-East or Northern Ireland can play their part in the national expansion and prevent the drift to the Midlands and the South-East. All these things may be helped by new technological inventions, by North Sea gas or by a Channel Tunnel, but basically they depend upon the exertions of the British people themselves.

30. The Development of the Old Dominions

CANADA

CANADA presented a number of problems for the home government after the defeat of the French during the Seven Years War, 1756–63. In 1774 the Quebec Act was passed which established a nominated council of Canadian citizens to advise the British Governor. It recognized French civil law but introduced English criminal law. It protected the lands and titles of the Roman Catholic clergy. It also declared that the land between the Ohio and the Mississippi was annexed to Canada. By this act a clear attempt was made to secure the loyalty of the French Canadians.

The success of the Americans in the War of Independence had political repercussions in Canada. The United Empire Loyalists who emigrated from the United States settled in some numbers in Nova Scotia, New Brunswick, Prince Edward Island and Newfoundland, and had also settled in Ontario, or Upper Canada, west of Quebec. There was also some immigration from Britain especially Scotland. The result of this change of the balance of population was the Canada Constitutional Act of 1791 which created two provinces, Upper Canada (Ontario) and Lower Canada (Quebec). There was a Governor for the provinces together, and there were Lieutenant Governors for each separately with an Executive Council nominated by and responsible to him. In Upper Canada English civil law as well as English criminal law was established, Lower Canada retaining French civil law and English criminal law as before. In each province there was a nominated Legislative Council and an elected Assembly which could present laws concerning taxation and other local matters to the Lieutenant-Governor but could not compel their acceptance if the home government disallowed them.

This Act did not, however, solve the problems of a country where two different peoples were demanding more and more powers for themselves. This difficulty became acute in Lower Canada where the Assembly was almost entirely French while the Governor, whose chief advisers were British, could overrule the Assembly. There were economic grievances too, especially when, in 1833, the newly-established British American Land Company started to settle the area with non-Catholic newcomers. The result was religious, economic and political strife.

In British Upper Canada there was also discontent. One of the main grievances was the favouritism shown, in land distribution and in political appointments, to the United Empire Loyalists who had entered Canada after the defeat of Britain by the American colonists in 1783. This meant that later immigrants were penalized. The clergy reserves were also a cause of discontent, for this involved the control of large areas of land by the English and Scottish Established Churches. Fortunately the other British-American colonies, New Brunswick, Prince Edward Island, Nova Scotia and Newfoundland, remained reasonably satisfied with their representative government.

However, in 1834 Grey's Whig Government sent out a special commission, which reported in favour of suspending representative government in the provinces. This was seen as an attempt to thrust the settlers back into the narrow mould of colonial dependence on Britain.

Rebellion, 1837, and the Durham Report

Discontent turned into open rebellion in 1837 under Papineau in Lower Canada and Mackenzie in Upper Canada. Although these rebellions were suppressed, Melbourne's Government sent out Lord Durham, a utilitarian Radical and friend of the great imperialist, Edward Gibbon Wakefield. Wakefield wanted to change the whole attitude of people and Government at home to the question of colonies which, in the words of one statesman, were commonly regarded as 'millstones round our necks'. Wakefield saw them as being important in two ways – namely, to receive Britain's surplus population and to promote valuable two-way trade once their resources had been developed by the new settlers. For this purpose he set up companies to promote emigration to New Zealand and South Australia particularly. Durham had considerable sympathy with this policy and took Wakefield to Canada with him as his adviser.

The Durham Report on Canada expressed a number of general political principles which influenced British government during the nineteenth century in dealing with the colonies, and indeed has been considered the foundation upon which the Commonwealth is based. He advised the reunion of Upper and Lower Canada, hoping that thus the peoples of the two provinces would soon be fused into one Canadian people. He proposed that there should be a Governor with Executive and Legislative Councils and that there should be an elected Assembly with equal numbers of members from each Province. Durham also advocated the early establishment of responsible government for all local affairs, including finance; constitutional changes, foreign affairs, defence, the regulation of trade and commerce, the disposal of undeveloped land being reserved for the home government.

Durham was convinced that the change to responsible government in Canada would strengthen the Empire and not, as many feared, lead to its disintegration. Events proved him right and his many critics wrong, at least until the era after the Second World War. Durham was guilty of a number of ill-advised acts while Governor-General in 1838 – he deported eight ringleaders to Bermuda and threatened Papineau and others who had fled with execution if they returned. He was therefore recalled in November 1838 and immediately resigned. His masterly Report was issued in 1839.

The Canada Act, 1840

The Canada Act, 1840, was the direct outcome of the Durham Report. It implemented many of its suggestions. Upper and Lower Canada were united. There was to be a nominated Legislative Council of life members and a House of Assembly with equal members from each province, an arrangement which led to a majority of British members. A gradual approach was made towards responsible government and this was achieved in 1847 when Lord Elgin, Durham's son-in-law, was Governor-General.

Durham had concentrated his efforts on the two Canadas and had shown little or no interest in the other British-North American colonies. Of these Nova Scotia attained responsible government in 1846, and New Brunswick and Newfoundland in 1847.

Canada and the United States

Relations between Canada and the United States during the nineteenth century were complicated. The two Canadas bore the brunt of the War of 1812–14 with the United States, and French and British Canadians co-operated in the defence of their country. The competition – or conflict – between the two countries greatly increased after the opening of the Erie Canal by the United States in 1825. The canal ran from Buffalo on Lake Erie to the Hudson River and established water communication with New York. The Canadian reply was to construct the Welland Canal between Lakes Erie and Ontario and there was mounting commercial rivalry for the internal trade of North America.

In 1817, Castlereagh, the British Foreign Secretary, had secured an agreement with the United States by which Britain and the United States removed all war vessels and fortifications from the Great Lakes, and in 1818 the boundary westward from the Lake of Woods to the Rockies was fixed at the 49th parallel. This, however, left the area from the Rockies to the Pacific still open, and led to conflict between American and Canadian fur traders and settlers. The Americans wanted to take over the whole of this area, and to cut off Canada from the Pacific. Serious tension developed between the British and United States Governments (the slogan in America became fifty-four forty or fight'), but in 1846 the boundary was finally established at the 49th parallel. Another point of dispute was the Maine boundary which was settled by the Ashburton Treaty of 1842, which was, in the eyes of Canadians, far too favourable to the United States.

The main Canadian trade routes ran north and south and Canada continued to depend on American trade. This situation strengthened

Canada's economy so long as the U.S.A. did not take action against her. For example, the ending of a commercial treaty by the U.S.A. in 1864 caused much difficulty.

The Dominion of Canada, 1867

Some of Canada's problems arose from Gladstone's free trade policy, for the preferences formerly given to Canadian timber in the British market were withdrawn. It was clear that Canada must develop internally and expand her markets for her chief products. It was above all necessary to link up the maritime provinces with the others by the promotion of railways. The American Civil War of 1861–5 hit Canada's trade and also revealed the weaknesses of the United States form of federation. This was a great shock to those Canadians who in the past had advocated the union of Canada and the U.S.A. Canada was thrown sharply on to her own economic and political resources in the later nineteenth century. From a realization of her weakness arose the demand in Canada for the strong union of the provinces into a federal system. The actual federal scheme was devised in Canada and not imposed by Britain. Discussions began at the Quebec Conference in October 1864 between the representatives of the Canadas (Ontario and Quebec) and the Maritime Provinces (New Brunswick, Nova Scotia, Newfoundland, Prince Edward Island) and went on for two years. The Fenian invasion from the U.S.A. in 1866 spurred on the determination to achieve a settlement, and later in 1866 a conference was held in London. Under the terms of the resulting British North America Act, 1867, Upper and Lower Canada were again separated, becoming the provinces of Ontario and Quebec. This arrangement met the fears of the French in Lower Canada that they would be swamped by the increasing immigration from Britain in these early years. Only Ontario, Quebec, New Brunswick and Nova Scotia (very unwillingly) joined the federation, but provision was made for others to come in as their populations increased. Manitoba joined in 1870 and Prince Edward Island in 1873. British Columbia was admitted in 1871 and Alberta and Saskatchewan became provinces in 1905. Finally Newfoundland, which had been a dominion in its own right was accepted as a province in the Dominion of Canada in 1949. The Hudson's Bay Company's territorial rights were bought out in 1869, and the vast northern territories came under federal administration, not without some difficulty, as a French-Indian trapper led a rebellion on the Red River in 1885 which was put down by a British force under Wolseley.

All the main tasks of government – defence, taxation, postal services and external trade – went to the new Federal Government at the new capital, Ottawa. The provinces were given powers in certain specific spheres. All other powers belonged to the federation. The Act also dealt with the railways. Up to that time Canadian trade had been dependent on the American railways. The Act of 1867 provided for railways to link all the provinces. When complete the line ran from the St Lawrence to Halifax in Nova

Scotia, with a long and costly detour to avoid the American state of Maine. It was completed in 1876 and known as the Inter-colonial Railway.

Canadian Pacific Railway

After the admission of British Columbia to the federation in 1871 the Federal Government agreed to promote another railway linking British Columbia with the eastern railway system. In 1886 a railway was completed across the Rockies to the Pacific coast, successfully surmounting immense natural obstacles. The Canadian Pacific Railway linked Montreal with the Pacific over a distance of 2,500 miles. Every province except Prince Edward Island was now connected, and later the North Canadian Pacific Railway and the Grand Trunk Railway consolidated the system. The economic and political unity of Canada, mainly promoted by her railway system, led to the rapid growth of certain towns – for example, Winnipeg, which had 215 inhabitants in 1870, had 192,000 in 1926. Wheat production was immensely stimulated, for internal and external markets could now be reached cheaply and efficiently. The wheat production of central Canada rose about seventy times between 1880 and 1930.

This later phase in the development of Canada is especially associated with the great Canadian Prime Minister, Sir J. Macdonald. His policies led to the proper financing of the Canadian Pacific Railway project. He also introduced a high protective tariff against American goods, a symbol of Canadian confidence and independence.

During both world wars Canada contributed a great deal to the Allied cause. After 1945 the country was a prominent member of N.A.T.O. Canada also played a large part in the economic reconstruction of Western

The last spike being driven into the Canadian Pacific Railway, 7 November, 1885.

Europe and has remained closely linked with her old Commonwealth partners by bonds of common interest and culture. Inevitably her links have also grown much stronger with the United States which has become Canada's main trading partner. Although the country has been largely preoccupied with the development of her vast economic potential since 1945, the picture has been slightly marred by a recurrence of tension between the French-speaking population of Quebec and the predominantly Anglo-Saxon inhabitants of the other provinces.

AUSTRALIA

In 1788, eighteen years after Captain Cook's voyage of discovery, Captain Arthur Phillips arrived at Botany Bay with a party of seven hundred and fifty male and female convicts. They brought cattle, implements and seed and made their first settlement at Port Jackson. The transporting of criminals to Australia had begun after the American War of Independence had deprived Britain of a North American convict dumping-ground. In 1793 the first free settlers arrived and worked their land with convict labour. This gave rise to many difficulties and led to widespread violence and brutality. Most convicts remained in Australia when their sentences ended, being unable to afford their passage home. It took Australia many years to

Caged prisoners being shipped out to the penal settlements in Australia.

develop a satisfactory social system out of the problems left by the convict-settlements. The free settlers gradually persuaded the home Government to stop transportation. Eventually the Whig Government of 1832–7 set up a Commission of Inquiry which advised the abolition of the system. A start was made when, after 1840, no more convicts were sent out to New South Wales, but it was not until 1866 that the practice ceased altogether with the closing of the convict settlement in Western Australia. This encouraged emigration by respectable settlers and led to increased trade between Australia and the home country – a trade which amounted to over £16,000,000 in 1860.

Sheep and gold

Wool and gold were the basis of the early Australian economy. Towards the end of the eighteenth century Captain Macarthur had successfully introduced Merino sheep to Australia from the Cape of Good Hope, but it was the discovery in 1812 of excellent pasture beyond the Blue Mountains which led to the development of a thriving industry.

The quick fortunes which sheep farming offered led to much speculation in land and animals in the 1820's. But production developed so fast that the wool producers of Europe were soon driven from the export market altogether and the British woollens industry became heavily dependent on Australian produce.

In 1851 a miner from California discovered gold near the Australian settlement of Bathurst, and there was an immediate rush to the area. In 1852, 84,000 immigrants arrived at Melbourne. Many sheep farmers gave up their flocks in favour of gold-mining. The old convict elements were completely swamped by newcomers in search of gold.

The economic and political effects of sheep and gold were profound. New banks and companies were set up in the main towns to finance these developments. This in turn led to increasing imports of mining and other equipment from Britain, whose exports to Australia of capital goods of all kinds became an important part of British trade. The need for improved communications led to increasing imports of British railway stock. The advantages which Gibbon Wakefield had claimed would arise from emigration to Australia had become a reality.

Government in Australia

These striking economic developments led to the early demand for self-government by the various states. In 1826 New South Wales had become a Crown Colony directly under the control of the Governor-General and the home Government, but in 1842 the Council, formerly nominated by the Governor of the State, was allowed to have two-thirds of its membership elected. In 1850, Victoria separated from New South Wales and election to the Council was introduced. Government responsible to an elected assembly was established in New South Wales, Victoria, South Australia and Tasmania in 1855, in Queensland in 1859 and Western Australia in 1890.

Federation

The Union of the Australian States into a federation took longer than in Canada. The vast area with a thin population made federation particularly difficult. There was also a great difference in economic life between the two main groups of States – Victoria, New South Wales and Queensland had an early industrial development, whereas Tasmania, South Australia and Western Australia were mainly agricultural. Their interests conflicted, for the States with industries wanted protective tariffs on manufactured imports in order to assist their own infant industries, whereas the agricultural States wanted free trade in order to obtain their manufactured goods cheaply from abroad. The agricultural States also feared that a protective tariff on manufactured imports would lead to retaliation against their own exports.

Communications in the first half of the century were poor and, indeed, the continent was still being explored with great difficulty, but increased immigration and economic development changed the picture, especially after 1870. Between 1870 and 1880 nearly 3,000 miles of railway were constructed and the telegraph widely introduced. As isolation lessened, some form of central government became feasible. The decisive stimulus to federation came from external pressures. The colonization of the Pacific by the Great Powers after 1880, especially by Germany and Japan, was seen as a possible threat to the future of Australia. An effective central Government was needed for defence, and this became even more urgent after the replacement of Bismarck in 1890 by ministers more favourable to German imperial expansion. The expansionist policy of Japan, seen in the war of 1894 against China, brought the danger home even more forcefully. Australians became acutely aware of the vulnerability of their coasts, especially in the uninhabited area now known as the Northern Territories. In 1890 came the first attempts to establish a federation, and eventually in 1901 the new Federal Constitution set out in the Commonwealth of Australia Act was adopted. To overcome difficulties between the States, a new capital, Canberra, was built to house the Federal Parliament. As in Canada, the Federal Government had control over most important matters, but in the Commonwealth of Australia, powers not definitely given to the central Government remained with the six States which were thus much stronger than the Canadian provinces.

Australia, like Canada, played an important part in the Allied effort in both the world wars. In the First War Australians and New Zealanders were particularly prominent in the ill-fated Gallipoli campaign and in the Second War, which was much closer to their own homes, they fought in both the European and the Far Eastern Campaigns. Indeed for a while Australia became the headquarters of General Macarthur after the Americans had been driven out of South-East Asia in 1942.

Australia's links with Britain have remained very close in every aspect of life from sport to trade. However, Australian Governments have also adopted an independent line in many fields, including foreign policy. In 1951 Australia and New Zealand joined the United States in the A.N.Z.U.S. pact of which Britain was not a member. More recently Australia has sent troops to help the Americans in Vietnam while Britain has held aloof. Economic links with America have also been strengthened and Australia and New Zealand always have to bear in mind that their trading privileges with Britain may well disappear if the latter joins the Common Market.

NEW ZEALAND

From the time of Captain Cook's annexation in 1769 until the early nineteenth century the home Government neglected New Zealand. The main British contact with the country was through missionaries and traders from Australia. A few far-seeing individuals tried to convince the Government of New Zealand's potential value to the Empire. Edward Gibbon Wakefield (see also p. 56) established a New Zealand Association to encourage and assist emigration and settlement. Wakefield's ideas were not well received at first by the Whig Governments of the 1830's. However, he had many friends among the Radicals and in 1838 after a Parliamentary inquiry into his schemes, his Association was given the status of a chartered company. The Whig Government feared that the French might step in if Britain made no positive move, and negotiations opened with the New Zealand Maoris to obtain sovereignty for Great Britain.

The Treaty of Waitangi, 1840

By this important treaty Britain gained sovereignty in New Zealand, but the Maoris were guaranteed the possession of their land. It was agreed that Britain should have the right to purchase any native lands which were to be sold. However, this agreement worked out very badly, for land was obtained from the Maoris by unscrupulous means and settlers and officials showed a callous and hostile attitude towards them. The missionaries for their part did their best to prevent colonization. In effect, the New Zealand Company ignored the treaty and poured scorn on an arrangement made with 'naked savages'. This produced constant conflict between Maoris and settlers until the Maoris on the North Island rebelled in 1848.

Sir George Grey

While Sir George Grey was Governor (1845–53) things began to improve. He had already been Governor of South Australia from 1841 to 1845 and was again to be Governor of New Zealand (1861–8) and later Prime Minister

(1877–9). A man of high ideals and great humanity, he put an end to legalistic trickery at the expense of the Maoris and gained their confidence and support. He secured the purchase of the whole of the South Island for the British Crown and dissolved the New Zealand Company. After 1850 land settlement in New Zealand became purely the business of the Crown.

In 1852 an Act of Parliament established the New Zealand federation, which joined together the six main areas of settlement. A central federal legislature was set up with six elected councils for each of the provinces. This federal system was still directly under the supervision of the Governor on behalf of the home Government, but in 1856 self-government was introduced. At this point the Maoris were excluded from the franchise, which was limited to those who could speak and write English. In 1876 federation and the provincial assemblies were abandoned and the country was ruled by a single Parliament and Government at Wellington. This last development was primarily due to the great increase of settlers from 60,000 in 1856 to 350,000 in 1878. Improvements in transport and trade had, of course, accompanied this immigration. In fifty years New Zealand had passed through the stages of Crown Colony, federation under Crown control, then self-government and finally unitary government at Wellington.

The Maoris
Despite Grey's efforts, further trouble broke out between settlers and Maoris after his departure in 1853. This was mainly due to the tremendous pace at which land was taken up by white settlers between 1856 and 1860. By 1859 over 32,000,000 acres of the South Island had been settled. This alarmed the Maori chieftains whose people's livelihood and tribal traditions appeared to be threatened. Between 1860 and 1870 in the North Island, war was almost continuous between Maoris and settlers, chiefly over land sales. Against the superior military equipment of the settlers the Maoris waged a courageous but losing battle. Moreover, their numbers were being rapidly reduced by diseases like measles which the settlers had brought with them and which proved deadly to the natives. British policy under Grey's second period as Governor (1861–8) was more conciliatory. In 1867 he secured the direct representation of the Maoris in the New Zealand Parliament, and at length a land settlement was reached which secured half the North Island for the Maoris.

Economic development of New Zealand
The influence of Socialism was considerable in New Zealand long before it had any effect in Britain. The New Zealand Labour Party was powerful at a particularly early stage and great extremes of wealth and poverty were avoided from the first. A system of graded taxation and measures of social insurance were introduced. The even spread of wealth prevented the development of the sharp class divisions existing in the countries of Europe. New Zealand production rapidly increased in the second half of the nine-

The capture of a Maori redoubt, August 1863.

teenth century. Between 1855 and 1859 her wool exports to Britain rose tenfold – from £30,000 to £317,000 and by 1870 her total exports of all goods amounted to £4,700,000; After a period of decline between 1870 and 1890, immigration revived again at the end of the century.

During the twentieth century New Zealand, like Australia, has developed a greater independence from Britain in foreign policy as she already had in domestic affairs. However, both economically and in ties of sentiment the country is probably closer to Britain than any of the other dominions.

31. From Empire to Commonwealth

INDIA

Economic and social problems after the Mutiny

The suppression of the Mutiny was followed by heavy British investment in the Indian economy. This capital investment was largely for railway development, which was not only valuable to English cotton and jute manufacturers, who set up their factories in India, but would help mobilization against any further attempted risings. This development undoubtedly brought some advantages to the Indian people themselves, but the main purpose was to help British manufacturers in India. British money was widely invested in irrigation systems, canals, water supplies and modernization of plantations, for all these secured a Government-guaranteed return of five per cent.

Indian nationalism

This swamping of India by British capital was regarded with strong disfavour by those educated Indians who wanted India's economic and political life to develop along their own traditional lines. Moreover, it produced the same social problems from which Britain had suffered at the time of her Industrial Revolution. British manufacturers in India employed young children under seven years of age for as long as thirteen or fourteen hours a day, the very conditions which Robert Owen and the Earl of Shaftesbury had fought against in Britain. The benefit to the manufacturers in India lay principally in the supply of cheap labour, and they were disgusted by the first Indian Factory Act introduced in 1881 to improve these conditions.

This exploitation contributed greatly to the rise of the Indian National Congress established in 1885. The Congress agitated against the suppression of native craft industries, against the appalling conditions of the workers in the towns, and against the obvious intention of the British to keep a tight hold on the Indian Civil Service. This latter policy meant that British officials in India, however well-intentioned, were greatly overworked and could not give adequate attention to the people under their care. In fact, about 5,000 officials were expected to govern a country which in 1880 already had over 300 million inhabitants. There was no organized attempt on the part of Britain to educate and employ the Indians themselves, and in 1914 the Indian Civil Service was still 95 per cent British. The intelligent and educated Indian was being excluded from the sources of power in his own country, and independence from British control came to be the main demand of the followers of Mahatma Gandhi, the Congress leader. It is interesting to note, however, that the leaders of the Congress movement in the late nineteenth century were demanding self-government for India on parliamentary lines which they had learned in Britain.

British reforms in India
It was Gladstone in his second ministry of 1880–85 who first clearly supported the ultimate aim of Indian self-government. He took the important decision to attempt to introduce representative methods of government on the British model. The Viceroy, Lord Ripon, agreed with these ideas and his period of office set the tone for future British political reforms in India. He set up municipal committees and district boards, the majority of whose members were elected by the local taxpayers. These local committees had considerable powers over education, public works and health, and certain forms of taxation. Lord Ripon's successor, Lord Dufferin, went further in the Indian Councils Act, 1892, which extended the system of election to the councils of the provinces and to some councils concerned with legislation for the whole of India.

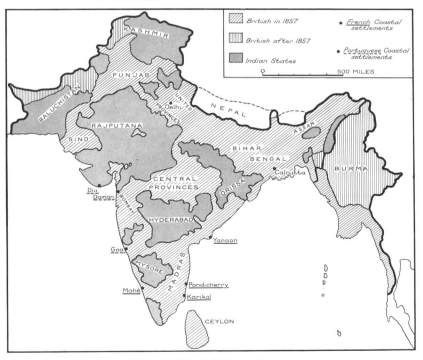

FIG. 12. British India.

These reforms were important because they enabled an increasing number of educated Indians to take part in political affairs, and gradually the old British attitude that only the British could govern India was undermined. However, the educated Indian was still jealously excluded from most key positions. The Indian Civil Service examination was held only in London, and this alone barred many educated Indians from competing for high executive posts. In 1883 there was an outcry from the Europeans when it was proposed to allow Europeans to be tried in courts presided over by Indian judges, and the measure was withdrawn. It was the limited and grudging nature of these concessions by the British that had led to the formation of the Indian National Congress in 1885. The annual meetings of the Congress became the arena in which Indian grievances could be fully discussed, and from the beginning it had European supporters and sympathizers. The Congress remained for some years an Indian middle-class movement tending to support progressive British measures, but in 1905 the Viceroy Lord Curzon cut off Eastern Bengal and Assam from Bengal proper against Hindu popular feeling, and from that time the movement came to represent a wider section of the Indian people. Congress also voiced economic discontent, especially over the drain of Indian wealth to Britain through railway and industrial dividends.

The Morley-Minto reforms, 1909
The Liberal Government in 1909 took further steps towards Indian self-government. Lord Morley, the Secretary of State for India, and the Viceroy, Lord Minto, produced a new scheme for provincial representative councils. The provincial councils of Bengal, Bombay and Madras were to have elected Indian majorities, and the Legislative Council for all India was to have a larger Indian representation, though not a majority. Indian members were also added to the Viceroy's Executive Council and the Secretary of State's Council in England. However, these councils were still only advisory bodies to the Viceroy without legislative powers. They could not in any way control the men chosen by the Viceroy to govern India. While some members of the Indian National Congress welcomed these changes, others began to demand stronger action against British rule.

The Delhi Durbar, 1911, an occasion of great pageantry, was marked by a declaration by King George V that Delhi would be restored as the capital of India, and that partition of Bengal would be ended. Even more important concessions were won in the First World War, in which Indians gave valuable and loyal support to Britain. In 1917 Lloyd George made it clear that democratic self-government for India was the definite aim of British policy.

The Montagu-Chelmsford reforms, 1919
In 1917 the Secretary of State for India, E. S. Montagu, went to India to confer with Lord Chelmsford, the Viceroy, and to sound Indian opinion. Their

conferences led to the Government of India Act, 1919. By this Act the Council of State was to consist of sixty members (some nominated, some elected) and the Legislative Assembly and the provincial legislatures were to have a majority of elected members. However, foreign policy, law, the armed forces, the police and finance were classified as 'reserved' matters which were in the hands of the Viceroy's Executive Council which, though enlarged, was not answerable to the legislature for its actions. A similar system held in the provinces. In other words, the key sources of power were still as far away from Indian hands as ever, and the reforms were violently denounced by the Indian National Congress, now increasingly influenced by Mahatma Gandhi. Anti-British feeling had already been inflamed by the massacre at Amritsar in 1919 when, on the orders of General Dyer, troops fired on a prohibited meeting of many hundreds of Indians; over four hundred were killed and more than a thousand wounded. Nevertheless many Indians did take office in provincial Governments, and gained valuable experience.

India in the inter-war years

Gandhi, by the simplicity and sincerity of his life, was able to gain the support of the Indian peasantry and working class as no other leader before him had succeeded in doing. By fasting, by the refusal of all human luxury, by humility of approach to all, he achieved the status of a saint. He preached above all non-violent action – the boycott of British goods, and the refusal of Indians in the Civil Service and elsewhere to work with the British. During the period of Lord Irwin's Viceroyalty, 1926–31, Gandhi attempted direct negotiation with the British and a Round Table Conference was called in London to devise a form of dominion status for India. However, the Government refused to give the Congress leaders a pledge of complete self-government, and the meeting broke down.

By the Government of India Act, 1935, the provincial Governments were made fully responsible to the legislatures and the system by which police powers had remained in British hands was abolished in the eleven most advanced provinces. The central House of Assembly was to consist of members elected by the provincial legislatures and the Council of State was made up chiefly of members elected to represent various interests and religions. The central administration remained a dyarchy, with representative members accountable to the Assembly on certain subjects, but the most important matters, such as foreign affairs, finance and defence remaining 'reserved' to the Viceroy and his advisers. Both the Viceroy and the provincial Governors also kept the right of emergency legislation. It was also proposed to create a federal system for India which would include the states of the Indian Princes which had not come within British India. Just before World War II the Congress Party had formed Governments in a number of provinces, but the Moslem League under Mr Jinnah opposed the federal idea and called for the protection of Moslem interests against the Hindus by the creation of a separate state for Moslems to be known as Pakistan. This solution had special difficulties, because the Moslems did not live in one compact area of India. However, after considerable violence, partition was the solution agreed on by the post-war Labour Government of Clement Attlee. The self-governing dominions of India and Pakistan were created in the India Independence Act of 1947.

India and Pakistan

The partition did not bring peace to the Indian subcontinent. Indeed the status of Kashmir, a largely Muslim state whose Hindu ruler took it into the Indian Union in 1947, is part of the inheritance of the partition and it was over Kashmir that the Indians and Pakistanis fought a full-scale war in 1965. However, since independence the British have naturally been less deeply involved in this area. Both countries have become republics within the Commonwealth and both have continued to receive a good deal of British economic and military aid. On the other hand their foreign policies have long ceased to be closely aligned with that of Britain. India, both under Nehru and his successors, has been one of the most important unaligned nations even after she had fought a border war with China in 1962. Pakistan was one of the founder members of the Baghdad Pact (now C.E.N.T.O.) and of S.E.A.T.O. the two main anti-Communist alliances in the Middle East and South-East Asia. Yet by the 1960's these bonds were of decreasing importance and Pakistan had established many links with Communist China while still accepting aid from the West.

Burma, Ceylon, Malaya, Singapore

The dissolution of the British raj in India was soon followed by the granting of independence to other parts of Asia. Burma not only became independent but also left the Commonwealth in 1947 and Ceylon became an independent Dominion within the Commonwealth in 1948. In Malaya, the British had to fight a protracted jungle war with Communist guerrillas, but eventually the rebels were crushed. In August 1957 the Federation of Malaya became an independent state within the Commonwealth. It comprised the nine Malay States and the Straits Settlements, Malacca and Penang. Singapore was not included in the Federation and became a self-governing state in June 1959, but with the limitations that defence and external affairs remained in the hands of Britain. In September 1961 Singapore agreed to enter the Federation of Malaya. In September 1963, the wider Federation of Malaysia was formed. It included not only the Federation of Malaya and Singapore but also Sarawak and Sabah (North Borneo) but not Brunei, which remained a British protected state. The formation of the Federation of Malaysia led to the confrontation with Indonesia and hostilities in Sarawak and Sabah and elsewhere; it was not ended until August 1966. In August 1965, Singapore seceded from the Federation, and became a fully independent state.

The end of empire in India. (above) *The Ceremonial: the last British troops parade in front of Government House in Delhi.* (below) *The Aftermath: Indian troops patrol the deserted streets of a town in the Punjab after communal riots.*

AFRICA

Introduction
At the beginning of the nineteenth century Britain possessed few territories in Africa, and these only on the west coast. They comprised scattered forts which had been centres for the slave-traders, and the colony of Sierra Leone. By purchase from the Dutch and Danes and by wars against the Ashanti tribes, the Gold Coast territory was extended under British rule, but it was only towards the end of the century that Britain and the other powers really showed an interest in taking over more territory in Africa. Lord Salisbury and Joseph Chamberlain were the first politicians to make a decisive move towards the foundation of a new British Empire in Africa. They gave support to Cecil Rhodes (p. 161), and also to the private companies who did the pioneering work of expansion.

The Gambia
The oldest British settlement in West Africa was made in 1664 at Fort James near the mouth of the Gambia river as a protection for British merchants against the Dutch. Trading connections had been made there as early as 1588. The present capital Bathurst was founded in 1816, and the Gambia became an independent colony in 1843. For a time after 1865 it became one of the West Africa Settlements administered from Freetown, but in 1888 it became a separate colony again. The Gambia Protectorate was established in 1894 over some 4,000 square miles stretching 200 miles inland along the Gambia river. After a series of constitutional advances, the Gambia became an independent state within the Commonwealth in February 1965.

Sierra Leone
English connections with Sierra Leone began early in the seventeenth century and Bunce Island was fortified by the Royal African Company in 1672. The coast of Sierra Leone was particularly favourable for slave traders. The Sierra Leone of today really dates from the settlement at Freetown in 1787 of freed slaves from London, followed by freed slaves from Nova Scotia. To these were added larger numbers of Africans freed from slave ships. After a chequered early history Freetown was made a Crown Colony in 1808. The colony expanded in the nineteenth century when Freetown was the headquarters of the Court of Mixed Commission set up to enforce the ban on the slave trade and also of British administration in West Africa. In 1896 a British protectorate was declared over a considerable hinterland and this led to a serious rising in 1898. The original colony and the Protectorate now form the state of Sierra Leone. It passed through a number of constitutional changes before it became an independent nation on 21 April 1961.

Ghana

Ghana today has taken the name of an ancient empire which existed in medieval times far to the north of the present state. Ghana today is made up of the territory earlier known as the Gold Coast, Ashanti and the Northern Territories. The Gold Coast had connections dating centuries back through the gold and slave trades not only with the British but also with the Portuguese and Dutch. Serious British attempts at administration date from the early nineteenth century and are particularly associated with the name of Captain George Maclean. His successor, Governor Hill, negotiated the Bond of 1844 with Gold Coast chiefs and this was held to establish a British protectorate over the region. In time the Danish and Dutch forts were purchased and the British were left as the only European authority. The Report of the Parliamentary Select Committee of 1865 made it clear that the British regarded their stay in Lagos, the Gambia and the Gold Coast as temporary, but temporary proved to mean till 1957. The British had their troubles, particularly with the powerful Ashanti, and it was only after two quite serious wars that Ashanti was declared part of the Gold Coast colony. The protectorate over the Northern Territories was declared in 1898.

Successive constitutional advances were made after World War II, especially when nationalist pressure mounted, led first by Dr J. B. Danquah, and then by Dr Kwame Nkrumah and his Convention People's Party. The chief of these constitutions were those of 1951 and 1954. The latter led directly to independence on 6 March 1957. From then on there developed a strong one-party state with a strong presidential government under Dr Nkrumah, who was at length dismissed by the National Liberation Committee on 24 February 1966.

Nigeria

British traders penetrated the Niger coast in the first half of the nineteenth century, before other nations were directly involved. After the abolition of the slave trade, the trading value of palm oil became the main attraction. Mungo Park had explored a great part of the River Niger and died during that exploration in 1805. After many attempts, the exploration of the River Niger was completed by the brothers Lauder in 1830 who found that the long-known Oil Rivers were the mouths of the Niger. French and Germans were also engaged in the exploration of the region, especially the German, Dr Barth, who worked with an expedition supported by the British Government. Trade was the chief aim along the Niger and prominent among the pioneers was Macgregor Laird whose steamships sailed up the river. Missionaries sometimes followed, sometimes preceded the traders. Britain was also keeping a close watch on the slave trade and it was an attempt to crush the activities of the ruler of Lagos that led the British Government to annex the island of Lagos in 1861. This became the first British colony on the Guinea coast, the Gold Coast being at first a vague protectorate. British interest in the Niger region continued to grow, and so did the interests of the Germans and French, the latter establishing trading stations on the lower Niger. In reply to this, Sir George Goldie, who also had trading interests on the Niger, evolved a scheme for uniting all British trading interests and creating a British Niger Province. For this purpose he had established the United African Company in 1879 and proceeded to buy out the French interests. In 1886 this company was granted a royal charter and became the Royal Niger Company. Through it British control of coastal Nigeria was established. In order to protect their gains from the French on the northern and western frontiers and from the Germans in the Cameroons, the company secured important political treaties with the Mohammedan rulers of the interior, and trained a special army of the Hausa people under British officers. Chamberlain, who was Colonial Secretary under Salisbury, created a special West African Frontier Force and the Niger Company gave up all its political rights to the British Crown at the beginning of 1900. The Company became once again a purely trading concern. Two British Protectorates of Northern and Southern Nigeria were created. Chamberlain's policy had proved an effective counter to French and German ambitions and enabled Britain to negotiate favourable frontier settlements with both Powers.

Lord Lugard
In 1900 British influence in Northern Nigeria was very slender, and this territory was brought effectively under British control by the first High Commissioner, Lord Lugard. An administrative capital was established at Zungeru, but there was opposition from the rulers of adjoining provinces. Lugard directed a campaign against them and replaced them with rulers who committed themselves to the suppression of the slave trade and to the recognition of British sovereignty. Lugard then established English Residents in the provinces and set up a system of provincial courts and a supreme court. In the main, however, he relied on 'indirect rule' by which most of the governing was left to the Mohammedan emirs under British supervision. The Residents interfered with the emirs' rule only when it was necessary to check abuses. The collection of taxes, for instance, was left to the emirs' officers, and a proportion – up to a half – was handed over to the British administration for the development of roads, railways, agriculture, and public health. In 1912–14 Lord Lugard was given the difficult task of amalgamating Northern and Southern Nigeria whose tribal and social structures were very different. He was appointed as the first Governor-General, and retired at the end of the Great War in 1918, having strongly established British power in Nigeria.

The recent political development of West Africa
Nationalist movements developed rather later in Africa than they did in Asia and it was not until after the Second World War that new young

leaders like Kwame Nkrumah in the Gold Coast and Azikiwe in Nigeria began to win mass support for fairly radical nationalist parties. Most of these leaders spent at least some time in gaol during their struggle for independence like their Indian counterparts, but generally there was much less violence in West Africa than in India. Nkrumah and others were given places on Government councils before independence so that when it came there was continuity and the new leaders were very well experienced in the process of Government.

The British for their part were quite willing to grant independence in West Africa both because the area was politically well developed and because the situation was not complicated by the presence of large bodies of white settlers. Thus the Gold Coast was granted independence in 1957 and was followed soon afterwards by Nigeria (1960), Sierra Leone (1961) and Gambia (1965). Both Ghana and Nigeria have suffered from considerable political difficulties since independence and both face enormous economic problems. It is even doubtful whether Nigeria will continue to exist as a unified state. On the other hand the new nations of West Africa have been extremely active members of the United Nations, and made an important contribution to the policing of the Congo at the height of its internal crisis. Although there have frequently been disagreements with Britain, especially over her policies in Rhodesia, all the West African states have remained within the Commonwealth and have retained close economic links with Britain.

East Africa

British influence in East Africa was at first exercised through trading agreements with the Sultans of Zanzibar, who controlled a great part of the East African coast. In 1877 the Sultan offered to Sir William Mackinnon, founder of the British India Steam Navigation Company, a lease of all his territories on the mainland, but the Foreign Office refused to agree. However, ten years later, when German penetration of East Africa had advanced a long way, a lease of those mainland areas not occupied by the Germans was accorded to the Imperial British East Africa Company. The Germans in Tanganyika proved a formidable rival as they put forward claims to districts conceded by the Sultan to the British East Africa Company. In 1888 a British expedition was sent out to the Victoria Nyanza and then, in order to counteract the activities of the Germans under Karl Peters in Uganda, advanced into Uganda. In 1890 an agreement with Germany gave Britain trading rights in Uganda and from these developed the British protectorate over that area.

The home government refused to support the Company's plans to build a railway from Mombasa to the Victoria Nyanza and other financial difficulties arose which finally forced the British Government to buy out the company in 1893. In 1895 the East Africa territory was taken over by the Foreign Office as a protectorate. Soon afterwards, Chamberlain and Salisbury decided that it was in the British interest to build the Mombasa-Victoria Nyanza railway. This was begun in 1896, and finished in 1903 at a cost of £7 million. Besides securing effective British penetration of the interior and providing access to Uganda, it opened up the Kenya highlands which were ideal for farming and European settlement.

White settlement of Kenya

From 1902 onwards applications for grants of land in the highlands were considered by the administration. The arrival of large numbers of prospective purchasers from South Africa set a problem for the administration, especially as some of the best land was reserved for the use of the Masai tribes. The first British settler was Lord Delamere, with whose name the early development of the highlands is closely associated. After much controversy between the home Government and the local administration, the policy of dividing the land into small farms for development by the individual settler rather than allowing the sale of large areas for speculative resale or rental was adopted. After the Great War of 1914–18, a considerable number of ex-service men from Britain received grants of land. At this time the main labouring work of the settlements was undertaken by the Kikuyu people. In 1919 the Europeans were allowed to elect seven representatives to the legislative council for the first time. The Indians, who were a substantial proportion of the population, also demanded representation. In 1920 the protectorate became the Crown colony of Kenya.

A division of opinion between the British Government and the white settlers was a very early feature of political and economic life in Kenya. In the Devonshire Report issued by the British Government in 1923 it was declared that 'the interests of the African natives must be paramount' and in the event of native interests and those of the settlers conflicting 'the former should prevail'. Compulsory native labour for Europeans and other non-natives had been prohibited in 1920, and the policy of developing the native reserves had caused the European settlers to fear that their supply of labour would decline. Lord Delamere campaigned in the 1920's for complete white supremacy by means of an elected majority on the legislative council, while the home Government continued to oppose him. They reiterated their policy of trusteeship on behalf of the natives – a trusteeship with which the white settlers were to be associated.

Since World War II Kenya has moved on to independence under African control and within the Commonwealth. This great change which took place in 1963, was the result of reasoned development and violent pressure after 1945. In 1948, representative government with an unofficial majority (i.e. a majority of members who were not officials) was established but there were only four Africans in the Legislative Council. A considerable proportion of the white settlers resisted the idea of an African independent state and many left Kenya. The Mau-Mau terrorist campaign undoubtedly hardened their views, and prevented further progress until 1955 when a Council of Ministers was set up. In 1957 the first African elections were held. In 1960 the State of Emergency which had been declared in 1952 was ended. Two conferences were held at Lancaster House, and Mr Jomo Kenyatta, who had been detained under the Emergency regulations, was released. In December 1963, Kenya became an independent state with Jomo Kenyatta as Prime Minister, and when in August 1964 Kenya became a republic within the Commonwealth Kenyatta became President. Many white settlers have accepted citizenship in the new state in view of the conciliatory attitude of the President in recent years. Thus Kenya appears to offer an example of genuine multiracial co-operation between its African, Asian and European citizens.

Zanzibar

Britain had had relations with the Sultans of Zanzibar since the beginning of the nineteenth century. Her chief interest in him and his territories was the restriction and ultimate prohibition of the slave trade which was finally agreed to by Sultan Barghash in 1873. Zanzibar was also a centre from which explorers began their journeys and from which missionaries set out. The Sultans claimed suzerainty not only over the coast but also over the interior of East Africa, and their position was threatened when Europeans began to regard East Africa as a sphere for colonial expansion. Hence arose the offer of a lease to Sir William Mackinnon in 1877 mentioned above, and hence, too, arose the eventual partition of East Africa by which Kenya, Uganda and Zanzibar fell under British jurisdiction, and Dar-es-Salaam and its hinterland became German East Africa. From 1890 Zanzibar became a British protectorate. Though the Sultans continued to rule, Britain had effective control. At length after various constitutional advances, Zanzibar became independent in December 1963. The minority rule with the Sultan at its head was unlikely to last, and in January 1964 the Sultan was deposed and a republic established. In April 1964 this was linked with Tanganyika in the United Republic of Tanganyika and Zanzibar which in August 1964 became Tanzania.

Tanganyika

By the Anglo-German Treaty of 1890, Tanganyika, Ruanda and Urundi became German East Africa. While the Germans endeavoured to develop the country's agriculture and to introduce German settlers, their system of administration led to serious discontent which culminated in the Maji-Maji rebellion in 1905-7. In spite of the unpopularity of their rule, the Germans were able to maintain resistance in the First World War right up to 1918.

After the War Tanganyika became a British mandated territory, while Ruanda and Urundi were administered by Belgium. In the period 1925-30, Sir Donald Cameron as Governor developed indirect rule of the type used by Lord Lugard in Northern Nigeria. Tanganyika was never technicall᾿ a British possession, and the advance towards independence after th᾿ Second World War was more rapid than elsewhere in East Africa. In Ma᾿ 1961 Tanganyika attained full self-government, and in December 1961 i᾿ became independent with Dr Julius Nyerere as Head of State. As mentionec above Tanganyika formed a union with Zanzibar (now Tanzania) in Apri᾿ 1964.

Uganda

By the Anglo-German Treaty of 1890, Uganda became a British sphere o᾿ influence, and in 1894 it was made a protectorate under the Foreign Office It was particularly important to Egypt and the Sudan, and therefore t᾿ Britain, as the source of the White Nile. It was not an easy area to contro᾿ owing to the rivalries of Moslems and Christians, and of Protestants an᾿ Catholics, as well as the rivalries between the predominant Buganda, an᾿ other kingdoms, especially Bunyoro. Considerable control over Bugand᾿ was allowed to its King, the Kabaka, and its Parliament, the Lukiko. I᾿ 1905 the Colonial Office took over responsibility for the Protectorate fron᾿ the Foreign Office, and in 1907 a Governor was appointed in place of ᾿ Commissioner as formerly. The Kenya-Uganda Railway greatly assistec᾿ the economic development of the country, and this was further stimulatec᾿ at a later date by the completion in 1954 of the Owen Falls hydro-electri᾿ scheme.

From 1921 gradual constitutional advances were made. Progress wa᾿ difficult owing to the demands of Buganda for independence from th᾿ Protectorate which led to the temporary exile of the Kabaka. In Marcl᾿ 1962 full self-government was attained by Uganda. In October 1963 th᾿ Kabaka Mutesa II became President of the independent republic witl᾿ Dr Milton Obote as Prime Minister. In 1966 the Kabaka was exiled b᾿ Obote, but in 1971 Obote was himself overthrown by a military coup unde᾿ General Amin, who then directed a vigorous campaign to drive out th᾿ Ugandan Asian population.

Central and Southern Africa

Southern Rhodesia became self-governing under the Crown in 1923. When the British South Africa Company's rule came to an end, the settlers in Rhodesia chose by a narrow majority to become a Crown colony rathe᾿ than to join the Union of South Africa. In the Constitution the British Government reserved to itself certain powers, including an oversight o᾿ legislation regarding mining rights and the status of Africans. A commor᾿ franchise qualification was established for Europeans and Africans, bu᾿ this was fixed at a level which made it impossible for any but a relativel᾿ small number of Africans to qualify. The Government was thus in the᾿ hands of the white settlers.

Northern Rhodesia lying to the north of the Zambezi was partly under

he British South Africa Company from 1894 and partly under the British
Crown. In 1911 the two territories were combined as Northern Rhodesia
and in 1924 they became a protectorate under the Crown.

Nyasaland became a protectorate in 1892. In 1904 responsibility for it
passed from the Foreign Office to the Colonial Office, and in 1907 a
Governor was appointed. It was difficult of access and poor in natural
resources.

Some kind of working agreement between these three countries would
obviously be to the economic advantage of all of them. Nyasaland supplied

*A romantic view of British Imperialism: Matabele attack a British
laager, 1893.*

many labourers to Southern Rhodesia and the copper of Northern
Rhodesia had to pass through Southern Rhodesia on its way to the
markets of the world. Southern Rhodesia itself hoped to control the
Federation if it was formed. In 1951 a Conference in London proposed a
Federation of the Rhodesias and Nyasaland, and in July 1953 this was
established by Order in Council in spite of the opposition of Africans in all
three countries who feared a perpetuation of white rule. The Federal
Government was given wide powers, including external affairs and defence,
but there was provision for the reservation of Federal legislation which
affected African interests for Her Majesty's pleasure.

Though there were important projects like the Kariba Dam and the
improvement of communications which were beneficial to all members of

the Federation, African discontent continued. The Monckton Commission in 1960 recommended increased African representation in the Federal Parliament and that racial discrimination should be illegal. It also recommended that members of the Federation should be allowed to secede, and this is what first Nyasaland (Malawi) in January 1963 and then Northern Rhodesia (Zambia) in January 1964 did on attaining independence.

The break-up of the Federation caused much bitterness in Southern Rhodesia which was re-named Rhodesia. Though ties of sentiment were strong between Britain and Rhodesia for many reasons, including the outstanding support Rhodesia had given in the Second World War, the restrictions imposed by the Constitution of 1923 were increasingly resented. Macmillan's 'wind of change' speech of February 1960 fell unpleasantly on Rhodesian as well as South African ears. South African apartheid policy

FIG. 13. Africa in 1967. Note: *Rhodesia declared independence unilaterally in 1965 but this was not recognised by Britain or the United Nations.*

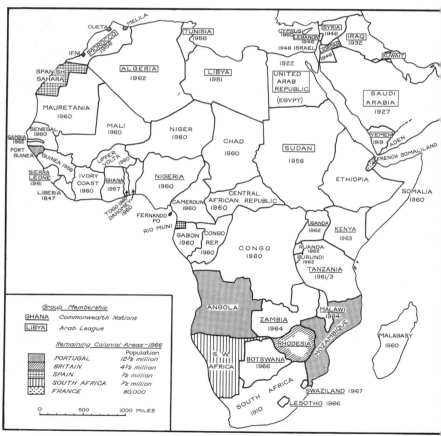

which led to her withdrawal from the Commonwealth in 1961 was viewed sympathetically by some Rhodesians. Some constitutional changes were made but the feelings of the settlers were reflected in the return of governments progressively more and more determined to maintain white supremacy for the foreseeable future. Thus the Unilateral Declaration of Independence by Ian Smith's government in November 1965 was not a surprise. It has posed a problem that neither the imposition of sanctions nor meetings of ministers has begun to solve. The question remains a threat to the Commonwealth itself.

In Southern Africa the problems have been different. The Union of South Africa had been an independent dominion for half a century before it left the Commonwealth and became a Republic in 1961.

The Boers or Afrikaaners had no strong ties with Britain and many of the English-speaking sections of the white population were divorced from the British in political attitudes. As for the Boers, South Africa was to them their country. In a Commonwealth in which the United Kingdom, the white dominions and the new Asian and African states enjoyed equality, South Africa, with racial discrimination its avowed policy, was the 'odd man out'. The withdrawal of South Africa was acknowledged by the South Africa Act 1962, a typically British measure by which South Africa retained the same trading privileges as Commonwealth countries and Britain retained the right to use the Simonstown naval base.

There remained the former High Commission territories, Botswana (Bechuanaland), Lesotho (Basutoland) and Swaziland, all of which were economically dependent on South Africa. The first of these became independent in September 1966 and the second in October 1966. They are both poor and will need much help from Britain. Swaziland, the most prosperous, attained independence in 1967.

EGYPT

Lord Cromer and British policy in Egypt

During the years 1883–1907 Sir Evelyn Baring, who became Lord Cromer in 1892, was the virtual ruler of Egypt. The Khedive was still nominally under the suzerainty of Turkey, but Cromer was the most powerful influence in the development of the country. Although Britain made numerous declarations promising eventual independence to Egypt, there were few signs of such a development before the 1914 war. A legislative council existèd, but it had no real powers. Cromer acted in economic matters on his declared principle that the 'interests of the bondholders and the Egyptian people are identical'. To meet the demands of the British and other bondholders of the Egyptian national debt it was necessary to increase Egyptian exports of cotton and Cromer's reforms substantially increased the cotton yield in these years – from about £8 million in 1883 to £30 million in 1907. This was mainly achieved by the allocation of £1 million by Cromer to improved irrigation. The completion of the first Aswan Dam in 1898 meant that the part of Egypt thus irrigated could raise two crops a year instead of one. This turned the Egyptian Government's deficit on foreign loans into a surplus and the debt was accordingly reduced. At the same time Cromer went ahead with the development of the railway system. His social reforms also helped to secure more justice for the Egyptian peasant (the *fellah*) and this in its turn boosted production. He succeeded in reducing nearly every form of taxation and, by curbing corruption in the administration, he ensured a more fruitful use of the actual income from taxation. He prohibited the beating of the *fellaheen* with the rhinoceroshide *kurbash*, he stopped the corvée or forced labour for the state, and he greatly improved the administration of justice. Such was the improvement in the general condition of Egypt that in 1901 Arabi Pasha, who had been in exile in Ceylon, was permitted to return.

Egyptian nationalism

Cromer was officially only 'adviser' to the Egyptian Government, but he opposed any idea of Egyptian independence, and just before his retirement strongly denounced the new nationalist movement which was beginning to develop. The early nationalist movement was anti-European, and anti-Christian, being based on the idea of the union of all Moslems in the pan-Islamic brotherhood. An incident at Denshawai in 1906 when fighting broke out between villagers and British officers and very severe punishment was meted out to the Egyptians involved led to further agitation for self-government. Cromer's own high-handed attitude gave unnecessary offence to the Egyptians. He often failed to consult the Khedive on important matters and tended to treat Egyptian officials with contempt.

Policy of Liberal Government, 1906–14

Campbell-Bannerman's Government increased the influence of the Egyptians in administration. More Egyptians were admitted to the Civil Service and the property qualification for the franchise was reduced. The Legislative Assembly was given the right to question and criticize Government policy. However, the development of the Young Turk movement and the establishment of a new constitution in Turkey encouraged the Egyptian nationalists to press forward with more radical demands for complete self-government. The Prime Minister who had advocated the extension of the Suez Canal Company's concession was assassinated by nationalists. In the Assembly the Nationalist Party had gained sufficient influence and representation to vote against the renewal of the concession, and they gained the secret support of the Khedive himself. When Lord Kitchener became Consul-General in 1911 he took severe measures to repress nationalist activities. At the same time he accorded the Assembly the right to delay legislation and to debate a number of hitherto prohibited topics such as foreign affairs. He also increased the proportion of elected members of the Assembly in relation to those nominated. Nevertheless, at the outbreak of war in 1914 the Egyptian nationalist movement, far from being satisfied by these concessions, was demanding independence even more vociferously.

Egypt during the First World War
Soon after the outbreak of war in 1914 Britain abolished the nominal suzerainty of Turkey over Egypt, deposed the pro-Turkish Khedive and placed his more amenable son on the throne. At the same time Britain proclaimed a protectorate over Egypt. After the war the nationalist leader Zaghlul organized a delegation, the Wafd, to put the case for Egyptian independence to the Versailles Peace Conference, but despite the high ideals of self-determination expressed by President Wilson and by France and Britain, Zaghlul Pasha received short shrift and was deported to Malta. This led to a serious anti-British rising in Egypt and the Wafd became the main organization of nationalist resistance. Lord Allenby was appointed High Commissioner and insisted on the release of Zaghlul. Though the British made considerable concessions these did not amount to full independence for Egypt. Britain proclaimed the independence of Egypt in 1922, but British troops were retained for the defence of the Canal and events showed that independence was merely a façade. Egyptian discontent increased, and relations between Egypt and Britain deteriorated. Zaghlul was allowed to return to Egypt in 1923, and soon became Prime Minister.

This tension was made worse by the murder in 1924 of Sir Lee Stack, Governor-General of the Sudan. Allenby was now given military reinforcements, and presented an ultimatum to the Egyptian Government which contained, among other items, the demand that Egypt pay a substantial fine and withdraw her units from the Sudan. All demands except the fine were rejected and the British replied by occupying key points in Alexandria. Zaghlul Pasha, the Prime Minister, resigned.

The Anglo-Egyptian Treaty, 1936
In 1936 outside pressures helped to improve the situation. The invasion of Abyssinia by Mussolini and his avowed intention of creating a new empire in Africa on the Roman model, caused Zaghlul Pasha to modify his own terms for a settlement. A treaty between Britain and Egypt was drawn up. By this, British troops were to remain in Egypt for a further twenty years, but were to be mainly stationed in the Canal Zone. Egypt gained complete control of her own affairs, though the Sudan was to remain under British control.

In the Second World War the Egyptians did not declare war against Germany and Italy; nor did they impede Britain's efforts. During the war the Egyptian Government, headed by Nahas Pasha, agreed to reduce the cotton crop in Egypt in favour of cereal growing with the help of a British subsidy in order to save shipping space which would have been needed to bring foodstuffs into Egypt.

After the war there were many changes in this area. The British left the Canal Zone in 1954 and apart from the ill-fated invasion in 1956 (see p. 276) Britain has had no further part in Egyptian affairs. The Sudan became a completely independent republic outside the Commonwealth in January 1956. In 1968 the British withdrew from Aden. The result has been that in the Middle East as elsewhere British control has almost vanished.

THE CARIBBEAN

During the latter part of the nineteenth century all, except Barbados and the Bahamas, of the British West Indian islands which had long had constitutions with Governor, Council and Assembly gave them up and became Crown colonies. The economic position of the colonies was weak although various crops were developed to reduce the dependence on sugar. Schemes for closer co-operation and federation were considered, and reforms were made in Crown colony governments. It was, however, not until after the Second World War that real progress was made with the grant of responsible government to various territories and the establishment of the Federation of the West Indies in January 1958. The members of the Federation were Jamaica, Trinidad and Tobago, Barbados, Antigua, Dominica, St Kitts-Nevis, Montserrat, St Lucia and St Vincent. Among those remaining outside were the Bahamas, British Honduras and British Guiana. Unfortunately jealousies and differences of long standing were not resolved by the formation of the Federation, and when, in 1962, first Jamaica and then Trinidad and Tobago broke away and became independent states the Federation was at an end. Since then British Guiana has become independent Guyana and Barbados has also become independent. The Leeward and Windward Islands have formed a federation in association with Britain.

32. Education

Elementary education

Elementary education in the nineteenth century was cheap and narrow. By using older children, or monitors, to do most of the teaching wage bills were kept to a minimum and the annual cost of educating a child at Lancaster's Borough Road School (see p. 51) was 16s. 6d. As a result, however, children left school with scrappy and often inaccurate information and that on a most narrow curriculum. The courses were so restricted

The development of British education: a village school. In the early nineteenth century this was the best education most children could hope for.

because the bodies such as the British and Foreign Bible Society (see p. 114) who were responsible for elementary education regarded it as a means of inculcating Christianity and little else. As a result children were taught to read, write and calculate and to study the Bible. This moral aspect of education was further emphasized by the London Statistical Society which was at pains to show that crime rates were lowest where there were most elementary schools. However, the very bodies which encouraged education for religious purposes opposed any liberalization of the curriculum, for they believed that, for example, the study of imaginative literature would lead to moral depravity and political discontent.

The introduction of 'payment by results' (see p. 124) in the revised Code of 1862 had a number of bad effects. In the first place, the old idea that the working class should be kept to its station in life was clearly re-affirmed

Elementary education at the turn of the century; pupils at the Gordon Memorial School, Kilburn in 1908.

by Lowe himself. Higher education was not for them. They should be educated, declared Lowe, in order that they 'may defer to a higher education when they meet it'. The Code itself, which lasted until the 1890's, maintained the concentration on reading, writing, arithmetic and the Bible which had characterized early nineteenth century education. It led to an immense amount of parrot-like learning from books dictated by the Education Department. One inspector reported that he could tell how long the pupils had been at school by the stupidity and vacancy of their faces! It led to reading without understanding – a fact deplored by Matthew Arnold himself as an inspector. He advocated more interesting and meaningful reading for young people, but his advice was ignored for many years (see Chapter 11.)

What exactly did elementary education achieve in the nineteenth century? The Code of 1862 made the curriculum very narrow, for what little science had been attempted before was even further reduced, while history and literature were used mainly in condensed and 'potted' forms for mechanical reading practice in preparation for the yearly examination of pupils on which the existence of the school and the teachers' salaries depended. In 1851 it is probable that three million out of five million children were still without any schooling and in 1867 the number was still about two million. Forster's Education Act of 1870 greatly increased the numbers at school, but unfortunately the official figures given for the 'literacy rate' are not a good guide.

Secondary education
During the first half of the nineteenth century secondary education was confined to the public schools, to private schools, and to the old endowed grammar schools. In all these, conditions for the children of the middle class who attended them left much to be desired. Many, especially the private and grammar schools, had a narrow and inadequate curriculum. Many were dominated by the old classical curriculum of the sixteenth century – the charters of the endowed grammar schools often compelled them to keep rigidly to Greek and Latin studies. In 1805 an attempt by Leeds Grammar School to widen the curriculum to include modern studies was frustrated by a legal judgement of Lord Eldon. However, by the Grammar Schools Act of 1840 the law courts were enabled to interpret the charters more liberally so that changes in the curriculum could be made. Even so it was still many years before there were substantial reforms.

In other schools another type of narrowness existed. In order to concentrate on mental discipline and subjects such as commercial arithmetic useful to the merchant and trader, the study of literature was omitted altogether. The Benthamites thoroughly approved of this. The learning of literary extracts to train the memory and for mental discipline found favour with the utilitarians, but they deplored the study of literature and the arts for imaginative enjoyment. In some respects the great public schools such as Eton, Harrow and Rugby were as set in their ways as the grammar and private schools. Indeed, English literature was included in their curriculum only for the purpose of translation into Greek and Latin!

The Clarendon Commission of 1861–4 inquired into the conditions prevailing in the public schools and the Taunton Commission 1864–8 did the same for the endowed grammar schools. Both strongly advised the broadening of the curriculum. This improvement was encouraged by the inclusion of English literature as a subject in the Indian Civil Service examinations in 1855 and the inclusion of the subject in the list of examinations in the 1870's for the Home Civil Service, the armed forces and entrance to the universities. In the same way the study of science also became more widespread, especially when Britain realized the superiority of continental education in this respect.

Pioneers of secondary education

The reform of secondary education was stimulated by a number of outstanding headmasters. Thomas Arnold of Rugby based his reforms on the twofold foundation of religion and a liberal culture. He was a strong believer in the educational value of the classics, but he also set a high value on history. The development of the prefect system was a key part of his work, and 'muscular' Christianity was certainly a product of it. Many of the great headmasters were trained by him, and many of the grammar schools attempted to follow the Rugby example. On the other hand, Butler at Shrewsbury introduced a much wider curriculum including mathematics, science, history and literature. Another great pioneer was Edward Thring, headmaster of Uppingham from 1853 to 1887. His aim was to suit the curriculum to the aptitudes of the pupils rather than forcing them all into one recognizable 'public school' mould. He added craft subjects, music and art, to the traditional classical studies. These public school pioneers influenced both the grammar schools and the new public schools founded in the mid-century, such as Marlborough, Wellington, Clifton, Cheltenham.

A number of private boarding-schools for girls of the middle class existed in the early nineteenth century. The curricula of these schools in some ways offered a better education than the boys' schools. As women were generally regarded as the producers of children and keepers of the home as well as decorative social assets, they were allowed to read romantic literature, take lessons from drawing masters, play the piano, sing and learn other social accomplishments which did not imply any competition with men but rather competition *for* them. The requirements of the 'marriage market' dominated women's education. However, Queen's College, London, was established in 1848 to train governesses, and this was a beginning of university education for women. Then in 1850 Miss Buss established the North London Collegiate School for girls and in 1858 Miss Beale began her outstanding period as headmistress of the Cheltenham Ladies' College.

Secondary education in the twentieth century

The importance of Balfour's Education Act of 1902 has already been emphasized (see Chapter 16). In effect, it abolished the school boards of 1870 and all State education was put in the hands of the local authorities, mainly the county councils and the county boroughs – in whose hands it has remained since. The authorities undertook the building of new grammar schools and helped the old ones with grants from the rates. Under the Liberal Government in 1907, the scholarship system was introduced to provide grammar school places for pupils from the elementary schools. Under this act all secondary schools receiving aid from the rates were to reserve 25 per cent of their places for scholars from the elementary schools. This was one of the most important changes made since Governments began to take any interest in education. It widened educational opportunity and helped to open up university and technical education to working-class children. It led on to the introduction of State Scholarships from secondary schools to the universities and also the system of County Major Scholarships. In 1944 the Education Act introduced by Mr R. A. Butler abolished the payment of fees in State secondary schools, and arranged the selection of pupils for grammar, technical or modern schools,

Fourth of June celebrations at Eton in 1937. Between the wars full secondary education was limited to the public schools and the grammar schools and was only available for those who could pay the fees or had won scholarships.

by a test given at the age of 11. Since 1945 secondary education has been changing rapidly. The first comprehensive schools were established during the period of the Labour Governments, 1945–51, and many more have been created since. These schools, with between 1,000 and 2,000 pupils, educate all children between 11 and 19, thus abolishing the divisions between grammar, modern and technical, and making any selection at 11 a purely internal matter for the schools.

During the 1960's there has been more and more concern with the way in which education, and especially secondary education, should be organized. This in its turn has led to a number of commissions on education the most important of which have been the Newsom Commission on secondary education which reported in 1963 and the Robbins Commission report on higher education, including the training of teachers, which reported the same year. The Labour Party strongly espoused the idea of comprehensive schools and have asked all local authorities to draw up plans for a reorganization of their secondary schools into some sort of comprehensive system. In the meantime they also appointed Sir John Newsom to investigate another aspect of secondary education, the public schools.

Technical education: the Mechanics Institutes

At the beginning of the nineteenth century there was very little technical education in Britain. It was confined to a few Schools of Industry in elementary schools whose object was to teach children a trade. Some private schools for middle-class children also taught technical subjects. The beginnings of organized technical education are to be found in the Mechanics Institutes established under the influence of the utilitarians who wished to teach science to working men. Their aim was to produce better workers and to counteract the dangers of crime and revolution which the utilitarians always associated with ignorance. The prime movers were Lord Brougham and Dr Birkbeck. In 1823 the London Mechanics Institute was founded, with Dr Birkbeck as its first president. He himself had established classes in Glasgow for the teaching of applied science as early as 1800. The London Mechanics Institute was the prototype of those which sprang up throughout the country in the next forty years. Their main aim was to teach science to working men by means of lectures. The first lecture of the London Mechanics Institute was attended by about 900 working men – a sign of the thirst for knowledge amongst the workers. By the middle of the century there were over 700 Mechanics Institutes in Britain.

Difficulties of the Mechanics Institutes

Conditions of employment in the early nineteenth century militated strongly against the success of the institutes. After twelve hours or more in factory or mine, it required remarkable stamina and faith in the value of education to bring working men to another hour or two of evening lectures. There were also various influential opponents of the Mechanics Institutes. Many Tories feared that instruction would make the workers discontented with their station in life. From the opposite direction, the Radicals, of whom Cobbett was typical, opposed the institutes because they would tame the spirit of the workers. At a later stage the Chartist movement attracted a great number of workers away from the institutes. The managements of the institutes showed great reluctance to widen the curriculum to include 'controversial' subjects, which working men often wanted but which were regarded by other classes as dangerous.

The result of these difficulties was that, although the Mechanics Institutes undoubtedly did important work in spreading a knowledge of science, their success was limited. The very illiteracy of the working class, which the elementary school system was so slow to remedy (see p. 125), proved a great barrier to progress. In many areas the middle class gradually pushed the working class out of the institutes – in 1840, for example, only one member in twenty of the Yorkshire Union of Mechanics Institutes was of the working class. It was noticeable that as the institutes became dominated by the middle class, controversial subjects such as history, philosophy, and literature were introduced.

Partly to meet the demand from the working man for more controversial subjects, Frederick Denison Maurice established the Working Men's College in London in 1854 (see also p. 116). But even here the middle-class supporters quickly outnumbered the wage-earners.

Developments after 1850

The trade unions became thoroughly disillusioned with the Mechanics Institutes and attempted to do something themselves to further technical as well as general adult education. Here the pioneer organization was the London Artisans' Club established with trade union support in 1869. In 1872 the Royal Society of Arts began classes in technical subjects and their examinations were taken over by the City and Guilds of London in 1880. This was followed in 1881 by the foundation of the first technical college in Britain – the Finsbury Technical College, and in 1882 the Regent Street Polytechnic was opened. These pioneer colleges were the first great breakthrough in technical education.

By an Act of 1889 direct state grants were given to technical education. These grants were used by the newly established county councils to set up technical classes. The Act was partly a result of the Royal Commission on Technical Instruction set up during Gladstone's second ministry, 1882. The commission had pointed out the lack of technical instruction compared with states such as Germany. In Britain a serious decline in apprenticeship had occurred during the nineteenth century and it was very necessary that technical education should compensate for this. However, the Act of 1889 still limited state aid to technical education for the 'industrial class' – that is, working men. This retarded the development of technical education on a wider scale. It was partly because of this that the Germans so far surpassed Britain in the production of electrical equipment and some important industries had been entirely lost to them. In Germany the state education of all classes in both arts and sciences had obviously enabled them to forge ahead. Yet before 1914 the state had done very little to advance technical education in Britain.

The period between 1918 and 1964 has seen an immense advance in technical education. In Britain, numerous technical secondary schools were established before 1939, and since the end of the Second World War there has been the further development of Institutes of Advanced Technology whose final examinations carry degree status. Increasing numbers of secondary schools have also developed technical instruction. With the drain of some of Britain's leading scientists and technologists to the United States the Government is now faced with the problem of providing adequate facilities for research and adequate salaries for those carrying it out. Efforts are also being made to persuade a greater proportion of secondary school leavers and university graduates to take up technical posts involving applied rather than pure science. The future of Great Britain may well depend on the success of these efforts.

Higher education

The development of higher education in Britain is worthy of a chapter in itself but here we do not have space for more than a very quick survey.

At the beginning of the nineteenth century there were only two universities in England, four small ones in Scotland and one in Ireland. Their courses were mostly limited to a very narrow range of subjects and they were open only to the few young men who could afford the luxury of several years without income. This situation changed very slowly during the century. New universities opened at Durham in 1832 and London in 1836 which offered a wider range of subjects and gave women their first chance of higher education in this country. Women also began to seek entry to the older universities but it was many years before their colleges were fully recognized. Towards the end of the century many more universities were

Part of the University of Sussex designed by Sir Basil Spence.

founded in the large towns, often based on existing colleges of various sorts. Manchester University opened in 1880 and it was followed by Leeds, Liverpool, Birmingham, Bristol and a number of others before the First World War. Thereafter a number of university colleges were established taking London external degrees. In due course these colleges achieved full university status themselves: for example, Exeter, Southampton, Nottingham, Reading and Leicester. The most rapid expansion of higher education came, however, in the sixties. It came as a result of a growing realization that Britain's future depended very largely on the educational opportunities it offered to young people. State and county grants based on a means test meant that any boy or girl could now afford to go to university, but there were just not enough places for those who were qualified for higher education. Completely new universities were founded in places such as Brighton (1961), York (1963) and Lancaster' (1964); at the same time colleges of advanced technology and teachers' training colleges (now known as colleges of education) were either given full university status or were allowed to give courses leading to degrees.

This rapid expansion of higher education, however, has been slower than that achieved in other countries. Britain still offers a lower proportion of her school-leavers the opportunity of a university education or its equivalent than many other industrialized countries and the result is a great shortage of qualified experts, especially in technical fields.

33. Science and Technology

DURING the past three hundred years, and particularly during the period covered by this book, man's knowledge of the material world has developed more rapidly and more profoundly than at any time in history. Europe, and later North America, have been at the centre of this scientific revolution, and almost all countries have made some contribution. From at least the sixteenth century English and Scots men of learning were in touch with friends and colleagues throughout Europe, so that the story of science and technology in modern Britain includes what Britain learned from outside as well as what Britain had to teach the world.

The inquiry into the nature of things (that is *science*) and the application of new knowledge to useful practical purposes (that is *technology*) have led to a profoundly changed view of the nature of the universe and man's place in it, and to a vast range of new powers and resources: machines, tools, textiles, foodstuffs, heating and lighting, transport, communications, and, sadly, means of destruction. These developments and the men who made them possible are the subject of this chapter.

The Scientific Societies

Up to the beginning of the nineteenth century, scientific and technical education were almost non-existent. Most science was carried out by amateurs, usually well-to-do middle-class men, often trained as doctors but sometimes for the church, the law or business. The oldest surviving scientific society, the Royal Society of London (founded in 1660), whose membership is today limited to scientists of the greatest eminence, was originally little more than a club for the discussion of a philosophical hobby. In the eighteenth century other societies were formed, such as the Lunar Society of Birmingham (about 1776) which had Erasmus Darwin (p. 378), Joseph Priestley (p. 383), James Watt (pp. 370–1), and Josiah Wedgwood as members, and was important for the way in which it brought industrialists and pure scientists together. There was also the Society for the encouragement of Arts (1754), now the Royal Society of Arts, which offered prizes for practical inventions and processes and there were also many provincial societies.

In the nineteenth century, the whole picture changed. The increasing growth of scientific knowledge led to the formation of specialist societies for the study of botany, geology, chemistry and so on. Then as more and more scientists ceased to be amateurs and used science as a means of livelihood, professional organizations were formed like the Royal Institute of Chemistry. Today there are very many such specialist societies and professional organizations. Similar changes have come over science education. Science courses were introduced in the new universities in the second half of the century, to be followed by an explosive expansion in the twentieth century. The upshot is that, whereas in 1800 there were only a few hundred scientists in the whole of Britain, today the Royal Institute of Chemistry alone has over 20,000 members.

POWER FOR MACHINES

Steam power
Much of the impetus for change came from the demands of industry. In Britain the main fields of industrial development were the textile industry (and chemical manufacture, which was closely associated with it), and the coal and iron industries.

Textiles in particular had long been the most important home and export industry. In the eighteenth century, the rapid growth of cotton textiles, and the great overseas demand for them, led to a series of inventions whereby machines for spinning and weaving were introduced, with a far greater output than the traditional hand methods. These machines were grouped in factories, and they needed power to drive them. This was first provided by water wheels (the first power-driven cotton factory was set up by Arkwright at Cromford on the banks of the River Derwent in 1779). But water-power had the disadvantage of limiting the location of the factories to places where there were fast-running rivers. It was at this moment that one of the greatest technological advances in history took place: the decisive improvements made by James Watt in 1782 to the efficiency of the steam engine and the inventions which made it capable of driving rotary machinery.

Newcomen. The steam engine was not a new device. Early in the eighteenth century, Savery (1650–1715) and then Newcomen (1663–1729) had invented steam engines. But these early engines were really just pumps working on atmospheric pressure. That is to say, steam was introduced into a cylinder fitted with a movable piston, and was then cooled down and condensed to form water. This created a partial vacuum behind the piston, and atmospheric pressure from outside forced the piston along the cylinder. Newcomen's engines were extensively used in the eighteenth century, about 360 being built for use in pumping water out of mines, where they greatly increased the productivity of the coal industry. However, they were extremely inefficient and wasted most of their heat alternately heating and cooling the cylinder.

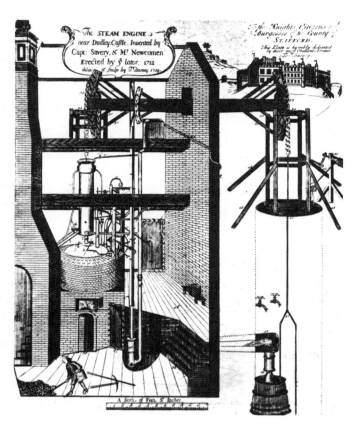

An engraving of the earliest known Newcomen engine, erected by him near Dudley Castle in 1712.

Watt. James Watt (1736–1819), working on a model Newcomen engine in Glasgow University, had the idea of condensing the steam in a special condenser separate from the working cylinder, which could then be kept at a constant temperature. This invention, which Watt patented in 1769, revolutionized the efficiency of the steam engine – at first as a pumping device. However when it was combined with Watt's subsequent device (1783) for transforming the up-and-down motion of the steam pump into rotary motion, it made steam power available as a direct source of power for machinery. Watt had by now joined his abilities to those of a practical manufacturer, Matthew Boulton (1728–1809), who was able to organize the building of Watt's engines at his famous works at Soho in Birmingham. By 1800, when Watt's patent expired, there were about 500 Boulton and Watt engines in use throughout the country, plus an almost equal number of 'pirate' engines, illegally built by other manufacturers. The steam engine had begun its long reign as the principal source of power throughout the nineteenth century.

Locomotives. Many improvements were made in the Watt engine, but it was still essentially a vacuum engine, operating near to atmospheric pressure. The use of high-pressure steam to drive the piston, instead of the air acting against a vacuum, was developed by Richard Trevithick (1771–1833); and he was the first man to build a steam locomotive to run on rails, in 1804. The development of the steam locomotive was due chiefly to George Stephenson (1781–1848). Stephenson's *Rocket* engine of 1829, driven by high pressure steam, incorporated features such as boiler tubes, which made it recognizably the forerunner of the machines which were to dominate land transport for a century, and which is only now being superseded.

The Rocket *in 1829.*

Further developments of steam. The development of the steam engine was now fundamentally advanced by scientists who were studying the theory of energy. James Prescott Joule (1818–89) showed how much heat is generated by a given amount of mechanical work. This was one of the foundations of the highly important theory of the *conservation of energy* (i.e. energy is never lost, but only converted from one form to another), which was formulated independently by several people about 1848. William Thompson (later Lord Kelvin, 1824–1907) was one of the leaders in this new science of 'thermodynamics' which was of immense theoretical importance. The Scottish engineer, William Rankine (1820–72), led in the direct application of the new principles to the steam engine.

Meanwhile, between 1800 and 1850 the efficiency of the steam engine improved greatly by empirical means, such as the introduction of compound working (i.e. using steam from one high-pressure cylinder to do further work in a low-pressure cylinder). The high-pressure engines also demanded better boilers and a more accurate manufacture of all moving parts. The pioneer in this field was Henry Maudslay (1771–1831) who constructed machine tools which could produce not only better quality machines, but almost identical interchangeable parts.

Steam ships. The steam engine had been applied to ships very early in the century. The first steam ship to cross the Atlantic was the *Curacao*, built at Dover in 1826. In 1838, the *Great Western*, a paddle ship 236 feet long, did the journey from Bristol to New York in the hitherto unheard-of time of fifteen days. The replacement of the paddle wheel by the propeller was a big step forward (the Cunard Company began to fit its mail steamers with propellers in 1862). This was followed by the introduction of the compound engine which finally established the superiority of steam over sail.

Parsons and the steam turbine. In 1800, the average Watt engine was of about 15 horse power. By 1850 the average steam unit could develop about 40 h.p. However, despite all improvements, these engines had one great disadvantage: they only produced motion in a straight line; the movement of the piston had to be converted into a relatively slow rotary motion by a system of cranks and levers. With the development of electricity in the second half of the century (see p. 374) a new type of steam engine was required – one which would turn a dynamo shaft at the fantastically high speed necessary to generate electric current. After many unsuccessful attempts an English inventor, Charles Parsons (1854–1931), devised an engine in 1884 in which the direct action of steam on the vanes of a wheel produced rotary motion. In Parsons' first steam 'turbine', as it was called, the steam passed through fifteen sets of blades, all on the same shaft, and turned the shaft at the hitherto unheard-of speed of 18,000 revolutions a minute. In 1894 the experimental vessel *Turbinia* demonstrated the enormous superiority of the steam turbine, which soon replaced the 'reciprocating' engine both in steam ships and in the generation of electricity. Even nuclear energy for the generation of power still depends on the steam turbine as an intermediary, since there is as yet no direct means of converting nuclear energy into electricity.

Parson's Turbinia *at speed in 1894.*

Magnetism and electricity
The nineteenth century opened with striking discoveries in electricity, followed by further discoveries about the relationship between electricity and magnetism which were to transform both the understanding of the physical world and the technological basis of society. Important, in some cases the most important, parts of this work were carried out in Britain.

Early discoveries. Static electricity had been known and studied for a long time. In 1800 Volta in Italy showed how the juxtaposition of two metals could produce a continuous current of electricity: he had in fact invented the first electric battery. Nicholson and Carlisle in England then showed that this current could be used to decompose water (that is break it up into its elements), and Humphry Davy (1778–1829) used this process of *electrolysis* to isolate several new metallic elements (sodium, potassium, calcium, barium). He also suggested that an electric charge might be the fundamental force uniting the elements in a chemical combination. His even more brilliant assistant Michael Faraday (1791–1867), working at the Royal Institution in London, discovered the laws which governed the amounts of electricity in chemical action. This was to lead eventually to large-scale chemical manufacture by means of electricity.

Faraday pulling a bar magnet out of a coil of wire and so producing an electric current, detected by an astatic galvanometer.

Faraday. Faraday, one of the greatest of all scientific geniuses, now made a fundamental discovery of incomparable influence: that of electro-magnetic induction. Following up the work of Oersted and Ampère on the magnetic effects of electric currents, he showed in 1831 how a change of magnetic field near a wire produced an electric current. In his first successful experiment, he moved a magnet (in the shape of a metal bar) through a hollow coil of wire; movement of the bar produced an electric current in the wire. Not only did this achieve the important theoretical aim of establishing the fundamental relation between electricity and magnetism; it also led to an immense technical advance, by showing how a continuous supply of electrical energy can be obtained by the continuous application of mechanical energy (in the form of movement) – and vice versa. Faraday had in fact discovered the principle of the dynamo and of the electric motor.

Development of electric power. The word 'dynamo' was not actually used until 1865, when it was applied to the generators at the Paris Exhibition. There was in fact a considerable time-lag between Faraday's discovery, and the widespread use of electricity. The first commercial use of electricity was for the electric telegraph, invented in 1838 (see p. 392). But it was another fifty years before large-scale demand for the generation of electricity was created by electric lighting. Davy had shown in 1810 how an electric current is carried across the gap between two carbon poles producing a brilliant 'electric arc'. This effect was first used to provide street lighting in Britain in 1880. For domestic use however, the arc lamp was unable to compete with the incandescent lamp, in which a wire is made to glow white hot by an electric current. The first commercially successful form of this lighting was made in 1879 by Joseph Swan (1828–1914) who used a carbon filament in an evacuated glass bulb.

The popularity of the new electric lighting led to the establishment of electric generating stations (the first being opened at Deptford in 1889) using dynamos driven by Parsons' newly-invented steam turbines (p. 372). The consequent increase in the supply of electricity meant that current was now available to drive machines, and for use in transport (trains and trams). A century after Watt's first steam engine, a new form of power was now available – one which required for its use no skilled mechanical knowledge, which could be used in small units, and could be started or stopped at a moment's notice. Science had in fact provided the power for really extensive mechanization, not only in the factory, but also in the workshop, the farm and the home.

The London Electricity Supply Corporation's Works at Deptford in 1889.

ASTRONOMY

Of less immediate practical importance but of enormous influence on the way in which men thought were the advances in astronomy.

Exploring the universe. Since ancient times five planets had been known to scientists: Mercury, Venus, Mars, Jupiter and Saturn. In 1781 a new planet, Uranus, was discovered by William Herschel (1738–1822), a German musician who had settled in Britain. Herschel began as an amateur observer but he soon radically improved the optical telescope and began a systematic survey of the heavens. He was able to show that the stars were not scattered at random but formed a coherent system. He suggested that some nebulae (stars which appear as a cloudy disc) were star systems outside our own galaxy, the Milky Way. He also showed that the sun was moving through space and that there were double stars which revolved around each other as if obeying Newton's law of universal gravitation.

Newton's theories of mechanics and gravitation were verified in other important ways. In the early nineteenth century, from the movements of the planet Uranus, mathematicians worked out theoretically the existence and likely position of another unknown planet which we now call Neptune. Eventually, in 1846, a telescopic search confirmed its existence.

These were only some of the ways in which the laws of nature, discovered on earth, were shown to extend throughout the universe. Such discoveries were to set off fierce controversies throughout the century, the place of Man in the Universe being always the chief point at issue.

Technical developments in astronomy. Two new methods of investigation widened the scope of astronomy enormously. One was photography (see below, p. 394), which allowed the astronomer to work away from the telescope with a permanent record of what he had seen. The other was spectroscopy. In 1859 Bunsen and Kirchoff, two German scientists, showed that many elements could be identified by the particular spectrum of colour each imparted to flames. Astronomers, including Herschel's son, John (1791–1871), used this method to demonstrate that certain elements we are familiar with on earth also existed in the sun and the stars. A distinguished British astronomer, Sir William Huggins (1824–1910), also used spectroscopy to measure the velocity of stars. This was later to become extremely important in connection with the Theory of Relativity (see p. 383), which has deeply affected men's thinking about the structure of the universe and its origins.

British observers at the Royal Observatory (formerly at Greenwich, now at Herstmonceux) and elsewhere made important contributions to the study of astronomy, especially in relation to navigation and time keeping. For many years the largest telescope in the world was the enormous 72″ telescope belonging to Lord Rosse who was Charles Parsons'

Lord Rosse's 72 in. telescope, for many years the largest telescope in the world.

father. However, the climate of Britain is not very suitable for optical telescopes and recently the most important work in this field has been done in the clearer mountain air of observatories such as Mount Palomar in the United States. Today, Britain is once more making an important contribution to observational astronomy through the invention of the radio-telescope, which is unaffected by limitations on light. One of the finest and most productive radio-telescopes in the world is at Jodrell Bank, operated by the Physics Department of Manchester University.

ORIGINS OF THE EARTH: EVOLUTION

Geology

The structure of the solar system and the place of Earth in it had been established by Newton and his successors. But as the origins and develop-ment of Earth itself came to be studied, scientists began to have serious doubts about the Biblical description of the creation of the Earth and all its creatures in a matter of six days. There had long been controversy about the nature of fossils – which appeared to be evidence of a very remote past, but which theologians, who believed that the earth was only 6,000 years old, held were accidental imitations of living species. The first serious new theory of the formation of the Earth's surface was put forward by James Hutton (1726–97) who asserted that the features of the Earth had been formed by the very gradual action of natural forces – the sun, wind and water. His work was followed by that of William Smith (1769–1839), who showed that the age of rocks was revealed by their fossil content, and by Sir Charles Lyell (1797–1875) who assembled a vast amount of evidence in his *Principles of Geology* (1830–33) to show that the world as we see it is only one stage in an immensely long process of continuous change.

Later in the century Lord Kelvin estimated that the earth was not 6,000 but about 40,000,000 years old, but before long biologists and geologists were showing that even this was not nearly long enough. But by this time scientists' thinking – and indeed the thought of all education men – had been deeply affected by a new biological concept: Darwin's theory of evolution.

Darwin and the theory of evolution
Early theories. Since at least the seventeenth century, scientists had been worried by the Biblical theory that said every plant and animal produced offspring of the same kind as itself. Examples were observed of seeds which grew into plants which clearly differed slightly from the parent plant and from other plants in the same species. Eighteenth-century naturalists studied these 'variations' in species and put forward various theories of progressive change or *evolution*. An important contribution to this problem was made by Erasmus Darwin (1731–1800), Charles Darwin's grandfather. In *Zoonomia, or the Laws of Organic Life* (1794) he asserted that the struggle for existence caused organisms to acquire new characteristics, which were then transmitted to their offspring. The French naturalist Jean Baptiste Lamarck (1744–1829) also supported this theory of the 'inheritance of acquired characteristics'.

The belief in an initial act of creation, in which all living things were given an immutable form, was therefore being challenged before Charles Darwin (1809–82) came on the scene. However, Charles Darwin was to transform not only this discussion, but much of the science of biology as well. The foundation of his theory was laid on a long sea voyage.

The voyage of the 'Beagle'. During the eighteenth and nineteenth centuries, a good deal of new knowledge was gained in botany, astronomy and many other fields by scientists making journeys to little known parts of the world. The most important of all such voyages was that made by Charles Darwin in the *Beagle* in 1831–34. During his voyage round the world, Darwin made a detailed study of the animals and plants of the islands in the Pacific ocean. He was particularly struck by the differences which existed between species on neighbouring islands. In considering the mass of evidence he had accumulated, Darwin was influenced by Lyell's *Principles of Geology* and by the work of the Rev. T. R. Malthus (1766–1834). Malthus had put forward a famous but fallacious theory that populations increase faster than the means to feed them, and that increase in population will therefore be limited by starvation, as a result of which the weakest will be eliminated. Under the influence of these two writers, Darwin developed a revolutionary theory. On the one hand he took the concept of evolution – that is to say that small variations in a species may be passed on by heredity, and that gradually an accumulation of these variations could produce important changes within a species. He then related this idea to the belief that all forms of life have to struggle to exist, and that those forms

Man and monkey: a contemporary cartoon ridiculing Darwin's theory of evolution.

of life that are best adapted to their surroundings will survive. Thus those strains in plants and animals whose minute variations equip them best for this struggle will be preserved, and the species will gradually develop its special organs and instincts.

It was necessary, of course, to assume that deviations could in fact be inherited. But Darwin did not explain how inheritance took place. The mechanism by which this was done was later to be discovered by others, starting with Mendel, who first propounded laws of inheritance in 1866, and culminating in our own day with the discovery by Crick and Watson in Cambridge (1953) of the 'genetic code' – the precise mechanism by which inheritance occurs.

'The Origin of Species'. Darwin worked on his theory throughout the 1840s, but it was not until 1859 that he published his famous *Origin of Species*, one of the world's great books. To support his argument in this book, he pointed not only to his observation of wild creatures, but also to the specialized breeding of domestic animals, where the breeder deliberately encourages certain features in his herds by the selection of those animals which are mated to produce the next generation. Darwin claimed that in nature this choice is made by the relation of the individual animal or plant to its environment. The 'variant' which fits best into its surroundings will survive and breed; the less well-fitted will leave no successors. In this way, throughout the ages, the whole of animal and plant life has developed from one original, simple form of life to its present state of variety and complexity. Darwin later applied his theory to the human species in *The Descent of Man* (1871) in which he showed that man and the apes had a common ancestor.

Darwin's theory of evolution provoked a barrage of criticism from both scientists and laymen. Richard Owen, the first Director of the Natural History Museum, bitterly attacked the idea that species might change. Even more violent attacks came from those who believed that Darwin's theory would undermine the Bible and all religious belief. The most famous clash came at the 1860 meeting of the British Association in which Samuel Wilberforce, Bishop of Oxford, denounced Darwin's ideas, only to have his own intellectual position demolished by Darwin's most able supporter, Thomas Henry Huxley (1825–95).

Darwin's theory that there was a simple and universal mechanism which produced changes in the forms of living creatures soon affected, not only the biological sciences, but many other branches of intellectual life. The philosopher Herbert Spencer (1820–1903) for instance, extended the theory of evolution into the fields of political and social theory and it was Spencer who coined the phrase 'The Survival of the Fittest'. The wider application of Darwin's theory gave powerful impetus to the notion of human progress, though it was misapplied by those who took the theory of the 'survival of the fittest' to justify their opposition to social reform which would protect the under-privileged.

PHYSICS

New concepts. Faraday was the outstanding British physicist in the early part of the nineteenth century, but there were other innovators. Joule and Kelvin developed our modern concepts of energy (p. 371). Thomas Young

(1773–1829) showed that light was probably a wave-motion. A fundamental advance was made by James Clerk Maxwell (1831–79), who not only expressed in a few differential equations the whole science of electromagnetism, but also related this to light, showing that electromagnetic waves travel through space in the same way as light waves. The consequences were remarkable, in particular the production by H. R. Hertz (1857–94) of electromagnetic waves, which obeyed the same laws of reflection and refraction as light, and were later to be used in wireless telegraphy (p. 393).

The nuclear atom. Maxwell was the first of a long line of brilliant men who directed the Cavendish laboratory in Cambridge, where some of the most revolutionary discoveries in modern physics were made. In particular, a great deal of the fundamental work on the structure of the atom was done here. Following Dalton's atomic theory of 1803 (p. 384), the atom had been regarded as the smallest possible particle of matter, the difference between one element and another being the basic difference between their immutable atoms. Gradually, however, this concept was destroyed. Since the time of Faraday, scientists in Britain and Germany had studied the light emitted when an electric current passes through a rarefied gas. For a while it was thought that the 'cathode' rays which were produced were a fourth state of matter – not solid, not liquid, not gas. But in 1897 J. J. Thomson (1856–1940), working in the Cavendish Laboratory, showed that they must be minute particles of about 1/2000th the mass of a hydrogen atom which had previously been the lightest known entity. These particles were found to be present in all matter. The discovery at about the same time of X-rays by Röntgen in Germany, and of radioactivity by Becquerel in France, showed that all previous ideas about the constitution of matter had to be entirely reconsidered.

Eventually the work of Ernest Rutherford (1871–1937) in Cambridge, and of the Dane, Nils Bohr (1885–1962), produced the concept of the atom as consisting of several constituents – a positively charged nucleus surrounded by a system of negatively charged electrons. In 1932 Cockcroft and Walton at the Cavendish Laboratory proved the existence of a particle within the atom which was neither positively nor negatively charged, the neutron; and in 1926 P. M. Dirac, a Cambridge mathematical physicist, predicted the existence of a positron (positive electron) which was later proved experimentally. The upshot of all these discoveries was to show that all matter throughout the Universe was made up of the same constituents; variation between one element and another resulted from the differing arrangement of electrons, neutrons and positrons within the atoms of each element. This world-wide study of atomic structure, to which British scientists had contributed so much, was to culminate in the discovery in Germany of atomic fission – or the splitting of the atom, with a consequent enormous release of energy. This led both to the production of the atomic bomb and the peaceful use of nuclear energy.

X-Ray crystallography. One other British discovery of the greatest consequence was the technique of X-Ray Crystallography (invented by W. H. and W. L. Bragg, father and son, in 1914), by which it became possible to determine the positions of atoms, at first in fairly simple molecules, and in recent times in the molecules of extremely complex substances on which the nature of life itself depends (e.g. the DNA molecule*). This immensely powerful method brought the Braggs a Nobel prize in 1917, and has transformed our understanding of the molecular structure of countless substances.

Sir William Bragg with his X-ray spectograph by which he revealed the structure of crystalline solids.

*DNA is the abbreviation for deoxyribonucleic acid. This molecule passes on hereditary characteristics from generation to generation.

Einstein and relativity. Many streams of scientific research, conducted both in Britain and elsewhere, contributed to the profound and far-reaching work of the German scientist, Albert Einstein (1879–1955). Attempts by Morley and Michelson to establish the speed of the earth's movement through space by experimental means, and the observations of many other physicists and astronomers during the late nineteenth century, produced puzzling results which were incompatible with the laws of absolute time and space assumed in Newtonian physics. Inspired by the work of the Irish mathematician, G. F. Fitzgerald and the Dutchman, H. A. Lorentz, Albert Einstein attempted to produce a theory which would resolve these contradictions. His *Special Theory of Relativity*, published in 1905 and his *General Theory of Relativity*, published in 1917 cannot be explained here, but some mention must be made of their influence and implications. Einstein was able to show that for very fast moving objects the concept of absolute time and space had no application, and that these dimensions existed only in relation to the observer. His famous equation $e = mc^2$ (where e is energy, m is mass and c is the velocity of light) was the algebraic expression of a further development of his theory.

The Theory of Relativity suggested new approaches to the structure of the Universe, which became the subject of prolonged controversy amongst astronomers. Today the debate about the origin and fate of the Universe has been intensified through the discoveries of the radio-astronomers such as Lovell and Ryle, and the new theories of mathematicians such as Fred Hoyle. The debate (like the observations and calculations) continues.

One result of Einstein's theory has affected all our lives. He showed that matter and energy are equivalent, so that when matter is annihilated, energy is released in its place. Early in World War II, Einstein wrote a now-famous letter to President Roosevelt of the U.S.A., which said that the controlled conversion of matter into energy on a massive scale by means of a bomb was now a practical possibility. The result was the atomic bomb of 1945. British scientists played their part in its production and after the war they led the world in the development of nuclear energy for peaceful purposes. Electric power generated in nuclear power stations has not yet brought about an economic revolution, but the many nuclear reactors from Calder Hall to Dungeness have shown what may one day be possible.

CHEMISTRY

Britain made notable contributions to the science of chemistry throughout the nineteenth century, and continues to do so. In industrial chemistry she sometimes led and sometimes lagged.

Dalton's atomic theory. During the eighteenth century Lavoisier in France, and British chemists such as Black, Priestley and Cavendish were responsible for many important advances, such as a new concept of what constitutes a chemical element, which together effected a revolution in chemical theory. This revolution was completed by the atomic theory of John Dalton (1766–1844). In 1803 Dalton, a Manchester Quaker teacher, who had already made important discoveries in the physics of gases, laid the basis for all subsequent progress in chemistry. He revived the idea of the classical Greeks that all matter was made up of minute atoms, but he went on to show how the atoms of the different elements could be given a quantitative value and so related to each other.

ELEMENTS

		W.t				W.t
☉	Hydrogen	1	⊕	Strontian		46
◑	Azote	5	✳	Barytes		68
●	Carbon	54	Ⓘ	Iron		50
○	Oxygen	7	Ⓩ	Zinc		56
◑	Phosphorus	9	Ⓒ	Copper		56
⊕	Sulphur	13	Ⓛ	Lead		90
◖◗	Magnesia	20	Ⓢ	Silver		190
⊖	Lime	24	⊛	Gold		190
◫	Soda	28	Ⓟ	Platina		190
◍	Potash	42	✳	Mercury		167

REPRODUCTION FROM THE ORIGINAL IN THE POSSESSION OF THE MANCHESTER LITERARY & PHILOSOPHICAL SOCIETY

DALTON DIAGRAMS
SYMBOLS AND ATOMIC WEIGHTS

One of John Dalton's early lecture diagrams showing atomic weights.

Dalton was followed by other distinguished workers, such as Edward Frankland (1825–99) who was one of the founders of the theory of *valency*, and Newlands and Odling, who prepared the way for the periodic classification of the elements which was the great achievement of the Russian Mendeléeff.

Fine chemical industry. Despite these and other outstanding theoretical advances, however, Britain lagged in the industrial development of chemistry. Even when important discoveries were made they were not often developed in Britain. For instance, it was an Englishman, William Perkin (1838–1907) who made the accidental discovery of the first artificial dye-stuff, mauve, in 1856. But his discovery was then developed commercially in Germany, which led for a long time in the manufacture of fine chemicals – dyes and drugs. It took the 1914–18 war, which of course stopped imports from Germany, to stimulate British manufacture to recover the lost ground.

Drugs and anti-biotics. In the half-century since then, however, the British fine chemical industry has moved into the front rank with developments which have revolutionized medical science. Ever since Pasteur discovered the germ-theory of disease in France in the 1860s, scientists had been searching for chemicals which would destroy germs without harming the human body – 'magic bullets' as a famous German bacteriologist described them. In 1935, following leads from Germany and France, chemists in the laboratories of May and Baker Ltd produced on a large scale the first of the 'sulpha' drugs (sulphonamides) to fight bacteria. The drug was called M & B 693, after the number of the laboratory notebook entry, and it brought about miraculous cures for killer-diseases such as pneumonia and meningitis, for which there had previously been no treatment at all.

There now followed probably the greatest discovery in the treatment of human disease – penicillin, the first antibiotic. Discovered in 1929 by Alexander Fleming (1881–1955), and first made in quantity by Florey and

Alexander Fleming at work in his laboratory.

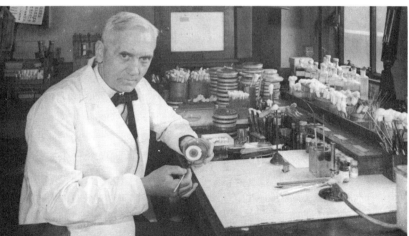

Chaim in Oxford in 1940, it killed a great many germs which had been quit untouched by the sulpha drugs. As Fleming himself wrote, 'Penicillin and other antibiotics have made it necessary to rewrite all the textbooks o medical treatment. We certainly live in wondrous times . . .' As a result o these and other discoveries, the British drug industry is now an importan factor not only in the nation's health, but in its commerce as well.

Heavy chemical industry. On the heavy chemicals side, progress was bette maintained during the nineteenth century. The heavy chemical industr was closely connected with textile production, since alkali products (sod and bleaching powder) were mainly used in the bleaching of cloth. Th two most important areas of alkali production were Scotland, and Lanca shire and Cheshire, both of which were also thriving textile manufacturin areas. The industry began to diversify during the nineteenth century. Fror the production of soda and bleaching powder it spread to sulphuric aci and glass, to explosives and later to chemical fertilizers and syntheti materials. The industry developed rapidly between 1880 and 1920, and i 1926 a number of companies merged to form Imperial Chemical Industrie Ltd, which is now one of the largest chemical producers in the world.

NEW MATERIALS, AND FOOD

The chemical industries grew out of ancient craft processes which converte natural materials into more useful forms, e.g. soft clay into hard potter During the nineteenth century the development of new materials an processes had most important effects on the lives of the ordinary peopl They provided new forms of lighting and heating, a new variety of food stuffs and clothing, and a new and more versatile range of materials fror which everyday goods could be made.

Coal gas. The fuel of the early 1800s was coal. In 1806, gas was successfull extracted from coal to provide artificial lighting. In 1812 the Gas, Ligh and Coke Company was formed to supply street lighting in London, an the method spread to most other towns during the century. Gas late came into use for domestic lighting, where it began to displace the tradi tional candles and oil lamps. The open gas flame soon faced competitio from electricity. However, the invention, in 1885, of the incandescen mantle, of high efficiency and brilliance gave a new lease of life to ga lighting in the home. Although gas was eventually replaced by electricit for lighting, it has retained great popularity for both domestic and industria heating and for cooking. The recent discovery of natural deposits of ga under the North Sea will no doubt increase the domestic and industria use of gas.

The coal-gas industry had a further importance: the chemical industrie became largely dependent on it for a wide range of chemicals originating from its by-product, coal-tar.

Petroleum. Petroleum began to be the material for an industry from about 1860. The demand for it arose from the discovery in 1850, that an excellent lamp oil called paraffin could be distilled from oil-shale in Scotland, or from the mineral oil called petroleum, which had been discovered in America. Apart from its use as fuels and lubricants, petroleum has today become, like coal, the source of a wide range of chemical products such as detergents, plastics, synthetic fibres and rubber, etc. The most spectacular use of petroleum, of course, has been to make possible the era of the motor-car. In this respect it shares the honours with rubber.

Rubber. Rubber was one of the most important vegetable products to be converted to industrial use during the nineteenth century. It was long known in its soft pliable form and was used to waterproof fabrics by Charles Macintosh in 1823. Later it was turned into a tough durable material by vulcanization (hardening by treatment with sulphur), a process discovered by Charles Goodyear in 1832. In 1888 J. B. Dunlop invented a pneumatic rubber tyre for bicycles, and rubber tyres were soon in use on all forms of road transport. There have been many attempts to make synthetic rubber, but it is only recently that they have met with any success.

Plastics. Much more success has been achieved with various synthetic plastics. It had long been observed that some chemical reactions produced materials which resembled natural products like horn or ivory. In 1865 Alexander Parkes of Birmingham mixed gun cotton (a derivative of cellulose) with alcohol and camphor to produce a hard substance which could be moulded under heat, and his experiments led to the discovery of Xylonite – later called Celluloid. Celluloid came to be used for a wide range of articles, including photographic film. Unfortunately, it was inflammable – unlike Bakelite, which was discovered in 1906. Since that time there have been many similar materials produced both in this country and in America. A notable British invention in 1939 was polyethylene, known by its trade names 'polythene', 'alkathene', etc. This substance is distinguished by its chemical inertness and unique electrical properties – which were of great value in war-time radar.

Synthetic fibres. From the middle of the nineteenth century there were also many attempts to produce artificial fibres to replace the natural fibres – wool, cotton and silk. The earliest commercial success came in 1892 with the production of Rayon, or 'artificial silk' as it was called, by Cross and Bevan. Rayon, and later 'Celanese', were both products of cellulose (which was obtained from wood-pulp). In 1935 the American Du Pont company produced a synthetic fibre which came not from cellulose but from simple chemicals. Nylon was the first of many commercial substances produced in this way and was followed in 1946 by the important British invention, Terylene.

These synthetic materials have played an ever more important part not just in clothing, but in many other aspects of everyday life in industrial countries in the last two generations.

Food supplies and food preservation
Preserving. New methods of food preservation developed during the nineteenth century had an almost revolutionary effect upon the lives of ordinary people. They made available a wider range of foodstuffs throughout the year and led to new standards in food hygiene. For centuries some food had been preserved by pickling, drying and smoking; then in 1850 the German chemist Liebig produced evaporated meat extracts which could be preserved indefinitely. Evaporated milk had already been produced in 1843, but it was not widely available until the Nestlé Company began commercial manufacture in Switzerland in 1866.

Canned foods were first produced by a Frenchman, Appert, who opened a canning factory in 1815; but it was not until the Americans developed the pressure cooking of canned foods in the 1870s that this method became really popular. The consumption of canned vegetables alone rose from 4,000,000 cases in 1870 to 55,000,000 in 1914.

Early preserved foods. Some of these tinned foods produced in the Boer War had hardly deteriorated when they were opened more than fifty years later.

Refrigeration. Of equally great importance was the refrigeration process. Men had preserved food with natural ice for many centuries, but the pioneer of artificial freezing was the French inventor, Carré, who produced a vacuum freezing machine in 1850. His method was enormously improved by A. C. Kirk in England in 1862, and from about 1880 really efficient machines were being manufactured for domestic use. One of the most important applications of refrigeration was in the transport of meat. The first Argentinian chilled beef arrived in London in 1877, and two years later the first shipment came from Australia. Thereafter there was an enormous increase in the import of cheap meat, with very adverse effects on British stock farming.

Cheap food. The upper and middle classes were slow to patronize the new processed foods, and for many years showed a preference for English meat. But for the working classes the cheapness and variety of preserved foods brought about a revolution in consuming habits, which was reflected in their health and well-being. In recent years high-speed drying and freezing processes have meant that some preserved foods reach the table in better condition than the so-called fresh foods, which have spent a long time in markets and shops.

NEW METHODS OF TRANSPORT

Of all the changes brought about by scientific advances in the last 150 years, those in transport and all forms of human communications have been amongst the most revolutionary in their effects.

Road transport

There was a rapid development in railways and shipping after the first quarter of the nineteenth century (see Chapter 29), but for a long time road transport lagged far behind. After 1830 competition from the railways ruined many of the turnpike trusts and the old coaching companies. There were a few attempts to apply steam power to road transport, but it was inefficient and costly. In 1865 the railway interests obtained the passage of the 'Red Flag' Act, which limited the speed of mechanically powered road vehicles to five miles an hour in the country and two miles an hour in towns. Powered vehicles also had to be manned by three men, including one walking ahead with a red flag. This act effectively put an end to powered road transport for a generation.

During the mid-century there were some improvements in the surfacing of roads. In 1860 steamrollers were used to lay asphalt macadam surfaces, and in 1865 the first cement roads were laid in Scotland. There were also new forms of horse-drawn transport in the towns, such as the hansom cab (1834) and horse-drawn trams in the 1860s. The first electric trams were introduced in about 1890.

The motor-car. The real revolution in road transport came with the invention of the internal combustion engine in the 1880s. The most important commercial developments of the motor-car before 1914 took place in France, Germany, and America. However, there were a number of British-produced cars on the roads as well as imported models. The Red Flag Act was repealed in 1896 and main roads were treated with hot bitumen to withstand the pressures of fast-moving rubber tyres.

The 'tube'. In the later years of the nineteenth century urban traffic, especially in London, became extremely congested. One solution to this problem was the construction of underground railways. At first trains were drawn by steam engines, and ran through shallow cuttings which were only partly covered; but between 1887 and 1890 London got its first 'tube', a deep-level railway using electric traction in a tunnel constructed by new techniques (the Greathead Shield) and lined with cast-iron rings to form a continuous iron tube.

Traffic congestion. During the twentieth century there has been no great technical revolution in land transport, but there has been a fantastic growth in the volume of road traffic. In 1919 there were 330,000 cars on the roads; in 1939 this had grown to 3,000,000 and in 1966 there was a total of 8,000,000 licensed vehicles. The roads of Britain have not proved adequate for this traffic, despite the construction of motorways and complicated urban road systems in the 1950s and 1960s. Urban congestion is now one of the major social problems, and new experimental vehicles such as monorail trains and hovercrafts are not yet in a position to offer any immediate relief.

The Age of Road replaces the Age of Rail: the Caerphilly Castle *being transported to the Science Museum.*

The aeroplane

At about the time when men first flew lighter-than-air craft (balloons) at the end of the eighteenth century, Sir George Cayley was constructing successful models of heavier-than-air craft and laying down the fundamental principles of mechanical flight. Experiments continued throughout the nineteenth century in several countries.

The pioneers. By 1900 steam-powered models had been made which were capable of *sustained* flight, but inventors had still not overcome the difficulties of *controlled* flight. This required a light engine and a means of control in the air. The first was supplied by the internal combustion engine which was successfully developed at the turn of the century. The second was supplied mainly by the inventiveness of the brothers Orville and Wilbur Wright in the United States. After long experience with gliders they accomplished the first man-carrying, powered, sustained, controlled flight at Kittyhawk in Florida in 1903. In 1909 A. V. Roe became the first man to make a powered flight in Britain, and in the same year Louis Blériot flew the English Channel. A contemporary newspaper headline 'Britain no Longer an Island' neatly summarized the long-term impact of aviation on British history.

Between the wars. The war of 1914–18 gave an enormous stimulus to aircraft design and manufacture. By 1918 thousands of aircraft had been built, many capable of carrying heavy loads. The year after the war, Alcock and Brown made the first non-stop crossing of the Atlantic. Commercial flying now grew rapidly. A daily service between London and Paris was opened in 1919, and in 1923 the government created Imperial Airways Ltd to develop European and Empire routes. A mark of confidence in the new form of transport was the opening of Royal Mail services. Routes were extended to Baghdad (1927), Karachi (1929) and Sydney (1934). Regular Atlantic crossings were being tried out just before the war broke out in 1939.

Jet engines. During World War II, aircraft grew not only in size and complexity, but also in fundamental structure. The famous Spitfire (unlike the Hurricane, which looked basically the same) was built on a new type of self-supporting metal-alloy shell and proved to be one of the most successful aircraft of the war. At the end of the war Sir Frank Whittle developed the gas turbine or jet engine. Within a few years it opened up vast new possibilities for aircraft development. British design produced the Comet aircraft in the 1950s, but the early disasters allowed the Boeing 707 to take the lead as the major long-distance high-speed aircraft. However, the lead in jet design remained with the British companies, and Britain has always been very successful with shorter distance machines. Modern aviation design and production requires vast resources and for this reason Britain has begun to co-operate with France, notably in the production of the supersonic airliner, the Concorde.

TELECOMMUNICATIONS

The telegraph. Modern telecommunications began in the 1830s with the invention of the electric telegraph. In 1838 Cooke and Wheatstone produced the needle telegraph system (an electrically controlled needle pointing to letters of the alphabet on a dial). At the same time Morse in the U.S.A. invented his dot-dash system. The telegraph was first used by the railway companies But the postal reformer Rowland Hill pointed out its advantages for business in general, a point made clear when the stock exchanges of London and Paris were brought into contact by the first cross-channel cable in 1851. In the same year Reuters News Agency was set up in London, and the modern business of immediate news transmission over great distances had begun. In 1866 the first transatlantic cable was laid, and in 1870 a line was opened between Britain and India.

The telephone. The next step was the transmission of the human voice. After many experiments, the first successful transmission was made in 1876 by Alexander Graham Bell in America. Two years later the first commercial telephone system was in operation in America and in 1878 the first tele-

The steamship Goliah *laying the first submarine cable across the Channel to Cape Gris Nez.*

Marconi in 1896 with his wireless telegraphy equipment.

phone exchange was opened in London. At first telephones were operated by private companies; but in 1912 the National Telephone Company had established a virtual monopoly and it was nationalized under the control of the Post Office.

Wireless. Telephone systems were soon linked on an international network throughout Europe. But long-distance communications were really established by the invention of wireless by Guglielmo Marconi (1874–1937). Marconi's experiments were based on the belief that the nature of electromagnetic waves, as postulated by Clerk-Maxwell and experimentally proved by Hertz (p. 381), would make possible a system of space telegraphy. In 1895 he sent a Morse code message over a distance of one mile; the next year he came to England and demonstrated his method to the Post Office officials. In 1901 the first wireless telegraph message was sent across the Atlantic from Poldhu in Cornwall to Newfoundland, a distance of over 2,000 miles. Marconi's revolutionary discovery was followed in 1904 by the invention of the thermionic valve by Sir John Fleming, which made further rapid development possible. Wireless became an invaluable communications device for shipping, and was well established on British vessels by 1914. During the war the transmission of speech was achieved and this led on to general broadcasting. The British Broadcasting Company was set up under government sponsorship in 1922, and became a public corporation in 1926. It very quickly developed into a major medium for education and entertainment.

Television. A further development was the transmission of images as well as sounds. The pioneering work was done in Britain by John Logie Baird (1888–1946) in the 1920s. Although there were public transmissions in the 1930s, Baird's system was too clumsy to produce a really good picture. However, the development of a means of scanning the image with a weightless electron beam, made higher definition transmissions possible by 1936. After the war the B.B.C. rapidly introduced an efficient service. Here again, a new technical process has had a profound effect on people's social and intellectual life.

Electronics. The technology centring round the thermionic valve and the cathode-ray rube, together with the recently developed transistor, has become known as 'electronics'. It has been one of the fastest growing branches of technology during our lifetime. Its products include television itself, radar, the electron microscope, and the computer, which is replacing countless human beings by 'electronic brains' and is making possible the development of 'automation' – the control of machines by machines instead of by men.

PHOTOGRAPHY AND PRINTING

Photography
One of the few technical innovations which can be said to have introduced an entirely new element into Victorian life is photography. Early chemists had observed that sunlight darkened some substances, notably silver compounds. Thomas Wedgwood (1771–1805) made some scientific attempts at recording by this means about 1800, but neither he nor Humphry Davy could make the image permanent. The first success based on the reaction of silver compounds to light was that of L. J. M. Daguerre (1787–1851), made public after long experiments in 1839. This was the Daguerreotype, a picture formed in silver mounted on a copper plate. In the same year an Englishman, W. H. Fox Talbot (1800–77) began to experiment with a method which would reproduce photographs on sensitized paper. This process produced negatives and could therefore be used to make any number of copies. Before long, innumerable family photographic portraits became an essential decoration in Victorian homes, and by the end of the century photographs were being used in books and newspapers.

The cinema. The natural extension of photography was the presentation of a succession of still photographs at high speed to simulate motion. No one person can be credited with the invention of the cinematograph. Successful experiments were made in France, America and Britain which laid the foundation of the modern cinema around 1896. After the World

The first photograph of a latticed window in Lacock Abbey taken by Fox Talbot in 1835.

War I the 'movie' became an established part of the entertainment industry and the first 'talkies' were produced in 1929. Since that time the film has become a powerful medium both for informing and entertaining mass audiences.

Printing and paper

Books were fulfilling a major role in education and leisure long before inventors had ever dreamed of films, radio and television. Far from being replaced by the new media, they have also benefited from technological improvements and are now reaching a wider audience than ever before. In the eighteenth century all printing was done by the impression on individual sheets of paper of pieces of metal type set on a flat bed. Except for an increase in size there had hardly been any changes for several hundred years. However in 1815 the proprietors of *The Times* began experiments with printing from rollers. By 1866 *The Times* was being printed on both sides of a continuous roll of paper simultaneously from two printing rollers. The type itself was a 'stereotype' or solid metal plate cast from the impression of the original hand-set type and curved to fit on to the roller. From this process modern newspaper printing has developed. The application of new machines, powered at first by steam power and later electricity, encouraged the growth of a cheap popular press. The process was completed in the late nineteenth century with mechanical typesetters and the development of a process for printing photographs from special blocks.

The production of cheap newspapers, and later cheap books, was also helped by new papermaking techniques. In the eighteenth century paper was made from pulped linen rags which were produced one sheet at a time on a kind of flat sieve. Early in the nineteenth century a method of making continuous rolls of paper was invented. After 1840 abundant wood-pulp from Sweden and Canada replaced rags as the basis for cheap paper.

These changes had the most profound effects upon English life. Cheap newspapers and books, especially informational books, were one of the most powerful educative forces in the nineteenth century. In the twentieth century the process has been extended still further by the 'paperback revolution' which has made all types of books available for a few shillings.

Science, Technology and Society

The advance of science and technology in this century has been so rapid and has had such far-reaching consequences that it would be impossible to review it all in this short space. Medicine has been revolutionized by new drugs, by the development of brain surgery and by the ability of doctors to fit artificial parts to the body. Radio messages and television pictures can be flashed around the world in a matter of moments. Rockets have landed on the moon and men have walked in space. Computers have become an everyday part of business and academic life and man has at his disposal not only the natural produce of the earth, but a vast range of synthetic materials.

Yet science has produced many enormous problems as well, and it has not solved some of the most urgent questions which face mankind. Men now possess powers of complete destruction but not the social organization to prevent it ever being used. One part of the world enjoys all the benefits of an advanced technological civilization while another, far greater, part exists at or below starvation level. Automation and electronic devices have relieved men of much back-breaking work, but we still have to learn how to use leisure wisely and constructively. These are problems which face not only the people of Britain but the whole world.

Appendices

MONARCHS

George III	1760–1820
George IV (son)	1820–1830
William IV (brother)	1830–1837
Victoria (niece)	1837–1901
Edward VII (son)	1901–1910
George V (son)	1910–1936
Edward VIII (son)	1936–1937
George VI (brother)	1937–1952
Elizabeth II (daughter)	1952

PRIME MINISTERS

Lord Liverpool	1812–27
George Canning	1827
Lord Goderich	1827
Duke of Wellington	1828–30
Lord Grey	1830–4
Lord Melbourne	1834
Sir Robert Peel	1834–5
Lord Melbourne	1835–41
Sir Robert Peel	1841–6
Lord John Russell	1846–52
Lord Derby	1852
Lord Aberdeen	1852–5
Lord Palmerston	1855–8
Lord Derby	1858–9

Lord Palmerston	1859–65
Lord Russell	1865–6
Lord Derby	1866–8
Benjamin Disraeli	1868
William Gladstone	1868–74
Benjamin Disraeli	1874–80
William Gladstone	1880–5
Lord Salisbury	1885–6
William Gladstone	1886
Lord Salisbury	1886–1892
William Gladstone	1892–4
Lord Rosebery	1894–5
Lord Salisbury	1895–1902
Arthur Balfour	1902–5
Henry Campbell Bannerman	1905–8
Herbert Asquith	1908–16
David Lloyd George	1916–22
Andrew Bonar Law	1922–3
Stanley Baldwin	1923–4
James Ramsay MacDonald	1924
Stanley Baldwin	1924–9
James Ramsay MacDonald	1929–35
Stanley Baldwin	1935–7
Neville Chamberlain	1937–40
Winston Churchill	1940–5
Clement Attlee	1945–51
Winston Churchill	1951–5
Anthony Eden	1955–7
Harold Macmillan	1957–63
Sir Alec Douglas-Home	1963–4
Harold Wilson	1964–70
Edward Heath	1970–74

Questions

The following questions may provide useful topics for discussion and subjects for further reading.

Chapter One. Britain in 1815
(1) What changes were occurring in the English 'social pattern' in 1815?
(2) What was the basis of Cobbett's social criticism?
(3) What was the Speenhamland System?
(4) Give some account of the armed forces in 1815.
(5) Why did the monarchy sink low in general esteem in the years 1811 to 1830?
(6) What 'freedom of opinion' was there in the years 1815–30?

Chapter Two. Crisis and Repression, 1815–21
(1) Is it justifiable to condemn Liverpool's policy for being *laissez-faire*?
(2) List the main reasons for discontent in Britain in these years.
(3) Were the Six Acts justified? If not, what was the possible alternative?
(4) What were the causes and results of the 'Peterloo Massacre'?

Chapter Three. The 'Enlightened Tories'
(1) What conditions made 'enlightened Toryism' possible?
(2) Estimate the importance of Huskisson in the economic history of Britain.
(3) What was the importance of the penal reforms of Sir Robert Peel? What influences were making themselves felt for penal reform before and after 1815?
(4) What circumstances led to the achievement of Catholic Emancipation and what were its effects on the Tory Party?

Chapter Four. The Foreign Policy of Castlereagh and Canning
(1) What were the chief aims of Castlereagh in foreign policy?
(2) What part did Castlereagh play in the settlement of Europe after 1815?
(3) What were the main problems Canning had to deal with as Foreign Secretary?
(4) On what principles was Canning's foreign policy based?

Chapter Five. The First Reform Bill, 1832

(1) Why did parliamentary reform become much more of an issue after 1815?

(2) What position was taken up on the question of parliamentary reform by Bentham, Brougham, Joseph Hume, Cobbett, Henry Hunt, Sir Francis Burdett, Thomas Attwood?

(3) What political developments, domestic and foreign, aided the cause of parliamentary reform in the years 1829–32?

(4) What was the real significance of the 1832 Reform Bill?

(5) Why do you think the secret ballot in elections was not adopted?

Chapter Six. The Whigs and Social Reform, 1832–41

(1) What were the basic ideas of utilitarianism as expounded by Bentham?

(2) Outline the career of Robert Owen.

(3) What was the importance of the Factory Act of 1833?

(4) What were the varied *motives* which led Parliament to sanction the first grant of education in 1833?

(5) Why was Poor Law reform necessary in 1834?

(6) Why did the Poor Law Amendment Act take the form it did?

(7) What was the state of local government before the Municipal Corporations Act of 1835?

(8) How would you account for the attitude of the Whig administration to Owen's trade union activity?

(9) Why was there a slowing-down of social reform under Melbourne's administration?

Chapter Seven. Robert Peel and the Repeal of the Corn Laws

(1) What was the importance of the Tamworth Manifesto?

(2) What difficulties faced Peel's administration in 1841?

(3) What were Peel's motives in introducing free trade measures, and what were the results of these measures?

(4) Why was the Bank Charter Act of 1844 promoted by Peel?

(5) Show the importance of the Earl of Shaftesbury in social reform in the years 1841 to 1850.

(6) How would you account for Peel's attitude towards O'Connell's agitation?

(7) Why was the Anti-Corn Law League successful?

Chapter Eight. The Chartist Movement

(1) What factors gave rise to Chartism?

(2) What were the various trends of thought in the Chartist movement?

(3) What were the Six Points, and why were they opposed by Parliament?

(4) Write brief notes on the following: Feargus O'Connor, William Lovett, Bronterre O'Brien, George Julian Harney, Thomas Attwood, Joseph Sturge.

(5) Why was the Chartist movement unsuccessful in achieving its aims?

Chapter Nine. Lord Palmerston
(1) What were the main principles underlying Lord Palmerston's foreign policy?
(2) Why did Palmerston regard the Belgian question as of great importance for Britain?
(3) Why was Palmerston concerned over internal events in Spain?
(4) What was the real importance to Britain of the career of Mehemet Ali?
(5) How would you account for Palmerston's policy towards China?
(6) Why was Britain's influence abroad beginning to weaken by 1865?

Chapter Ten. The Crimea, the Mutiny and the Second Reform Bill
(1) Why were the old party systems undergoing change in these years?
(2) What is the real significance of the Crimean War in the history of Britain?
(3) What were the main causes of the Indian Mutiny?
(4) How would you account for the ferocity shown by both sides during the mutiny?
(5) Why did agitation for a second Reform Bill arise during these years?
(6) What was the parliamentary situation which enabled the Second Reform Bill to be passed?

Chapter Eleven. The Victorian Outlook
(1) Why was the Victorian period an age of question and doubt?
(2) How would you account for the element of optimism in the Victorian outlook?
(3) What aspect of Victorian thought and action was represented by the works of Samuel Smiles?
(4) What was the average Victorian idea of success?
(5) What was the position of the monarchy in this period?

Chapter Twelve. The Welfare of the Body and Soul
(1) What were the causes of high infant mortality in the first half of the nineteenth century?
(2) What were the bad results of the 'miasmatic' theory of disease?
(3) What was the importance of the work of Edwin Chadwick?
(4) In what ways was London a pioneer city in regard to public health?
(5) What was the importance of the work of J. Y. Simpson, Louis Pasteur and Robert Koch?
(6) What was the importance of the work of Florence Nightingale?
(7) What were the main stages in the development of insurance after 1850?
(8) How would you explain the rise of Methodism?
(9) Give a brief account of the ideas and influence of John Henry Newman.
(10) What were the aims and influence of the Christian Socialists?
(11) What was the importance of the work of General William Booth?

(12) How would you account for the great interest shown in religion in the Victorian period?

(13) What influences have challenged basic religious ideas in the period 1815–1939?

Chapter Thirteen. Gladstone and Liberal Reform

(1) What was Gladstone's attitude to (a) warfare as a part of national policy (b) income tax (c) the paper duties (d) thrift?

(2) What were the general results of Gladstone's economic policies?

(3) Explain why the land question was the fundamental problem in Ireland in the nineteenth century.

(4) Why was the First Land Act of 1870 ineffective?

(5) How would you account for the development of the Home Rule movement in Ireland?

(6) Why was the question of elementary education taken up so strongly by Gladstone?

(7) What factors had caused attention to be focused on the condition of the British armed forces in 1870?

(8) Why did Gladstone become unpopular with the trade union movement by 1874?

Chapter Fourteen. Disraeli and Tory Democracy

(1) What were the main reasons for Gladstone's defeat in 1874?

(2) Why was there increased concentration on matters relating to housing and health in these years?

(3) What changes were made by the Factory Acts of 1874 and 1878?

(4) On what grounds did Gladstone oppose Disraeli's imperial policies?

(5) What difficulties arose for Disraeli in the years 1878–80?

(6) What is the place of Disraeli in British history and in the history of the Conservative Party.

Chapter Fifteen. Gladstone and Salisbury, 1880–95

(1) What were the internal party problems facing Gladstone in 1880?

(2) Why did the Irish question come to dominate politics in these years?

(3) What would you consider were the motives of the Irish Land League in opposing Gladstone's land courts?

(4) What was the political importance of the Phoenix Park murders?

(5) How did Gladstone deal with the problems of South Africa and Egypt?

(6) Why did Gladstone's imperial policies tend to weaken his position at home?

(7) Explain the changes made by the Third Reform Bill of 1884.

(8) What were the effects on the Liberal Party of the defeat of Gladstone's First Home Rule Bill?

(9) Why was Salisbury able greatly to reduce social turmoil and discontent in Ireland?
(10) Explain the changes made by the County Councils Act, 1888.
(11) Why was the term 'splendid isolation' applied to Salisbury's foreign policy?

Chapter Sixteen. Conservatism and Imperialism, 1895–1905
(1) What was Joseph Chamberlain's main work for Birmingham?
(2) Enumerate the main political ideas advocated by Chamberlain.
(3) Show how the Uitlander problem contributed to the outbreak of the South African War.
(4) Show how Rhodes and Kruger came into political conflict.
(5) What was the importance of the Jameson Raid in the history of Boer-British conflict?
(6) What was Salisbury's policy towards (a) Egypt (b) Turkey (c) Germany (d) Russia (e) France (f) Japan?
(7) What circumstances brought about the *Entente Cordiale*?
(8) Estimate Salisbury's achievements in respect of Ireland.
(9) Why did Chamberlain's tariff reform proposals have an adverse effect on the Conservative Party?
(10) What were the main factors in the defeat of the Conservative Party in 1906?

Chapter Seventeen. Liberalism and Reform, 1906–11
(1) In what ways was the Liberal Government of 1906 a break from the nineteenth-century tradition?
(2) What was the importance of the People's Budget of 1909?
(3) What changes were made by the Parliament Act of 1911, and what was their importance?
(4) What Acts were passed by the Liberal Governments of this period affecting the welfare of the working classes?
(5) Why was there social unrest in the period 1906–14?
(6) Describe the events leading up to the Curragh 'Mutiny'.
(7) What were the reasons for the Anglo-Russian agreement and the formation of the Triple Entente?
(8) What were the main reasons for the conflict between Serbia and Austria?
(9) What are the principal causes of the Great War of 1914–1918?

Chapter Eighteen. The First World War and the Post-war Settlement
(1) Why did the German initial plan of campaign fail?
(2) How would you account for (a) the common British view that the war would be a short one and (b) the fact that it continued for over four years?
(3) What controversies at home arose over the conduct of the war?

(4) What was the importance of Lloyd George during the war period, both before and after he became Prime Minister?

(5) What were some of the problems left by the Versailles settlements?

Chapter Nineteen. Post-war Britain, and the First Labour Government

(1) What were the economic and social effects on Britain of the First World War?

(2) How did Lloyd George deal with the immediate post-war problems?

(3) Give an account of the Irish problem, 1918–23.

(4) Explain the main peace settlements and the part played by Lloyd George.

(5) What forms did social unrest take after 1921?

(6) How would you account for the end of the Coalition in 1922?

(7) Describe the work of the first Labour Government and account for its fall.

Chapter Twenty. Baldwin and the General Strike

(1) Explain the foreign policy of Baldwin's second Government.

(2) What were the causes and results of the General Strike?

(3) Explain the main social and economic reforms of this period.

(4) How would you account for the decline in Conservative strength in the election of 1929?

Chapter Twenty-one. MacDonald and the Economic Crisis

(1) What were the main points of MacDonald's foreign and imperial policies at this time?

(2) List the main points of the economic and social legislation of the second Labour Government.

(3) What circumstances led to the fall of the second Labour Government in 1931?

Chapter Twenty-two. Depression and Recovery, 1931–39

(1) For what reasons was there an overwhelming victory for the National Government in the election of October 1931?

(2) Explain the work of Neville Chamberlain as Chancellor of the Exchequer.

(3) Describe the main principles behind National Government domestic policies in the years 1931–39. To what extent were they successful?

(4) Write brief notes on (a) the hunger marches (b) the Special Areas (c) Unemployment Act, 1934.

Chapter Twenty-three. Crisis and Appeasement, 1931–39

(1) How was the Irish question settled?

(2) What were the principles underlying MacDonald's foreign policy?

(3) Why did the 1932–34 Disarmament Conference fail?

(4) What was the 'Stresa Front'?

(5) Describe the policies of the National Government towards Japan (Manchuria) and Italy (Abyssinia).

(6) How did the Spanish Civil War affect British politics in the years 1936–39?

(7) Explain British defence policy in the years 1936–39.

(8) Why did Chamberlain seek to reach agreement with Hitler?

(9) What are the possible explanations of the Chamberlain Government's attitude to Soviet Russia?

Chapter Twenty-four. The Second World War

(1) How would you account for the early successes of Hitler?

(2) What was the importance of the battles of Stalingrad and El Alamein?

(3) What was the role and importance of the R.A.F. and the Royal Navy during the Second World War?

(4) How was Britain organized during the war?

(5) Why was national unity so great during the war?

(6) Explain the aims and importance of the various official reports published between 1940 and 1945.

(7) How would you account for the victory of the Allies in the Second World War?

Chapter Twenty-five. Post-War Britain under Labour Government, 1945–51

(1) What were the main reasons for the success of the Labour Party in the 1945 election?

(2) Describe the economic condition of Britain at the end of the Second World War.

(3) Briefly outline the organization of the post-war economic system, 1945–51.

(4) What problems arose for the first two Labour Chancellors of the Exchequer, and how did they meet them?

(5) Describe the main legislation which implemented the idea of the Welfare State.

(6) Describe the main trends of British foreign policy, 1946 to 1951.

(7) How would you account for the ending of post-war Labour government in 1951?

Chapter Twenty-six. Conservative Government, 1951–64.

(1) Describe the approach of the Churchill Government, 1951–55, to Britain's problems.

(2) Examine the importance of the Suez crisis in the history of Britain.

(3) How were Britain's economic problems dealt with during the Macmillan administration, 1957–63?

(4) What were the main lines of defence policy under the Conservative administrations of 1951–64?

(5) Write notes on (*a*) the Cuba crisis (*b*) the Nuclear Test-ban Treaty (*c*) Britain and the Common Market.

(6) What were the main controversies in the Labour Party in the years 1951–61?

(7) How would you account for the general strength of Conservatism during the years 1951–61?

(8) What caused a decline in Conservative support in the years 1961–64?

Chapter Twenty-seven. Labour Government, 1964–70

This chapter may serve as the basis for discussion of the contemporary problems of Britain and what she must achieve. Can national aims be clarified and agreed upon, and how can a sense of united purpose be created? Important issues are trade union reform, removal of outdated parliamentary procedures, foreign policy, 'east of Suez', the independent nuclear deterrent, the future of the Commonwealth, education, housing, race relations, drugs and delinquency.

Chapter Twenty-eight. The Development of the Trade Unions and the Rise of the Labour Party, 1848–1970

(1) What were the aims and methods of the craft unions?

(2) How did the Trades Union Congress originate?

(3) What was the importance of the Dockers' Strike of 1889 in the history of trade unionism?

(4) In what connection are the following mentioned: Friedrich Engels, Henry Mayers Hyndman, Keir Hardie, Annie Besant, Tom Mann, Joseph Arch, John Burns?

(5) Describe the origins of the Labour Party.

(6) What was the importance for the trade unions of the Taff Vale and Osborne judgements?

(7) Why were the trade unions militant in the years 1906–14?

(8) What was the importance of Ernest Bevin and Walter Citrine in the trade union movement of the inter-war years?

(9) What was the effect on the trade union movement of the failure of the General Strike?

(10) What have been the main changes in the composition and organization of the unions since 1945?

(11) What have been the greatest difficulties facing the trade unions since 1960 and how have they faced them?

Chapter Twenty-nine. The British Economy, 1815–1970

(1) What were the main causes of the rapid development of the railways?

(2) What were the economic and social results of railway development?

(3) What were the main stages in the development of the steamship, and what was its value to Britain?

(4) How far had Britain gone on the road of industrialization at the time of the Great Exhibition?
(5) What were the main reasons for mid-Victorian prosperity?
(6) What exactly is meant by the economic 'depression' of 1873–1900?
(7) What were the reasons for agricultural decline in the years 1870–1900 and what remedies were attempted?
(8) What effects did the First World War have on Britain's industry and trade?
(9) What efforts were made in the years 1919–39 to revive industry and agriculture?
(10) Compare the pattern of exports and imports in the period 1919–39 and 1945–60 and account for the differences.

Chapter Thirty. The Development of the Old Dominions
(1) What were the causes of discontent in Canada which led up to Lord Durham's mission?
(2) What was the importance of the Durham Report?
(3) What factors brought about the creation of a federal system for Canada?
(4) What circumstances made Australian federation difficult, and what factors brought about eventual federation?
(5) Write notes on the following: Edward Gibbon Wakefield, the Treaty of Waitangi, Sir George Grey, the Maori problem.

Chapter Thirty-one. From Empire to Commonwealth
(1) Trace the stages of British reform in India after the Mutiny.
(2) Why did the Indian National Congress gain increasing support?
(3) Outline the development of British control in Nigeria.
(4) What circumstances caused Britain to take a more decided interest in East African colonization?
(5) What differences of opinion existed between the home Government and the British settlers in Kenya?
(6) Trace the main activities of the Egyptian nationalist movement from 1900.
(7) In what ways did British attitudes to the Empire change during the years 1919–39?
(8) Why was India partitioned in 1947?
(9) Outline the steps by which independence was gained by the British colonies in West Africa.
(10) Show how independence was won by the British territories in East and Central Africa.
(11) Why does Rhodesia present such a difficult problem to Britain and the Commonwealth?

Chapter Thirty-two. Education

(1) What were the main reasons for the demand for elementary education?

(2) Attempt some statement of the over-all results of elementary education in the nineteenth century.

(3) What part did the public schools play in changing the nature of British education in the nineteenth century?

(4) Explain the importance of the Butler Education Act, 1944.

(5) Describe the development of technical education during the last 150 years.

(6) What are the main weaknesses in British education at the present time and what steps are being taken to solve them?

Chapter Thirty-three. Science and Technology

(1) Why was the steam engine the most important technical advance of the Industrial Revolution?

(2) What was the importance of the early scientific societies?

(3) What was the importance of Faraday's discovery of electro-magnetic induction?

(4) What important advances were made in astronomy in the nineteenth century?

(5) Explain how Darwin arrived at the theory of natural selection as stated in the *Origin of Species*.

(6) On what grounds did people (*a*) oppose Darwin, (*b*) support him?

(7) What important results followed from the discovery of radioactivity?

(8) List some of the important new materials developed since the eighteenth century.

(9) What advances were made in food preservation in this period?

(10) What were the main stages of air and telecommunications?

(11) Explain the origins and importance of the relativity theories of Einstein.

(12) Identify the following: Joseph Black, James Prescott Joule, William Herschel, Charles Darwin, Samuel Wilberforce, Clerk-Maxwell, Madame Curie, Lord Rutherford, Charles Goodyear, François Appert, Cooke and Wheatstone, Alexander Graham Bell, Louis Blériot.

(13) What are the most important problems which advances in scientific and technical knowledge have brought during the past twenty-five years?

Books for Reference and Further Reading

Some of the following books are advanced works, others are simple introductions. As far as possible, this list attempts to guide the reader to the sort of book he or she needs.

1. GENERAL HISTORIES

David Thomson, *England in the Nineteenth Century*, and *England in the Twentieth Century* and H. Pelling, *Modern Britain, 1885–1955* are good introductions to the period.

Asa Briggs, *The Age of Improvement, 1783–1867*; R. J. White, *Waterloo to Peterloo*; H. W. C. Davies, *The Age of Grey and Peel*; G. L. Woodward, *The Age of Reform*; R. C. K. Ensor, *England 1870–1914*; A. J. P. Taylor, *English History, 1914–1945*; and C. L. Mowat, *Britain Between the Wars, 1918–1940* provide more detailed treatment of their respective periods. D. Thomson, *Europe Since Napoleon* and I. Crowley, *Background to Current Affairs*, will help to put British history in its European and world context.

They Saw It Happen, Vol. III, 1689–1897 by T. Charles-Edwards and B. Richardson and *Vol. IV, 1897–1940* by Asa Briggs contain interesting extracts from contemporary accounts of great events.

2. SOCIAL AND ECONOMIC HISTORY

General introductions to the whole period are to be found in G. M. Trevelyan, *Illustrated Social History of England*; P. Gregg, *A Social and Economic History of Britain from 1760 to 1955* and W. B. H. Court, *A Concise Economic History of Britain from 1755 to Recent Times*. H. L. Beales, *The Industrial Revolution, 1750–1850*, is a good short account and G. P. Jones and A. G. Pool, *A Hundred Years of Economic Development*, covers the period 1840–1940. T. K. Derry and T. Williams *A Short History, of Technology*, gives a manageable account of the technical developments in the Industrial Revolution. Lord Ernle, *English Farming Past and Present*, is the standard authority on agriculture and amongst the many more advanced books on the economy, J. H. Clapham, *An Economic History of*

Modern Britain, provides a massive and authoritative account of nineteenth-century developments. I. M. Livingstone, *Britain and the World Economy,* gives an excellent short description of the post-1945 difficulties which Britain has faced.

M. D. George, *England in Transition* (on the early nineteenth century), Asa Briggs, *Victorian Cities* and *Victorian People,* J. L. and B. Hammond, *The Bleak Age* (on the Chartists), G. S. Turner, *The Road to Ruin* (on social conditions in the nineteenth century), E. Moberly Bell, *Storming the Citadel* (on women's rights especially in the medical profession) are all useful detailed studies.

R. Graves and A. Hodge, *The Long Weekend, a Social History of Great Britain, 1918–1939,* gives an excellent description of the inter-war years and G. D. H. Cole, *The Post War Conditions of Britain,* deals with the decade after 1945. Ronald Blythe, *The Age of Illusion: England in the Twenties and Thirties,* and Michael Sissons and Philip French, *The Age of Austerity,* highlight both political and social developments in a lively way which is within the grasp of 'O' level students. There are colourful descriptions of conditions in the Depression in J. B. Priestley, *English Journey,* and George Orwell, *The Road to Wigan Pier.*

G. D. H. Cole and Raymond Postgate, *The Common People – 1746–1946,* provides a general account of social conditions with special reference to the working man. F. Engels, *Conditions of the Working Class in England, in 1844* and Henry Mayhew, *London Labour and London Poor,* are worth looking at for powerful contemporary descriptions of the condition of the people. G. D. H. Cole, *A Short History of the Working Class Movements,* provides a good introduction to a subject dealt with in more detail by H. Pelling in *History of British Trade Unionism,* and *Origins of the Labour Party,* and by S. and B. Webb in their massive *History of Trade Unionism.*

F. Smith, *History of English Elementary Education 1760–1902* and R. L. Archer, *Secondary Education in the Nineteenth Century,* provide useful background material.

3. BRITAIN OVERSEAS

The Cambridge History of the British Empire, is the standard account. There are shorter outlines in C. E. Carrington, *The British Overseas,* W. R. Brock, *Britain and the Dominions,* D. C. Somerwell and H. Harvey, *The British Empire and Commonwealth,* and J. A. Williamson, *A Short History of British Expansion.*

Individual areas are dealt with in J. H. Parry and P. M. Sherlock, *A Short History of the West Indies*; P. G. Creighton, *The Story of Canada*; A. G. L. Shaw, *The Story of Australia*; K. Sinclair, *A History of New Zealand*; and P. Spear, *A Short History of India.* On Africa there are many excellent volumes in the Penguin African Series. In particular J. Fage and

R. Oliver provide the background in *A Short History of Africa*, and Basil Davidson looks at future prospects for the continent in *Which Way Africa?* A useful treatment of most recent problems can be found in *An Atlas of African Affairs* by P. Van Rensburg and A. Boyd, and a broader view in *An Atlas of African History* by J. Fage.

4. FOREIGN POLICY

Most detailed studies of British foreign policy are rather difficult reading for the beginner.
R. W. Seton Watson, *Britain in Europe, 1789–1914*, is long but clear.
M. R. D. Foot, *British Foreign Policy Since 1898*, is a good shorter account.
E. H. Carr, *International Relations between the Two World Wars*, is valuable for reference on a complex period. M. Gilbert, *Britain and Germany between the Wars*, is a useful short account, and information on post 1945 questions is easily available in A. Boyd, *Atlas of World Affairs*.

5. IRELAND

J. C. Beckett, *A Short History of Ireland,* and B. Inglis, *The Story of Ireland*, are good introductions. C. Woodham Smith, *The Great Hunger,* is a fine account of the famine in Ireland. Edgar Holt, *Protest in Arms,* and Richard Bennett, *The Black and Tans*, give more detail on the 'troubles' of the Twentieth Century.

SCIENCE AND TECHNOLOGY

F. Sherwood Taylor, *The Century of Science*, is an excellent introduction. R. J. Forbes, *Man the Maker*; R. J. Forbes and E. J. Dijksterhuis, *A History of Science and Technology*; *Engineering Heritage* Vol. I and II; Shyrock, *Development of Modern Medicine*, H. Pingle, *The Century of Science* and T. K. Derry and T. Williams, *A Short History of Technology*, are all useful works of reference.

7. MILITARY HISTORY

Cyril B. Falls, *A Hundred Years of War, 1850–1950* and B. H. Liddell–Hart, *The Revolution in Warfare*, provide interesting general studies. There is an enormous literature on the two great wars of the Twentieth Century. A. J. P. Taylor, *The First World War*, is a very stimulating outline. M. F. Cruttwell, *History of the Great War*; B. H. Liddell-Hart, *A History of the*

412 A HISTORY OF MODERN BRITAIN

World War 1914–1918; C. Falls, *The Second World War* and J. F. C. Fuller, *The Second World War, 1939–45*, provide straightforward accounts. Sir Winston Churchill, *The Second World War*, is a fascinating work of reference with many personal insights.

The books on specific campaigns are too numerous to list in detail. Cecil Woodham Smith, *The Reason Why*, gives a colourful picture of the mid-nineteenth century army as well as a description of the Battle of Balaclava. Barbara Tuckman, *August 1914*, is much more than a military history. Arthur Marwick, *The Deluge: British Society in the 1st World War* and David Marshall, *Women on the Warpath: The Story of Women in the 1st World War*, give interesting descriptions of the home front.

8. RELIGION

E. E. Killett, *Religion and Life in the Early Victorian Age*, L. E. E. Brins, *Religion in the Victorian Age*; H. G. Wood, *Belief and Unbelief Since 1850*; E. W. Watson, *The Church of England*; H. Davies, *The Free Churches* and E. I. Watkin, *Roman Catholicism in England from the Reformation to 1950*, may all be consulted by the advanced student.

9. BIOGRAPHY

There are an enormous number of biographies available on the greater and lesser figures of the last hundred years. Many of these are very detailed and often have little relevance for G.C.E. courses. *The Clarendon Biographies*, which include E. G. Collieu, *Queen Victoria*, and C. L. Mowat, *Lloyd George*, are suitable for 'O' level candidates. Amongst other relatively easy biographical studies are Lytton Strachey, *Queen Victoria* and *Eminent Victorians*, which are amusing and irreverent but not always accurate, Cecil Woodham Smith, *Florence Nightingale* and Lord David Cecil, *Lord M.* (on Melbourne).

R. Jenkins, *Herbert Asquith*, R. Rhodes, *Balfour*; A. Bullock, *Ernest Bevin*; R. Rhodes, *Lord Randolph Churchill*; R. Blake, *Disraeli*; Sir H. Nicolson, *George V*; P. Magnus, *Gladstone*; T. Jones, *Lloyd George*; H. C. Bell, *Lord Palmerston*; A. H. Ramsay, *Peel*; A. L. Kennedy, *Salisbury, 1830–1903*; J. W. Bready, *Lord Shaftesbury and Social and Industrial Progress*; G. Longford, *Victoria R. I.*; Philip Guedella, *The Duke* (Wellington) cover some of the outstanding political figures until most recent times. For the period since 1939 there are many books of memoirs and autobiography, especially on the war.

Index

National Insurance, 112, 177, 264
Nationalization, 260–1, 282
New Zealand, 337–9
Newman, John Henry (Cardinal), 115–16
Nigeria, 347
Nightingale, Florence, 90, 111, 112
Normandy landings, 255
North Atlantic Treaty Organization, 268
North-West Frontier, 138
Nuclear deterrent, 279, 282
Nuclear Test Ban Treaty, 280
Nursing, 111
Nyasaland, see Malawi
Nylon, 388

O'Connell, Daniel, 29–31, 41, 63–4
O'Connor, Feargus, 70–5
Old Age Pension, 174, 176, 221
Oliver (spy), 18, 19, 21
Opium wars, 79–80
Organization for European Economic Co-operation, 267
Osborne Judgment, 178, 298
Ottawa Conference, 230
Owen, Robert, 17, 47–9, 50, 54, 55
Oxford Movement, 115

Pakistan, 345
Palestine, 270–1
Palmerston, Lord, 76–86, 88, 92
Pankhurst, Emmeline, 179
Paper duties, 119
Parliament Bill, 1911, 175
Parnell, Charles Stuart, 141, 143, 148, 151
Parsons, (Sir) Charles, 372
Party System, 44
Pasteur, Louis, 111, 112
Peace Ballot, 238
Pearl Harbor, attack on, 253
Peel, (Sir) Robert, 24, 26, 28–9, 30–1, 41, 45, 58–68, 67
Penicillin, 385

Penjdeh incident, 147
Penny post, 57
'People's Budget', 174
Perkin, (Sir) William, 385
Peterloo massacre, 20–1
Petroleum, 387
Philosophic Radicals, 41, 47
Phoenix Park murders, 144
Photography, 394
Place, Francis, 17, 28–9
Plastics, 387
Plevna, siege, 136
Plimsoll, Samuel, 133–4
Plug riots, 72
Pocket boroughs, 40–1
Poland, guarantee of, 247
Police, 28
Poor Law, Amendment Act, 52–3, 69, 109
Poor relief, 6
Post Office Savings Bank, 120
Potsdam Conference, 265
Press, Freedom of, 13
Prince Consort, 56, 106
Prince Regent, see George IV
Printing, 395
Public Health, 108–13
Public Health Act, 1848, 63, 110; 1875, 132
Public Schools, 361–3

Quadruple Alliance, 34, 35
'Queen's Affair', 22–3
Quintuple Alliance, 35

Radio-telescope, 377
Railways, 310–12, 390
Railway mania, 56, 60, 311
Rationing, post-war, 262
Rayon, 387
'Red Flag' Act, 289
Redmond, John, 175, 180, 186
Reform Bill, First, 42–5; Second, 96; Third (1884), 148

Regency, 13
Relativity, 383
Religious movements, 113–17
Rennie, John, 8
Representation of the People Act, 200, 221
Rhodes, Cecil, 153, 160, 161, 166, 346
Rhodesia, 162, 281, 352
Roads, 7
Road transport, 389
Roberts, Lord, 166
Rome, Treaty of, 280
Roosevelt, F. D., 243
Rotten boroughs, 38
Royal Society, 368
Royal Society of Arts, 368
Rubber, 387
Russell, (Lord) John, 30, 41, 44, 83, 84, 85, 87, 88, 96, 97
Russo-Finnish war, 249
Rutherford, Ernest, (Lord), 381

Salisbury, Lord, 149, 150, 154, 167, 168
Salvation Army, 116
Samuel Commission, 219, 302
Sankey Commission, 207, 301
Sebastopol, siege, 91
Secret ballot, 129
Security scandals, 283
Serbia, 185
Sévres, Treaty of, 212
Shaftesbury, Earl, 50, 61, 114
Sicily, invasion of, 254
Sidmouth, Lord, 15, 18, 19, 21
Sierra Leone, 346
Simon, (Sir) John, 220, 229–30
Sinn Fein, 180, 181
'Six Acts', 21
Slavery, abolition, 49
Smiles, Samuel, 104
Smuts, Jan, 166
Social Democrat Federation, 294
Socialism, 101, 103

South Africa, 139, 158–66, 173, 281, 354–5
Soviet-Nazi Pact, 248
Spa Fields riots, 18
Spanish Civil War, 240, 241
Spanish marriages, 80
Special Areas, 233–4
Speenhamland System, 6, 52
Statute of Westminster, 224
Steam power, 10, 369
Steam ships, 312, 313, 372
Steel industry, 309
Stephenson, George, 310, 371
Straits (Dardanelles) Convention, 79, 92
Stresa Conference, 237
Sudan, 146, 167
Suez Canal, 135, 275
Suez crisis, 275, 276
Suffragettes, 179
Sulpha drugs, 385
Super tax, 175
Syndicalism, 298

Taff Vale decision, 172, 174, 296, 297
Tamworth Manifesto, 58
Tanganyika, 349, 351
Tariff Reform, 171, 323
Telecommunications, 392
Telegraph, 374, 392
Telephone, 392
Television, 273, 394
Telford, Thomas, 7, 8
Ten Hours Movement, 61, 63
Terylene, 388
Test Act, repeal, 30
Tolpuddle martyrs, 55, 56, 57
Townshend, Lord, 4
Trades Disputes Act, 1906, 174; 1927, 220; repeal, 262
Trade Unions, 28–9, 54–5, 127–9, 133, 178, 207, 219–21, 291–306
Trade Union Acts, 293
Trades Union Congress, 291, 306